Acquisition Management

Acquisition Management

R. Marshall Engelbeck

ᚎ

MANAGEMENTCONCEPTS

Vienna, Virginia

(((
MANAGEMENTCONCEPTS

8230 Leesburg Pike, Suite 800
Vienna, Virginia 22182
Phone: (703) 790-9595
Fax: (703) 790-1371
Web: www.managementconcepts.com

Printed in the United States of America

Library of Congress Cataloging-in-Publication Data

Engelbeck, R. Marshall, 1933–
   Acquisition management handbook / R. Marshall Engelbeck.
     p. cm.
   Includes bibliographical references and index.
   ISBN-13: 978-1-56726-128-8 (hc.)
   ISBN-10: 1-56726-128-0 (hc.)
   1. Government purchasing—United States—Handbooks, manuals, etc. 2. Public
contracts—United States—Handbooks, manuals, etc.   I. Title.

JK1673.E55 2001
352.5'3'0973—dc21

                                      2001044185

Dedication

I dedicate this book to my wife, Ronnie Engelbeck, who patiently tolerated my preoccupation with writing this book.

About the Author

Marshall Engelbeck retired from the Air Force after 28 years of service. He has a B.S. in General Business and an M.S. in Logistics Management. While in the Air Force, he had over eight years experience working with government contracts. In the Air Force, he also held positions of Base Commander, Logistics Support Group Commander, Director of Logistics, Integrated Logistics Support Staff Officer, and Aircraft Maintenance Officer. After retiring from the military, Marshall spent ten years as a Senior Contract and Proposal Manager with the Defense Communications Division of Rockwell-Collins in Richardson, Texas. During this period, he also taught Management of Government Contracts and Contemporary Contracting at the University of Dallas Graduate School of Management. He has also been active in governing the Town of Trophy Club, Texas, serving on the Town Council and as Mayor.

Table of Contents

Preface

It goes without challenge that the federal government is the biggest buyer of them all. The record shows that in fiscal year 1999, the federal government spent more than 183 billion dollars to acquire goods and services. At the same time, government procurement policies and procedures were undergoing their most extensive overhaul in government procurement history. Not only was the federal government moving toward a paperless contracting process, but it also was changing its policies and procedures to meet post-Cold War needs. The objective of these new ways of doing business, often referred to as "acquisition streamlining," was to make the process more flexible and responsive. Another goal was to reduce the time required to develop, procure, and deliver the products needed to satisfy requirements.

To accomplish these objectives, many government acquisition managers looked to adapting commercial practices to the federal acquisition process as much as possible. Another way it was determined that the acquisition process could be streamlined was to place greater emphasis on the use of individual judgment and business sense. Members of the acquisition workforce are now being encouraged to use their own initiative and to make decisions within their areas of responsibility.

The story goes that Baron Fredrich Wilhelm von Stuben (1730-1794), a German officer in American service during the Revolutionary War, when asked how the American soldier differed from his European counterpart, answered: An American needs to understand why something is to be done prior to beginning the task, whereas the European is more likely to act obediently without question. During my career in the military, industry, and local government, I found Baron von Stuben's observation to be true: People perform best when they understand the purpose and objectives behind what they are being asked to do.

Acquisition Management is written with this thought in mind. It is directed to government and contractor personnel working together in the acquisition process as members of a cross-functional team. One of the assumptions on which the book is based is that government and contractor personnel are more effective when they both have knowledge of the rules and regulations as well as an understanding of the principles on which those rules and regulations are founded.

When implementing the Acquisition Streamlining Act of 1994, the government included a set of "guiding principles for the Federal Acquisition System" in the Federal Acquisition Regulation (FAR), which is the primary source of uniform policies and procedures for acquisitions by all executive agencies (FAR 1.101). These guiding principles are intended to provide direction and consistency of purpose to those involved in the acquisition process. Key to an understanding of the process is knowledge of the core principle—"the vision of the Federal Acquisition System to deliver on a timely basis the best value product or service to the customer, while maintaining the public's trust and fulfilling public policy objectives" (FAR 1.102). This vision is intended to inspire and guide all involved in the federal acquisition process.

Acquisition principles are also intended to provide a standard for decisions by contracting officers as well as other members of multi-functional acquisition teams. The FAR includes a set of four performance objectives: (1) to satisfy the customer in terms of cost, quality, and timeliness of the delivered product or service, (2) to minimize administrative operating costs, (3) to conduct business with integrity, fairness, and openness, and (4) to fulfill public policy objectives (FAR 1.102-2).

One of my primary complaints is that we seem to have gotten side-tracked. The primary purpose of the contract document is to clearly define contractual obligations and establish the completion criteria. In other words, the contract needs to first serve as the common language between the buyer and seller. Its primary purpose is not to protect one party from the other in the event of litigation. Therefore, this book is organized so that it covers the numerous multi-functional tasks as they are scheduled to be accomplished during the various phases of the acquisition process.

One of the reasons I wrote this book is that other procurement texts are organized and written strictly from a legal perspective. Therefore, they are difficult to follow and use as references. *Acquisition Management* presents material from the FAR at the applicable point in the acquisition phase. It also incorporates recent changes to the Department of Defense's 5000 series directives and instructions governing the management and operation of the defense acquisition system.

To assist the reader, this book also combines detailed information on the rules and procedures contained in the FAR with information on subjects not included in the FAR. These include: the importance of time in acquiring goods and services; management of integrated acquisition teams; the importance of managing interfunctional as well as buyer-seller relationships; management of risks and opportunities; making tradeoffs; the importance of acquisition planning; market research as an essential element of the requirements determination process; intellectual property; win-win negotiations; managing variances to contract baseline; and cooperative strategic agreements.

These subjects are incorporated into the text at the point in the acquisition process where they are applied. This is important because acquisition is a synergistic process that links the contractor to the ultimate user. The postulate of the acquisition principles is that the customer is best served when functional specialists operate as a part of an independent and integrated system. Government policies and concepts are oriented on a functional basis. It is essential that all members of this integrated team understand the rules and tasks involved in acquiring goods and services so they can work together efficiently and effectively.

Chapter 1, Reform of the Federal Acquisition System, illustrates how the federal government is responding to pressure from its constituents and is initiating action to make the process more responsive and cost-effective. The chapter also provides an historical perspective to the guiding acquisition principles.

Chapter 2 describes the federal acquisition process, the integrated acquisition team and its role, as well as management of the risks and opportunities that are present in every acquisition.

The requirements determination process and procurement planning are covered in Chapter 3. Emphasis is placed on the role market research plays in determining requirements as well as the importance of identifying potential risks and opportunities early in the process.

Chapter 4, The Solicitation, describes the process the federal government follows when asking for information or requesting that potential contractors submit proposals. The quality of the solicitation document is emphasized because it becomes the initial draft of the contractual agreement between the buyer and the seller.

The primary objective of Chapter 5 is to provide information about the preparation of bids and competitive proposals. One of the goals of this chapter is to emphasize that potential contractors need to clarify all ambiguities early in the process as a means of mitigating risk.

Chapter 6 covers the subjects of source selection and contract award. Topics include contractor qualifications, competitive sealed bidding, competitive negotiated procurements, the best value continuum, the evaluation process, exchanges after receipt of proposals, establishing the competitive range, notification of unsuccessful offerors, proposal analysis, making the source selection decision, discussions and negotiations, contract award, and protests.

In Chapter 7, Contract Performance, emphasis is placed on three factors: the importance of contract administration services, the significance of defining and understanding the contract baseline, and the need for an effective interorganizational relationship between the government buyer and seller.

Contract closeout is covered in Chapter 8, the final chapter. Information is provided on settlement of all outstanding contractual issues and assurance that all parties have met their contractual obligations, as well as documenting the contract file.

As noted, the core acquisition principle is to deliver on a timely basis the best-value product or service to the customer, while maintaining the public's trust and fulfilling public policy objectives. This means that the acquisition process should be carried out in a manner that serves the interests of the buyer as well as the seller. To accomplish this, participants must understand their mutual interests and how both parties must interact for the vision to be achieved.

It is my sincere desire that *Acquisition Management* will help those participating in the federal acquisition process understand what is behind all the rules and regulations.

Marshall Engelbeck
Colonel USAF (Ret.)
August 2001

Acknowledgments

During my careers in the Air Force and industry, I have been influenced by countless outstanding and dedicated people who gave me a helping hand along the way. In writing this book, I wish to especially thank David V. Lamm, Ph.D., Associate Professor of Acquisition Management at the Naval Post Graduate School, who provided encouragement when the paper was blank. I also thank Catherine A. Kreyche of Management Concepts, Inc., for her patience and support. John Nevitt, Bill Bellamy, and Fritz Weigl Ph.D., of Rockwell-Collins, as program managers, rounded out my perspective during my years at the Defense Communications Division of Rockwell-Collins. And of course I must recognize Khalid bin Rasheed, Major Royal Saudi Air Force (Retired), who demonstrated the ins-and-outs of negotiations during our trips to the rug suq in Riyadh.

Reform of the Federal Acquisition System

This book is written for members of the acquisition team, especially contract managers, to show how they can meet the challenges of change brought about by: (1) the crusade to make the federal government more efficient and user friendly, (2) the end of the Cold War, and (3) improved communications technology. A book on this subject is important because the "Reinvention of Government" initiative of 1994 has kicked off the most extensive revolution in acquisition and logistic processes since the end of World War II. In addition, everyone involved in the buying or selling of goods and services in the federal market must understand the doctrine upon which these changes to the acquisition process are founded and how they will affect how the federal government does business.

The Department of Defense (DoD) adopted the term *acquisition* in 1970 as an alternative to the term *procurement*. Acquisition became part of the government-wide regulatory system in 1984 with the issuance of the Federal Acquisition Regulation (FAR).[1] In *The Government Contracts Reference Book*, the authors point out that the terms *acquisition* and *procurement* are synonymous. *Procurement* is used in the United States Code, while *acquisition* is usually used in the FAR.[2] Acquisition is defined in the FAR as:

> . . .the acquiring by contract with appropriated funds of supplies and services (including construction) by and for the use of the Federal Government through purchase or lease, whether the supplies or services are already in existence or must be created, developed, demonstrated, and evaluated. Acquisition begins at the point when agency needs are established and includes the description of requirements to satisfy agency needs, solicitation and selection of sources, award of contracts, contract financing, contract performance, contract administration, and those technical and

management functions directly related to the process of fulfilling agency needs by contract.[3]

A successful acquisition is built on relationships. Not only is a constructive association between the buyer and seller necessary, but real-time linking between their functional staffs and collaborative relationships within the integrated acquisition team are vital as well. In part this is due to the exponential growth of the Internet and its by-product the Website. These tools are erasing the time, place, and organizational barriers that once made acquisition a line-flow process. The hypothesis of this book is that a proactive approach to acquisition management is a prerequisite to providing the user with a best-value product when and where it is needed. Keys to achieving this objective are to reduce procurement cost through: (1) understanding that the key element in the development of a product or service is a strategic relationship between the contractor and its suppliers, (2) enhancing market research techniques, (3) implementing a cross-functional integrated acquisition team approach, (4) focusing on managing the risks and opportunities associated with the acquisition, (5) using the contract agreement as the common language by all members of an integrated acquisition team, and (6) maximizing the use of electronic data transfer.

The objective of this first chapter is to illustrate how the federal government is responding to pressure from its constituents by being more responsive and cost-conscious. An outgrowth of this initiative has been an effort to change how government will purchase goods and services in the post–Cold War era. Reinvention of the acquisition system started over six years ago when the federal government revised its primary acquisition directive, the Federal Acquisition Regulation (FAR). Among the many changes made to this document was, for the first time, the development and inclusion of a statement of guiding principles and standards. These guiding principles define the core vision of the federal acquisition system. This chapter also addresses the performance standards that were included with the guiding principles because the standards define the critical factors of an effective and efficient acquisition system.

This chapter will also explain why the government's acquisition system needed to be reinvented by reviewing some of the most significant characteristics of the government market, and then briefly summarizing the history of government acquisition over the past 60 years or so.

CHARACTERISTICS OF THE GOVERNMENT MARKET

In procuring its needs, the federal government wears two hats. First, it acts in a contracting capacity and is expected to exercise good business judgment when determining requirements and purchasing a wide variety of goods and services from every sector of the economy. Second, the government also is the defender of the taxpayer's interest and is expected to act even-handedly while implementing social and political policies.

The dollar value and number of purchases, i.e., $183.1 billion from 487,264,000 contractual transactions in fiscal year 1999, make the federal government by far the largest buyer of goods and services in the world.

Ten years ago approximately 50 percent of the total dollars spent by the federal government were for supplies and equipment, with other services, excluding R&D, A&E, and ADP services, totaling just over 25 percent. As Table 1-1 shows, expenditures for supplies and equipment in 1999 fell to around one-third of the total. The reduction in defense spending was a major factor in this decrease. On the other hand, the amount spent for services rose to 41 percent. This trend illustrates an increase in outsourcing service-related tasks to contractors in the private sector as well as the effect of government's increased dependence on electronic data interchange.

In FY 1999 the Department of Defense spent $123.2 billion, or 67% of the total federal contract dollars spent in that fiscal year. The next five top government spenders were the Department of Energy ($15.6 billion), the National Aeronautics and Space Administration (NASA) ($10.9 billion), the General Services Administration (GSA) ($7.6 billion), the Department of Health and Human Resources ($4.1 billion), and the Department of Veterans Affairs ($4.0 billion).[5] What is significant is that DoD expenditures exceed the other five by $82.4 billion. DoD procurement exceeded the amount purchased by the next four agencies by a factor of three. Consequently, its domination of government acquisition no doubt has a great deal of influence on the policies and procedures contained in the FAR.

Dr. J. Ronald Fox, former professor of business at Harvard and Assistant Secretary of the Army, in his book *Arming of America: How the U.S. Buys Weapons*, cites the 1962 study of the defense market by Merton J. Peck and

Table 1-1 Major Categories of Federal Government Purchases[4]—1999

Major Category	Dollars (Billions)	Percent of Total
Supplies and equipment	$57.0	32
ADP equipment, purchases/leases	6.4	3
Research and development	24.5	13
Construction	16.0	9
Architect & engineering	1.7	1
Real property, purchase/lease/maintain	.8	1
ADP services, including installation and maintenance	11.8	6
Other services	64.9	35
Total	$183.1	100

Frederic M. Scherer of the RAND Corporation. They concluded that the defense market differs from the commercial market in that it is not determined by supply and demand. First Congress determines how much the DoD will spend and for what. This decision is influenced by political and economic conditions as well as international events and the interests of the members of Congress.[6] A market system does not now exist in the weapon acquisition process . . . a market system in its entirety can never exist for the acquisition of weapons.[7]

The government market as a whole is also described as being a monopsony, i.e., consisting of only one buyer. Writing in *Contract Management* magazine, W. Gregor Macfarlan states, "as a monopsony, the government inherently regulates the marketplace to its own ends through defined requirements and specified processes that satisfy those requirements. The more influential the monopsony, the fewer the opportunities for the marketplace to express its competitive dynamics."[8]

It is only when the government purchases off-the-shelf items on the commercial market that the true forces of supply and demand apply. A majority of goods and services in this category have traditionally been procured through the sealed bidding method. Sealed bid purchases, although high in the number of contracting actions, historically have represented a relatively low percentage of the total dollar value of purchases in any one fiscal year. Negotiated procurements have traditionally led in the number of solicitations and dollar amount. In 1990 solicitations for negotiated procurements equaled 85.4 percent of the total action and 93.1 percent of the total dollars.[9]

Fair and open competition is the core philosophy of our supply-based economic system. It is widely believed that competition generates low prices and promotes efficiency, innovation, and quality. To realize these benefits, federal procurement policy is founded on giving every potential responsible supplier an equal opportunity to meet the government's needs. For over 100 years procurement procedures also have been directed toward full and open competition, while government contracting officers have aspired to protect the "integrity of the acquisition system." Separate studies by the RAND Corporation, the Battelle Memorial Institute, and the Office of the Secretary of Defense concluded that a reduction in contract price of 25 to 30 percent can be realized when genuine price competition exists.[10] The perception that potential price reductions can best be realized from competition also is prevalent in Congress and has been a factor in the government's efforts to launch such policies as dual-sourcing and leader-follower development contracts and to perform fact-finding and post-award as a replacement for competition.

When the criteria for classifying a procurement competitive were limited to goods and services purchased via advertised bidding, less than 50 percent of all procurements were judged to be competitive.[11] Then in 1984,

Congress passed the Competition in Contracting Act (CICA), in which it reemphasized the need for the government buyer to reap the benefits of competition. The act also states that negotiated procurements can be considered competitive when there is more than one prospective seller. The percentage of purchase actions classified as competitive increased from 44 percent in 1984 to 67 percent in 1990. Stanley Sherman, then Professor of Purchasing at George Washington University, points out that this occurred at the same time the broader private economy, especially manufacturers of commercial products, were experiencing an unmistakable trend toward fewer competitive purchases.[12]

An agreement between the buyer and seller in the commercial sector is subject to the Uniform Commercial Code (UCC).[13] On the other hand, purchases by the federal government are governed primarily by the FAR. Compared to the FAR, the UCC is broad and flexible. The FAR, which was codified on April 1, 1984, is "designed to prescribe, structure, and control the method and procedures by which is conducted in a defined segment of our economy—government procurement."[14] Further executive orders, regulations, rules, and procedures are frequently issued that are designed to provide additional detailed instructions to the operation agencies within the Executive Branch while:

- Ensuring fairness of contract award by affording all interested and responsible suppliers equal opportunity to obtain the contract
- Giving the government the right to change its mind and cancel a procurement, with reimbursement limited to cost incurred and profit limited to items delivered
- Requiring contractors to disclose their cost or pricing data in order to ensure the price is fair and reasonable
- Giving a share of contracts to small business, small disadvantaged business, contractors in labor surplus areas, and minority groups.[15]

Sherman believes the greatest distinction between the public and private sectors is the absence of a profit-and-loss standard in the public sector. The bottom line provides a means to measure success. The commercial firm can purchase the stated requirement directly, without so much oversight, and is graded on its competitive position in the market and its profitability. The federal government does not have such a single standard for success. Instead it has multiple goals, including cost, schedule, and technical performance as well as the social and economic goals of the nation.[16]

THE FEDERAL ACQUISITION SYSTEM: THE PAST 50 YEARS

After more than 50 years of war and near–world war confrontations, the American taxpayer was ready for a peace dividend in the form of lower taxes and an end to deficit budgets that hindered economic growth and their standard of living. This period in our nation's history began in 1940 with President Franklin Roosevelt's call to the nation to be the "great arsenal of democracy,"[17] which occurred just a year prior to the United States entering into war with Germany, Italy, and Japan. For the next five years the nation's industry and procurement system built and supported a two-ocean navy and a military of over seven million troops fighting simultaneously in Europe and the Pacific theaters. Materiel and supplies produced in this country also helped maintain the war efforts of our allies. After a short respite, during which U.S. military capabilities were cut back, the American people were again called to deter an external threat. This time it was communism, exported by the Soviet Union. The next 40 years would be known as the Cold War period, beginning with the European Recovery Program (Marshall Plan) in 1947, continuing through the Korean War (1950–1953) and Vietnam War (1964–1973) and ending with the collapse of the Soviet Union from within in the early 1990s. During this time the American economy not only supported significant defense and foreign aid expenditures, but also significantly increased its social programs.

At the end of the Cold War the balance sheet showed our national economy had been able to build and support an armed force second to none while providing the commercial sector with countless commercial goods and also expanding social services. A review of the Gross Domestic Product (GDP) between 1968 and 1998 (Figure 1-1, Federal Budget Catego-

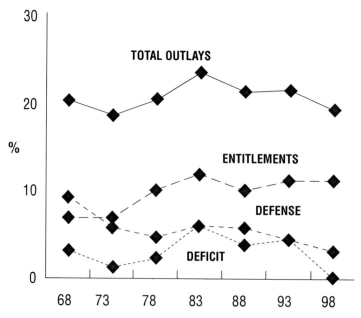

Figure 1-1 Federal Budget Categories as a Percentage of GDP[19]

ries as a Percentage of GDP), shows that the percentage of GDP allocated to entitlements increased 4.4 percent, while defense spending fell from 9.4 to 3.2 percent of GDP. This represents a reduction of almost one-third of the amount spent for defense in 1968. During the same period total outlays decreased by 0.9 percent, and the budget deficit as a percentage of GDP decreased from 3.2 to 0.3. Note that as entitlements rose from 6.9 percent of GDP, the deficit was decreased by 1.9 percent. The legacy of the era has downplayed how economic expansion enabled the nation to meet commercial and defense needs simultaneously. Instead, commentary concentrated mainly on the inefficiencies of the federal government. Public opinion[18] questioned the federal government's ability to operate effectively and efficiently. This apprehension was fueled by budget deficits, the individual tax burden, and stories in the media of unsuccessful programs and government purchases gone wrong.

THE FEDERAL ACQUISITION SYSTEM: VIEWED FROM THE INSIDE LOOKING OUT

Acquisition management is a well-established activity within government, with a set of management responsibilities that are perceived to be broader in scope than procurement.[20] This is because it traditionally has focused on large-scale purchases of major defense systems, usually under the direction of a project or program manager. Acquisition follows an integrated systems approach with applicable technical and management disciplines collaborating to achieve the goals of the acquisition. This integrated team often includes members from logistics, production, quality assurance, finance, contract management, and the appropriate technical disciplines.[21]

An acquisition of a product or service often consists of multiple procurements. The term *procurement*, when applied to the government environment, includes all stages of the process of acquiring property or services, beginning with the determination of a need for the property or service and ending with contract completion and closeout. In the private sector it is comparable to materials management, which is a concept that integrates the flow and control of materials and services, beginning with identifying the need and ending after delivery to the ultimate user.[22] "Both [acquisition and materials management] are interface functions that interact with both supplier's and customer's organizations as well as with internal functions and activities."[23]

In the federal government, Congress is the source of funds and thereby exercises the ultimate control over government procurement. The executive branch and its associated agencies have been given the authority to regulate the acquisition system. Over the past 200 years, both Congress and the executive branch have relied on legislation to fulfill their constitutional responsibilities to protect the public interest and ensure fairness through common treatment. As Figure 1-2 (Most Significant Procurement Legislation, 1795–1994) illustrates, there has been a noticeable increase in the amount of legislation regulating procurement since the end of World War II.

Over the past few years writing directives to solve the issues has not been left solely to Congress. Agencies within the executive branch have issued supplements to regulations and have developed unique rules and practices in the acquisition process. The DoD FAR supplements are a prime example. The practice has been that whenever there is a snafu, the bureaucracy has responded by revising or writing a regulation to ensure that the problem doesn't recur. The result was a maze of intertwined legal and accounting rules.[24]

The purpose of the Truth in Negotiations Act (TINA) of 1962,[25] and subsequent revisions, was to "assure that the Government is placed on an informational parity with contractors in price negotiations and avoid excessive contractor prices and profits. Failure by a contractor to disclose current, accurate, or complete cost or pricing data may result in over pricing and government recovery of excess cost."[26] The contractor also can be charged with fraud if the disclosure is intentionally incorrect. TINA provides the buyer information on the seller's cost, which is unique to government acquisition. It can also be viewed as a way the government obtains information compensating for the absence of the market forces and en-

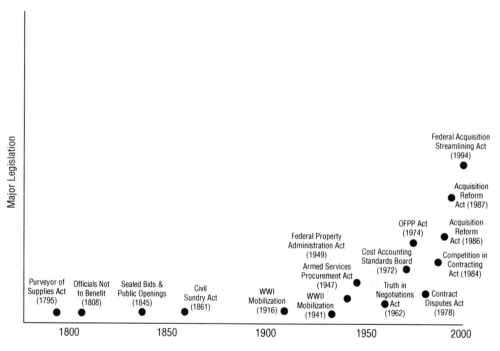

Figure 1-2 Significant Procurement Legislation, 1795–1994

hances its bargaining power. The requirement to provide cost or pricing data does not apply to sealed bids but does apply to modifications to contracts awarded under the sealed bidding process.

The requirement for consistency in a contractor's accounting practices was the subject of PL 91-379, which was passed as part of the Defense Production Act in 1970. This law was the result of criticism by Admiral Rickhover, the father of the nuclear submarine, of the government's ability to identify properly the contractor's cost to specific contracts.[27] He also stated, "the single most serious deficiency in government procurement was the lack of uniform standards," in testimony before the House Committee on Banking and Currency in 1968. This motivated the Senate Banking Committee to direct the Comptroller General to study contractor accounting practices. The end result was a law in 1972 requiring the establishment of a Cost Accounting Standards Board, which would from time to time review accounting practices and promulgate cost accounting standards. As a condition of contracting with the government, other provisions of the law are: (1) defense contractors and subcontractors with more than $10 million in contracts and subcontracts must disclose their accounting practices, and (2) there must be a contract price adjustment, with interest, for any increased cost paid by the government because of the contractor's failure to follow the cost accounting standards created by the board.[28]

The Competition in Contracting Act (CICA) of 1984 (PL 98-369) represents another significant legislative initiative. The goal of this legislation is to make the government operate more as a business by requiring more competition.[29] It represents a reaction by Congress to stories of inefficiencies, e.g., $400 hammers and $3,000 coffee pots. CICA was an alteration of Congress's "historic preference for formal advertising....; it reversed nearly two centuries of tradition..." by "placing negotiated procurement (a World War I innovation to gain flexibility) on the same level as formal advertising."[30] Statistics reported in his book *Government Procurement Management* led Dr. Stanley N. Sherman to conclude that the upward trend in modifications to ongoing contracts between 1985 and 1990 may have offset an apparent increase in competitive procurements.[31]

The "federal buying system is undoubtedly the most thoroughly examined, carefully thought-out, and fully documented procurement system in existence."[32] There have been investigations and studies of the federal procurement process, their stated objective often being to make the government operate more like a business.

In the 1980s there were two major examinations by commissions composed of distinguished citizens from the private sector. Both had charters to hold hearings, make site visits, and submit recommendations on ways to "fix" the procurement system. In 1983 the Grace Commission analyzed the procurement process and submitted recommendations on how to improve federal acquisition. Next, the president's Blue Ribbon Commission on Defense Management, headed by former Deputy Secretary of Defense David Packard, issued a report in June 1986 titled *Quest for Excellence.* The Packard Commission had a broader scope than did the Grace Commission, addressing national security planning, military organization and command, acquisition organization and procedures, and government industry accountability.[33] Both commissions submitted recommendations that resulted in passing new or revised laws and issuing more regulations.

The net result of legislation and procedures created by Congress and executive agencies themselves was placed in perspective in a 1987 study by the Center for Strategic and International Studies (CSIS) titled "US Defense Acquisition: A Process in Trouble." The study found "procurement regulations alone total more than 30,000 pages and were issued by 79 different offices." In addition, "defense activities were monitored by 55 subcommittees of 29 congressional committees, assisted by more than 20,000 staff and supporting agency members."[34] Laws, regulations, check lists, and oversight had replaced individual responsibility and accountability.

This all adds up to thousands of pages of regulations and instructions, some of which may even have the force and effect of law because they have been authorized by Congress.[35] Under a unique concept called the "Christian doctrine," when a federal procurement contract does not contain a clause that is required either by statute, regulation, or executive order, then it is automatically "incorporated by operation of law." The roots of this doctrine can be traced to a 1963 court case that ruled the Termination for Convenience of the Government clause, required by regulation, that had been excluded from a contract is to be read into a contract whether or not it was physically included in the contract, unless a proper deviation from the contract has been obtained.[36] The Christian doctrine became a method whereby contracting officers (COs) could argue that a required clause is automatically incorporated into the contract by operation of the law. A more recent case law provides clarification. For the Christian doctrine to be applied, the clause must express or implement a deeply ingrained strand of public procurement policy, and then only if its incorporation is not sought by the party who is intended to benefit from the clause's presence.[37]

In his book *The Death of Common Sense,* Phillip K. Howard reports that since the 1950s the nation has experienced, in the name of due process, the rise in the use of rules and regulations as a way to minimize discretionary government administrative decisions: "Our regulatory system has become an instruction manual. Detailed rule after detailed rule addressing every eventuality, or every situation the lawmakers and bureaucrats can think of."[38]

> Maintaining an even playing field is key to the government procurement process. All potential suppliers are to be offered an equal opportunity to bid on a potential contract, and the CO must be able to justify the contract award decision publicly. This is a constraint purchasers in the private sector do not enjoy. Therefore, being

able to base the award on objective criteria, i.e., written specifications and lowest price, has traditionally been essential to defending the award in the event of a protest by an unsuccessful bidder. Various critics of the process have noted that constraint-driven management may be the enemy of goal-driven management.[39]

THE FEDERAL ACQUISITION SYSTEM: VIEWED FROM THE OUTSIDE LOOKING IN

Examples of $400-hammers and $3,000-coffee pots have initiated numerous audits and investigations, editorials, and jokes on late-night talk shows. However, this is not a recent phenomenon. The fear of profiteering from the sale of goods and services to the government is as old as the nation itself. History cites examples at Valley Forge, during the Civil War, the war with Spain, and World Wars I and II.[40] The American public has looked with a judicious eye at selling to the government for quite some time, especially in the defense industry, where the thought of anyone profiting from war is especially disturbing. *U.S. National Survey: Public Attitudes in Defense Management*, published in 1986 as part of the final report to the president by the Blue Ribbon Commission on Defense Management (Packard Commission) reported, "four in five Americans think that defense contractors should feel an obligation, when doing business with DoD, to observe ethical standards higher than those observed in their normal business practices."[41] The report concluded that "the lack of confidence in defense contractors may affect public support for important defense programs, and thus weaken our national security."[42]

Jacob Goodwin, in the *Brotherhood of Arms: General Dynamics and the Business of Defending America*, relates the story of Harry Truman, then a senator from Missouri and chairman of a Senate committee investigating the nation's defense program, during a visit to the Consolidated plant in San Diego in the early 1940s. Senator Truman, getting tired of hearing about the virtues of Consolidated's latest aircraft, interrupted the owner, Reuben Fleet, saying, "Dammit, I want to see your books, Fleet. I'm not interested in your rise from rags to riches story."[43]

Over the past 50 years, American industry has become divided into two segments, i.e., contractors who specialize in government contracts and those who do not. However, industry as a whole has become more and more reluctant to participate in the defense market. In 1988 Dr. David V. Lamm of the Naval Postgraduate School published the results of a study conducted to determine why companies refuse to participate in defense contracts. The conclusion, which was based on a response of 427 of the 1,300 firms surveyed (33 percent), was that almost 50 percent of the responding firms indicated they did not want defense contracts. The most prevalent reasons they gave were burdensome paperwork and bidding methods, inflexible policies, and more attractive commercial opportunities.[44]

A CORE VISION FOR THE FEDERAL GOVERNMENT IN THE 21st CENTURY

In 1993 President Bill Clinton asked Vice President Al Gore to work on making government function more efficiently and cost less. The challenge was to regain public confidence in the federal government's ability to solve problems by fostering partnerships and community solutions.[45] The vice president formed a National Performance Review (NPR) team, which issued a report in September 1993. The NPR report, *From Red Tape to Results: Creating a Government That Works Better and Costs Less*, called for revising federal procurement regulations into guiding principles instead of rigid rules, decentralizing authority to purchase computers, testing an electronic marketplace, increasing the small purchase threshold, and relying more on off-the-shelf commercial products.[46]

In October 1994 the president signed into law the Federal Acquisition Streamlining Act (FASA), which is the most significant attempt to reform the government's acquisition process since World War II, and is a flow-down of the core vision and guiding principles from the NPR. The act also includes 20 recommendations on procurement from the NPR team's report. FASA charges the executive branch with reinventing the acquisition process by increasing personal initiative and decreasing mandatory controls. The overall goal of FASA is to streamline the contracting process through eliminating non–value-added rules and procedures, shortening procurement lead times, encouraging the use of automated purchasing procedures, using electronic commerce to the maximum, encouraging the use of commercial products to satisfy government requirements, and using proven contractors as a way to reduce risk.[47]

Playing a major role in this reform effort is the Office of Federal Procurement Policy (OFPP). Created by Congress in 1974, the OFPP is located organizationally in the White House under the Office of Management and Budget. OFPP is charged with the distribution of uniform policies and procedures and the maintenance of the Federal Acquisition Regulation System. The FAR, a part of that system, had replaced previously existing regulation systems in 1984.[48] In his 1990 book, *Procurement and Public Management*, Steve Kelman, later to become administrator of OFPP, describes federal procurement "as a system in trouble"[49] and the government industry relationship as "a culture of distrust."[50] Mr. Kelman instructed the task force assigned to oversee the administrative aspects of revising the FAR to incorporate such business practices as:

- Placing greater reliance on the good sense and business judgment of the procurement workforce
- Satisfying the customer's needs
- Reducing unnecessary layers of review

- Emphasizing the importance of timeliness of the procurement process
- Stressing best value judgment in making contract awards.[51]

Over the next year many revisions were written, reviewed, commented on by the public, and issued as amendments to the FAR.

It is never easy to put a mechanism in place that fosters a change in the way business has been done over many years. It can be compared to a large ocean liner changing its course. Deputy Under Secretary of Defense for Acquisition Reform Colleen Preston summarized the situation facing government procurement as the "most unavoidable challenge facing acquisition reform....[was] going through the needed cultural change."[52]

THE IMPLEMENTING ACQUISITION VISION

To facilitate this challenge, the revised FAR incorporates a "statement of guiding principles" early in the process. This statement includes: (1) a vision statement, or mission statement, for the Federal Acquisition System, (2) organizational relationships, and (3) standards for performance that apply to all acquisition participants. This "statement of guiding principles" is an expression of the mission of the Federal Acquisition System and how the federal government intends to acquire goods and services. For the first time, a written statement of acquisition doctrine, clearly defining the core objectives of the system and the performance standards of the federal acquisition system, has been articulated to participants in the process (see Figure 1-3).

This implementing vision statement complements NPR's core vision for the federal government. It declares that the primary goal of the acquisition system is "to deliver on a timely basis best value product or service to the customer, while maintaining the public trust and fulfilling public policy objectives." It also concludes that participants can best achieve the primary goal by "working together as a team empowered to make decisions within their areas of responsibility."[53]

The implementing vision answers the question, "What business are we in?" First and foremost, the goal of every acquisition is to deliver on a timely basis the best value product or service to the customer while maintaining the public trust and fulfilling policy objectives. Further examination of the vision provides the following insight into its meaning:

- The customers are "the users and line managers acting on behalf of the American taxpayer."[54]
- The primary purpose of each acquisition is service to the customer, not the process itself.
- The use of the term "best value product or service" means that the government buyer can use subjective judgment to procure a product

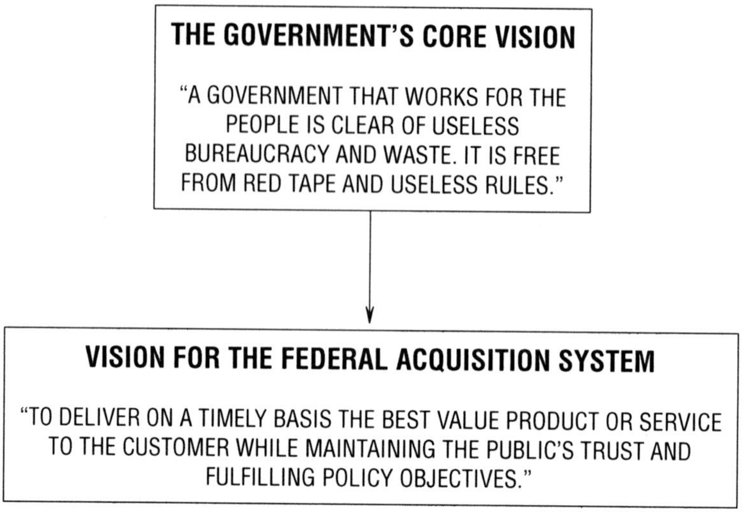

```
┌─────────────────────────────────────┐
│    THE GOVERNMENT'S CORE VISION      │
│                                      │
│   "A GOVERNMENT THAT WORKS FOR THE   │
│      PEOPLE IS CLEAR OF USELESS      │
│   BUREAUCRACY AND WASTE. IT IS FREE  │
│    FROM RED TAPE AND USELESS RULES." │
└─────────────────────────────────────┘
                    │
                    ▼
┌───────────────────────────────────────────────┐
│    VISION FOR THE FEDERAL ACQUISITION SYSTEM   │
│                                                │
│ "TO DELIVER ON A TIMELY BASIS THE BEST VALUE PRODUCT OR SERVICE │
│   TO THE CUSTOMER WHILE MAINTAINING THE PUBLIC'S TRUST AND      │
│          FULFILLING POLICY OBJECTIVES."        │
└───────────────────────────────────────────────┘
```

Figure 1-3 Implementing Vision for the Federal Acquisition System

that provides the greatest overall benefit to the customer. The 1997 rewrite of FAR Part 15.101, The Best Value Continuum, rather than using the term "best value," used the term "tradeoff." This was because: (1) there was no standard definition of "best value," and (2) an accurate reflection of what occurs during source selection, when price is not the only determining factor for contract award, is a tradeoff between the factors and subfactors that are mandated by statute. These are cost or price, quality (technical merit and other measures of the proposal's worth), and past performance (unless the Contracting Officer has made a written determination that it is not applicable to the instant acquisition).[55]

• The required product must be available when and where the customer needs it. The economists refer to this as "time and place utility," meaning that a product or service has no value unless it is at the required place at the required time.

• The participants in the acquisition process must apply high ethical standards and maintain the public trust through openness, fairness, and integrity.

The vision also decrees that implementation can best be achieved when an integrated acquisition team works together and when all members are authorized to make decisions within their areas of responsibility. The FAR describes the integrated acquisition team as "including not only representatives of the technical, supply, and procurement communities but also the customers they serve and the contractors who provide the products and services."[56] Including the contractor as an advisor to the integrated acquisition team is a departure from the "past arm's-length" relationship and represents an attempt to restore a closer buyer-seller relationship. It also recognizes that a positive buyer-seller relationship is vital to the success of any contract. In the case of small procurements or routine purchases, the integrated acquisition team can be limited to the line manager, contracting officer, and seller's purchasing agent.

The DoD has implemented a process management concept called Integrated Product and Process Development (IPPD), which integrates all activities from product concept through production and support, to optimizing simultaneously the product and its manufacturing and sustaining processes to meet cost, schedule, and performance objectives. Key to the success of this management concept is the Integrated Product Team (IPT). The IPT is a multifunctional team that is assembled around a product or service and is responsible for advising the project leader, program manager (PM), or Milestone Decision Authorities (MDA) on cost, schedule, and performance of the product.[57]

Each integrated acquisition team member is expected to "exercise personal initiative and sound business judgment in providing the best value product or service to meet customer needs."[58] Authority (and hence accountability) to make these decisions must be delegated to the lowest level within the system permitted by law.[59] Business judgment, based on the core values, includes establishing objectives, developing plans, and identifying potential risk and opportunities associated with each acquisition. Prior to contract award the team's tasks include establishing the project's objectives and developing plans that consider the potential risk and opportunities associated with meeting or exceeding the objectives. After award the integrated acquisition team focuses on the variances from the original objectives by managing risk and opportunities.

Acquisition doctrine places a great deal of importance on the use of integrated acquisition teams. In addition, including the user and contractor as members of the team highlights the need for synergy and timely decisions that can only be achieved through effective communications. Acquisition doctrine is also an admission that the traditional stovepipe-like organizational relationships make it difficult to communicate laterally among disciplines, especially when separate organizations are involved. The integrated acquisition team is designed to facilitate organizational and individual interaction by creating a multifunctional critical mass so that the acquisition functions (i.e., product design, test and evaluation, production, purchasing, logistics support, and contracting) will "sign up" to a shared objective and thus have a greater sense of commitment to the acquisition process.

In discussing the role of the integrated acquisition team, the FAR states that "the contracting officer must have authority to the maximum extent practicable and consistent with law, to determine the application of rules, regulations, and policies on a specific contract."[60] Ralph C. Nash, Jr., founder of the Government Contracts Program at The George Washington University, suggests that placing the contracting officer (CO) on the integrated acquisition team is very important because it ensures that the CO will function as a member of a team and not as the person responsible for the back end of the procurement process.[61]

The strongest endorsement of using individual initiative in the acquisition process is the FAR policy statement: "if it is in the best interest of the Government and not addressed in the FAR, nor prohibited by law (statute or case law), Executive order, or other regulation that the strategy, practice, policy or procedure is a permissible exercise of authority."[62] This policy ends an age-old question as to whether or not a course of action not specifically prohibited by law or policy is permitted to be implemented. To many it represents another departure from previous practice.

PERFORMANCE STANDARDS: A GUIDE TO DECISIONS AND EVALUATION

The FAR also includes four performance standards that provide a framework for decision making (see Figure 1-4). These standards—customer sat-

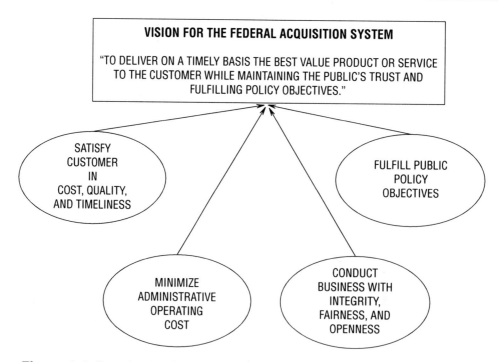

Figure 1-4 Standards of Performance for the Federal Acquisition System

isfaction, minimizing operating cost, maintaining the public trust, and fulfilling public policy objectives—provide criteria upon which participants in the process can measure how well they performed. All acquisition officials and members of the integrated acquisition team are advised to keep these standards in mind when performing their duties, remembering that they come before policies, practices, and goals.

Customer Satisfaction

The first standard, customer satisfaction, is a restatement of the implementing vision that the primary objective is to satisfy "the customer in terms of cost, quality, and timeliness of the delivered product or service."[63] It means that the product is more important than the process. This key performance standard has seven elements (Figure 1-5, Key Elements of Customer Satisfaction):

1. It is a recognition that the ultimate user's needs are paramount.
2. Continuous communication with the customer is key to define, and often refine, the performance characteristics of the product or service.
3. The potential offeror's track record is to be taken into account when selecting contractors to provide the product or perform the service.

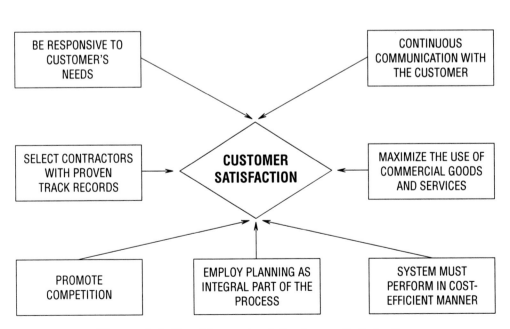

Figure 1-5 Key Elements of Customer Satisfaction

4. The early use of market research is vital to identifying sources within industry that have the capability to furnish the designated goods or services.
5. Effective competition must be promoted.
6. To be successful, the acquisition system must deliver a high-quality product when it is needed, where it is needed, and in a cost-effective manner.
7. Advanced planning is an integral part of the overall process, but the system must retain the capability to be flexible.

Satisfy the customer in terms of quality and timeliness of the delivered products or service: The purpose of this principle is to remind all participants in the acquisition process that all actions should be directed to supporting the needs of the customer, who is the ultimate user. It is also important to point out that the contemporary meaning of the term *quality* includes the ultimate user's performance, reliability, and maintainability needs, which are defined during the requirements determination and refined product design phases of the acquisition through a series of tradeoffs.

Principal customers are identified as the users and line managers acting on behalf of the American taxpayer. How responsive the integrated acquisition team is to the needs and concerns of the customer is a critical factor upon which the team is evaluated. Customers usually view their needs primarily in terms of performance and schedule. They want to receive exactly what they ordered—no more, no less, no substitutes, no defects, and at the agreed-upon delivery date. However, fiscal constraints are a reality that all who participate in the acquisition process must recognize, and everyone must be willing to make tradeoff decisions. Therefore, the integrated acquisition team must know how much it will cost to provide the customer the desired level of quality and service early in the life cycle of the product. For example, in the DoD the PM, supported by the Cost/Performance IPT (CPIPT), is tasked to conduct all program cost and performance tradeoff analysis. The CPIPT's analysis may result in performance or engineering and design changes, provided they do not violate threshold values in the Operational Requirements Document (ORD) and Acquisition Program Baseline (APB).[64]

Continuous communications: This is about the management of information—converting ideas into concepts and then into products or services that meet the needs of the customer. Meeting this standard requires establishing a communication protocol and maintaining an effective feedback process within the entire integrated acquisition team. Including the customer as a member of the integrated acquisition team facilitates meeting the customer's goals. The open communication process includes using the intranet, extranet, video conferencing, and traditional written and verbal means.[65] After contract award the common language for communicating within the team must be the contract document. This document represents the contract performance baseline that was the product of the negotiated agreement and encompasses the characteristics of the product or services to be delivered as well as the how, where, and when. Which documents should be designated for use as the performance baseline depends on the complexity of the acquisition. Examples of appropriate documents are: specifications, requirements-traceability matrices, statements of work, work breakdown structures, integrated master plans, integrated master schedules, earned value systems, system maturity matrices, and technical performance indicators.

Select contractors with proven track records: Acquisition policy now makes it mandatory that the past performance record of all offerors be evaluated for all source selections for negotiated competitive acquisitions expected to exceed $100,000, unless the contracting officer determines competition is not an appropriate factor for the acquisition.[66]

This standard strongly endorses the use of a contractor's demonstrated past performance record, or demonstrated current superior ability to perform, to establish the contractor as a primary candidate for a government contract. The value of this practice to the government is that there is supposedly less risk in selecting a contractor with a proven track record than one that is relatively unknown. This belief is based on practices being adopted by industry and Deming's philosophy, i.e., the value of developing long-term relationships that lead to reduced cost and improved quality by working together.[67] Implementing this standard will not be easy. It requires the buying office to address questions such as: (1) What in a contractors' past performance history is considered relevant? (2) Does a contractor's past performance experience have a shelf-life? (3) How will corporation mergers and downsizing be considered? and (4) How will firms without a history of past performance on a government contract be evaluated and compared to one with a history?

Maximize the use of commercial sources: Acquisition policy emphasizes maximum use of commercial and commercial non-developmental[68] items. This policy was implemented because of the technology explosion, especially in electronic data interchange, and the realization that commercial items can satisfy a large majority of government requirements. Also, by using commercial or non-developmental sources, cost will be reduced, lead times shortened, and the industrial base enhanced. Commercial contractors must be considered not only as prime contractors but subcontractors as well. Whenever practical to maximize competition, innovation, and interoperability, the DoD charges its acquisition managers to capitalize on commercial technologies for the acquisition of products and services.[69]

This performance standard also charges the integrated acquisition team to communicate with the commercial sector during the requirements determination phase to identify available capabilities that will satisfy the user's needs. This recognizes the vital role market research plays in determining requirements. Market research is defined as "the process that is used to collect, organize, maintain, analyze, and present data for the purpose of fully understanding the technology, competitive forces, and capabilities of the marketplace to meet an organization's needs for supplies and services."[70] The goal of market research is to find the most suitable supplier, product, or service available to satisfy the customer's needs. To be successful, early participation in the market research process is required by all members of the integrated acquisition team.

Selection of a commercial product or service can also be viewed as a way to accelerate the acquisition process because it identifies goods or services already available. This strategy bypasses the design and product development phases of the acquisition process. It mitigates the cost, schedule, and performance risk inherent in the development of items unique to the government.

For systems, the CO should now focus on developing strategic partnerships because the private sector is depending more and more on strategic sourcing as part of supply chain management. Selecting the right partner who will participate in joint planning early in the process is critical. As suppliers build their businesses around their specialized knowledge and core competencies, strategic alliances with these suppliers become increasingly important to the design and development of a system and ensure long-term support. Consequently, supplier assessments of the potential supply base must be more detailed and precise.[71]

At this point it is appropriate to point out that the laws, rules, regulations, policies, and procedures used by the federal government can easily discourage a commercial contractor from doing business in the public sector. One of the most significant laws is TINA, which requires designated categories of contracts and contractors to furnish the government cost or pricing data upon which the product or services cost was based. TINA also requires some contractors to disclose their accounting practices to the government.

Promote competition: Acquisition policy has traditionally emphasized "full and open competition" as the way to ensure that quality goods and services are obtained at a fair and reasonable price. This means that all responsible sources are permitted to compete.[72]

In a competitive situation, both the seller and buyer will attempt to exploit the situation for their own advantage. The seller will ask as high a price as it feels it reasonably can. The buyer will not pay more than necessary to obtain the needed item. "Which prevails will depend on relative bargaining strength, and this will depend on the interaction of such factors as the number of buyers and sellers of the product, the costs, the amounts of profit, the intensity of demand, and the alternatives available to both buyers and sellers."[73]

As discussed earlier, studies by the RAND Corporation, the Battelle Memorial Institute, and the Office of the Secretary of Defense concluded that contract price reductions from 25 to 30 percent can be realized in an atmosphere of genuine price competition.[74] Price reductions on government contracts through competition are prevalent. Congress has made clear that competitive procurements are mandatory, and sealed bids and negotiated procurements fit the competitive award criteria that "full and open competition" exists.[75] Inclusion of negotiated procurements, which permit award without discussion, and the implementation of the best value and past performance standards, means the award will no longer be left only to the low bidder.[76] Low price is not a fair way to measure competition because, as Deming points out, "price has no meaning without a measure of the quality being purchased."[77]

Early in our history, contracts were awarded primarily on price because it was believed that lowest price represented the "best value" to the government. This policy created "the strict conformance standard"—a process in which lowest price begets the lowest possible interpretation of requirements, i.e., no more, no less. Today, as part of acquisition streamlining, government policy encourages greater use of performance specifications. This, coupled with continued advances in technology, means that requirements have become more complex and that the number of variables to consider when evaluating proposals has increased. Consequently, the 1991 DoD appropriations bill changed the law to enable the use of "best value" criteria. Best value is consistent with Deming's fourth point, i.e., "to end the practice of awarding business on price tag alone."[78] The contractor's approach to meeting the requirement, delivery schedule, contractor's past performance, and life cycle (support) cost are also major factors to be considered when selecting the supplier.[79]

The system must perform in a cost-effective manner: This standard relates to reducing policy and procedural constraints on the acquisition system that cause it to be characterized as non-responsive and inefficient. The requirement for the system to perform in a timely, high-quality, and cost-effective manner embraces one of the major initiatives of the vision, i.e., acquisition employees must be empowered to exercise their individual initiative and judgment. James Wilson points out that we want government to be both fair and responsive; but the more rules we impose to ensure fairness, the harder we make it for government to be responsive.[80] Herbert Kaufman is quoted as saying that red tape is of our own making: "Every restraint and requirement originates in somebody's demand for it."[81]

The DoD inspector general reported that in the case of procurements under $500,000, cost and pricing data were still requested 75 percent of the time, even though they were not required by the regulations.[82] Empowering employees to make decisions in their areas of responsibility is a message that a significant cultural change is required. FAR paragraph 1.102,

Statement of guiding principles for the Federal Acquisition System, states that members of the integrated acquisition team must be empowered to make decisions in their area of responsibility for the system to become more responsive. The FAR vision further encourages members of the team to exercise initiative when it is in the best interest of the government to do so. If it is not prohibited by law or regulation, and it makes good business sense to initiate an action, then do it.[83] Members of the team can address tasks in their areas of responsibility from the perspective that if it does not add value, and the regulations or policies are silent on the subject, then why do it?

Emphasis is also being placed on the government adopting best commercial practices when and where it makes good business sense to do so. In the 1980s commercial industry began to focus on the total system cost. This change in perspective occurred when the private sector realized that almost 60% of the cost of goods sold went to purchase supplies and services from subcontractors and vendors. Top management realized that they needed to change their perspective to be more competitive. The primary measures of success no longer were price, keeping the production line moving, and the cost of operating their departments. Effective management of outside suppliers was recognized in the private sector as a competitive weapon. Purchasing and supply managers began to focus on: (1) value-added benefits, such as the quality of purchased material and services, and (2) cutting the total cost of acquiring, converting materials to finished goods, moving, and holding inventories. At the same time, supply strategies were developed and integrated into marketing, production, and financial strategies. This has led to three major developments in industry:

1. Using cross-functional commodity teams to identify sources or develop new products
2. Developing and managing the organization's supply chain
3. Developing collaborative supplier partnerships and strategic alliances.[84]

An efficient acquisition system is also the outgrowth of the skills and training of its personnel. As the government downsizes, contracting professionals are assuming an increased workload and becoming generalists specializing in business management–type duties. Therefore, job training and qualification requirements must be revised to meet the government employee's future needs.

Planning is an integral part of the acquisition system: The acquisition team must participate in the planning and budgeting process. All members are also charged to participate in the requirements determination and acquisition planning steps of this process. The integrated acquisition team must be formed early so that each appropriate discipline can translate operational and support needs into program requirements. Participation in program definition, market research, and the subsequent preparation of the documentation describing the requirement ensures that all factors are considered. Depending on the size of the acquisition, these documents can be multidimensional; it is therefore vital that all appropriate members of the integrated acquisition team participate in initial planning. This performance standard also cautions members of the team to be flexible so they can adjust to unforeseen changes to requirements as conditions dictate.

Minimizing Administrative Cost

The next performance standard is *minimizing administrative operating cost*. This has always been important, but the scale of importance increases exponentially in periods of declining funds. Some examples of ways to minimize administrative cost are: (1) shortening procurement cycle time through the use of electronic communications; (2) eliminating the use of paper through the use of electronic commerce; (3) using purchase cards for small dollar purchases; (4) taking advantage of the bulk purchasing power of the government; (5) using blanket purchase agreements, multiple-award indefinite quantity contracts, and single agency procurements; (6) integrating product and process; and (7) relying increasingly on commercial products.

Avoiding excessive checking is another way to reduce administrative cost. "There is an optimal level of 'waste' in any organization, public or private. It is at that level below which further savings are worth less than the cost producing them."[85] The benefits derived from added product testing and inspection fit the same law of diminishing returns. Acquisition managers must determine by cost-benefit analysis if the cost of avoiding risk entirely is worth the expenditure. Other prime candidates for cost-benefit evaluations are performance requirements, process standards, product modification, product and reliability testing, data items, and size and structure of the integrated acquisition team itself.

Dr. Paul Kaminski, former Under Secretary of Defense for Acquisition and Technology and one of the architects of acquisition reform, recalled how as a program manager in the Air Force he had evaluated recommendations from the engineering support organization on required specifications and data items. He determined their merit by using the risk-reward (cost-benefit) technique.[86] Following Dr. Kaminski's lead, questions to ask when determining the requirements to be incorporated into the specifications, processes, and data to be delivered to the government include:

1. Is it vital to product performance and the customer's mission?
2. Does it enhance management of the program, or is it a "just in case" requirement?

3. What is the impact on the purchasing cycle time and the personnel cost of the integrated acquisition team?
4. Can it be accomplished in a less costly way?

Maintaining the Public Trust and Managing Risk

Maintaining the public trust: When framing the Constitution, our founding fathers recognized the crucial role public opinion plays in influencing what laws would be written, what their content would be, what funds would be requested, and how those funds would be allocated. Alexander Hamilton recognized in *The Federalist Papers* that "legislative discretion is regulated by public opinion."[87] This performance standard highlights the importance of maintaining the public trust, calling on each member of the integrated acquisition team—government as well as contractor—to ensure the integrity of the acquisition system by handling public resources wisely, fairly, and openly. The standard states that each member of the team is "responsible and accountable for the wise use of public resources as well as acting in a manner which maintains the public's trust. Fairness and openness require open communication among team members, internal and external customers, and the public."[88]

As part of the government's fiduciary responsibility to the taxpayer, government personnel have traditionally performed oversight of contractor performance. This often includes full-time personnel assigned to review the contractor's performance on site or performing periodic visits to the contractor's plant to inspect and accept the deliverable product. Contractor progress is also monitored by reports, often covering numerous details, submitted by the contractor via contract data requirements lists (CDRL). This practice has sometimes led to the government approving performance plans after contract award and creating decision points where government permission is required prior to the contractor advancing to the next step.

Acquisition doctrine has moved government surveillance to a higher level without sacrificing the public's interests. Emphasis is now being placed on increased use of performance-based contracting, which is designed to increase the contractor's accountability for achieving the designated performance factors. In exchange for accepting this increased risk, the contractor is given a much greater amount of flexibility in the way it performs under the contract.[89]

Draft solicitations now can be sent to prospective offerors prior to issuing the solicitation. This means that a performance requirement document fully describing tasks and performance requirements can be developed in conjunction with the contractor prior to issuing the formal request for proposal. The integrated acquisition team can then monitor contractor performance through the use of performance indicators, e.g., metrics. Under this concept the contractor also is able to incorporate its current processes into the requirements document rather than create a hybrid process, as has been the case in the past.

Managing risk: Another way to earn the public trust is to empower officials to exercise initiative and apply sound business judgment to the management of the risks associated with each acquisition. The goal is to be proactive by shifting the objective of decisions from "risk avoidance" to "risk management." This is opposed to "eliminating risk" through the adoption of all-inclusive processes and extensive test programs.[90]

Managing risk increases the acquisition team's readiness to address possible problems. Risk is defined as "the probability of unwanted consequences of an event or decision." Every risk has a probability of occurrence, an impact, and choices that will affect outcome.[91] Risk can also be described as a potential problem dealing with the possibility of failing to achieve a designated objective. It is not limited to any one source and can be categorized by type, e.g., cost, schedule, technical performance, supportability, and programmatic risk. The contractor is also subject to business risk, such as a subcontractor going out of business, failure of a subcontractor to deliver on time, or a component part becoming obsolete.

A historic obstacle in managing risk is the real-life situation in which managers are more often busier correcting today's problems than preventing or mitigating tomorrow's. A large part of the reason for this condition is that the reward system recognizes those who solve current problems and rarely recognizes those with the foresight to prevent problems from occurring.

DoD Directive 5000.2 defines risk management as "an organized method of identifying and measuring risk and developing, selecting, and managing options for handling these risks. The types of risk include, but are not limited to, schedule, cost, technical feasibility, threat, risk of technical obsolescence, security, software management, dependencies between a new program and other prgrams, and risk of creating a monopoly for future procurements."[92] Risk management is a systematic approach rather than an "art or science."[93] Identifying and managing risk is an important part of each integrated acquisition team's responsibilities. Policy has shifted the team's focus from total risk avoidance to risk management.

Members of the integrated acquisition team can manage risk by: (1) reducing the probability of the problem occurring; (2) developing a contingency plan to work around the problem, should it occur; (3) transferring the risk to another party; and (4) eliminating the risk completely. In most cases the cost of completely eliminating a risk is prohibitive.[94]

Policy initiatives are also addressing risk from the top down. One leading example in which risk management has been implemented through policy is the performance standard that maximizes the use of commercial products or services in the FAR.[95]

An additional example of risk management is the emphasis placed on the contractor's recent past performance in making the source selection.

Theoretically, there is less risk when a proven performer is awarded a contract. The FAR performance standard is: "When selecting contractors to provide products or perform services, the Government will use contractors who have a track record of successful past performance or who demonstrate a current superior ability to perform."[96]

From the contractor's point of view, almost every acquisition also represents a potential window of opportunity. For example, it provides the contractor the opportunity to improve its sales position and return on invested assets. It also means that the contractor can maintain a positive record of performance that will enhance its ability to obtain subsequent business. It could represent an opportunity to launch a new product line or enhance the contractor's competitive position within the industry. In addition to receiving the needed product at a fair and reasonable price, the government also benefits from mission success, improving organizational efficiency and effectiveness, and enhancing the industrial base.

The key point regarding these windows of opportunity is that they are often of short duration. Therefore, management must be alert to the opportunity potential present and develop contingency plans before the window slams shut.

Fulfillment of Public Policy Objectives

Congress is the primary authority for turning public policies into law. Not only does it establish the foundation for rules that govern the acquisition process, but it also initiates social and economic policies through legislation. However, interpreting the legislation is the function of the executive branch of government, with help from the judiciary and case law. The magnitude of social and economic policies addressed in the FAR is immense and complex. Table 1-2 below lists the categories of social and economic programs.

This performance standard also requires the acquisition system to attain goals adopted by Congress and the president while ensuring efficient use of public resources.[98] The social economic programs that have the greatest affect on the acquisition process are small business, small and disadvan-

---

Table 1-2 Categories of Social Economic Programs[97]

Programs that Improve Working Conditions
Programs to Favor Selected or Disadvantaged Groups
Programs Favoring Purchase from American Companies
Programs to Protect the Environment and Quality of Life
Programs to Achieve Other Government Purposes

taged business, equal opportunity, affirmative action programs, and wage protection given to construction and service contract labor.

THE INFORMATION REVOLUTION

If the reasons cited above were not enough to encourage reforming the government acquisition process, the fact that we are also entering the Information Age adds gravity to the situation. In his book *Megatrends: Ten New Directions Transforming Our Lives,* Peter Naisbitt claims globalization of the information society occurred in 1957, when white-collar workers in technical, managerial, and clerical positions first outnumbered blue-collar workers. For the first time in our history, more people worked with information than labored to produce goods or services.[99]

The federal government has had a major role to play in developing the computer and what we refer to as electronic data interchange. The first working computer, the ENIAC, was developed for military needs during World War II. Early in the Cold War, the military requirement for an "early warning system" in the Canadian Arctic enabled IBM to design and manufacture working computers in substantial numbers.[100] The Internet, which is a group of academic, commercial, and government computer networks, was developed in 1965 under the auspices of the Advanced Research Project Agency (ARPA) and the National Science Foundation to link scientific computers for technical research purposes.[101]

The capability to move data electronically means that people can exchange information without paper. Computer-to-computer exchange has had a phenomenal influence on how business information is processed, transmitted, and stored. It can be accomplished through a wide range of information technologies that include electronic data interchange (EDI), electronic funds transfer (EFT), electronic mail (e-mail), document imaging, and facsimile (fax) transmissions.

E-mail includes any technology that permits the interchange of electronic data between e-mail users. EDI is a computer-to-computer exchange of routine business documents using transaction standards agreed on by both contracting parties.[102] Document imaging technology scans the characters from paper and then stores the electronic image on an optical or laser disk. This technology permits storage and retrieval of thousands of documents within seconds without the operator leaving the workstation.[103] Document imaging, when combined with e-mail and EDI, is not only making a paperless office a reality but also is revolutionizing the flow of work within the organization and between the buyer and seller.

EDI is a powerful communication tool that carries a variety of message formats, including technical drawings, and that can interconnect with a variety of e-mail networks.[104] E-mail fosters communication among buyers, sellers, and members of an integrated development team because it is not constrained by organizational or even national boundaries.

One of the primary benefits of EDI is a faster and concurrent flow of information to members of the integrated acquisition team. The Internet and sharing of common databases has greatly reduced the information float (that is, the amount of information that cannot be accessed because it is in the mail between sender and receiver[105]). Another advantage of EDI is greater efficiency due to the elimination of data entry errors and a reduction of personnel costs by reducing handling and storing of documents. Other revolutionary methods by which data is exchanged include:

1. Electronic funds transfer (EFT), which is the electronic transmission of payments and remittance information. The Department of the Treasury's Financial Management Service (FMS) and the Department of Defense Finance and Accounting Service (DFAS) are the agencies that manage invoices and vouchers for the civil and defense acquisition, respectively. Both prefer paying via EFT because it reduces paper-handling cost substantially. The benefit to the contractor is that it receives payment three to five days sooner than payment via a mailed check.[106]

2. Facsimile (fax) transmissions, which occur when typed characters on a page are converted into electronic impulses that are transmitted over telephone lines to a fax machine for conversion into readable text. Documents can be faxed over an already existing telephone system integrated into a computer or stored in a document imaging system.[107]

Within the organization, EDI, E-mail, and document imaging are electronically integrating information used by such traditional business functions as product design, manufacturing, acquisition, inventory management, physical distribution, accounting, and finance. Rather than waiting for information on the design of a new product to be sent to manufacturing, that information can now be pulled from the design database, thereby compressing product development time. This same technology permits the buyer and seller to do business electronically.

The use of EDI for business purposes was advanced with the passage of the Electronic Signatures Act in June of 2000. Under this legislation electronic signatures and documents have the same legal validity as manual signatures and hard-copy documents. Key provisions of the act are that: (1) a signature, contract, or other record relating to a transaction in interstate or foreign commerce may not be denied legal effect, validity, or enforcement solely because it is in electronic form; (2) a contract relating to such a transaction may not be denied legal effect, validity, or enforceability solely because an electronic signature or electronic record was used in its information; and (3) rules for retention of electronic records are set.[108]

Peter Drucker has stated that "with the advent of the computer, information became the organizing principle for work."[109] Beginning in the 1950s, in most commercial firms such tasks as physical distribution, manufacturing support, and purchasing were organized functionally, and management followed a vertical protocol. Since that time, as new methods to move and share information have been introduced, organizations have begun to refocus their orientation away from function operations and have learned to operate interdependently, rather than independently. This requires rethinking how work is actually going to be done as well as the internal management structure. The information-based organization is a group of specialists with separate bodies of knowledge that are linked in a network but that function as independent agents. These specialists are viewed as interacting with the suppliers as well as the ultimate customer. This interaction occurs across internal functions on a network basis rather than by formally reporting to a specific manager. Success comes from a commitment to managing the overall process rather than remaining loyal to the organizational structure.[110]

In an article appearing in the *Acquisition Review Quarterly*, the authors state that information technology "is changing the role of the government's purchasing department from a transaction-oriented function to a more managerial function focused on establishing and maintaining relationships with suppliers, third parties, and internal customers, and leveraging corporate buying power. In its new role, procurement will also manage the technological infrastructure necessary either to automate transactions fully or to empower end users to perform many transactions without direct involvement of purchasing personnel."[111]

It is important to point out that the term *procurement* as used above has a broader meaning than the word *purchasing*. Procurement takes place in many departments. It is the systematic process of deciding what, when, and how much to purchase; the act of purchasing it; and the process of ensuring that what is required is received on time in the quantity specified. In other words, purchasing is a subset of procurement.[112]

To purchase goods and services effectively, the government acquisition process must be able to interface effectively and efficiently with processes used in the private sector. Management in the commercial sector, because of its significant contribution to the bottom line, is looking to reduce the organization's total material cost. They are therefore reviewing their purchasing history and systems. The results will then be used to develop procurement plans and to form strategic alliances with key suppliers, creating a synergistic relationship between purchasing, materials management, and the product's supply chain.

CONCLUSION

Performance by the arsenal of the United States was a major reason for the victory in World War II and the end of the Cold War. The threat of a world war between superpowers is lower than it has been in over 50 years.

In the last half of the 20th century, the American economy was able to deliver both guns and butter. Nevertheless, there was a price to pay: a budget deficit, higher taxes, and doubts among the citizenry as to the efficiency of the federal government.

Philip Howard points out that the public's dissatisfaction with government is not caused by the goals but by government techniques.[113] The bureaucracy is subject to conflicting objectives, e.g., satisfying the customer while at the same time protecting the integrity of the procurement process.[114] Over the years procurement laws, regulations, checklists, and continuous oversight have been the way to protect the integrity of the system. Thousands of pages of law, rules, and regulations have given the appearance that following the process was more important than delivering a product to the ultimate user on time at a reasonable price. Rules and regulations have eclipsed common sense and individual responsibility, thereby creating this balance.

In the early 1990s it was clear something needed to be done to make the federal acquisition system more efficient. Public opinion, the end of the Cold War, and the move into the Information Age and the changes it will bring, e.g., electronic data interchange, the Internet, and strategic alliances with suppliers, provided the motive for the nation's leadership to seize the opportunity to make the changes needed. As Alexis de Tocqueville observed, a democratic form of government "often unintentionally works against itself; but its aim is more beneficial [than the aristocracy's] . . . for all its faults, [a democratic government] is the best suited of all to make society prosper." Being able to adjust past law and policies is "the great privilege of the Americans."[115]

David N. Burt's 1984 book *Proactive Procurement* focuses on the importance of procurement in containing cost, improving quality, increasing productivity, shortening concept to delivery times, and integrating materials management through the use of modern technologies. Burt, collaborating with Michael Doyle on *American Keiretsu* (1993), addresses the need for strategic relationships among buyers and suppliers and the fact that the supply chain is a competitive weapon.[116] Although their ideas are directed toward the private sector, the business practices of the commercial sector are also models for acquisition reform.

Reinventing government and streamlining federal acquisition were the methods selected to renovate the process. A customer-oriented goal for the federal acquisition system has been stipulated as doctrine for all to follow. Standards of performance have also been articulated that provide a framework to measure compliance and a set of continuous improvement targets. However, it would be remiss to leave the reader with the impression that government procurement will become the mirror image of the commercial market. The fundamental objectives of the federal acquisition process also include the need to be fair and maintain the public trust while at the same time fostering social and economic programs. These objectives must also be viewed with the understanding that federal contractors must comply with the Cost Accounting Standards as well as furnish the buyer cost or pricing data in absence of adequate competition. Therefore, the two markets will never be totally integrated.

In a paper titled *The Road Ahead*, the Under Secretary of Defense J.S. Gansler outlines a course the Department of Defense must follow to build on the past achievements of acquisition and logistics reform. The initial implementing action is "increased reliance on an integrated civil-military industrial base in lieu of a defense-unique industrial base." The paper celebrates the successes of the department's revolution in business affairs and the forging of a "strong partnership between the Congress, the administration, industry, labor unions, our acquisition community, and our ultimate customer, the warfighters." It also establishes the following implementing actions, which are designed to build on the successes of the past, i.e., "a more efficient and effective acquisition and logistics environment that will deliver high-performance weapon systems and support to our warfighters in less time, and at a lower total cost of ownership":

- Increase reliance on an integrated civil-military industrial base in lieu of a defense-unique industrial base
- Extend military specification and standard reform to re-procurements through the use of performance-based acquisitions to enable logistics reform
- Provide incentives for suppliers by using acquisition strategies that give contractors flexibility to innovate and access commercial solutions as a way to reduce acquisition cost and cycle time
- Migrate DoD oversight and buying practices to management of suppliers, not supplies, through establishment of strategic alliance relationships among buying commands and suppliers
- Expand the use of performance-based acquisitions by streamlining procurements for the services through use of commercial processes, products, and practices
- Expand the use of price-based acquisition for research and development by shifting significant risk to contractors and having alternatives available
- Adopt a new approach to systems acquisition in which price and schedule play a key role in driving design development and systems are reviewed by portfolio
- Develop a way to look at programs on a portfolio basis, which provides the flexibility to meet current threats by having viable alternatives to specific acquisition programs that have common architecture and information exchange requirements that facilitate interoperability with other programs or legacy systems

- Address the cost in the Operational Requirement Document (ORD) to determine what a system is worth compared to other capability needs and their costs
- Implement time-phased requirements and evolutionary acquisition as a way to reduce acquisition cycle times
- Transform its mass logistics system to a highly agile, reliable system that delivers logistics on demand
- Implement DoD Logistics Transformation Plans, DoD Logistics Strategy goals, and objectives metrics
- Identify Section 912(c) Pilot Program production support reengineering initiatives
- Assess the feasibility of developing new Product Support Working Capital Fund business areas to support legacy systems
- Establish logistics system architecture to coordinate integrating and reengineering business practices and to support information technology systems so that they operate to achieve total supply chain management in a unified manner
- Reduce the DoD acquisition infrastructure and overhead functions
- Continue to implement Service RDT&E infrastructure efficiency initiatives
- Reduce DoD facilities and bases
- Provide the DoD workforce with the requisite skills to operate efficiently in its new environment and perpetuate continuous improvement
- Deliver team training courses for commercial practices and services
- Implement Phase II continuous learning to transition to a learning organization by improving individual and organizational performance through seeking out and adopting best practices
- Adapt the key facets of the DoD Corporate University to the Defense Acquisition University to facilitate acquisition reform further.[117]

With acquisition reform as the backdrop, Chapter Two explains the role of the integrated acquisition team and relationships within it and shows how the team can satisfy the user's needs through increasing reliance on business judgment in making cost-benefit tradeoffs and focusing its efforts on the management of risk and opportunities. Subsequent chapters concentrate on the tasks of the integrated acquisition team, using the phases of the acquisition process as the framework.

NOTES

[1]Sherman, Stanley N. 1991. *Government Procurement Management.* Wordcrafters: Germantown, MD, 21. Stanley points out that the adoption of the word *acquisition*

instead of *procurement* indicates a tendency in government to invent terminologies that relate to similar or overlapping activities to reflect attitudes and approaches of individuals, groups, or agencies.

[2]Nash, Ralph C., Steven L. Schooner, and Karen R. O'Brien. 1998. *The Government Contracts Reference Book: A Comprehensive Guide to the Language of Procurement.* 2d ed. Washington, D.C.: The George Washington University, 408.

[3]FAR 2.101.

[4]Federal Procurement Data System, Total Federal Snapshot Report. Actions Reported Individually on SF279, Fiscal Year 1999 through Fourth Quarter, as of January 15, 2000.

[5]Federal Procurement Data System, Federal Contract Actions and Dollars by Executive Department and Agency. Actions reported individually on SF279, Fiscal Year 1999 through Fourth Quarter, as of January 15, 2000.

[6]Fox, J. Ronald. 1974. *Arming of America: How the U.S. Buys Weapons.* Boston: Harvard University, 37.

[7]Fox, 26.

[8]Mcfarlan, Gregor. 2000. The Buyer as a Business Manager? *Contract Management* (August): 28.

[9]"Total Federal Snapshot Report." SF 279 and SF 281 Federal Procurement Report, Fiscal Year 1990.

[10]Fox, 256.

[11]Sherman, 257.

[12]Sherman, 278.

[13]The Uniform Commercial Code is a U.S. model law developed to standardize commercial contracting law among the states.

[14]Sherman, 107.

[15]Alston, Frank, Franklin Johnson, Margaret Worthington, Louis Goldsmith, and Frank DeVito. 1984. *Contracting with the Federal Government.* New York: John Wiley and Sons, 9.

[16]Sherman, 12.

[17]Fireside Chat radio broadcast, December 29, 1940.

[18]For our purposes, public opinion is a combination of citizen beliefs, statements by the nation's intellectuals, and commentaries from the news media.

[19]Air Force Association. 1999. *Air Force Magazine.* (May): 58.

[20]Sherman, 20.

[21]Sherman, 21.

[22]Sherman, 14.

[23]Sherman , 8.

[24]Sourwine, Darrel. 1992. Contracting—Law+Accounting. *Contract Management* (May): 10.

[25]10 U.S. Code 2304.

[26]Galimore, Carl R. 1982. *Accounting for Contracts.* Chelsea, Michigan: Bookcrafters, 272.

[27]Gallimore, 280.

[28]Gallimore, 280.

[29]Many point out that it is unrealistic to compare a purchase by the federal government to a similar one in the private sector. This is because the executive and legislative branches implement social and economic programs and establish accounting practices/standards through legislation and because in many cases the federal market is a monopsony.

[30]Sherman, 117.

[31]Sherman, 361.

[32]Sherman, 6.

[33]Blue Ribbon Commission on Defense Management, Final Report to the President. 1986. *A Quest for Excellence.* Washington D.C. June, xv.

[34]The Center for Strategic and International Studies. 1983. The CSIS Acquisition Study. *U.S. Defense Acquisition: A Process in Trouble.* Washington D.C.: Georgetown University. March: 3.

[35]Cibinic, John Jr., and Ralph C. Nash, Jr. 1986. *Administration of Government Contracts.* 2d ed. Washington, D.C.: The George Washington University, 14.

[36]*G.L. Christian and Associates v. United States,* 160 Ct.Cl.1, 312,F.2d 418,160 Ct. 902.

[37]Wyatt, John B. III. 1993. The Christian Doctrine: Born Again But Sinfully Confusing. *Contract Management.* (November): 25.

[38]Howard, Phillip K. 1994. *The Death of Common Sense.* New York: Warner Books, 11.

[39]Wilson, James Q. 1989. *Bureaucracy: What Government Agencies Do and Why They Do It.* Basic Books, 128.

[40]James A. The Sinews of War: Army Logistics 17751953 *Army Historical Series* Office of the Chief of History United States Army, Washington D.C.

[41]Blue Ribbon Commission, 77.

[42]Blue Ribbon Commission, 77.

[43]Goodwin, Jacob. 1985. *Brotherhood of Arms: General Dynamics and the Business of Defending America.* New York: Times Books, 49.

[44]Lamm, David V. 1988. Why Firms Refuse DOD Business: An Analysis or Rationale. *National Contract Management Journal* Winter, 54.

[45]Gore, Albert, Jr. 1997. Introduction. *Blair House Papers.* Washington, D.C. (www.whitehouse.gov/WH/html/Blair_VP.html)

[46]Gore, Albert, Jr. 1993. *From Red Tape to Results: Creating a Government That Works Better and Costs Less.* Report of the National Performance Review, 26–31.

[47]Lumer, Mark and Donna Ireton. 1994. *Acquisition Reform under the Federal Acquisition Streamlining Act of 1994, Vol. 2, Synopsis and Implications.* NCMA, i.

[48]Public Law 93-400, 1976.

[49]Kelman, Steve. 1990. *Procurement and Public Management.* Washington, D.C., 1.

[50] Welsh, Bill. 1997. A Look Back at Acquisition Reform with Steve Kelman. *Contract Management* (November): 42.

[51]Kelman, Steve and Susan Alesi. 1995. Guiding Principles for the Federal Acquisition System. *Contract Management.* (March): 28.

[52]Preston, Colleen A. 1997. Colleen Preston on Acquisition Reform. *Program Manager* (January-February): 26.

[53]FAR 1.102, Statement of guiding principles for the Federal Acquisition System.

[54]FAR 1.102-2 (a) (1).

[55]Rider, Melissa, Kenneth D. Brody, David B. Dempsey, and Bernard L. Weiss. 1997. *Understanding The FAR Part 15 Rewrite.* Vienna, VA: National Contract Management Association, 19.

[56]FAR 1.102 (c) (1).

[57]DoDI 5002.2, 2001. Enclosure 2.

[58]FAR 1.102 (d).

[59]FAR 1.102-4 (b).

[60]FAR 1.102-4 (a).

[61]Nash, Ralph C., Jr. 1997. Training the Contracting Officer of the Future. *Contract Management,* (March): 16.

[62]FAR 1.102 (e).

[63]FAR 1.102(d).

[64]DoD 5000.2R. 2001. Part 7, paragraph 7.6.4.

[65]The terms *intranet* and *extranet* are defined as "a private internal network that operates within a company and is usually insulated from the outside world via an electronic or hardware impedance called a firewall" and "a close relative of an intranet, the difference being that both specified trading partners and remote company offices not confined to the corporate location can securely access it via the Internet," respectively. Shaw, Jack. 1999. *Surviving the Digital Jungle: What Every Executive Needs to Know about eCommerce and eBusiness.* Marietta, GA: Electronic Commerce Strategies, Inc., 104.

[66]FAR 15.304 b(3) (i).

[67]Walton, Mary. 1986. *The Deming Management Method.* New York: The Putnam Publishing Group, 35.

[68]A commercial non-developmental item is defined as one being customarily used for governmental needs that was: (1) developed with private funds and (b) sold on a competitive basis (FAR 2-101).

[69]DoDD 5000. 2000. Paragraph 4.2.3.

[70]Rumbaugh, Margaret G. 1997. Conducting Market Research. *National Contract Management Association Workshop Series.* Vienna, VA: National Contract Management Association, 3.

[71]Duffy, Roberta. 1999. Where Are We Headed. *Business Briefing: Global Purchasing and Supply Chain Management.* World Market Research Center, Proceedings of the 11th World Congress of International Federation of Purchasing and Materials Management, 17–19 November, Milton Qld, Australia, 102–107.

[72]FAR 6.003.

[73]*Armed Services Pricing Manual.* 1986. Chicago: Commerce Clearing House, Inc., 2–5.

[74]Fox, 256.

[75]Sherman, 123.

[76]Delane, John. 1997. A Contractor's Perspective on Procurement Reform. *Contract Management.* (September): 43.

[77]Walton, Mary. 1986. *The Deming Management Method.* New York: The Putnam Publishing Group, 62.

[78]Walton, 35.

[79]Menker, Janice M. 1992. Best Value Contracting: Debunking the Myth. *Program Manager,* (September): 16.

[80]Wilson, James Q. 1989. *Bureaucracy: What Government Agencies Do and WhyThey Do It.* New York: Harper Collins, 326.

[81]Wilson, 317.

[82]Preston, 29.

[83]FAR 1.102-4 (e).

[84]Dobler, Donald W. and David N. Burt. 1996. *Purchasing and Supply Management* 6th ed. New York: McGraw-Hill Companies, Inc., 11–15.

[85]Wilson, 324.

[86]Kaminski, Paul G., Under Secretary of Defense for Acquisition. Interview by Dr. J. Ronald Fox. 1997. *Program Manager,* Special Edition. (January-February): 4.

[87]Hamilton, Alexander. 1961. *The Federalist Papers,* Number 84. New York: Penguin, 514.

[88]FAR 1.102-2 (c) (1).

[89]Dayton, Charlotte A., and Jean-Anne Erickson. 1999. Insights. Oversight: Can the Government Make the Change from Task-Based to Performance-Based Contracting? *Contract Management* (October): 48.

[90]FAR 1.102-2 (c) (2).

[91]Gammer, Art. 1997. Risk Management: Moving Beyond the Process. *Computer* (May): 38.

[92]DoDI 5000.2, Operation of the Defense Acquisition System. Paragraph 4.7.3.2.3.4.1.

[93]Stevens, Michael R. 1997. Addressing Risk Management in Non-Developmental Items Acquisition Programs. *Acquisition Review Quarterly* (Winter): 41.

[94]Gammer, 38.

[95]FAR 1.102 (b) (1) (i).

[96]FAR 1.102-2 (a) (3).

[97]Sherman, 347.

[98]FAR 1.102-2 (d).

[99]Naisbitt, John. 1984. *Megatrends: Ten New Directions Transforming Our Lives.* New York: Warner Books Inc., 2.

[100]Drucker, Peter F. 1990. *The New Realities.* New York: Harper & Row, 48.

[101]Drake, Daniel. *Procurement Manager's Guide to EC/EDI*. Vienna, VA: Holbrook & Kellogg, 2–18.

[102]Drake, 2–3.

[103]Drake, 2–15.

[104]Drake, 2–13.

[105]Naisbitt, 15.

[106]Drake, 2–12.

[107]Drake, 2–14.

[108]Public Law 106-229.

[109]Drucker, 255.

[110]Bowersox, Donald J., and David J. Gross. 1996. *Logistics Management: The Integrated Supply Chain Process*. New York: McGraw-Hill Companies, Inc., 75.

[111]Gebauer, Judith, Carrie Beam, and Arie Segev. 1998. Impact of the Internet on Procurement. *Acquisition Review* 5(2): 167.

[112]Burt, David N., and Richard L. Pinkerton. 1996. *A Purchasing Manager's Guide to Strategic Proactive Procurement*. New York: American Management Association, 2.

[113]Howard, 173.

[114]Wilson, 127.

[115]de Tocqueville, Alexis. 1988. *Democracy in America*. Translated by George Lawrence, edited by J.P. Mayer. Harper & Row Publishers, Inc., 232.

[116]Burt and Pinkerton, ix.

[117]Gansler, J.S., Under Secretary of Defense. 2000. *The Road Ahead*. Washington, D.C. June 2, 2000.

CHAPTER 2

Introduction to the
Federal Acquisition Process

To provide a backdrop for further discussion on the integrated acquisition team, its role, responsibilities, structure, and relationships among team members, this chapter provides an overview of the federal acquisition process. It concludes with a presentation on the management of risk and opportunities (MR&O) technique, which focuses on the acquisition's objectives and is a way by which possible variances can be managed proactively to ensure that the risk of not achieving the objectives is mitigated and the window of opportunity to exceed expectations is not missed.

Peter Drucker suggests that we are now in transition from the traditional command-and-control organizational relationship to one based on the flow of information among bodies of knowledge. Drucker describes the information-based organization as a group of specialists linked to each other in a network but functioning as independent agents for their specialty. These specialists actively interact with customers and suppliers using the Internet and extranet in a computer-to-computer exchange of data. Organizationally, this interaction occurs horizontally rather than vertically and crosses functional and institutional boundaries. Distance, which once inhibited real-time communications, is almost no longer a concern. Organizations are becoming flatter, with fewer layers of management. Drucker also predicts that operations of large businesses will more likely resemble those of hospitals or orchestras than of typical manufacturing companies.[1]

Traditionally, contracting has been viewed as an exclusive relationship between a buyer and a seller, each concentrating on getting what they want from the other. This perception goes back to the era when the seller had the expertise and was able to perform a majority of the work using its own organic capabilities. However, as the technological content and complexity of products increased, dependence on outside specialists and subcontractors also grew because their special knowledge and capabilities were crucial to satisfying contractual requirements. Today, at least 60% of a product or service's cost is in the form of purchased supplies, equipment, material, and services. On average, 50% of a firm's quality problems can be traced to purchased materials.[2]

The postulate of acquisition doctrine is that control over cost and quality of goods and services purchased can be achieved more effectively when functional specialists in the buyer and seller's organizations operate as part of an interdependent and integrated system. The contracting officer (CO) as a business manager plays a leading role in this relationship. No longer can the COs act as if their primary role is to enforce the acquisition rules and regulations and when others get involved, view them with apprehension. It has been said, "Years of dictated regulated solutions have bred a contracting culture that avoids risk, that tends not to think creatively when devising solutions, and that has gained a reputation in many quarters for being toads in the road."[3] One of the goals of this book is to help eradicate this reputation. The prescription is to follow the acquisition principles, eliminating the adversary relationships through team building, managing risk and opportunities, and taking advantage of the communication capabilities afforded by technological advances in telecommunications.

THE ACQUISITION PROCESS

In this book the basic framework, or model, for obtaining supplies and services by the federal government will be referred to as the acquisition process. Acquisition must not be thought of as a function but rather as a process that links customer needs to customer satisfaction.[4] This process should be viewed as a series of steps and activities for converting specific inputs into specific outputs.[5] It includes determination of requirements, acquisition planning, preparation of the solicitation, source selection, negotiation, and contract award, performance, and closeout. The first step in managing the acquisition process is to identify the stakeholders. Stakeholders in an acquisition include the ultimate user, program managers, contracting officers, functional managers, engineers, manufacturers, marketing personnel, suppliers, stockholders, subcontractors, vendors, financial institutions, and taxpayers. Success in managing the stakeholder relationship can be measured using these critical success factors:

- Client acceptance
- Client consultation
- Top management support
- Acquisition plans and schedules
- Monitoring of feedback
- Communication
- Troubleshooting.[6]

The term *acquisition* is defined in the FAR at 2.101 as "acquiring by contract with appropriated funds of supplies or services (including construction) by or for the use of the Federal Government through purchase or lease, whether the supplies or services are already in existence or must be created, developed, demonstrated, and evaluated. The acquisition process begins at the point when the agency needs are established and includes the description of requirements to satisfy agency needs, solicitation and selection of sources, award of contract, contract financing, contract performance, contract administration, and those technical and management functions directly related to the process of fulfilling agency needs by contract."[7] In this book the process of fulfilling an agency's needs will be referred to as the *acquisition process*. DoD directives in the Defense Acquisition System, the 5000 series, also refer to the new acquisition process. In the DoD context, the acquisition process has traditionally been an acquisition management process structured in logical phases by major decision points called milestones, beginning with broadly stated mission needs that cannot be satisfied by nonmaterial solutions.[8]

The federal acquisition process consists of a network of tasks and activities associated with a sequence of discrete events designed to produce the timely delivery of the needed product to the customer. Figure 2-1 depicts this process, illustrating major events associated with the procurement of goods and services.

The requirements determination phase: All requirements begin with a determination of need. Government needs fall into one of four general categories: (1) a need to establish a new operational capability, (2) a need to improve an existing capability, (3) a need to exploit an opportunity to reduce cost or enhance performance, and (4) a need to preserve a current capability through maintaining or replenishing inventory. Included in this phase

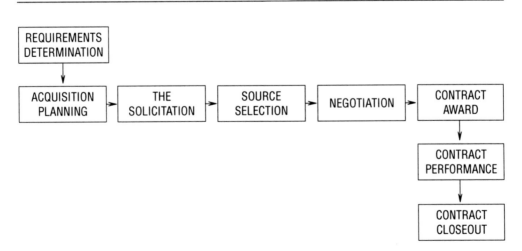

Figure 2-1 The Acquisition Process Model

are requirements forecasting, market research, development of initial acquisition strategy (external or internal source), and quantification of the funding requirement.

Acquisition planning: During this phase the acquisition cadre is formed, the user initiates the purchase request, market characteristics and industry practices are determined, and perceived needs are developed into more detailed statements of requirements. Specifications and statements of work, identification of sources, designation of the method of procurement, refinement of the procurement strategy, definition of evaluation criteria, and completion of procurement plans are examples of requirement documents. Initial tradeoffs are made and steps are taken to identify the cost, schedule, performance, and supportability risks, and assess their possible impact.

The solicitation: The solicitation phase includes all tasks and activities needed to refine the specifications, statement of work, and evaluation criteria into the proposal document or the request for bid, if the sealed bidding process is to be followed. Part of this task is determining the appropriate pricing arrangement; identifying government-furnished property needs, bonding requirements, and data needs; placing the appropriate requirements documents on the Internet; and announcing the business opportunity in the *Commerce Business Daily*. The pre-bid/proposal conference is held at this time, and amendments to the request for bid or proposal are also made during this phase.

Source selection: For negotiated procurements the integrated acquisition team evaluates potential contractors' proposals for technical content and cost analysis using the evaluation criteria defined in the solicitation. The team assesses the past performance records of prospective contractors, completes tradeoffs, and makes the competitive range decision. It then undertakes discussions with sources within the competitive range and makes the best value tradeoff determination. The team then finalizes the negotiation strategy and plan. If a sealed bid is involved, the team receives and administers the responses.

Negotiations: Negotiation is not an event but a process. There is a need to gather data and to prepare a negotiation plan before actual face-to-face bargaining. Therefore, negotiation planning overlaps previous steps in the acquisition process. In this phase the bargaining segment of negotiations is conducted. Agreement is reached, and appropriate changes are made to the draft contract (solicitation) to ensure that it conforms to the negotiated agreement and can be used as the contractual document.

Contract award: The parties execute the conforming contract, which represents common language for the integrated acquisition team and the foundation for managing risks and opportunities.

Contract performance: At this point a post-award conference is held, and the integrated acquisition team transitions to performing tasks and activities that focus on contract performance, such as risk and opportunity

(MR&O) variance analysis. Consent to subcontract is approved as required. Contracting officers implement change management procedures. Delivery schedules are monitored and action taken in the event of a variance. Quality assurance activity begins, and deliverables are tested, inspected, and accepted.

Contract closeout: Payments are processed and obligations discharged. In the event the contract is terminated for default or for convenience of the government, the tasks and activities necessary to settle all outstanding contractual issues and obligations are performed as part of this phase of the acquisition process.

THE INTEGRATED ACQUISITION TEAM

Today the probability of a successful acquisition is increased through the use of an integrated acquisition team. Members of the acquisition team are multi-organizational as well as cross-functional. This means that the ultimate user, contractors, suppliers, and the acquisition professional are organized into an acquisition team. The original skunk works, established by Kelly Johnson at Lockheed, was so organized.

The integrated acquisition team is an information-based organization that is composed of more specialists than in the traditional command-and-control organization. It is held together by the flow of information among the specialists in government and industry, regardless of organizational boundaries. Electronic data interchange (EDI) is greatly facilitating the exchange of project-related technical information among all members of the integrated acquisition team, regardless of their location.

Acquisition doctrine advocates including the customer as an active member of the integrated acquisition team. In addition, the prime contractor and major critical subcontractors contribute to the efforts of the team. This organizational relationship ensures that both the user and the supplier participate in tradeoffs among cost, schedule, performance, and supportability decisions as they are made. The characteristics of the product and method of procurement determine the tasks and activities performed by the integrated acquisition team because different products and contracting methods require diverse bodies of knowledge to procure the goods or services effectively. Therefore, tasks performed by the team vary from acquisition to acquisition.

Figure 2-1, The Acquisition Process Model, shows the events in the process occurring sequentially. A common electronic database often makes it possible to overlap events. Sharing a common database permits members of the team to work concurrently from the beginning to the end of the project, regardless of their physical location. The net result is real-time communication among team members, a reduction of rework, and a decrease in the amount of administrative lead time.

This integrated approach to acquisition management is not entirely new, having evolved from the program management[9] concept used by DoD in the 1950s. Program management developed because traditional organizational relationships were ponderous, geared to performing repetitive routine tasks, and slow to take action because of their functional focus. The goal of the project management concept was to achieve defined objectives by concentrating resources, e.g., specialists, funds, and equipment, in a group established to perform non-routine tasks.

By definition, a program or project has the following attributes:

- A boundary separating work on the product from routine work
- Non-routine multifunctional tasks
- A fixed beginning and scheduled completion dates
- An organizational structure tailored to the characteristics of the product
- Representation from all appropriate disciplines
- A high degree of interdependency between tasks and functions
- A need to coordinate and communicate directly and frequently with other members of the project
- A membership with the authority, responsibility, and accountability for decisions
- A commitment to mutual goals and a process for resolving differences
- A management information system containing cost, schedule, and performance data
- A control process that compares current status with the planned position.

Some integrated acquisition teams have failed to realize their potential because they: (1) lack senior management support, (2) have poorly defined goals, or (3) let personnel conflicts develop among functional specialists. Specialists often try to maximize one functional approach over another while trying to minimize their responsibility and accountability for attaining the overall objectives of the acquisition. This practice easily produces instability within the integrated acquisition team.[10] One of the most important tasks of the leaders in the integrated acquisition team is to set goals and establish accountability so that the members of the team can maintain an acceptable balance between areas where they have the authority to make decisions and their responsibility to achieve the objectives of the project.

The Program Manager/Project Manager

Although there are differences in the skills and training of a program manager and those of a project manager, in practice the two terms are often used interchangeably. *The Government Contracts Reference Book* describes the program manager (PM) as an individual who manages a system acquisition (typically a major system acquisition) program and whose tasks include developing acquisition strategies, promoting full and open competition, and sustaining effective competition between alternative major weapon system concepts and sources, as long as it is economically beneficial and practical to do so. In the DoD the program manager reports directly to the program executive officer on all program matters.[11] *The Government Contracts Reference Book* also defines the position of project manager as the official responsible for planning and controlling assigned projects to achieve program goals. Typical duties of the program manager that are related to the government acquisition process include establishing program objectives; developing requirements, including purchase requests containing specifications and statements of work; obtaining required approvals; scheduling, estimating, budgeting, and controlling projects; coordinating project planning with the contracting officer; and functioning as the contracting officer's representative or technical representative.[12] In this book, the term PM also refers to a project manager.

The PM's role is not to perform the work individually but to accomplish project objectives through specialists working in a group or, better yet, a team situation. "As part of this process PMs must become intimate with all project stakeholders (internal and external) in an effort to understand the drivers behind the customer needs and the organizational challenges that the project will help to resolve."[13] The PM needs a broad perspective on how to lead in an event-oriented environment, i.e., balancing functional objectives with overall project needs and milestones. To accomplish this, the PM must develop a team structure for the project as well as a sense of project identification. A typical duty of the PM is to translate the project's strategic objectives into achievable goals for the project.[14] The PM is essentially a manager of information and risk.

The PM is in charge of the program. However, the PM often has been described as having responsibility for the program but limited authority over the multifunctional and multi-organizational resources assigned to his or her integrated acquisition team. The imbalance between responsibility and authority means that the PM must accomplish things through negotiating with upper-level management and those functional managers who supervise technical specialists. Integrated acquisition teams can take on the characteristics of transient organizations because specialists become involved in the acquisition for relatively short periods at various times during the acquisition process. This means that the PM does not have direct authority over the personnel resources assigned to the project. It also means that the PM and other members of the integrated acquisition team, who have a collective responsibility to get the job done, are also vulnerable to decisions made by managers located outside the team. In their book, *The Manager as Negotiator: Bargaining for Cooperation and Competitive Gain,*

David A. Lax and James K. Sebenius refer to this situation as "indirect management" and state that it is faced by most PMs.[15] In this situation the
project manager requires cooperation from members of the team, who,
even when working directly for the project leader, are dependent on the
function for resources, backing, and even a "good job" when the project is
completed. The authors conclude that this circumstance calls for a management approach very different from the traditional "I say, you do"
method. Consequently, a significant part of the PM's job is to create and
maintain a series of agreements concerning the objectives and utilization
of resources on the project. With "shared authority and resources but concentrated responsibility...effective negotiation with the other shareholders
is often the key to success."[16] Figure 2-2, The PM As an Indirect Manager,
illustrates the environment in which the PM functions.

The success of every project requires collaboration of separate bodies of
knowledge, each having its own perceptions and objectives. Each profession (technical specialists) tends to regard itself as elite, with special values
that may get in the way of cross-disciplinary sharing.[17] This can easily lead
to conflict, thereby breaking down the process. The PM's task is to discipline the acquisition process and establish a climate and a communication
protocol that will ensure that the entire integrated acquisition team works
together.

Primary skills to consider when looking for a PM include good communication, negotiating, and interpersonal skills. General technical and contractual knowledge are additional requirements of the job. As noted above,
the role of the PM is to build a positive collaborative relationship among
technical specialists on the integrated acquisition team. With today's
highly specialized work forces and the inclusion of the user and contractor
on the integrated acquisition team, people involved in the project are often separated by distance and travel time.

Communication is the process by which information of the project is
exchanged and can be formal or informal, in written or oral form. Timely
communication is vital to the success of the project. The exchange of information among members of the integrated acquisition team using EDI is
not only an effective way to communicate, but it also allows all addressees
to share their knowledge with other specialists quickly and concurrently.
When projects are complex or are not well defined, no one person, function, or organization may know what the full depth or range is or where
the key issues reside. To take advantage of the broad technical knowledge
that resides with all members of the team, an EDI protocol bringing members quickly together to focus and solve a single problem is a powerful
management tool. Figure 2-3 shows how planning information, project
status, and problem solving can be facilitated through what has been described as a "spider web" communications network.[18]

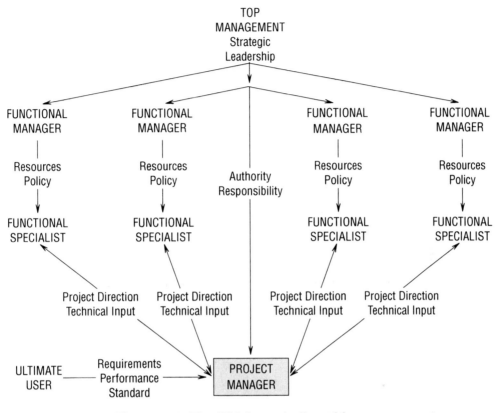

Figure 2-2 The PM As an Indirect Manager

To gain a sense of ownership, members of the team must also develop project objectives. This is most often accomplished by developing "micro-goals," which are evaluated and integrated into the overall project goal. Team participation gives members a sense of ownership and commitment to the common purpose as well as the plan on how the teams will get there. The members should also be evaluated on how well they participate in the team process by cooperating and sharing their knowledge.

The Contracting Officer

The Government Contracts Reference Book describes a contracting officer (CO) as an employee of the government with the authority to bind the government legally by signing a contract.[19] The CO is the person with the authority to enter into, administer, and terminate contracts, and to make determinations and findings.[20] The CO's role is to secure supplies and services from sources outside the organization. COs are also responsible for

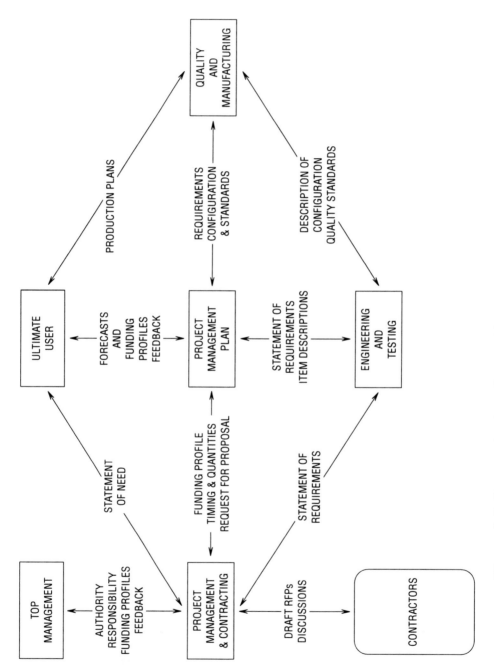

Figure 2-3 Communications Protocol for the Integrated Acquisition Team

ensuring performance of all necessary actions, employing effective contracting practices, complying with the terms of the contract, and safeguarding the interests of the United States in its contractual relationships.[21] In accomplishing this mission, the CO must understand the customer and its needs and maintain a good relationship with the cross-functional integrated acquisition team and the commercial contractors. There are four categories of CO, each having different tasks and responsibilities. The purchasing or procuring contracting officer (PCO) has authority to enter into a contract; the administrative contracting officer (ACO) strictly administers the performance of a contract; the termination contracting officer (TCO) is responsible for contract termination; and the corporate administrative contracting officer (CACO) performs selected contract administration functions on a corporate-wide basis.[22] The relationships between the PCO and ACO, as defined in Part 42 of the FAR, will be discussed in Chapter 7.

One of the most significant differences between the buyer-seller relationship in a government contracting environment and the buyer-seller of commercial goods is the fact that the government is not bound by unauthorized acts of its employees. Therefore, unless the act is authorized, the government is not obligated to comply. Consequently, it is difficult for those outside the government to determine the exact status of government employees they are dealing with. In this situation case law is clear: "...anyone entering into an arrangement with the Government takes the risk of having to accurately ascertain that he who purports to act for the Government stays within the bounds of his authority."[23]

The CO and CM can no longer consider themselves as independent agents viewing the integrated acquisition team from the outside. Rather, they are integral members of the integrated acquisition team. Dr. Ralph C. Nash, Jr., founder of the government contracts program at The George Washington University, feels that the Guiding Acquisition Principles made an important contribution by recognizing the CO as a member of the integrated acquisition team. The principles "speak primarily in terms of the integrated acquisition team," thus assuming that "the CO will function in the future as a member of a team and not as the person responsible for the back end of the procurement process."[24] The contracting profession will require that future contracting professionals be prudent business managers because of how the profession and the overall work force will change.[25] Today the CO must "understand, accept, and project corporate values, goals, and objectives instead of a more limited contracting view of the world."[26]

The PCO operates as an agent of the federal government whose authority and responsibilities are established by law and agency policies. Most have the power to execute two-party agreements, within defined limitations. The FAR's acquisition principles stipulate that the contracting member of the integrated acquisition team "must have the authority to the maximum extent practicable and consistent with law to determine the applicable rules, regulations, and policies on a specific contract."[27]

Acquisition doctrine encourages individual initiative and use of sound business judgment. Some of the rules that previously constrained CO performance have been removed. Policy now permits government members of the team to implement a specific strategy, practice, policy, or procedure that is in the best interest of the government when it is not specifically prohibited by the FAR, executive orders, and appropriate directives.[28] This policy statement initiative enables government personnel to be more proactive. The CO can add significant value to the overall product by bringing timely expertise to critical issues.

Professor Ralph Nash considers critical skills for COs in the 21st century to be: "knowledge or strategy and tactics; market knowledge and research expertise; and total familiarity with all of the various procurement tools available to purchase goods and services coupled with the ability to use them to the customer's advantage."[29]

The PCO is performing in the strategic role during the requirements determination and acquisition planning phases. The PCO makes a critical contribution during the determination of need phase of the acquisition process. At this time the PCO provides data on products available in the commercial market, characteristics of the market, and industry practices. Some of these data are valuable in developing the acquisition plan and negotiation plan and strategy. Although the users have final say in the selection process, it is the PCO who is responsible for providing qualified candidates. During acquisition planning the PCO is deeply involved in procurement planning, i.e., evaluating the extent of competition that is achievable, selecting the contracting method, determining the most appropriate contract type, and defining how risk and opportunities will be addressed in the solicitation. The PCO's tactical knowledge is used during the negotiation and contract award phases. At this time the PCO assumes a dominant role in source selection, negotiation, contract award, and the subsequent development of the conforming contract.

With the increase in communication between functions brought on by the use of electronic data interchange (EDI), the role of the procurement office is changing from being oriented mainly toward transactions to managing the procurement system. This is a significant change, as the buying offices had previously limited their role through procurement rules and regulations.[30] The CO must have a systems view. As the federal government re-engineers itself, procurement can now be easily linked with functions such as finance, inventory management, receiving, property management, and payment. It is quickly becoming an integrated system that cannot be separated. COs must understand these interfaces and functional relationships so that any changes to procurement procedures are compatible with the overall integrated system.[31]

The contract document should be thought of as "common language across the government/contractor team...." Placing the contract on the project's home page, where it is easily accessible to the integrated acquisition team, helps ensure that the document can easily be read and understood. Therefore, it is imperative that the entire contract document not only record the negotiated agreement so that the intent of the parties is clear, but it must also facilitate the administration of work, provide an incentive for the contractor to perform, allocate risk, and describe terms of payment. The conforming contract has taken on even greater importance than before because with today's capabilities of EDI and the ability to have a home page dedicated to a single project, it is now easily accessible to all. The modern contract, with an Integrated Master Schedule (IMS) and Integrated Master Plan (IMP), provides a plan that can be referenced by the entire integrated acquisition team. Therefore, its function as a document that will stand up in a court of law, although still very important, is not the only reason for its existence.

In addition to defining requirements, the conforming contract is a primary source of information that can be used to determine if there are any variances from contract baseline.[32] The PCO is responsible for managing contract changes and, therefore, must maintain continuous communication with his or her counterpart in industry as well as other members of the integrated acquisition team. Contract closeout or termination requires the contracting officer to orchestrate the final disposition of property, deliverables, data, and final payments.

An integral part of the integrated acquisition team organization during all phases is the local area contract administration activity of in-plant government representatives. They can assume part of the administrative workload and are a valuable conduit for information on contractor performance for the entire integrated acquisition team. To ensure their participation, the PCO must define specifically the supporting administrative functions to be performed by the ACO. The tasks to be performed at the contractor's plant by the ACO should be specifically delineated in a delegation agreement between the ACO and PCO. This agreement also should be coordinated with the PM to ensure that it is consistent with the allocation of tasks and activities of the team.

In the private sector, quality and reduced time to market have replaced price as the key to increased market share and profit margins.[33] In addition, in the private sector approximately 70 percent of major U.S. manufacturing firms have adopted a materials management concept that coordinates all planning, organizing, and controlling activities related to material and inventory. This action was taken because of the interdependency of such functions as purchasing, inventory management, production planning, scheduling, transportation, receiving, materials handling, and warehousing. These functions, which had traditionally been located in different departments, are in reality subsets of what is now called a materials management system. Therefore, functional policies and activities must be coordinated on a macro basis. This is done in one of two ways: (1) establishing a set of reporting, communicating, and control procedures designed to foster coordinated decision making; or (2) by arranging the organization to consolidate some of these individual functions in a single organization under one manager. In many materials management organizations the purchasing process has been complemented by what has been called a procurement function. In industry the procurement function now has a strategic focus that includes developing material and service requirements, performing market studies, performing make-or-buy analysis, formulating suppliers' product and quality standards, and contracting for transportation services.[34]

What is the future role of the CO? In November 1999 the Contract Management Institute (CMI), the National Contract Management Association (NCMA), a not-for-profit foundation, published the results of a research report by PricewaterhouseCoopers LLP titled "Survey of Contracting Professionals—Emerging Demands of a Changing Profession." Respondents to the survey were from the public and private sectors as well as professional associations. The survey found that while many of the best practices best-value contracting and managing supplier relationships had not yet been well established, "...the role of the contracting and purchasing professional is far less clerical than it was only a short time ago, more strategic and team-oriented in its contribution to successful outcomes, more specialized in its requirements for effective competencies and skills, more responsible for results, and more conscious of the needs to use time as a critical component." Although "contracting was considered a secondary business-management function that was too process- and rules-oriented..." the respondents also "predicted that the success of contracting and purchasing officials would be measured by business-management performance metrics rather than volume of transactions."[35]

Other Government Team Members

Acquisition doctrine calls for forming multi-disciplinary teams working to facilitate the delivery of a specific product or service to the ultimate user. The integrated acquisition team's goal is to optimize the product by involving all functional bodies of knowledge through integrated decision making. Implementing a risk management and opportunities program also rests with the integrated acquisition team.

One of the project manager's first duties is to assemble the integrated acquisition team. While organizing the team, the PM must determine what bodies of knowledge (specialists) will be required during the life cycle of the project. Any body of knowledge that will have an effect on the performance and ownership cost of the product must be represented on the team. Factors such as product characteristics, the probable contracting method, and the type of contract also must be considered when determining the knowledge and skills needed. Knowledge and skills required by the team also change as a project progresses through its life cycle. The size of the team is also a function of what phase of the life cycle the product is in. Figure 2-4, Bodies of Knowledge Involved in a Project, is a menu of the bodies of knowledge the PM should consider when building the integrated acquisition team.

The bodies of knowledge often found on an integrated acquisition team are contracting, logistics, planning and control, engineering, quality assurance, configuration control, information systems, reliability and maintainability, testing and evaluation, manufacturing and production, property management, subcontract management, cost estimating, financial, and legal.[36] The organization's functional staff is responsible for supporting the integrated acquisition team, which includes human resources management aspects, such as technical competency and development. To be effective each team member must have the resources and be empowered to achieve the project's objective.

The availability of EDI and the Internet has enabled representatives from other geographic locations to participate in the collective decision-making process. An example of communications within the team was illustrated in Figure 2-3.

Figure 2-5 illustrates three types of integrated acquisition teams and their interrelationships. (It is based on the DoD model described in Part 7 of DoD 5000.2R, dated January 4, 2001.) The integrated acquisition team is a multifunctional organization assembled around the product or service being procured. Members advise the PM. The concept is to manage the acquisition by integrating all acquisition activities, from determining the requirement through its deployment to simultaneously optimizing the product and its manufacturing and sustaining processes to meet cost, schedule, performance, and cost-of-ownership objectives. Note that Figure 2-5 lists an Overarching Integrated Acquisition Team. This team provides assistance, oversight, and review through the acquisition process. The Overarching Integrated Acquisition team is led by an individual at least one supervisory level above the PM. It is also responsible for chartering the Intermediate Integrated Acquisition Team and the Working-Level Integrated Acquisition team. At the lowest level there is a Working-Level Integrated Acquisition Team, whose role is to help the PM plan program structure, document and resolve issues, and develop and administer the MR&O Handling Plan. The role of the Intermediate Integrated Acquisition Team, which is formed at the working level, is to coordinate the efforts of the Working-Level Integrated Acquisition Team and handle issues assigned to another team. The Intermediate Integrated Acquisition Team and the

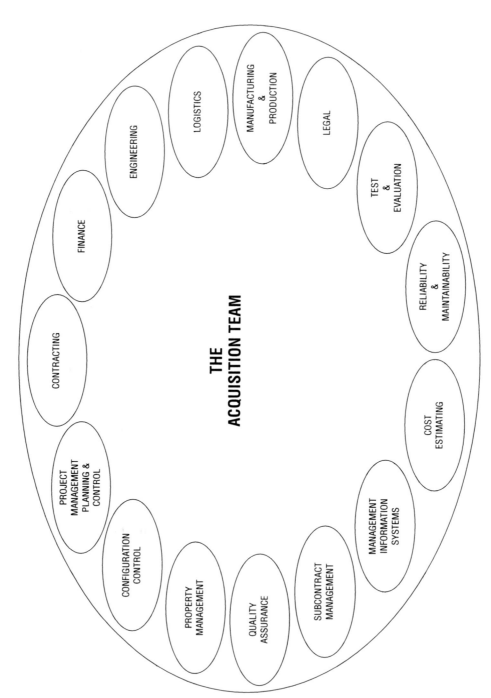

Figure 2-4 Bodies of Knowledge Involved in a Project

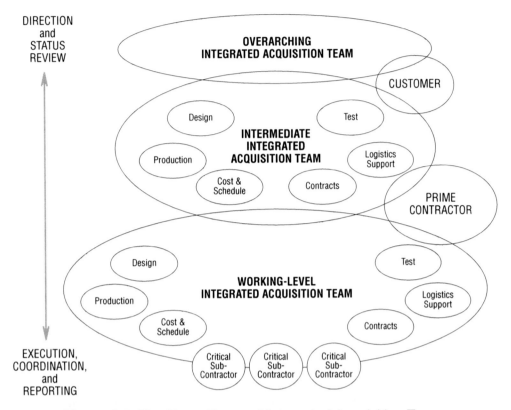

DIRECTION
and
STATUS
REVIEW

EXECUTION,
COORDINATION,
and
REPORTING

Figure 2-5 The Three Types of Integrated Acquisition Teams

Working-Level Integrated Acquisition Team are normally led by the PM or representative of the PM. (Because of the size of the acquisition, only the Working-Level Integrated Acquisition Team will be required to satisfy the work load.) The customer may also participate in meetings of the Overarching Integrated Acquisition Team. Industry representatives, including support contractors, provide information, advice, and recommendations to the team, although they are not formal members of a team. Because of the sensitive nature of discussions, industry representatives do not participate in deliberations by any integrated acquisition team.

Although the structure of an organization does not guarantee success, effective communication and coordination are essential among the various bodies of technical knowledge not only within the government's buying office but between the contractor and critical subcontractors as well. The integrated team concept represents a departure from the traditional functional orientation, which is characterized by vertical communication via the chain of command, often described as resembling a stovepipe. An integrated product team is built around the product, with both vertical and horizontal communication.

The ability to coordinate and communicate horizontally is evident in this organizational chart. The overarching level of the integrated acquisition team includes the PM and the leadership of the government agency as well as senior representatives from the customer (ultimate user) and participation by the prime contractor. Their role is to provide direction, including funding, and to review the project's status.

At the working level are the technical specialists associated with the bodies of knowledge in the government's buying office. This is the original integrated acquisition team cadre of technical specialists who have been instrumental in performing market research, working with the customer in developing the requirements, developing the acquisition plan, finalizing and issuing the solicitation, evaluating proposals, and making the contract award. After contract award this group is retained to manage the project and the risks and opportunities associated with meeting the acquisition objectives.

Participants in the contractor segment of the working level are the same as the government's. Critical subcontractors are also included so that information on their product, production, and product support requirements can be shared with the integrated acquisition team on a real-time basis. The contractor and critical subcontractors are also responsible for participating in managing the risks and opportunities associated with the acquisition.

A study by RAND of risk management in the Air Force's F-22 Engineering and Manufacturing Development Program noted that the acquisition team cited the lack of understanding of the requirement as one of the three basic causes of risk.[37] Participation by the customer as a member of the integrated acquisition team is one way of managing the risk of not understanding the customer's desires. Including the customer on the integrated acquisition team from the beginning greatly facilitates communication and coordination. An example of this can be found in the Ford Motor Company, which in 1979 consulted with customers, including a car-rental company, a women's committee, and other consumers, when designing the Taurus automobile. This was done rather than relying on the engineers and manufacturers to anticipate the customers' needs as they had done in the past.[38] The net result was a design that focused on the customer and a car that turned around the fortunes of the Ford Motor Car Company.

The Contractor As Member of the Integrated Acquisition Team

Historically the relationship between the buyer and seller in this country has been more adversarial than fraternal. Suppliers were played off against each other and squeezed for lower prices.[39] There has since been a growing realization that the needs of the customer must be integrated into the manufacturer's design and production process as early in the acquisition as possible. Therefore, including the contractor as a participant in meetings of the integrated acquisition team is an attempt to realize the advantages of a positive buyer-seller relationship. Dr. Deming said: "Purchasing should be a team effort, and one of the most important people on the team should be the chosen supplier."[40]

Industry also has recognized that to meet the competitive demands of today, the procurement effort must be proactive rather than reactive. Commercial firms are focusing attention on increasing productivity, shortening delivery times, and integrating materials management into the total operations of the organization. The heart of this concept is the cross-functional procurement team as part of the Integrated Procurement System (IPS). This team includes representatives of design engineering, manufacturing engineering, purchasing, manufacturing, and quality control, as well as key suppliers.[41] Suppliers work as members of the team under a strategic alliance, long-term contract, or blanket purchase order.

In large or complex programs, contractor participation as members of the acquisition team should also involve the key suppliers. Earlier in this chapter it was noted that, on average, contractors contract over 60 percent of the goods and service content of a product. This percentage can go even higher as the technical content of products increases and outsourcing is seen as a way to cut costs and accelerate development time. Long-term strategic alliances are being formed, and firms are becoming more interdependent. This means they are learning to share information to make product and product decisions jointly. Ravi Vankatesan is quoted as saying, "Today manufacturing focus means learning not to make things—how not to make the parts that divert a company from cultivating its skills—parts its suppliers could make more efficiently."[42]

DoD Implementation of the Integrated Acquisition Team Concept

"I am directing a fundamental change" were the words used by then-Secretary of Defense William Perry on May 10, 1995, when he endorsed the implementation of integrated product and process development (IPPD) through the use of integrated product teams (IPTs).[43]

IPPD is described as "a management process that integrates all activities from product conception through production and support, using a multifunctional team, to simultaneously optimize the product and its manufacturing and sustaining process to meet cost, schedule, and performance objectives.[44]

Figure 2-6, The Generic IPPD Iterative Process, shows the IPPD as an open process, i.e., it is influenced by factors outside its environment. These factors include annual funding, changes in political priorities, oversight, policy of regulatory agencies, suppliers, changes to the threat, and competitive products. The IPPD process recognizes the comprehensive requirement to modify and align team structures, analytical and decision tools,

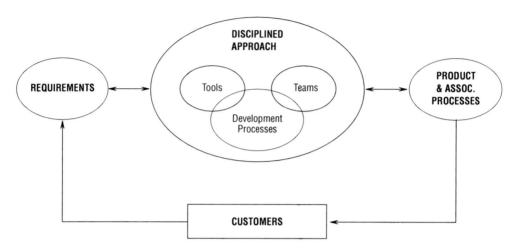

Figure 2-6 The Generic IPPD Iterative Process[45]

and process to achieve optimal performance as defined by the customers' criteria.

The IPPD model represents a disciplined approach used to organize activities, scope out issues, identify and manage risk, and pursue opportunities. Requirements are initiated based on input from the ultimate customer and are refined through market research. The iterative process enables the integrated team to focus on several product issues simultaneously. Tools available to the team include documentation, data systems, and methodologies that enable cross-functional experts to share and integrate information and make decisions at the lowest level commensurate with the magnitude of the issue involved. As noted earlier, teams are made up of the stakeholders, who are empowered to make decisions in their areas of expertise. Output is the product that measures the success of the integrated team.

This IPPD concept means that the IPT can optimize the cost, schedule, performance, and supportability objective of the acquisition. The IPPD requires bodies of knowledge represented by members of the multifunctional team, who can interact simultaneously. The integrated team can also receive input from the outside environment. The IPPD/IPT management framework remains functional for the entire life cycle of the product or service.[46]

DoD guidance states that the chain of command includes the program manager, program executive officer, Component Acquisition Executive (CAE) reporting through the Head of the Component, and Under Secretary of Defense for Acquisition, Technology, and Logistics (USD AT&L) or Assistant Secretary of Defense for Command, Control, Communications, and

Intelligence (ASD C&I). However, to streamline the process, no more than two levels of review are to exist between the program manager and the Milestone Decision Authority.[47]

The Milestone Decision Authority shown in Figure 2-7 is an individual designated in accordance with the criteria established by the USD AT&L of ASD C&I to approve entry of an acquisition program into the next phase of the acquisition process.[48]

DoD 5000.2-R establishes the following basic tenets for the working-level IPT (WIPT):

- The PM is in charge of the program
- IPTs are advisory bodies to the PM
- Direct communication between the program office and all levels in the acquisition oversight and review process is expected as a means of exchanging information and building trust.

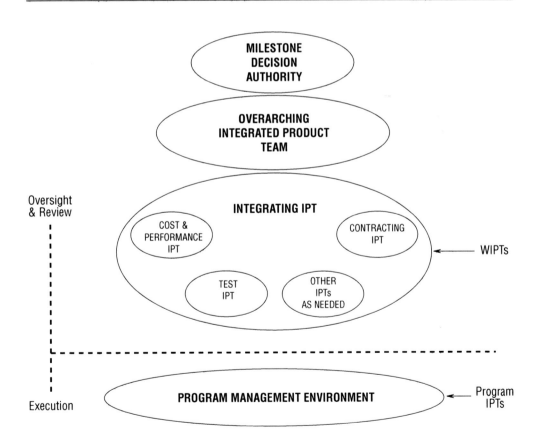

Figure 2-7 The DoD Integrated Product Team Structure for Oversight and Review

All WIPTs have the following roles and responsibilities:

- Assisting the PM in developing strategies and planning programs as requested by the OM
- Establishing an IPT plan of action and milestones
- Proposing tailored documentation and milestone requirements
- Reviewing and providing early input documents
- Coordinating WIPT activities with the OIPT members
- Resolving or elevating issues in a timely manner
- Assuming responsibility for obtaining concurrence on issues, documents, or portions of documents.[49]

Communications Protocol

One FAR performance standard for the integrated acquisition team is to conduct business with integrity, fairness, and openness. This requires open communication among team members, internal and external customers, and the public.[50] In 1996 the RAND Corporation published a review of the management of three DoD acquisition programs as a source for recommending improvements in acquisition management procedures, using lessons learned from other DoD major programs to serve as a basis of their assessment. Communication was one of the 10 critical success factors selected by RAND. The criteria for evaluation of the effectiveness of communication include the following factors:

- Was communication completely open?
- Were unique, innovative communication techniques being followed?
- Was communication, both verbal and written, continuous?[51]

RAND's study also cited the use of the contract as the "common language across the government/contractor team" by the F-22 System Program Office (SPO) as the way to ensure that the team was responding to a common set of plans, processes, and controls. This "common language" was found in the "specifications and a requirements-traceability matrix, the Statement of Work, Work Breakdown Structure, integrated master plan, integrated master schedule, Cost/Schedule Control System, system responsibility matrix, technical performance measures, and award fee plan (if applicable).[52] Most of these documents are, or can be, included as part of the contract. Not only do they establish the common language, but they also define the contract baseline. All members of the team must know what the contract says; therefore, it is a primary responsibility of both government and contractor personnel assigned to the integrated acquisition team to see that the contract is free of ambiguous legalese and that it reflects current requirements. It also must be accessible to all members of the team.

With the Internet capabilities available today, the contract can easily be included on the project's home page.

MANAGING RISKS AND OPPORTUNITIES

Planning is one of the most important functions a manager performs. Implementation of all acquisition decisions begins with a plan, which is key to getting the project off to a successful start. By setting the objectives of the acquisition, the plan establishes the course for the integrated acquisition team to follow. Without solid planning the buyer is forced to play catch-up, and the integrated acquisition team becomes reactive rather than proactive. Objectives developed during the planning process also provide the integrated acquisition team a road map and reference points that can be used to measure variances from the desired route. Effective management control relies on measurement of the variance from the desired point and enables the project leadership to evaluate performance and institute corrective actions where and when required. Acquisition reform efforts seek to change the program management environment from a risk-averse philosophy to one of risk management.[53]

A proactive technique to ensure that objectives are met or exceeded is called the "Management of Risk and Opportunities" (MR&O). The MR&O is a structured technique that concentrates management attention where it will benefit most. It should be thought of as an additional step in the planning process. The goal of the MR&O is to be in position to respond quickly to potential problems or opportunities if they occur. Chapter 1 defines risk as a potential problem and opportunity as a chance to improve on the state of the acquisition.

The last step in acquisition planning is to answer the following four questions:

- What potential problems (risks) might occur, and what opportunities are possible?
- What are the likely causes of problems or opportunities?
- What is the probability of these problems or opportunities occurring?
- What is the potential impact of the problems or opportunities?[54]

By looking into the future at the probable risks and opportunities, the acquisition manager can develop contingency courses of action that will alleviate the problem or position the project to capitalize on the opportunity. Art Gemmer of Rockwell International views it as performing in a "working smarter" mode rather than the "working harder" mode. He contends that acquisition programs that operate in the "work harder" mode spend most of their time dealing with the consequences of their past decisions, while programs that operate in a "work smarter" mode have anticipated change and can easily adapt to their environment because they have spent most of their time considering future options.[55]

Sources of Risk

Identifying the risks associated with an acquisition is a function of logic, reason, experience, and intuition. Because one is looking for future potential problems, experience and intuition are especially useful guides. Historically, risk falls into five categories: political, financial, technical, human, and risks due to uncertainty. Figure 2-8, Sources of Risk, illustrates these categories.

Political factors include the internal influence of the functions and the other parties. In addition, each project is subject to labor and environmental regulations. Government contracts not only are subject to the potential ups and downs of annual appropriations, but priority changes by the executive and legislative branches can result in revised funding profiles and

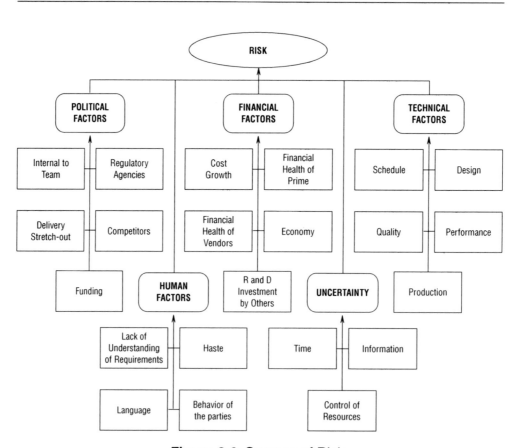

Figure 2-8 Sources of Risk

the lengthening of delivery schedules. New or updated products by competitors also have an effect on the acquisition.

Financial factors include the financial health of the prime contractors and subcontractors as well as interest rates and inflation. Cost growth related to contractor performance is a factor that is extremely important because it could lead to the termination of the procurement.

Technical factors include such elements as design, product performance, quality of the item produced, and the impact of all these subfactors on the schedule. For example, a study of 8,000 software projects in the U.S. by the Standish Group concluded that 84 percent did not finish on time, on budget, and with all the features installed.[56]

Human factors contributing to risk include the shortcomings of language and differing interpretations of the contract language and the contract itself. Rules of contract interpretation, which will be covered in Chapter 7, are important considerations to keep in mind when developing the contract. Government contracts not only allocate risk via the contract type, but they also contain risk allocation clauses that address deadline extensions or price adjustments should various contingencies occur or conditions not be as expected or represented. There are also risk allocation techniques, which have their roots in common law, that may serve as a basis for interpreting the scope of contract clauses.[57]

Uncertainty includes two dimensions. There is uncertainty as to when events will occur and the ability of the acquisition team to react to them. Uncertainty as to the adequacy and accuracy of the information used to make decisions is another important subfactor.[58]

Managing Risk

Acquisition doctrine emphasizes the "management of risk" rather than "risk avoidance." The FAR points out that attempting to avoid risk totally is cost prohibitive.[59] Dr. Saul W. Gellerman, former Dean of the Graduate School of Management at the University of Dallas, expressed it well by saying, "Managers are not paid to take risks, but to know what risks to take."[60]

Acquisition doctrine considers management an important part of each procurement. DoD Directive 5000.1 defines risk management as "an approach...that...encompasses risk identification, mitigation and continuous tracking, and control procedures that feedback through the program assessment process to decision authorities."[61] This philosophy represents a departure from past practices in which risk was avoided by instituting what proved to be costly specifications and processes that were unique to government contracts.

For example, risk management in DoD is a systematic process that includes four steps: risk planning, risk assessment, risk handling, and risk monitoring. Figure 2-9, Risk Management in the Acquisition Process, shows the flow of these risk management activities during the acquisition process, i.e., before the request for proposal, during the proposal phase, and after contract award.[62]

Risk planning: Risk planning is a process that includes developing, documenting, and organizing a comprehensive interactive strategy that includes methods for identifying and tracking risk areas as well as developing risk handling plans and performing risk assessments to determine how risks change during the course of the acquisition. The plan also includes determining resource requirements.[63] The risk management plan should serve the following functions:

1. It identifies possible acts that could prevent meeting a specific goal, e.g., late delivery of parts needed for assembly, inoperative government-furnished equipment, situations in which several people or organizations share responsibility, tight deadlines, or a complex technical problem.
2. It enables management to focus attention on future issues that may cause a variance from plan, e.g., the risk of a potential problem.

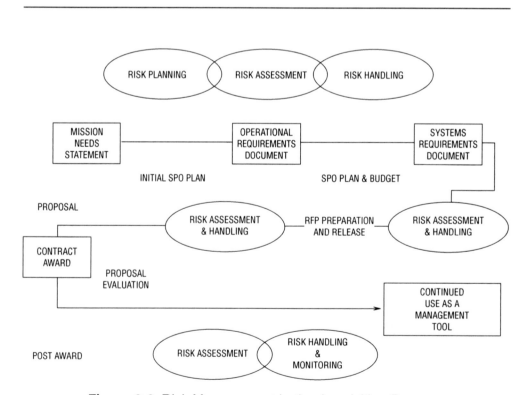

Figure 2-9 Risk Management in the Acquisition Process

3. It serves as the basis for determining where corrective action should be concentrated and establishes priorities among the actions needed.
4. It provides management with a tool for evaluating the status and improving the situation.

Risk assessment: The genesis of risk is usually found in the following three sources: organizational politics, finances, and technical and product support. Potential problems often arise when the outcome of a project depends on actions taken by others who are assigned to different internal or external organizations. A prime example is the relationship between the prime contractor and its suppliers. Another illustration can be found in the design and manufacture of a technically complex and multi-functional product that depends on the effective interface of numerous components to fulfill. In business, competitors that can change their pricing strategy or introduce an improved product are a potential source of risk. The same can be said about a hostile power that can introduce a new aircraft with increased capability. Potential financial problems are also present in every project. Government projects that are dependent on annual funding by Congress run the risk of budget cutbacks. Another example of financial risk is the possible bankruptcy of a key supplier. Technical uncertainty is a well-known source of risk. The design, manufacture, and testing of almost every product have varying degrees of technical risk. A highly risky technical project results from uncertainty associated with the various unknowns related to the requirement.[64]

Uncertainty about whether the job can be accomplished in the time allowed is a major cause of risk, as is uncertainty regarding the ability to react and accomplish a repair in the time allotted. The lack of direct supervision, i.e., total control, over the resources required to do the job is often perceived as a source of risk because of inadequate authority to establish priorities. The possibility of inadequate or inaccurate information on which to base a decision is also present in almost every management situation.[65]

To assess risk accurately, the analyst should follow a structured approach that includes: (1) identifying the risk and its characteristics, (2) estimating the probability of occurrence, (3) identifying the timeframe and probability distribution of the risk, and (4) determining the impact on acquisition goals and expectations.[66] The latter includes determining the impact on cost, schedule, performance, and logistics support. To describe the potential problem accurately, one needs to include additional characteristics, such as an estimate of the probability of occurrence if the situation is allowed to continue. Knowledge of the timeframe during which corrective action must be taken to relieve the situation is an important factor. However, the uncertainty regarding the probability of occurrence of a risk may also vary over time. Linking of one risk to other possible risks is an additional attribute. If the risk becomes a problem, it often triggers additional risks.[67]

Risk handling: In developing the risk-handling strategy the integrated acquisition team must consider the probability of occurrence, possible time frame of occurrence, and possible impact. All risk-handling actions involve a tradeoff between cost and benefits. As noted earlier, the benefits derived from improving the reliability of the product from 97 percent to 100 percent by increasing the amount of product testing may not be worth the cost.

The risk-handling strategies implemented during the request for proposal (RFP) and proposal evaluation phases include:

- Risk mitigation, which is the reduction of the probability that a problem will occur or of its impact.
- Risk avoidance, which is the complete elimination of the possibility of occurrence. This may be costly or require creating other risks that might make an acceptable impact on the acquisition.
- Risk transfer, which includes getting another party to assume the risk or share the consequences. Examples include selection of contract type, warranties, and insurance policies. Contract terms and conditions are other vehicles whereby risk can be shifted or shared.
- Risk acceptance is the determination that, based on its impact, an acceptable strategy would be to track the risk and take action only when it becomes a problem.[68]

Changes to government acquisition policies are also being used to implement risk management. The following recent examples show how DoD policies are attempting to reduce risk:

- Including the customer and contractor as members of the integrated acquisition team to reduce the technical risk resulting from a lack of understanding requirements.
- Emphasizing the selection of commercial, off-the-shelf items to minimize the technical risk associated with development of government-unique products.
- Instituting a single-process policy in contractor manufacturing facilities to reduce exposure to the high cost of having different processes for the same products.
- Balancing cost objectives with mission needs under the policy of cost as an independent variable (CAIV), thereby diminishing the danger of acquiring non-affordable systems. The CAIV-based parameters will become part of the Acquisition Program Baseline (APB).
- Making past performance an evaluation factor in every source selection for negotiated procurements to reduce the cost, schedule, and technical risks related to contract award to contractors with a poor track record.

Management of risk must be an integral part of the acquisition process and is especially pertinent during acquisition planning, development of the solicitation, contract award, and contract formation.

Managing Opportunities

In some areas there are opportunities to exceed the project's expectations, which could result in a compensatory change to the contract. A cost-benefit tradeoff must be made to determine whether the extra or added performance is worth the added cost. This must be completed and approved contractually before any effort begins.

Figure 2-10, Cost Benefit vs. Performance Tradeoff, illustrates a relationship between cost, performance, and time. In this example time is fixed by the period of performance stipulated in the contract. Curve O A represents the contract level of performance. Curve O B represents a 10 percent improvement in performance by adding additional resources (cost) to the effort.

The greater the potential performance, the greater the cost. As you move from left to right on the cost/performance curve, the cost per increment of increased performance slowly increases until cost becomes exponential. It is the task of acquisition management to determine where the expected benefit from added performance equals the added cost. Above that point it is less than cost-effective, and the need must justify the cost.

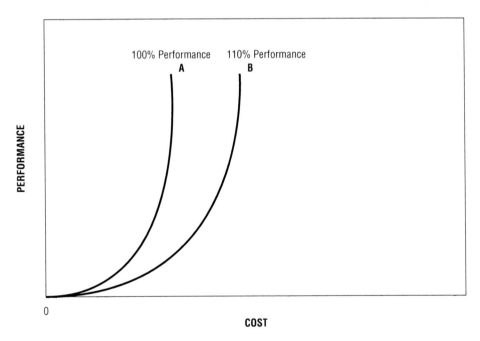

Figure 2-10 Cost Benefit vs. Performance Tradeoff

On the contractor's side, the primary objective of a business is to maximize the wealth of the shareholders (owners).[69] The contractor is motivated to achieve long-term profits by producing quality products and establishing a long-term relationship and repeat business. Contractors realize that the best way to achieve this goal is to meet the performance and schedule goals of the agreement within cost. The importance placed on past performance in source selection acknowledges this objective. Internally it is the return on assets (ROA) and return on investment (ROI) that measure the profitability of a business organization, i.e., the effectiveness with which capital is being utilized.[70] Delivery schedules, payment frequency, financing provisions, and other provisions of a contract can significantly affect a contractor's cash flow and ROA. An overall excellent performance by the contractor provides an opportunity for repeat business.

The FAR includes a procedure, i.e., the Value Engineering clause,[71] that can result in the sharing of any cost reduction. Under this procedure the contractor submits a Value Engineering Change Proposal (VECP), which can result in a reduction to the contract price without impairing the functions or characteristics of the product. In theory the VECP is intended to provide the contract or an incentive to develop ways to be more efficient by including a provision on how the cost avoided will be shared. Use of the VECP clause also avoids any question of defective pricing if the contractor changes the method of performance after its disclosure during negotiations and the certifying cost or pricing data.

The Value Engineering (VE) concept originated during World War II, when many essential materials used in production were scarce and creative engineers at General Electric (GE) used alternatives. Not only did the substitutes perform satisfactorily, but some turned out to be more reliable or cheaper. After WWII a purchasing agent at GE was given the job to develop "a systematic approach to the investigation of the function-cost aspect of existing materials specifications." The approach, referred to as value analysis by GE, is defined as "an organized creative approach which has for its purpose the efficient identification of unnecessary cost."[72]

As noted, to be more competitive many organizations in private sector procurement, or material management, have been given increased responsibility for the cost of purchased material. Therefore, it is their responsibility to provide incentives for suppliers to offer cost-saving suggestions during the product design process.

Potential functions that are subject to function-cost tradeoff include:

- Material composition and manufacturing operations and processes used in production parts and assemblies
- Acceptance and reliability testing
- Packaging specifications

- Design of operating systems
- Administration
- Transportation
- Production inventory.

Figure 2-11, Management of Risk and Opportunities, summarizes the MR&O technique and illustrates how it unfolds over the acquisition process. The x-axis represents the life of the contract. The y-axis depicts leadership by the entire integrated acquisition team to manage the risks and opportunities associated with controlling the variances from the planned acquisition. During the pre-award phase the risks and opportunities are incorporated into pre-award planning, solicitation, and contract award phases. Risks and opportunities on the diagram are separated by the center horizontal line, which represents the objectives of the acquisition.

During pre-award planning, risks and opportunities are identified and commitments made as to the expected outcome, along with the risk associated with attaining the stated acquisition goals. Risk-handling strategies designed to avoid, mitigate, or transfer risks will be incorporated into the

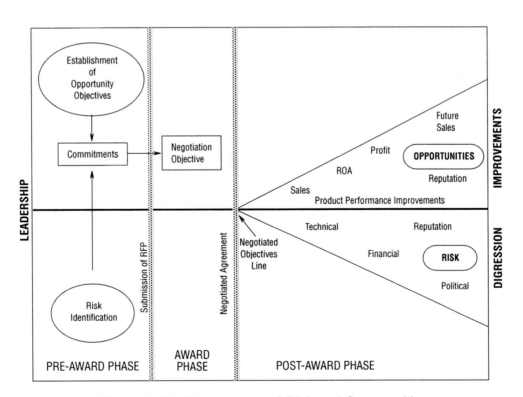

Figure 2-11 Management of Risk and Opportunities

solicitation for those risks whose potential impact is judged to be unacceptable. This process includes an implied management commitment to how risks and opportunities will be overseen. This becomes the foundation on which the source selection is made, the contract is awarded, and the contract document itself is formulated.

After the contract is awarded and the conforming contract is issued, the performance phase begins. Here both the government and the contractor must be involved in tracking the risks and opportunities as the performance phase evolves. Possible variations from contract objectives are shown on Figure 2-11; they diverge from the center line of balance as performance progresses. Opportunities for improvements, i.e., overall performance, deliveries, ROA, ROI, reputation, and future programs (contractor sales), are shown above the objective line. Below the line are the possible political, technical, financial, and supportability risks.

Figure 2-12, Handling Risks and Opportunities, illustrates how the management of risks and opportunities begins with defining the objectives of the acquisition during the requirements determination process. This method is a recurring process designed to improve acquisition planning and then monitor the plans process so the integrated acquisition team can mitigate risks that could potentially prevent attaining the acquisition objectives. The amount of time the integrated acquisition team spends on this process depends on the complexity of the procurement. For highly technical and complex projects or programs, a formal handling program is appropriate. Techniques used in the process include answering the following questions early in the requirements determination process:

- What are the risks and potential opportunities, i.e., what could happen that would prevent attaining objectives or provide an opportunity to exceed expectations?
- What are their likely causes, the probability of their occurrence, and their probable impact?
- What actions can be taken to handle the risks?
- What opportunities might be discovered during performance, and how should they be handled?

Answers to these questions are used in building a "How to Handle Plan." This plan has two parts. The first includes actions that can be taken to reduce risk or likely causes of problems. The second part of the plan should list what can be done to maximize the rewards associated with the opportunities. For each risk the plan should document: (1) a description of the possible cause, (2) the probability of occurrence, (3) a quantification of the impact or possible variance from the objective if the risk becomes a problem or an opportunity presents itself, and (4) a list of alternative actions, including contract provisions that would minimize or avoid any negative variance from the plan or steps that can be taken to improve the situation.

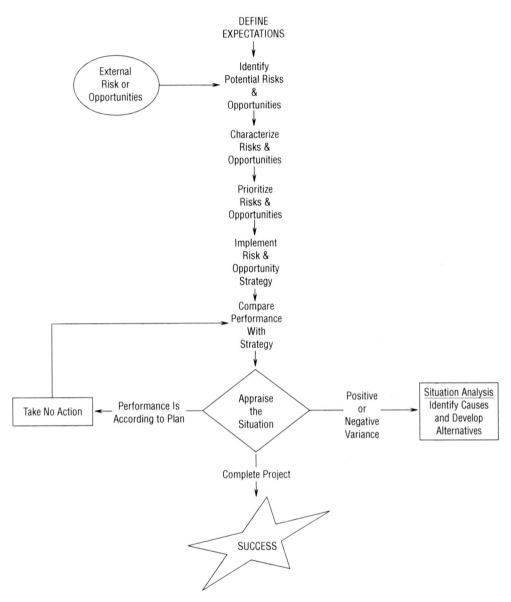

Figure 2-12 Handling Risks and Opportunities

CONCLUSION

It is clear that to be effective and efficient in the 21st century, the federal acquisition process must be structured to cope with increasing competition for scarce budget dollars, the need for flatter organizations, strategic alliances between suppliers, and an exponential growth in the area of electronic data interchange.

In recent years DoD has done much to improve its acquisition practices and policies through acquisition reform and to transform its logistics systems to integrated supply chains driven by modern information technologies and a wide range of best business practices that have been proven in the commercial sector.[73]

To add value to the acquisition process, the contracting community must become more proactive and innovative. Procurement is much broader than the purchase of goods and services—it involves activities that take place in many functions. "Organizations exercise the best control over cost and quality of purchased goods and services only when appropriate members of the various departments involved in the procurement process operate as an interdependent, integrated system. When this happens, a synergism takes place, with the result that the integrated efforts become greater than the sum of the individual efforts."[74]

It is clear that the capabilities of EDI are not limited to the further automation of the existing acquisition process. EDI has eliminated distance as an inhibitor to communications, thus creating common databases that not only will enhance communications but also will link organizations and their processes together. Contractors with good performance track records, along with effective supply chains and manufacturing processes, will have an advantage over their competitors. This capability will reduce the average acquisition cycle time and lower the cost of ownership.

In Chapter 3 we will begin our focus on the acquisition process and how acquisition doctrine extrapolates lessons of the past to the acquisition environment of the future.

NOTES

[1]Drucker, Peter. 1987. The Coming of the New Organization. *Harvard Business Review on Knowledge Management.* Cambridge, MA: Harvard Business School Press, 3.

[2]Burt, David N., and Richard L. Pinkerton. 1996. *A Purchasing Manager's Guide To Strategic Proactive Procurement.* New York: American Management Association, xi.

[3]Doyle, Gregory. 1999. Developing the Next Generation of Contracting Officers (and This Generation, Too). *Contract Management* (April): 43.

[4]*The Contracting Professional as a Manager: 2000 National Education Seminar.* 2000. Vienna, VA: National Contract Management Association, 1–5.

[5]Rummler, Gear, and Gordon Sellers. 1997. Pitfalls in the Strategic Deployment of Processes Improvement Management. *Excellence in Practice: Innovation and Excellence in Workflow and Imaging.* Lighthouse Point, FL: Future Strategies Inc., 193.

[6]*The Contracting Professional as a Manager: 2000 National Education Seminar.* 2000. National Contract Management Association, Vienna, VA: 3–4.

[7]Nash, Ralph C., Jr., Steven L. Schooner, and Karen O'Brien. 1998. *The Government Contracts Reference Book.* 2d ed. Washington, D.C.: The George Washington University, 9.

[8]DOD Directive 5000.1 "Defense Acquisition," March 15, 1991. DODI 5000.2. 2001 Operation of the Defense Acquisition System, January 4, paragraph 4.5 refers to the "new acquisition process" without defining the term.

[9]The two terms, i.e., project and program, signify differences in the estimated value of the acquisition. A program has more scope, is more complex, and has a higher fund value than a project. In this book we use the term *project manager* for simplicity. However, the material pertains to both to a varying degree.

[10]Hicks, Herbert G. 1972. *The Management of Organizations: A Systems and Human Resources Approach,* 2d ed. New York: McGraw-Hill, 270.

[11]Nash, Schooner, and O'Brien, 416.

[12]Nash, Schooner, and O'Brien, 418.

[13]*The Contracting Professional as a Business Manager: 2000 National Education Seminar.* 2000. National Contract Management Association, Vienna, VA, 3-2.

[14]Nash, Schooner, and O'Brien, 418.

[15]Lax, David A., and James K. Sebenius. 1996. *The Manager as Negotiator: Bargaining for Cooperation and Competitive Gain.* New York: The Free Press, 12.

[16]Lax and Sebenius, 14.

[17]Quinn, James Bryan, Philip Anderson, and Sydney Finkelstein. 1998. Managing Professional Intellect. *Harvard Business Review of Knowledge Management.* Cambridge, MA: Harvard Business School Press, 193.

[18]Quinn, Anderson, and Finkelstein, 201.

[19]Nash, Schooner, and O'Brien, 127.

[20]FAR 2.101.

[21]FAR 1.602-2.

[22]Nash, Schooner, and O'Brien, 127.

[23]Cibinic, John, Jr., and Ralph C. Nash, Jr. 1985. *Administration of Government Contracts* Washington D.C.: The George Washington University, Government Contracts Program, 23–24.

[24]Nash, Ralph C., Jr. 1997. Training the Contracting Officer of the Future. *Contract Management* (March): 16.

[25]*The Contracting Professional as a Manager: 2000 National Education Seminar.* 2000. Vienna, VA: National Contract Management Association, 1–2.

[26]Doyle, 42.

[27]FAR 1.102-4 (a).

[28]FAR 1.102-4 (e).

[29]*The Contracting Professional as a Manager: 2000 National Education Seminar.* 2000. Vienna, VA: National Contract Management Association, 1–10.

[30]Drake, Daniel J. 1996. *Procurement Manager's Guide to EC/EDI.* Vienna, VA: Holbrook & Kellog Inc., 5–17.

[31]Drake, 5–17.

[32]In the case of system acquisitions, the program baseline, which is expressed in terms of cost, schedule, performance, and supportability, and the contract baseline should be the same.

[33]Burt and Pinkerton, 4.

[34]Dobler, Donald W., and David N. Burt. 1996. *Purchasing and Supply Management*. 6th ed. New York: McGraw-Hill, 38.

[35]Macfarlan, Gregor. 2000. The Buyer as a Business Manager? *Contract Management* (August): 29.

[36]O'Brien, Dan. 1998. Briefing during 11th Annual Academic Conference for Contract Management Educators, National Contract Management Association. 29 October 1998, Monterey, CA.

[37]Johnson, Robert V., and John Birkler. 1996. *Three Programs and Ten Criteria: Evaluating and Improving Acquisition Program Management and Oversight Processes Within the Department of Defense*. RAND, National Defense Research Institute. Prepared for the Office of the Secretary of Defense, Santa Monica, CA, 41. The other two causes were the lack of mature technology to satisfy the requirement and lack of a planning and tracking system to measure progress.

[38]Taub, Eric. *Taurus: The Making of the Car That Saved Ford*. New York: Penguin, 131.

[39]Bowersox, Donald J., Patricia J. Daugherty, Cornelia L. Droge, Richard N. Germain, and Dale S. Rogers. 1992. *Logistics Excellence: It Is Not Business as Usual*. Burlington, MA: Digital Press, 34.

[40]Walton, Mary. 1986. *The Deming Management Method*. New York: Perigee, 64.

[41]Burt and Pinkerton, ix.

[42]Venkatesan, Ravi. 1992. Strategic Sourcing—To Make or Not to Make. *Harvard Business Review* (November-December): 98.

[43]Hocevar, Susan P., and Walter E. Owen. 1998. Team-Based Redesign a Large-Scale Change: Applying Theory to the Implementation of Integrated Product Teams. *Acquisition Review Quarterly*5(2): 147.

[44]DoD Regulation 5000.1. The Defense Acquisition System, Enclosure E, paragraph E2.1.6, 23 October 2000.

[45]Hocevar and Owen, 150.

[46]DoD Regulation 5000.2-R, paragraph E2.1.6.

[47]DoD Regulation 5000.1, The Defense Acquisition System, paragraph 4.5.6, 23 October 2000.

[48]DoD Regulation 5000.1, Enclosure E, paragraph E2.1.5.

[49]DoD Regulation 5000.2-R. Mandatory Procedures for Major Defense Acquisition Programs (MDAPs) and Major Automated Information System (MAIS) Acquisition Programs. Part 7, paragraph 7.6.3.

[50]FAR 1-102 (c).

[51]Johnson and Birkler, 9.

[52]Johnson and Birkler, 41.

[53]FAR 1-102 (c) (2).

[54]Spitzer, Quinn, and Ron Evans. 1999. *Heads You Win: How the Best Companies Think—and How You Can Use Their Examples to Develop Critical Thinking Within Your Organization.* New York: Simon and Schuster, 98.

[55]Gemmer, Art. 1997. Risk Management. *Computer* (May): 36.

[56]Hoch, Detlev J., Cyriac R. Roeding, Gert Purkert, and Sandra K. Linder. 1999. *Secret of Software Success.* Boston MA.: Harvard Business School Press, 94.

[57]Cibinic, John, Jr., and Ralph C. Nash, Jr. 1986. *Administration of Government Contracts.* 2d ed. Washington D.C.: The George Washington University, 178.

[58]Gemmer, Art. 1997. Risk Management. *Computer* (May): 38.

[59]FAR 1.102-2 (c) (2).

[60]Interview, August 17, 1998.

[61]DoD Directive 5000.1, Defense Acquisition, March 15, 1996, D.1.4 d.

[62]*The Contracting Professional as a Manager: 2000 National Education Seminar,* 2-5.

[63]Ibid.

[64]Gemmer, 37.

[65]Gemmer, 38.

[66]Ibid.

[67]Ibid.

[68]Ibid.

[69]Symonds, Curtis W. 1978. *Basic Financial Management.* New York: AMACOM, 4.

[70]Chisholm, William D. 1985. Return on Assets/Investment Considerations for Contract Managers. *National Contract Management Journal* (Winter): 58.

[71]FAR 52.248-1 and FAR 52.248-2.

[72]Burt and Pinkerton, 157.

[73]Gansler, J.S. 2000. The Under Secretary of Defense, Acquisition and Technology. Washington, D.C., 3.

[74]Burt and Pinkerton, 3.

CHAPTER 3

Acquisition Planning

In Chapter 2 we defined the process by which supplies and services are procured and briefly discussed the six steps or phases in the government acquisition process, i.e., requirements determination, acquisition planning, negotiation, contract award, performance after contract award, and contract closeout. In this chapter we will discuss the requirements determination and procurement planning phases of the acquisition process.

The word requirement means "need," not product or service type, which is a solution to a need. All procurements begin with the determination of need. The need is translated into products or services, which then direct us to potential suppliers and the cost of the solution.[1] This chapter will emphasize the significant role market research plays in this process and the early identification and management of the risks and opportunities as a way to increase the probability of a successful procurement.

It is the policy of the federal government to use electronic commerce whenever practicable or cost-effective.[2] For the micropurchaser,[3] the use of electronic commerce (e-commerce) is introducing a more integrated contracting process. The use of EDI to transmit purchase orders means that they can potentially move between the buyer and seller without human review and processing. Therefore, the data pertaining to what is being purchased, including the item description, quantity, price, contractual terms, and authentication of acceptance, are electronically integrated. Efficiency will be added through the use of electronic catalogs (e-cats) that provide online access to commercial firms as well as government agencies (e.g., General Services Administration, Defense Logistics Agency). The use of e-cats speeds access to contract and supply schedule items and improves sourcing, pricing, and the ordering process.[4] A detailed discussion of micropurchasing using e-commerce is beyond the scope of this book; therefore, this chapter will address the acquisition of goods and services in larger dollar categories.

Acquisition planning is more than just determining what to purchase and when. It addresses technical, business, management, and all other considerations that influence the acquisition decision, such as which items are to be developed or produced in-house and which procured from outside the immediate organization. Acquisition planning is designed to coordinate effectively the efforts of all personnel responsible for the multi-faceted aspects of procuring supplies and services.

A recent survey by the University of Houston concluded that the primary cause of program or contract failure is a lack of defining the program adequately at the beginning, i.e., inadequate definition of requirements.[5] Planning for the acquisition begins as soon as the need is identified. As acquisition doctrine reminds us, the goal of each procurement is to deliver the best-value[6] product to the ultimate user on a timely basis, while maintaining the public's trust and fulfilling public policy objectives.[7] The acquisition planning process demands teamwork. To be successful it requires all personnel involved in the acquisition to develop, coordinate, and integrate their body of knowledge into a comprehensive acquisition plan. Planning to acquire goods or services is an evolutionary process, beginning with the development of the mission needs statement and culminating in the solicitation. Procurement planning is a subset of the overall acquisition plan. The procurement plan should contain all applicable technical, contracting, fiscal, business, and program/project management factors that will govern the acquisition. The plan also must address potential problems, risks, and opportunities. The magnitude and detail contained in an acquisition plan should be tailored to fit the situation. For example, the detail of a plan to purchase supplies in economic quantities, covered in FAR 7.2, is significantly less than what is needed for more complex high-dollar items that will be procured via the competitive negotiation process.

PROCUREMENT LEAD TIME

Procurement lead time, which is defined as the time required to acquire supplies and services and then place them in the hands of the user, has two separate components: administrative lead time and development or production lead time. The administrative segment begins with identifying a material requirement and ends with awarding a contract for the needed item or service. Production lead time begins at contract award and concludes when the item or service is delivered to the ultimate user.[8] For such non-development items as replenishment of material inventories, procurement lead time represents the span of time required to replenish the inventory, including the time needed to accomplish such administrative tasks as inventory management, solicitation, negotiation, and contract award, as well as production and distribution of the item.

Acquisition doctrine states "timeliness of delivery" as one of the primary objectives of the Federal Acquisition System.[9] In the area of replenishment of inventory items, where demand is usually random, it is a tradeoff between the risk of not having the item immediately available and the cost of acquiring and maintaining an inventory at a supply point or points. A fundamental rule in the requirements determination process is that procurement lead times must be compensated for by the size of the inventory. Longer procurement lead times result in a larger investment in inventory to meet any demand that could occur during the time items are being ordered, produced, and delivered. In investment dollars this represents the one-time cost of the initial purchase of the item plus the continued cost of holding and managing the inventory.

As a general rule, procurement lead times for maintenance, repair, and operating (MRO) items in DoD are substantially longer than lead times in private industry, regardless of the type of commodity being purchased.[10] A study completed before acquisition reform, which compared procurement lead time profiles on 400 aircraft engine parts purchased by DoD and major U.S. airlines, concluded that: (1) procurement lead times for DoD were 4.6 times longer, and (2) the average DoD inventory investment was 2.1 times greater than that of the airlines.[11] In the period between FY 1984 and FY 1988, administrative lead times in DoD increased 104 percent, while production lead times grew 23 percent.[12] Much of this increase in administrative lead time is related to the increased processing requirements of the Competition in Contracting Act of 1984.[13] To illustrate how a change in policy often can have an indirect and unplanned effect, between FY 1984 and FY 1988, DoD's budgetary requirement for inventory increased from $8 billion to $24 billion to compensate for the increased procurement lead times.

The time it takes to replenish stocks directly determines the size of the inventory the using organization must retain. The use of e-commerce has shown that it improves coordination among firms and lowers the cost of searching for qualified goods and services. A study called "Restructuring Supply Chain Through Information Channel Innovation" refers to a cost analysis of the procurement process of a large European pharmaceutical firm that demonstrated that the administrative cost of electronic procurement processes was one-third the cost of the manual process.[14] The author states that some initial providers have used electronic markets to concentrate on systems biased to a particular supplier. (See Figure 3-1, Supply Chain Information Model.) However, he projects that in the long term buyers will realize that significant benefits from the electronic brokerage effect will drive almost all electronic markets toward being unbiased channels for purchasing products from many suppliers.[15]

In the early 1980s, Norman Augustine, a long-time participant in the acquisition process on both the commercial and government sides, developed a set of laws for major systems development programs. One of his conclusions was that most new systems become obsolete only slightly before they are born.[16] This is because the time it takes to develop a new

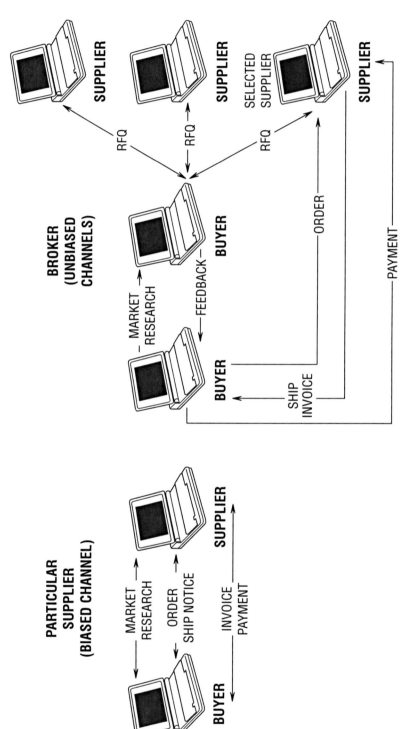

Figure 3-1 Supply Chain Information Model

system, including decision time and approval time, has consistently increased over the previous 15 years, while the life of technology has been decreasing. This problem became more acute in the 1990s because the half-life of technology continued to decrease at an increasing rate. Consequently, in the post Cold War–era, acquisition doctrine is challenging the acquisition community to reduce procurement lead times.

In obtaining products on the higher end of the technology spectrum, government also experiences longer procurement lead times than does the private sector. In an article in the *Acquisition Quarterly*, A. Lee Battershell compares the differences between DoD and Boeing in developing aircraft with comparable technologies, i.e., the Air Force's C-17 and Boeing's 777. The C-17 was selected because it does not have the complex subsystems that are characteristic of fighters and bombers.[17] It took well over 10 years to develop and deliver the C-17, compared to the Boeing 777, which took a little over four years to develop and deliver. The author concludes that where Boeing's focus is on cost, schedule, performance, and market competition, DOD's focus is mainly on performance.[18] It would be appropriate to add that the manufacturers of commercial airlines usually base their designs on previous models, whereas DoD contractors are more often required to make quantum leaps between models. The goal of a major system acquisition by the Defense Department is to provide the technology to support the strategy. Dr. Jacques S. Gansler, currently the Under Secretary of Defense (Acquisition and Technology), points out that the world and the strategy will undoubtedly change during the long period of time between the initial decision to develop a weapon system and actually fielding the system, which is often 10 to 15 years.[19]

Nevertheless, the importance to the national defense of having the technological advantage cannot be discounted. Military historians quickly point out that technology often provides the advantage in time of war. Former Secretary of Defense William Perry has cited people, readiness, and technology as the advantages the U.S. had during Desert Storm.[20] Other examples include the evolution of fighter aircraft by both sides during World War I that turned the tide of the air-to-air combat two or three times; the invention of radar by the British, which prevented Germany from attaining air superiority because the British could concentrate their limited fighter forces against the German bomber raids, thus precluding an invasion of England; and the development and use of the V-2 buzz bombs late in World War II, which could have drastically changed the complexion of the war in Europe had they been introduced a year earlier.

In the post–Cold War era, where the threat now comes from multiple sources, an evolutionary acquisition approach is required. Today's acquisition strategy is driven by rapidly changing operational requirements. This means that new capabilities must be selected, developed, and integrated into current forces using a block upgrade approach. Under this acquisition strategy the government will also be able to benefit from the changes to technology available in the commercial sector. For an evolutionary acquisition strategy to be effective, the acquisition community must look for ways to cut time out of the process by modifying the current sequential approach to acquiring goods and services.

Traditionally, the acquisition planning process has followed a gradual building up of the bodies of knowledge to be used to define the performance requirements as well as the contract and source selection information needed to award a contract. Developing an acquisition plan has traditionally been a push process—large batches of paper-based data are collected until they are complete and then assessed, placed in the proper format, and approved before being pushed to the next checkpoint, the solicitation. During this phase data are refined and information holes filled. When this process is complete, data are again placed in the proper format and, when approved, are pushed to another checkpoint on the path to evaluating sources. The difficulty with this approach is that it treats the information required as though it were a monolith, either entirely ready or entirely not ready for the next phase.

Following the traditional method has created queues of work in process everywhere, so that personnel have not always been productively engaged. Time is money, and backlogs of information waste time, cost money, and represent lost opportunities to reduce the cost of procurement. As noted above, past practices meant that information about the subject was held until it was virtually complete, and then was transferred to the next activity, where it was used by the next body of information to complete its part of the task. In reality, the data needed by another member of the team may be available and could be used concurrently. Overlapping of work will reduce the process time. By using modern electronic data interchange technology, which includes document imaging and workflow process technology, the phases leading to the development of a solicitation can overlap rather than follow a sequential approach. Overlapping relies heavily on the use of partial information and affects how the information is accumulated and how the user can pull it when it is needed.

Traditionally, most accounting and control systems have measured only cost. This has led management to measure performance on the degree of cost-effectiveness rather than on time. Only recently has procurement lead time been analyzed and monitored with the same fervor as cost. "It is essential that nonfinancial people also understand and be able to deal quantitatively with the financial value of time. Only when they are fluent in this language will they be able to challenge cost systems that delay development constructively."[21] Previously, when schedules were not met, attempts were rarely made to determine the impact on the cost of the operation. Improving the time taken to develop a product can be turned into an advantage for the ultimate user.

The just-in-time (JIT) movement has forced a reevaluation of our think-ing.[22] In manufacturing, JIT places emphasis on shortening the acquisition cycle, which results in reduced inventory requirements, especially the work-in-process (WIP) inventory. Benefits of just-in-time manufacturing are not limited to the reduction in the size of inventories; more important, JIT has forced the manufacturing sector to be more responsive to what the customer wants, when, and where. JIT reduces factory lead time so that orders are filled faster, mistakes corrected sooner, and forecasting becomes less critical. EDI is allowing the factory to be more responsive to the marketplace.

Sharing data systems means that JIT techniques can also be applied to transferring information between bodies of knowledge during the acquisi-tion planning process. The pull concept of JIT can be employed to obtain partial information. In the traditional procurement process, information was pushed downstream whether or not the recipient was ready to use it. It also meant that the recipient could not use the data until it was pushed to him or her. On the other hand, under a pull concept every person on the acquisition team can quickly exchange information regardless of where he or she is in the organization or is located geographically.

Using partial information requires the members of the acquisition team to be connected to each other electronically. Real-time communication is essential. "The effective use of partial information requires and supports the concept of close-knit teams."[23] Figure 3-2, Overlapping and Non-over-lapping Functional Tasks, illustrates how overlapping affects the point in time when information is available to another function. In the example at the top of the figure, the next activity cannot start until complete informa-tion is pushed to the next function. The 50-percent overlap example shows the pulling of information from the other function prior to comple-tion of the task. Because the information is incomplete, communication must go both ways for clarification and to provide feedback on how well it serves its intended purpose. The last example shows a close working rela-tionship, with the two tasks starting at the same time and being performed concurrently.

Useful multimedia tools include audio and video teleconferencing and electronic white boards, along with the Internet and an extranet.[24] There are both formal and informal opportunities for overlapping. Formal, as the name implies, means that procedures or tasks are part of an established communications network. Informal opportunities for overlapping arise every day as circumstances demand. A member of an acquisition team can meet his or her needs for data by using an electronic interface linked with other team members. Partial information may either be pushed to other members of the team or pulled from a common database. The pull ap-proach can be ingrained in the development team's normal operating pro-cedures by making it clear that it is the responsibility of the downstream function to ask for whatever information is needed. By making this

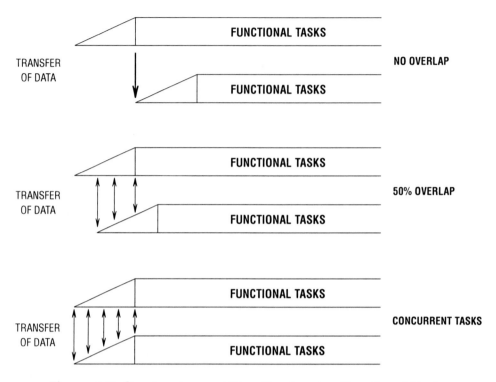

Figure 3-2 Overlapping and Non-Overlapping Functional Tasks

method the standard way of doing business, tasks will get started sooner, and the time required to issue the solicitation will be compressed.

The acquisition team members must be the ones to initiate the transfer of data. They should look for opportunities where they can compress the process by asking such questions as:

- What is the bare minimum of information needed to start the next task?
- What is the earliest date this information can be made available?
- Are there assumptions that are accurate enough to begin work?
- Will the likely consequences of a particular mistake be large or small?
- Can one save enough time by starting early to allow for making a mistake?
- Who could use the information I have to enable them to initiate another one of their tasks?[25]

Acquisition team members must also consider the risk associated with the possibility that the partial information is incorrect and should develop contingency plans for this eventuality.

The difference between the traditional push method of information management and an accelerated pull approach, which is designed to cut administrative lead times, is a matter of leadership within the acquisition team. In DoD such initiatives as Alpha contracting and the Air Force's One-Pass Contracting Process have been implemented to cut administrative lead times. Both concepts stress early and continuous parallel involvement by the buyer and contractor in the acquisition process, including jointly defining and refining requirements.

An initiative by the Air Force's Launch Systems Program Office presents an example of how the administrative lead time can be reduced through overlapping and transferring partial information. Motivated to meet the goals of the National Performance Review, the Delta II Integrated Product Team (IPT) set out to reengineer the traditional Engineering Change Proposal (ECP) process. Using Program Evaluation Review Technique (PERT) and Acquisition Management Information System (AMIS), they analyzed the cycle time of six ECPs, averaging over $700,000, that had followed the traditional ECP process (see Figure 3-3). The Delta II IPT discovered that it took an average of 46.5 weeks for these ECPs to navigate the standard administrative maze between the validation of need and contract award.

Figure 3-4, Overlapping the ECP Process, illustrates how the ECP process was reduced to 18.21 weeks based on changes initiated by the Delta II IPT.[26] The initial goal of the Delta II IPT's reengineering initiative was to reduce the ECP process cycle time by at least 50 percent. To achieve this objective, they implemented a comprehensive training program that emphasized teamwork, accountability, project management, and empowerment.[27] Overlapping in the revised process forces the government to work directly with the contractor early in the cycle, beginning with joint participation in defining the requirement. Under the new procedure the contractor works closely with the government during each step in the contract change process rather than waiting until information is pushed back and forth, as in the traditional ECP process. The IPT communicates continuously to develop jointly the request for proposal and then reach a consensus on the hours and materials required to complete the project before the proposal is actually submitted to the government. The result is that after the proposal is received, the government knows what it contains, which makes negotiating and writing the contract change document much easier. The six ECPs that followed this new process were then examined and found to have taken an average cycle time of 18.21 weeks.[28] The net result of overlapping and using partial information was a 60-percent reduction in the administrative lead time.

ACQUISITION PLANNING

Planning to acquire goods or services is an evolutionary process that begins with the development of the statement of need and culminates with

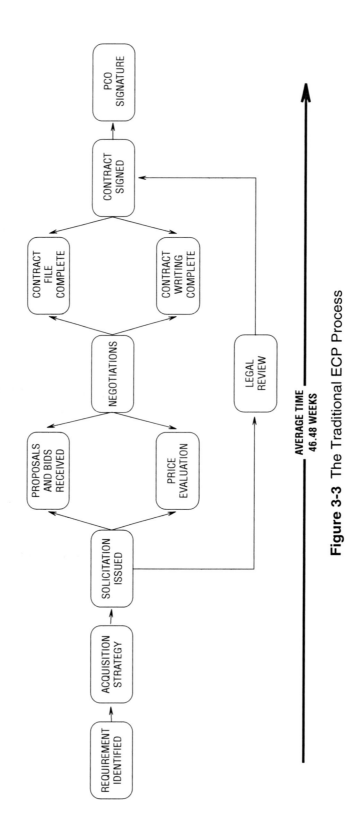

Figure 3-3 The Traditional ECP Process

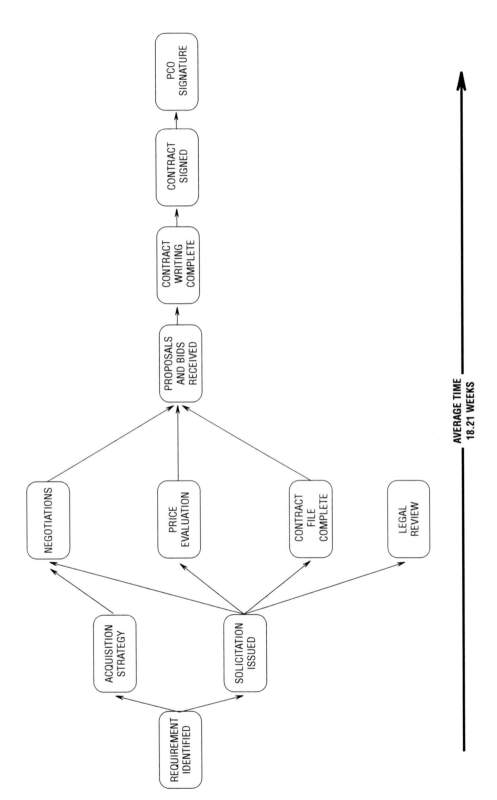

Figure 3-4 Overlapping the ECP Process

the solicitation. "This planning shall integrate the efforts of all personnel responsible for significant aspects of the acquisition. The purpose of this planning is to ensure that the Government meets its needs in the most effective, economical, and timely manner."[29] It is during the planning process that the acquisition team identifies risks and opportunities associated with the procurement. The MR&O process begins at this point in the acquisition process with the development of the "How to Handle Plan." Procurement planning is a subset of the overall acquisition plan. The plan should contain all applicable technical, contracting, fiscal, and business management factors that govern the acquisition. The magnitude and detail contained in an acquisition plan should be tailored to fit the situation. For example, details included in a plan to purchase supplies in economic quantities are significantly less than what is needed in a plan to acquire a major system.

Determining Requirements

The requirements determination phase includes such tasks as requirements forecasting, market research, defining risks and opportunities, developing initial acquisition strategy, and quantifying the initial budgetary estimate. This estimate is extremely important because it becomes the basis for initial planning and is often the initial amount cited in the fund request submitted up the chain of command. Numerous projects have suffered because they were saddled with an unrealistic initial budget estimate. The initial budget estimate must be realistic because subsequent management decisions must live with this fund projection.

It is a fundamental policy that all government requirements are based on a need that is tied to a mission. The mission must, by law, emanate from a Congressional authorization. Figure 3-5, Overview of the Requirements Determination Process, depicts the requirements determination process from perceived need to preparation of the solicitation/request for bid. This illustration will guide our discussion on how requirements are developed and solicitations/bids are requested.

Needs can be separated into four general sources, each with its own distinguishing characteristics: (1) the need to establish a new operational capability, (2) the need to improve an existing capability, (3) the need to exploit an opportunity to reduce cost, and (4) the need to preserve a current capability through maintaining replenishing inventory.

When maintaining existing equipment or replenishing inventories, the inventory manager originates individual procurement requests. Inventory replenishment is most frequently determined through the use of requirement determination models, which include such variables as past consumption and such mission factors as force size and flying hours, as well as planned distribution points, re-supply times, item value, and procurement

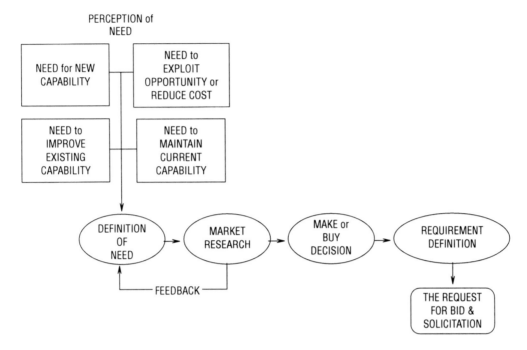

Figure 3-5 Overview of the Requirements Determination Process

and production lead times. With increasing frequency, stock replenishment orders can easily be handled by computer-to-computer exchange without human intervention. The sealed bid method of contracting, with its competitive bids and public opening of bids, is the method most frequently used to replenish inventories. In addition, indefinite quantity agreements and requirements contracts, which will be covered in Chapter 4, are very appropriate contracting methods in lieu of single-purchase contracts.

The remaining three sources of needs, i.e., the need for a new operational capability, the need to improve an existing capability, and the need to exploit an opportunity to reduce cost, are based on an assessment of current and projected capability and validated mission needs. The process begins with a broad statement of a requirement that cannot be satisfied with current resources or by nonmaterial means. It is during the requirements determination process that mission needs are translated into an Operational Requirements Document (ORD), which includes the operational and logistics support requirements. There must be a linking of this to possible mission failure. Requirements should be stated in terms of functions to be performed, performance parameters, and essential physical characteristics.[30] The supporting technical and program analysis and initial funding projections are important parts of the requirements determination process but are not discussed in any detail in this book.

For the purposes of our discussion of the requirements determination process, we will assume that the need has been approved and the acquisition team is on board and ready to begin the acquisition process. The mission needs statement has been translated into basic performance objectives.

Two common problems to keep in mind when developing requirements statements are:

1. The requiring activity fails to consider the cost implications of alternative approaches to describing requirements.
2. The CO and others members of the acquisition team fail to conduct systematic search and analysis of alternative solutions to providing the need.[31]

Initially the CO obtains a description of the basic attributes of the product and how it will fulfill the requirement. Using this information, market research is then used to locate alternative sources to satisfy a need. One of the reasons why it is difficult to initially define the desired characteristics of the product is that there is an assortment of technical knowledge that must be translated into an accurate description of the needed product characteristics. Acquisition doctrine calls for participation by the ultimate user in writing the requirements specifications. In the case of development programs, the user and engineer have a tendency to write product descriptions for different purposes. Traditionally, the user describes the performance characteristics. An engineer often tries to specify in minute detail how the product works. This difference can cause a problem because a poor initial description can lengthen the acquisition process. Everything downstream in the process depends on the initial description. However, the ultimate user is not the only stakeholder to determine what product will best satisfy the requirement. Other functions such as logistics (product support), manufacturing, quality assurance, and testing may also be written into the specifications, depending on the product and how it will be employed. Therefore, an acquisition team representing the user, engineering, manufacturing, and logistics must be involved from the outset because each of these areas has its own expertise to contribute. Another advantage to using the team approach to defining the requirement is that the team gains a sense of ownership of the project from the outset.

In 1994 DoD turned away from its traditional practice of using detailed specifications when it canceled many of its detailed MILSPECs and process-oriented MILSTDs. The purpose of this monumental change in policy was three-fold:

1. To reduce the cost of weapon systems and other material DoD sought by eliminating unique military requirements and procedures that drove up acquisition cost

2. To remove impediments to getting state-of-the-art technology into defense weapon systems, especially information systems, telecommunications, and microtechnology, where private R&D exceeded defense R&D by a ratio of 2 to 1
3. To facilitate the diversification into the commercial markets of firms that had produced goods for defense purposes.[32]

This change in policy enabled defense agencies to utilize commercial products and services to a greater extent than in the past. Acquisition doctrine now emphasizes the use of non-government standards, program-specific requirements, or tailored portions of MILSPECs and MILSTDs to the maximum extent possible. Rather than stating how the requirements are to be satisfied by using design specifications and citing MILSPECs and MILSTDs, requirements must now describe functions to be performed, performance parameters, and physical characteristics. The buying office is charged to look for different approaches to meeting the user's needs.

The order of precedence for documenting requirements is: (1) documents mandated for use by law; (2) performance-oriented documents; (3) detailed, design-oriented documents; and (4) standards, specifications, and related publications issued by the government outside the Defense or federal series for the non-repetitive acquisition of items.[33] Performance-oriented specifications emphasize that objectives, measurable performance requirements, and quality standards are to be used in the ORD and statements of work (SOW).

Another policy change introduced with federal acquisition streamlining is that the federal government has tried to make it easier to purchase commercial items. Therefore, the CO is authorized to tailor government contractual provisions and clauses to permit the acquisition of commercial items so they are consistent with standard commercial practices found in the commercial marketplace.

Contracts for acquiring commercial items are subject to the FAR. However, when a policy in the FAR conflicts with one applying to commercial items in FAR Part 12, Acquisition of Commercial Items, the policy in Part 12 takes precedence.[34] The CO may also use streamlined procedures for soliciting commercial items outlined in FAR 12.203. If the price of the items exceeds the simplified threshold but does not exceed $5,000,000, including options, the CO is instructed to follow the simplified procedures authorized by Subpart 13.5 to the maximum extent possible.[35] Contract types that are to be used to acquire commercial items are firm-fixed-price or fixed-price contracts with an economic price adjustment. (The various types of contract pricing arrangements are discussed in detail in Chapter 4.) Indefinite-delivery contracts are contracts in which prices are based on a firm fixed-price or a fixed price with an economic price adjustment.[36] Contracts for the acquisition of commercial items are also subject to a special contract clause, FAR 52.212-4, *Contract Terms and Conditions—Commercial Items.* Tailoring of contract clauses is permitted for all paragraphs of FAR 52.212-4, with the exception of assignments, disputes, payments, invoices, other terms and conditions, act of yielding, and compliance with the laws unique to government contracts.[37]

Product performance goals are always constrained. Figure 3-6, The Tradeoff Process, illustrates the e-tradeoffs the acquisition team is most likely to encounter during the process. Team members should participate in making these e-tradeoffs at the macro, or total product level, by making their interests known. This will also give team members a better understanding of the basic decisions that were part of the requirements determination process.

MARKET RESEARCH: STARTING THE MANAGEMENT OF RISK AND OPPORTUNITIES PROCESS

For years the commercial sector has undergone more extensive presales research than has the government. This is because in the private sector, there is a belief that if you wait until the receipt of the solicitation to learn

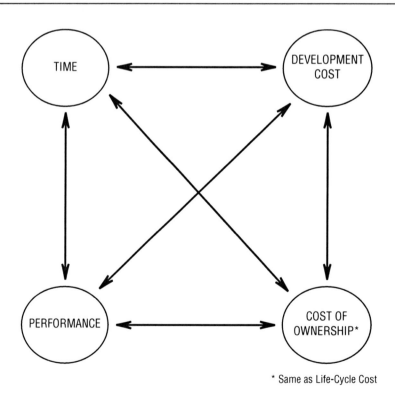

* Same as Life-Cycle Cost

Figure 3-6 The Tradeoff Process

about a proposed contract to get organized, you have missed the window of opportunity. The private sector believes in re-screening potential suppliers to eliminate the ones that are not qualified to perform according to the requirements.[38] This was because government buyers traditionally assumed that firms in the private sector would aggressively seek opportunities to do business with the government. This assumption, in addition to a policy requiring publication of business opportunities in the *Commerce Business Daily* before issuing the solicitation, ensured that the most qualified companies would compete for the government's business. This is not a valid assumption. As we saw in Chapter 1, not everyone wants to do business with the government.

On the other hand, government has only recently emphasized the need to be more proactive in the area of market research. Market research is more than merely advertising in the *Commerce Business Daily* to satisfy the need to consider using a commercial product and having the necessary documentation in the sole source file. Dr. Ralph Nash, Jr., professor emeritus of law at the George Washington University Law School, points out that buying practices of commercial buyers of the same product normally demonstrate an understanding of the market. "In my ideal world the CO would come to the acquisition planning meeting with full knowledge of the market (as well as information on all acquisition strategies), while technical people would come to the table with full knowledge of the needs of the agency."[39] The federal government deals in almost every commercial market. To have an effective market research program requires initiative and knowledge of what companies within each of these markets are selling. Market research has not been included in training programs because it has only recently been considered a subject most COs should know about. Previously, it was assumed that the sellers would seek out the government. In the post–Cold War environment, where the industrial base for many of the government's requirements has decreased, the CO must be more proactive in seeking alternative sources of supply.

The government's primary objective is then to obtain the best-value products or services that are available from the private sector. Today, acquisition doctrine emphasizes the use of commercial products to provide the ultimate user with the latest technology at lower cost. This is also seen as a way to simplify the acquisition process. Policy also emphasizes defining acquisition objectives in the form of performance objectives and then giving contractors the latitude to determine how to achieve the performance standards—and the incentives to achieve them.[40]

Performing market research is a prerequisite to developing new requirements documents. It is also required before soliciting offers that are expected to exceed the simplified acquisition threshold of $100,000 or when adequate information is not available and the circumstances justify the cost. (Outside the United States or in the event of a peacekeeping or humanitarian operation, the threshold is $200,000.[41]) When making micro-purchases, agencies are required to consult readily available sources, such as catalogs, to ensure that the goods or services purchased will meet the government's needs at a fair and reasonable price.[42]

Genesis of Market Research

Goods and services available in the commercial market are key sources of products that will meet the government user's requirements. The method by which the CO and other members of the acquisition team determine what is available in the commercial market is part of the market research process. The position of market research in the overall requirements determination process is highlighted in Figure 3-7. Analysis of the commercial marketplace was first mentioned as being a part of the acquisition process in a 1982 policy document issued by the Office of Federal Procurement Policy (OFPP).[43] It was not until passage of the Competition in Contracting Act (CICA) in 1984 that market research became closely associated with acquisition planning. In that act, government agencies were directed to perform market research to ensure that they obtained competition.[44] In the

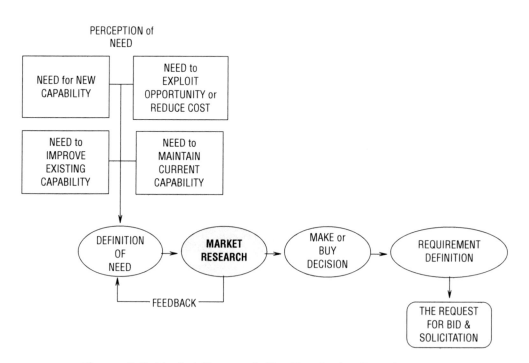

Figure 3-7 Market Research Position in the Requirements Determination Process

Federal Acquisition Streamlining Act of 1994, Congress mandated that the executive branch do a better job of conducting market research.

The use of commercial products to satisfy government needs has been promoted in policy statements for some time. The May 1990 edition of the FAR defined commercial products as "items sold or traded to the general public in the course of normal business operations at prices based on established catalog or market prices."[45] Many felt that this definition made procurement of commercial items too complicated because it was often interpreted differently by the various agencies. FAR 2.101 now defines a commercial item as "any item, other than real property, that is customarily used for nongovernmental purposes and that…has been sold, leased, or licensed to the general public, or has been offered for sale, lease, or licensed to the general public." In addition, a commercial item is defined to include:

- "Any item that evolved from an item described (above) through advances in technology or performance and not yet available in the commercial marketplace, but will be available in the commercial marketplace in time to satisfy the delivery requirements under a government solicitation
- Any item that would satisfy a criterion (described above) but for…modifications of a type customarily available in the commercial marketplace and minor modifications of a type not customarily available in the commercial marketplace made to meet Federal Government requirements."[46]

Support services for a commercial item are also included in the new definition if they are the same as those offered concurrently to the general public and federal government under similar conditions by the same work force. Commercial services are deemed to be included in the definition if such services are "offered and sold completely, in substantial quantities, in commercial marketplace based on established catalog prices for specific tasks performed under standard commercial terms and conditions."[47]

A non-development item is also included within the definition of a commercial item if the procuring agency determines that the item was developed exclusively at private expense and has been sold in substantial quantities, on a competitive basis, to multiple state and local governments.[48]

The Market Research Process

In addition to the CO, other members of the acquisition team who should be involved in market research include representatives of the user, technical personnel from the buying activity, price analysts, and industrial specialists. Small business specialists can also assist the process if required. Areas to consider when determining what type of information is needed include the complexity of the requirement (including an understanding of the state of the art), how much time is available until the user suffers harm, the dollar amount, and past experience with the item or service.[49] A tradeoff process should be followed when determining the amount of market research to undertake. One must determine the value of the information to be gathered on the suitability of items offered in the commercial market and the insight into the business practices of the market, and then compare this information to benefits of the time that could have been spent on other acquisition tasks.

Buyers can accomplish the following from market research:

- Determine if the items being considered achieved commercial market acceptance or have recently been satisfactorily supplied to a government agency to satisfy the same or similar requirements.[50]
- Determine how best to satisfy the stated need and predict the probable trend in technology development of the product line. Are there other sources or highly technical alternatives that will meet the user's needs more efficiently? This includes information on the existing commercial products and potential suppliers. What is the possibility of incorporating commercial items into the product at the component level? The iterative nature of the market research and definition of needs is illustrated in Figure 3-7. The point to be made is that market research often uncovers alternative means to satisfy the requirements that lead to amending the definition of need.
- Obtain data on the prevalent business practices of the industry—generally accepted methods in the industry related to production lead times, the production process, structure of the distribution system, and product support history of items delivered to the customer. The buyer can learn which buying practices of the industry, including types of contracts, are normally used. They can find out about industry practices regarding delivery and acceptance and information related to billings and discounts, variances in performance from different sources, logistics support cost of products of the various vendors, past performance history, bonding requirements, and information on which to make the determination of responsibility by the CO or the Certificate of Competency and Determination of Eligibility from the Small Business Administration.
- Determine if potential contractors can comply with the proposed terms of performance and have the financial resources necessary to do so. They can learn about labor laws and regulations that apply to the supplies or services needed.
- Gain an increased understanding of the risks and opportunities associated with the acquisition. How well did the same or similar goods or services meet the buyer's needs? Was the supplier competitive? What types of problems were encountered?

- Gain information for use in determining if the potential contractor is responsible and if it is debarred or suspended from doing business with the government.
- Develop information that can be used during discussions, source selection, and negotiations. This includes information on patents, copyrights, and ownership of technical data. The buyer can also obtain price-related factors such as seasonal, cyclical, lease versus purchase, mode of transportation, and type of contract.

The 1994 rewrite of the FAR removed many of the restrictions that previously had constrained exchanges of information between the government and the potential seller. This change in policy was intended to encourage joint planning by the buyer and seller on a strategic basis. However, discussions between the parties are nevertheless constrained because of the restrictions contained in the Procurement Integrity Act, the Trade Secrets Act, and 10 U.S.C. 2305. Industry is very protective regarding what information is disclosed, during discussions, especially if they view it as being proprietary or if they see it as the source of any competitive advantage they may have.

In the rewrite of FAR Part 15, one-on-one meetings between the parties have been identified as a primary means of exchanging information.Policy outlined in FAR 15.306 (e) requires that information revealed during the pre-solicitation conference also be furnished to potential offerors not able to attend the conference and be included in the next release of information.[51] Industry has asked what standard is to be used to determine what information is necessary to prepare the proposal. It has also expressed a concern about safeguarding proprietary information obtained during meetings that are not necessary for the preparation of the proposal.

The rewrite of Part 15 of the FAR also formalized the process by which possible offerors are invited to submit a capability statement or similar information to the government prior to their receipt of the proposal. These inputs are analyzed and the respondents notified regarding the likelihood that they would be viable competitors. This revision to the FAR also is careful to note that all respondents, regardless of the government's conclusion, may participate in the resultant acquisition.[52]

Table 3-1 shows possible sources of market research information.

The pre-solicitation notice and pre-solicitation conference are often used as preliminary steps in negotiated procurements to develop or identify interested sources, request preliminary information based on a general description of the supplies or services involved, explain complicated specifications and requirements to interested sources, and aid potential contractors in submitting proposals without undue expenditures of effort, time, or money.[53]

The requirements determination process culminates with the prospective user determining which of the supplies or services will be provided

Table 3-1. Sources of Market Information

Sources	Participants
Industry Specific	*Network*
Trade Journals	Accountants/Lawyers
Association Information	Investment Advisors/Brokers
Newspaper/Magazine Articles	Brokers
Pre-solicitation Conference	Other Government Officials
Company Specific	*Personal Network*
Websites	Friends/Family
Annual Report	Coworkers
Company Newsletters	Current Clients
Marketing Material	Suppliers
Dun and Bradstreet Reports	Competitors
On-site inspections	
Government Sources	*Extended Network*
SEC Reports	Other Contracting Offices
Real Estate Records	Calls to Users

using government capabilities or which will be purchased using the contracting process.

The Make-or-Buy Decision

One of the early decisions that must be made is if the requirement will, or can, be satisfied by the government utilizing its own capabilities. There are only two choices: Will the work be performed by the government's own employees, or will it be purchased or leased? This question involves many interest groups in both the public and private sectors. For the government, the decision involves productivity, equity, jobs, and the question, "What is our mission?" An inherently governmental function includes activities that require either the exercise of discretion in applying government authority, or the making of value judgments in making decisions for the government.[54]

Figure 3-8 shows how the make-or-buy decision fits into the overall requirements determination process. It shows the make-or-buy decision occurring after market research has been completed. Nothing would preclude this event from overlapping or being done concurrently with market research.

In his 1954 budget message to the Congress, President Eisenhower stated that it was government policy to rely on the private sector during peacetime for obtaining goods and services. He announced "... a policy of shift-

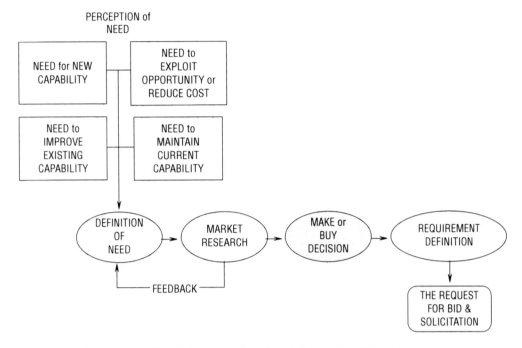

Figure 3-8 The Make-or-Buy Decision in the Requirements
Determination Process

ing from in-house operations to state, local, and private enterprise." Later
the Bureau of the Budget (the forerunner to the Office of Management and
Budget) published the following policy statement:

> It is the general policy of the administration that the federal govern-
> ment will not start or carry on any commercial activity to provide a
> service or product for its own use, if such product or service can be
> procured from private enterprise through ordinary channels....[55]

As a matter of policy, there are functions so intimately related to the public
interests that they mandate performance by government employees. These
inherently governmental functions include the act of governing, i.e., the discretionary exercise of government authority, interpretation and execution of
the laws of the United States, and monetary transactions. They do not include
gathering information for providing advice to government officials, building
security, mail operations, operating cafeterias, housekeeping, operating and
maintenance facilities, and warehouse operations.[56]

Probably the most important question for the buyer to have answered
when determining if the requirement will be outsourced is if there will be
sufficient administrative or technical expertise available within the government to perform and supervise the work. Another consideration in

making the make-or-buy decision is if it would be the least costly alternative. Making a cost comparison is complicated because it involves determining both direct and indirect costs.

The decision the CO and the acquisition team must make involves answering the following questions before progressing to further defining the requirement and developing the solicitation:

1. How should the project be subdivided between internal sources and contractors?
2. Should the requirement be contracted for as a system or group of subsystems, with the government acting as the systems integrator?
3. Are the specifications and other technical documents regarding the allocation of responsibilities and risk between the government and contractors sufficient and available?
4. Have all likely commercial sources been identified? Should additional sources be sought?[57]

PROPRIETARY INFORMATION (INTELLECTUAL PROPERTY)[58]

One of the major considerations in using commercial products is how proprietary information and intellectual property will be handled. As one would imagine, government policy encourages the use of commercial inventions while performing government contracts. It is also government policy to honor the rights in patents, technical data, and copyrights and to comply with the stipulations of the law when using or acquiring such rights.[59] However, some of the rules regarding the use of intellectual property by the government recognize the dominant relationship that the needs of the public have in relation to all other needs.

Part of the market research process is a requirement to obtain information regarding intellectual property that could be involved. Questions to ask are: (1) what intellectual information is needed to meet the acquisition objectives, (2) where is it, and (3) who owns it? The concern over location and ownership of intellectual property begins during product development and continues through the life cycle of the product. It is important to the government because it is technical information required to develop or modify products as well as detail on testing, training, operation, maintenance, and re-procurement. To the contractors it is their life's blood, and therefore it must be protected from use by outsiders. This is because maintaining control over intellectual property is viewed as the best way to remain competitive and profitable.

In 1919 not a single U.S. company could supply a complete radio transmitter or receiver to the U.S. Navy without an infringement on patent rights of other firms. The situation was finally resolved, at the prodding of the Navy, by forming the Radio Corporation of America (RCA). This new enterprise included General Electric (GE), AT&T, and Westinghouse as major shareholders. Key patent rights were leased from American Marconi. Thus the barriers that had prevented vacuum tubes from being supplied to produce radio transmitters and receivers were removed.[60] This obstacle to equipping the Navy with radio transmitters and receivers illustrates how the access to intellectual property, i.e., patents, copyrights, and other proprietary data or processes, plays a significant part in acquiring modern high-tech products.

Industry places a premium on innovation and strongly defends its rights to its intellectual property against being used by its competitors.[61] Many of today's products are an accumulation of technologies. "Cumulative systems technologies" exist when one innovation builds on another. To be successful, many products must draw on several related technologies.[62] Some firms can create marketable value from their innovation only by embedding their new products and processes into equipment produced by others. Examples of products with multiple technologies are electronics, semiconductors, aircraft, and automobiles.

One of the realities of the high-tech world we live in is that the competitive necessity to shorten the acquisition cycle times requires industry to speed up its innovative processes. With less time to create new products, or variations of established products, one corporation cannot possibly have the expertise within its walls to develop independently the cumulative technologies contained in today's components. Innovation requires that organizations evolve their products in concert with each other.[63] Therefore, it is essential that contractors look for ways to supplement their capabilities with the needed technology from outside the firm. This can be accomplished by working in close collaboration with others through license agreements for patented items, teaming arrangements, or subcontracting.

Patent Rights

A patent is a grant of a right given to the inventor to exclude others from the making, using, or selling of an invention during a specified time; it constitutes a legitimate monopoly.[64] This right is usually conferred by the government to the originator of the invention for a 17-year period. Government policy:

- Encourages the use of inventions in performing contracts, even though the inventions may be covered by U.S. patents and protection against infringement may be appropriate
- Encourages maximum use of commercial inventions made while performing government contracts
- Encourages the development of inventions under federally sponsored research contracts so that the general public can benefit from their use.[65]

In the private sector, any encroachment on the exclusivity rights of the patent holder, without legal permission, means that the person guilty of the infringement is subject to damages and is prohibited from continuing to use the invention in any way. Predictably, this often requires the government to enter into some form of license agreement with the owner of a patent if its plans for future use of the item dictate. This can occur because the government is either bound to pay a royalty on a patent because of an existing license agreement between the government and the patent holder or the government is obligated to pay a royalty on a patent involved in a prospective contract. In the latter case, the government acknowledges its obligation by including a clause in the solicitation identifying the owner of the patent.[66]

The Authorization and Consent clause (FAR 52.227-1) in included in most government contracts primarily to permit the contractor to continue to work on the contract uninterrupted even if a patient infringement has occurred.[67] Under this clause, the government authorizes and consents to the manufacture or use of an invention covered by a patent of the United States. A suit for infringement of the patent cannot be made against the contractor or subcontractor. It must be made against the government in a U.S. Claims Court. In any solicitation or contract, the CO is not to include (a) any cause whereby the government expressly agrees to indemnify the contractor against liability for patent infringement, or (b) any authorization and consent clause when delivery and performance are outside the United States, its possessions, and Puerto Rico.[68] There are two Authorization and Consent clauses in the FAR. One covers work specified in the contract. The other is used when the effort is primarily a research and development contract, and it gives blanket authorization and consent to use any invention.[69]

For contracts for supplies or services normally sold to the public in the commercial open market, including commercial items that have minor modifications, the Patent Indemnity clause is required.[70] This clause, which also applies to construction contracts, provides that the contractor will reimburse the government for the infringement of any patent used during performance of the contract. This is necessary because the government is liable for paying compensation to the owner of the patent.[71]

There are two schools of thought regarding who should retain title to intellectual property developed while performing federally funded contracts. One favors government retention of the title to the patent. The other point of view advocates the inventor retaining title to the patent while assigning a nonexclusive, nontransferable, royalty-free license to the government to use the invention for government purposes. The logic supporting the latter school of thought is that contractors are more likely to develop innovative technology with possible commercial applications when the title remains in their possession.[72]

The government obtains rights in technical data, including a copyright license, under an irrevocable license granted or obtained for the government by the contractor. "A license is a legal instrument granting permission to do a particular thing, exercise a certain privilege, carry on a particular business, or pursue a certain occupation."[73] The contractor or licenser retains all rights in the data not granted to the government. The source of funds used to develop the item, component, or process generally determines the scope of the license.[74]

In solicitations and contracts for experimental, development, or research work, the contractor is required to disclose all inventions it develops while working on the contract. Under FAR clauses 52.227-11 or 52.227-12, the contractor may elect to retain the entire right, title, and interest to these inventions throughout the world.[75] The government retains a revocable, nonexclusive royalty-free license to the inventions and the right to apply for additional rights to use the patents throughout the world. Deviation from the rules of granting title to inventions is limited to: (1) contractors not located in the United States or subject to the control of a foreign government; (2) contracts for the operation of government-owned, contractor-operated Department of Energy facilities; (3) exceptional circumstances when a restriction will better serve FAR policy objectives; and (4) occasions when granting title would endanger national security.[76] Most contractors favor retention of the title to the invention because they have the ability to use and commercially market the product or process.

Rights in Technical Data and Computer Software[77]

The government has unique requirements for technical data and computer software, making it more expensive to prepare and maintain than it would be for commercial users. For example, equipment and supplies used by DoD are often unique, and the product must not only be purchased, operated, and maintained at remote locations, but the technical information needed for its re-procurement also should be included in the acquisition contract. The government's long-term needs for technical data and computer software must be defined during the requirements determination process.

The basic government policy on rights to make use of technical data and computer software calls for the contractor and the government to reach a balance between: (1) the contractor's legitimate proprietary interests in the privately developed data and protecting it from disclosure, thereby compromising the contractor's commercial position; and (2) the government's need to obtain access to the data.[78] In other words, the policy states that the government should acquire only the rights to technical data and computer software that are needed for the contract, thereby relinquishing as much data as possible for private use by the developer.

There are two sets of rules in the areas of technical data and computer software. The FAR 27.400, Rights in Data and Copyrights, establishes the guidelines that pertain to commercial products. When it comes to needs of the Department of Defense, however, it is felt that DoD's technical data requirements differ from those of the civilian agencies, and a single government-wide procurement regulation on the subject is not feasible.[79] The Defense Acquisition Regulatory Council has the authority to implement separate policies and procedures for the acquisitions of technical data by DoD. These cover the right to use, modify, reproduce, release, display, or disclose data and are defined in a subpart of the Department of Defense FAR Supplement (DFARS) Rights in Technical Data.[80]

Technical data is often produced as a deliverable item during the performance of the contract. It constitutes data on the form, fit, and function item delivered under the contract. It can encompass test results and instructional training manuals as well as directions on the installation, operation, and maintenance of the items delivered under the contract. Ownership of technical data and computer software is usually determined by the source of the funds that paid for its development. When the government pays the full cost of developing the product and related data, it almost always claims "unlimited rights" to the data. When a contractor or subcontractor develops an item at its own expense, it is considered proprietary, and the government generally obtains "limited rights" in technical data. Department of Defense contractors obtain "government purpose rights" to data when they were developed with a mixture of public and private funds. All of these rights are license rights, with the contractor retaining the title to the data.

The release of data delivered under a government contract is subject to the data rights provisions of the contract, federal export control, and national security laws and regulations. The basic categories for government rights to technical data defined in the FAR include:

- *Unlimited rights data*: The government has unlimited rights to use, reproduce, modify, or disclose form, fit, and function data delivered under a contract (except for restricted computer software) to the extent it feels is required.[81]
- *Limited rights data*: These are "data that embody trade secrets or are commercial or financial and confidential or privileged, to the extent such data pertain to items, components, or processes developed at private expense, including minor modifications thereof."[82]
- *Restricted rights*: The rights of the government to computer software are restricted to what is negotiated as part of a collateral agreement and incorporated in the contract by the parties thereto.[83]
- *Limited rights data and restricted computer software*: The contractor is able to protect qualifying computer software by delivering only form, fit, and functional data in lieu of all data. To qualify, the data must

incorporate a trade secret or be commercial, financial, and confidential or privileged as well as pertain to components developed at private expense. When the buyer has a need for this data, the contracting officer can selectively request its delivery by specifying what data are to be delivered in the contract.[84]

- *Restricted computer software*: This term applies to data, other than computer software, developed at private expense that embody trade secrets or are commercial or financial and confidential or privileged.[85]

The contractor is able to protect qualifying limited rights and restricted computer software by withholding such data from delivery to the government and delivering form, fit, and function data in lieu thereof. (Form, fit, and function data means data relating to component processes that are sufficient to enable physical and functional interchangeability, as well as data identifying source, size, configuration, mating, attachment characteristics, functional characteristics, and performance requirements. For computer software, it includes data identifying source, functional characteristics, and performance requirements, but specifically excluding the source code, algorithm, process, formula, and flow charts of the software.[86])

As noted above, the Defense Acquisition Regulatory Council can prescribe regulations governing technical data rights under Public Law 102-190. These are included in the Defense Federal Acquisition Regulations System (DFARS), which defines DoD policies and procedures on data rights as they pertain to the defense agencies, and are intended to address unique military systems with no commercial counterpart.[87]

The government is also able to require delivery of limited rights data rather than allow the contractor to withhold such data. As part of the negotiation process, the contractor may specifically identify data not to be delivered under the contract or data that will be delivered with limited rights.[88]

COOPERATIVE AND TEAMING AGREEMENTS

A recent projection by the National Association of Purchasing Management (NAPM) and the Center for Advanced Purchasing Studies (CAPS) concluded that over the next five years, "as supply bases shrink, supplier alliances will become increasingly important and require purchasing and supply focus." The acquisition strategy of the government to rely increasingly on an integrated government industrial base requires "the establishment of strategic alliance relationships among buying commands and suppliers to gain insight into, and apply, business sector best practices in such processes as government property, material management and accounting systems, performance-based payments, single-process incentive, and past performance."[89]

Many commercial businesses view management of their acquisition process as a way to obtain a competitive advantage. Therefore, they manage their supply system strategically. "Strategic management is the design, development, optimization, and management of the internal and external components of the organization's supply system."[90] They are accomplishing this by forming strategic alliances with key suppliers, which enables them to establish integrated relationships with the suppliers supporting their core competencies. Establishing cross-functional teams that extend across corporate boundaries results in horizontal integration of functions. These integrated teams are able to participate jointly in forecasting, marketing, design, cost estimation, production planning, inventory planning, purchasing, quality assurance, personnel, and others tasks that are part of an integrated purchasing system.

Integration means that collaborative agreements are needed to enable companies to work cooperatively while maintaining their corporate interests, i.e., they become common stakeholders. It is through these agreements that businesses are able to keep their corporate entity while furthering their goals through agreements to pool or exchange resources. These agreements are fundamentally contracts between two parties and are governed by the Uniform Commercial Code (UCC). They are not contracts to sell good or services; rather, they are more like Memoranda of Understanding, which describe the intent of the partners and include an expectation to enter into more detailed agreements in the future.[91] These cooperative agreements define an area of focus, the value to be gained by each party, how intellectual property will be protected, and exit conditions. The goals of cooperative agreements are to:

- Improve performance in existing markets
- Improve shareholder value
- Achieve an innovation or breakthrough
- Maintain access to key supplier capabilities
- Gain name recognition in new markets.[92]

When a cooperative relationship is developed to perform a government contract, the document outlining the details of the alliance is commonly referred to as a teaming agreement. It is a contract in which: (1) two or more companies form a partnership or joint venture to act as a potential prime contractor, or (2) a potential prime contractor agrees with one or more companies to have them act as subcontractors under a specified government contract or acquisition program.[93] The first type of arrangement is often called a *horizontal teaming agreement*. The latter, and most common, is described as a *vertical teaming agreement*.[94]

It is the government's policy to recognize the integrity and validity of teaming arrangements, provided the relationship is disclosed in an offer, or before the arrangement becomes effective after the offer has been submitted. The teaming agreement must also not violate the antitrust laws nor limit the government's rights to require consent to subcontract, as well as determine the responsibility of the prime contractor, provide the prime contractor data rights owned by the government, pursue policies of competitive contracting and component breakout, or hold prime contractors fully responsible for contract performance.[95]

To the buyer these teaming arrangements are "desirable" because they enable contractors to "complement" their unique capabilities and to offer the government "the best combination of performance, cost, and delivery."[96] The contractor views teaming agreements as a way to improve its chances of participating in a government contract while protecting its intellectual property and the proprietary data exchanged during the bidding process. Smaller firms entering into a teaming arrangement often see it as a way to introduce their product by riding the coattails of a larger company.

The subject of teaming agreements will be covered in greater detail in Chapter 5, when we review the subject of proposal preparation.

THE ACQUISITION PLAN

Planning is a function of management. It is undertaken to define and coordinate the activities of the organization toward designated and agreed-upon objectives. By including the identification of potential risks and opportunities as part of the planning process, it can also take on a contingency aspect. The alternative to planning is random behavior. Implementation of a plan commits an organization, and elements within the organization, to a specific course of action. Therefore, plans must cover a time period long enough to fulfill the commitment made in the plan.[97]

Acquisition planning is more than just describing the who, what, and when of the purchasing process. The federal government defines acquisition planning as "the process by which efforts of all personnel responsible for an acquisition are coordinated and integrated through a comprehensive plan for fulfilling the agency need in a timely manner and at a reasonable cost. It includes the overall strategy for managing the acquisition."[98] The heads of government agencies are charged to prescribe a planning process that tailors the detail and formality of each acquisition plan to the complexity and cost of the prospective acquisition on a system or individual contract basis.[99]

For DoD, before the initiation of a program, each PM is required to develop and document a comprehensive strategy to guide program execution from initiation through reprocurement of systems, subsystems, components, spares, and services beyond the initial production contract award and during post-production support. A key component of this strategy is the contract approach, which includes such topics as:

- Major contracts planned
- Contract type
- Contract incentives
- Integrated contract performance measurement
- Integrated baseline reviews
- Special contract terms and conditions
- Warranties
- Component breakout
- Leasing.[100]

The FAR contains uniform policies and procedures on how federal agencies are to purchase supplies and services. The FAR has also identified categories of supplies and services that have unique contracting characteristics requiring distinctive policies and procedures. As part of the acquisition planning process, the acquisition team must categorize the supplies or services being purchased so that the unique policies and procedures pertaining to that family can be integrated into its acquisition plans. Differentiating policies and procedures from families of requirements is addressed in the following sections of the FAR:

- Supplies in Economic Quantities (FAR Part 7.2)
- Contractor Versus Government Performance (FAR 7.3)
- Equipment Under a Lease or Purchase Arrangement (FAR Part 7.4)
- Acquisition of Commercial Items (FAR Part 12)
- Major Systems (FAR Part 34)
- Applied and Basic Research and Development (FAR Part 35)
- Construction and Architect-Engineering Services (FAR Part 36)
- Services (FAR Part 37)
- Commonly Used Supplies and Services (FAR Part 38)
- Certain Automated Data Processing, Telecommunications, and Related Resources (FAR 39)
- Utility Services (FAR Part 41).

Contracts are awarded by one of two competitive methods: sealed bids (originally known as formal advertising) and competitive negotiated proposals. Under the latter, supplies or services are placed on contract after negotiations between the buyer and seller. Sealed bids are based on the idea that the price should determine the source. The sealed bidding process begins with the CO formally advertising the need. This method of contract award is most often referred to as "formal advertising" because it is based on the assumption that formally advertising the proposed acquisition satisfies the need to have full and open competition. Because price is the determining factor under the sealed bidding method, there is no need to have any meaningful discussion between the buyer and seller prior to contract award. Sealed bidding has historically been the preferred manner in which contracts are to be awarded. It was once the key metric by which Congress evaluated the percentage of contracts awarded competitively. Negotiated procurement, as the name implies, always includes discussions. With the passage of the Competition in Contracting Act of 1984, sealed bids and negotiated procurements were given equal standing. Today there is no single "right method" to place an item or service on contract. The CO is expected to use good business judgment and select the contracting method that best meets the government's needs. Required competitive procedures include two basic methods for purchasing goods and services. These are sealed bids and negotiated procurement. The simplified acquisition procurement method also meets the statutory requirement of full and open competition. Methods not meeting the requirement for full and open competition include sole source and the use of unsolicited proposals. FAR Part 17 includes information on multiyear contracts, options, leader-company contracting, and interagency acquisition.[101]

CONTENTS OF WRITTEN ACQUISITION PLANS[102]

Acquisition planning and market research are prerequisites to all acquisitions. The acquisition plan is prepared well in advance of the development of the solicitation. It is critical to effective procurements because it defines in advance the resources that will be needed to manage the procurement as well as the sequence of actions to be taken to meet the intended procurement objectives. On major programs the acquisition plan may cover numerous individual contracts. The plan involves such material as technical, financial, contractual, quality assurance, reliability, and logistics support. Its contents must be developed jointly by each function involved in the procurement to ensure their needs are included. By participating in the planning process, these functions also become committed to the priorities defined in the acquisition plan.

The format for a written acquisition plan provides a template for the acquisition team to use when they address all the technical, fiscal, legal, and policy aspects of an acquisition. The specific content of any acquisition plan, written or otherwise, will vary depending on the scope, complexity, cost, and timing of the acquisition.

FAR 7.105 contains an outline and instructions for the planner to follow when preparing acquisition plans. Table 3-2, Contents of Written Acquisition Plans, shows that the acquisition plan is divided into two major parts. The first addresses general information on the objectives of the purchase, followed by background information on the acquisition itself. The second is the actual plan of action. It addresses such topics as sources, how competition will be sought, source selection procedures, contracting considerations, budgeting, and funding.

Table 3-2. Contents of Written Acquisition Plans

Part I
Acquisition Background and Objectives

Statement of Need
Applicable Conditions Affecting the Acquisition
Related Cost Goals and Concepts to be Employed
Capability or Performance Characteristics
Delivery of Performance Period Requirements
Tradeoffs Among Cost, Capability, or Performance and Schedule Goals
Risks and Efforts Underway to Reduce Risks of Failure
Plans and Procedures to Streamline the Acquisition

Part II
Plan of Action

Gain Competition
Source-selection Procedures Including:
    Contracting Considerations
    Budgeting and Funding
    Produce or Service Considerations
    Method of Obtaining Priority Allocation and Allotments
    Contractor versus Government Performance
    Considerations Given to Inherently Government Functions (OFPP Letter 92-1)
    Management Information Requirements
    Considerations Given to Make-or-Buy Programs
    Test and Evaluation
    Logistics Considerations
    Government Property to Be Furnished, Including Material and Facilities
    Government-Furnished Information
    Environmental and Energy Conservation Objectives
    Security Considerations
    Contract Administration

Part One: Acquisition Background and Objectives

Statement of need: The objective of this part of the acquisition plan is to explain the events preceding this acquisition and the purpose of the procurement. It must answer the question of why the item being procured is needed. All acquisition programs are based in an identified, documented, and validated mission needs statement. Mission needs result from the need to develop a capability, to improve an existing capability, or to exploit an opportunity to reduce cost. In addition to a brief summary of the statement of need, a technical and contractual history of the acquisition includes other topics, such as feasible alternatives, the impact of prior acquisitions on those alternatives, and any other related in-house effort. (DoD components are charged to try first to satisfy mission need through non-material solutions, such as the changes in doctrine or mission.) Justification for general requirements is strengthened if it is related to a mission or capabilities. Re-supply requirements are generated by a review of inventories consumed as the agency performs its mission. Repair of equipment performing intended operational plans falls into the same category. The factors supporting the make-or-buy decision are also included.

Applicable conditions: Known cost, schedule, and capability or performance constraints can be found in this part of the acquisition plan. Under the design-to-cost concept, cost is a design constraint during the design and development phases and a management discipline throughout the acquisition and operation of the system or equipment.[103]

Compatibility with existing or future systems or programs also should be addressed, as well as the interface with other capabilities and the interoperability between other communication systems vital to national defense. Any deficiencies in this area should be identified, along with an explanation of how this deficiency will be eliminated by this procurement.

If the proposed acquisition is to follow an evolutionary acquisition process, a summary of the overall development plan, along with its status, must be included in this section of the acquisition plan. A primary example is the block upgrade approach to aircraft development, which involves the procurement of the initial block of the system that forms the base operational capability, which is then followed by subsequent blocks providing additional increments of capability.

Cost: This part of the acquisition plan also covers the cost objectives and how they were determined, i.e., the process, approach, and rationale used to arrive at the cost objective. The goal is to disclose the source of data used to develop the cost objective. Was it based on historic data or judgment? It goes without saying that the more vendor information and historic data are used in the development of the cost objective, the greater the level of confidence given to its credibility.

Financial constraints are a reality in each acquisition. Product performance, cost, and schedule are inextricably tied to each other and cannot be independent of one another.[104] The more technically challenging the product, the more costly it will be. In addition, it will have a longer development cycle, and there is a greater probability of error in accurately estimating its cost and development schedule.

This part of the acquisition plan should include descriptions of how the following tools will be applied during the acquisition, if they are applicable.

Life-cycle cost is the estimated "total cost to the government to acquire, operate, support, and, if applicable, dispose of the item being acquired."[105] It is a tool that highlights the cost drivers. How it will be considered, or why it is not appropriate, is described in this part of the acquisition plan. It is DoD policy to require an independent full life-cycle cost estimate for Major Defense Acquisition Programs (MDAP) prior to obtaining approval to enter into engineering and manufacturing development or production and deployment phases of the program.

Design-to-cost is a management concept that establishes cost elements as goals. It is used during the design process to achieve the best balance between life-cycle cost, acceptable performance, and schedule. Rigorous cost goals are established during the development of a system, and control of costs (acquisition, operating, and support) is achieved through practical tradeoffs among operational capability, performance, costs, and schedule.[106] This part of the acquisition plan should include a description of design-to-cost objectives and underlying assumptions and rationale for such factors as quantity, slope of the learning curve, and economic adjustment. A description of the related solicitation and contractual requirements, as well as how the design-to-cost objectives are to be applied, tracked, and enforced by the government and contractor members of the acquisition team, are also to be addressed.

Application of cost realism analysis to the procurement is also to be described in the acquisition plan. Cost realism analysis is particularly useful for efforts that are to be performed under a cost-reimbursement pricing arrangement because the government is obligated to pay the contractor allowable and allocable cost incurred in performing the contract, regardless of the initial proposal costs. Cost realism analysis not only verifies the offeror's understanding of the requirement; it also assesses the degree to which proposed cost accurately reflects the approaches or risk assessments made in the technical proposal and assesses the degree to which the cost included in the cost proposal accurately represents the proposed technical effort.[107]

Cost realism analysis differs from other cost evaluation methods in that it is an independent review and evaluation of specific elements of each offeror to determine if they are realistic. The results of the cost realism analysis are compared to the government's best cost estimate for the effort to determine the variances. The CO determines the scope of the cost realism review. The objective of any cost realism analysis is to predict the probable cost that will result if the offeror executes the proposed contract.[108] The results of this process are then applied to a specific negotiation with the contractor.

Cost as an independent variable (CAIV), which applies to DoD programs, is one of the most significant changes to the development and management of requirements since the end of the Cold War. The traditional DoD approach was to emphasize controlling cost and schedule while developing a needed product. Under the CAIV concept, the cost has the same level of importance as performance and schedule. It is based on the belief that the best time to reduce life-cycle cost is early in the acquisition process. Therefore, DoD policy charges the acquisition community as well as the technical, logistics, and requirements community to use the CAIV process to develop total ownership cost (TOC), schedule, and performance thresholds. The user is to treat cost as a military requirement.[109]

Capability or performance: This part of the plan should include a description of the required supplies or services in the form of performance-based standards. The description of the needed capabilities or standards must also relate to the user's needs. Performance specifications that do not tell the contractor how to build the product or perform the service should be used. This policy recognizes stating the user's needs in terms of form, fit, function, performance, and interface, although it avoided risk, was in the long run costly, and made it less likely that current technology could be purchased.

Tradeoffs: As noted earlier in this chapter, the goal of the requirements determination process is to translate objectives into requirements before issuing the solicitation. The attributes of these requirements not only establish the product's performance characteristics, but they also affect the cost of the project, the delivery schedule, and the life-cycle cost, i.e., the cost of ownership. Tradeoffs decisions are required throughout the life cycle of the project.

Figure 3-9 illustrates the interrelationship between cost, time, and performance objectives for the project. The three different parametric perfor-

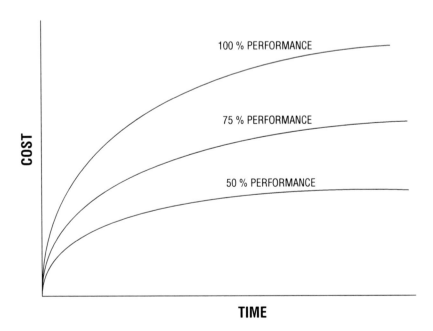

Figure 3-9 Interrelationship Between Cost-Time-Performance

mance curves show how cost and time for achieving the desired performance goals can vary depending on the desired level of performance. A change in cost, time, or performance usually results in an adjustment of one or both of the other two variables.[110]

In making tradeoffs, the acquisition team is often faced with complex decisions that involve uncertainty, multiple outcomes, and the diverse functional values that are held by different members of the team. Any analysis of the possible tradeoffs should emphasize the total systems approach because it recognizes that even the smallest change in a product or system frequently affects other attributes of the product.[111]

In Figure 3-10 (The Tradeoff Process),[112] we return to the six possible tradeoffs. This figure shows the potential tradeoff possibilities among project cost, product performance, time (delivery schedule), and life-cycle cost. It is important to realize that it is not possible to maximize all four objectives at the same time. Making these tradeoffs is an iterative process. After understanding the initial tradeoff, the team must then determine the impact on the other variables. For example, when making a change to the performance of the product, not only must the acquisition team estimate its impact on the development cost, but it must also look at what happens

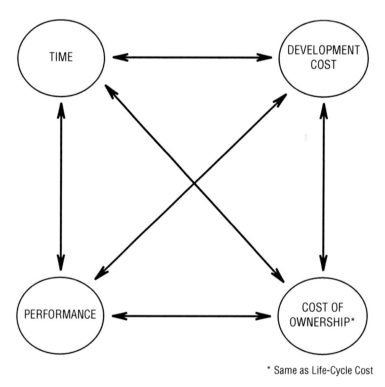

* Same as Life-Cycle Cost

Figure 3-10 The Tradeoff Process

to the schedule (time) and cost of ownership (life-cycle cost). To make wise tradeoff decisions, the acquisition team must know the relative importance of the project's objectives. The initial challenge for the team is to determine the relative value, i.e., the absolute essential performance requirements as well as those that would be desired but are less critical.

Figure 3-11, The Risk vs. Performance Tradeoff, illustrates how risk management affects possible tradeoffs. The left portion of the curve shows a performance strategy that avoids risk. Today's acquisition policy is willing to increase risk to an acceptable level. By doing so it can realize the benefit of added performance. Understanding the amount of risk being taken and not crossing the boundary between management and gambling is key.

Project cost represents the total research, development, and production cost associated with meeting and delivering the product to the user. It includes the recurring and non-recurring direct and indirect cost associated with the project. Categories of cost include labor, material, other direct charges (G&A), and overhead. If project cost is a primary concern, tradeoffs can be made to increase or decrease cost in the areas of:

- Product performance
- Delivery schedule
- Life-cycle cost.

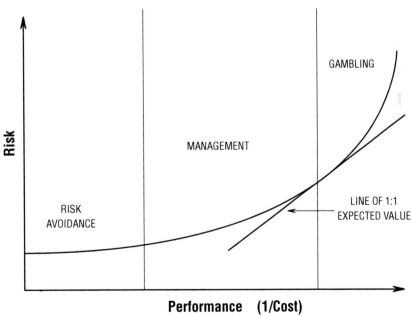

Performance   (1/Cost)

Adapted from Sweeney, John, Some Homespun Wisdom on Risk Management, *Program Management* (Fort Belvoir, VA: Defense Systems Management College), July-August 1995, p. 22.

Figure 3-11 The Risk vs. Performance Tradeoff[113]

To illustrate how an increase in performance would affect cost, refer to Figure 3-12, Performance-Cost Tradeoff. The total estimated cost of a widget to perform at a level of 100% is $5,000,000. The performance curve OAB shows the cost at performance level A to be equal to $2,100,000. This is approximately 76% of the projected possible performance, at a cost of approximately 42% of the estimated total cost of $5,000,000. However, at point A the increase in performance begins to diminish quickly in relation to cost. This begs the question, is it worth the added cost and time to achieve an additional 13% of performance to point B on the curve? Would a viable alternative be to increase performance by only 5%? The total estimated cost at a performance level of 86% would be $2,650,000. In this example the question now is, will the customer be satisfied with an 86% percent performance level? Maximizing performance requires longer schedules, higher costs, and a higher probability that the performance goals will not be achieved.[114]

Delivery schedule represents the cost associated with administrative and development or production lead times. Time and cost are interrelated in labor-intensive projects. The cost of maintaining the acquisition team or the overhead cost that must be absorbed by the contractor when schedules are changed are two examples of how cost increases when schedules are

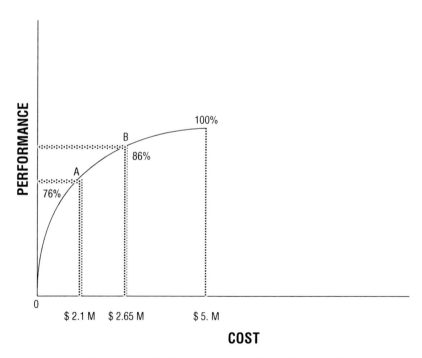

Figure 3-12 Performance-Cost Tradeoff

not met or are extended. An example of how cost can increase when schedules are reduced is the premium that is usually paid to vendors to expedite product delivery and contractor overtime requirements. It is difficult to quantify the impact on the user if the product is not available when deliveries are delayed. Changes to the delivery schedule can affect:

- Project cost
- Life-cycle cost.

As discussed earlier, life-cycle cost, or cost of ownership, is a systems engineering tool used to estimate the total cost to the government to acquire, operate, support, and, if applicable, dispose of the item being acquired. In periods when funding levels are declining, the affordability of new products or systems over their service life is important. Entering the system development and demonstration phase of an acquisition, along with technology maturity and a validated requirement, is one of the three determining factors. The affordability determination is made in the process of addressing cost as a military requirement. This includes considering the acquisition cost as well as life-cycle cost or TOC when available and approved. Transition into system development and demonstration also requires full funding, i.e., inclusion in the budget and the out-year program funding for all current and future efforts necessary to carry out the acquisition strategy.[115]

Figure 3-13, Life-Cycle Cost Model, illustrates that tradeoffs can also be made that affect the cost of ownership of the product being purchased.

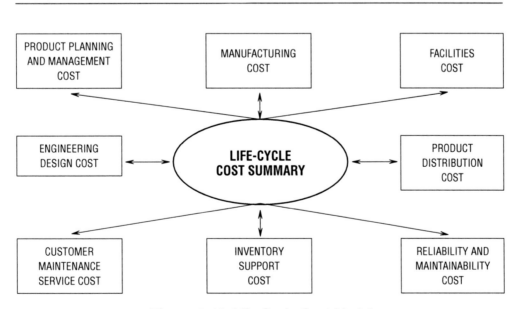

Figure 3-13 Life-Cycle Cost Model

This model portrays the major factors that affect the life-cycle cost of an item. It is the job of the acquisition team to look for alternatives that will minimize the life-cycle cost of the product.

It is essential to the program that the acquisition team minimize the cost of ownership as much as possible.For example, upon approval of the ORD, DoD policy requires the PM to formulate a CAIV plan as part of the acquisition strategy.[116] CAIV enables the acquisition team to refine requirements by considering cost and to make earlier tradeoffs between cost and performance in order to make affordable products. Setting a cost ceiling for a program and accepting what technology and contractual effort can deliver is a new way of doing business for government and industry. The previous DoD paradigm was to control cost and schedule. The CAIV concept is to control the requirements that drive cost and schedule.[117] This means that life-cycle cost is the independent variable; performance, schedule, and program cost are the dependent variables.

Technical, cost, and schedule risks: This part of the acquisition plan not only identifies the technical, cost, and schedule risks, but also presents that actions that are underway to reduce these risks and the consequences if project goals are not achieved.

In the area of risk, acquisition doctrine has shifted the focus from policies and procedures designed to avoid failure altogether to ones emphasizing making prudent management decisions by investing time and money where they will have the greatest payoff. In other words, it is a tradeoff between the desire to increase the amount of product testing to reduce the probability of failure and applying that cost to reducing the risk exposure in another area. Figure 3-11, Risk vs. Performance Tradeoff, illustrates the difference between avoiding and managing risk.

A management strategy that is designed to avoid the maximum amount of risk exposure operates in the lower parts of the curve. The other end of the curve, where the exposure to risk increases exponentially in relation to increases in performance, is classified as gambling.[118] In the middle is the area where the expected return from increased risk is greater than the increased cost. This is the area where a risk manager is expected to operate. A prudent risk management strategy realizes that it is not possible to avoid risk altogether. However, by identifying and understanding the causes and characteristics of the risk involved, the acquisition team can develop a risk management program that maximizes payoff and minimizes cost.

Technical risk is defined as the probability of failing to meet performance expectations. The higher the expectation, the greater the risk of underachievement. This truism is especially valid when the delivery schedule and initial budget estimate are ambitious or when funding is constrained or even cut during the project's life cycle. A study for the U.S. Air Force by the RAND Corporation of how risk was handled in seven large-scale USAF weapon systems development programs in the late 1980s concluded that three programs had acquisition difficulties. Three of the seven had important "holes" in the technology base that had been recognized but de-emphasized in the advocacy for the program.[119] Ways to manage technology risk include use of market research to understand the product line and market, greater reliance on proven commercial products to ensure that current technology is available to the user, and use of contractors with proven track records. Early testing and evaluation, application of modeling and simulations, product demonstrations and evaluations, and prototype testing are some methods that can mitigate risk.

The sources of schedule and cost risk are both internal and external to the organization. Schedule changes can come from inadequately projecting the product need date. This occurs from inadequately involving the user in the requirements determination process or changes in conditions. The accuracy of the projected requirements and the length of time consumed in the procurement cycle are directly related. The longer the development cycle, the higher the probability that the need will deviate from the original specification. Accuracy of the initial fund estimate and stability of the funding support by higher management are among the external sources of risk.

Another dimension of risk is the degree to which requirements are controlled. As technological advances are introduced after the acquisition program has been initiated, the user understandably wants the latest technology, and the program offices are quite naturally inclined to support the request. This is justified because products historically are in inventory for quite some time, and the contractual vehicle is already in place to initiate the change. Changes to requirements emanate throughout the cost, schedule, and technical performance aspects of the acquisition. Controlling the changes process and using preplanned product improvements or an evolutionary product growth through block upgrades are techniques that can be used.

The previously referenced RAND study concluded in the seven cases analyzed that "realistic cost, schedule, and performance goals, coupled with quality personnel, are keys to good risk management. Where significant acquisition problems arose...they were usually associated with schedules that were overly ambitious, budgets that provided no funds for contingencies and/or hedging, or a reluctance to adjust performance goals after the consequences of maintaining those goals were apparent."[120]

Acquisition streamlining: This section presents the plans and procedures to encourage contractor participation. Information to be provided relates to how draft solicitations, pre-solicitation conferences, and other techniques will be used to stimulate industry involvement. The goal of early participation by industry is to apply technology appropriately to the user's requirements during product design and development.

It is this area in which personnel resourcefulness can be exercised to streamline the acquisition process. Acquisition doctrine as discussed in

Chapter 1, encourages the implementation of innovative procedures, even when they are not addressed in the FAR, as long as they are in the best interest of the government.[121]

Individual meetings between government officials and an offeror or potential offeror are not prohibited provided that unauthorized disclosure or receipt of contractor bid proposal or government source selection information does not occur. For example, there is no prohibition against having more than one pre-solicitation conference. The United States Information Agency has taken advantage of this situation, and their COs routinely conduct one-on-one pre-proposal briefs. They have found that it is easier for contractors to ask questions about government requirements they don't understand when competitors are not present. The result has been that potential problems are addressed prior to contract award, thereby easing administration of the work and avoiding changes to the contract.[122]

Paperless contracting presents numerous opportunities to streamline the administrative segments of the entire acquisition process. In his book *Procurement Manager's Guide to EC/EDI*, Daniel Drake points out that emerging technologies can be used to streamline and integrate business processes, thus providing information between the acquisition organization and its contractors.[123] To do this effectively, the acquisition team must have access to computer networks that enable information to be shared with other departments and organizations. The goal is to make the process more efficient by unearthing opportunities that will: (1) minimize the handling of paper, (2) automate routine and repetitive administrative tasks, and (3) provide online information access.

An example of using the Internet and the personal computer in soliciting construction work was recently described in *Contract Management* magazine. By accessing the buying office's Web page, prospective contractors were able to view the solicitation, the drawing package, and the terms and conditions of the proposed contract. The author reported that by using the Internet, the time required to issue a solicitation was cut from 25 days to two days. In addition, time required by the staff to administer the bidders list and mail solicitations was reduced, as was printing cost.[124]

Part Two: Plan of Action

Sources: An important element of acquisition doctrine is the use of commercial developments and management innovations as primary sources to satisfy the users' needs. Throughout procurement history the trend has slowly been toward contracting more and more with the private sector for the needed goods and services. The amount of outsourcing has been primarily driven by technology needs rather than policies and practices. In 1979 the Office of Management and Budget openly encouraged the private sector to compete for work currently being performed by government employees using internal facilities.[124] However, the pace of outsourcing has accelerated with the end of the Cold War as DoD has downsized.

All decisions regarding sources for supplies and services begin with a decision as to whether procurement should be accomplished using the government's organic resources or if capabilities outside the government should be solicited. Federal government policy with respect to this decision was expressed in Bureau of the Budget (now the Office of Management and Budget) Circular A-76. A-76, which was issued in 1967, states that "the federal government will not carry on any commercial activity to provide a service or product for its own use, if such product or service can be procured from private enterprise through ordinary channels...."[126] This policy direction is founded on the following concepts:

- Jobs such as making policy, regulatory, and investigative decisions are inherently governmental and must be performed by government employees.
- Work that is commercial in nature currently being performed by government employees in government facilities is subject to a comparison between in-house and private sector sources to determine the lowest-cost method
- New commercial-like work should not be initiated when there are more economical private sector sources available.[127]

Policy regarding sources is further refined in FAR Part 8–Required Sources of Supplies and Services. This policy should be consulted when acquiring supplies and services because it establishes priorities for selecting government sources for the needed supplies or services as opposed to commercial sources.

For supplies, Part 8 of the FAR lists (in priority sequence) the following supply sources: agency inventories; excess from other agencies; Federal Prisons, Inc.; purchase lists from the Committee for Purchase from the Blind and Other Severely Handicapped; wholesale supply sources such as the General Services Administration, the Defense Logistics Agency, the Department of Veterans Affairs, and military inventory control points; Mandatory Federal Supply Schedules; and commercial sources.[128]

For services the sources are, again in priority sequence, those that are available from the Committee for Purchase from the Blind and Other Severely Handicapped; Mandatory Federal Supply Schedules and mandatory GSA term contracts for personal property rehabilitation; optional-use Federal Supply Schedules and optional-use GSA term contracts for personal property rehabilitation; Federal Prison Industries, Inc.; or other commercial sources, including educational and nonprofit institutions.[129]

Part 8 also provides specific instructions for such specialized products as jewel bearings, public utility services, printing and related supplies, automated data processing, telecommunications acquisitions, leasing of motor vehicles, strategic and critical materials excess from the GSA inventories, and helium.[130]

When considering contracting for services, it is the duty of the CO to determine whether the proposed effort is for personal or non-personal services. The difference between the two is that when performing under a non-personal services contract, the contractor's personnel are not subject to the supervisor-employee relationship. A personal services contract is defined as one that "by its expressed terms or as administered, makes the contractor personnel appear, in effect, Government employees."[131] Policy opposes contracting for services that are currently performed by government employees. Today more and more firms producing high-technology products are also including support services as part of the procurement package. FAR policy may prevent the government from taking advantage of these opportunities. However, a recent Office of Personnel Management statement may indicate a shift in policy.[132] In a case involving a temporary employee seeking disability benefits from the government, the Office of Personnel Management stated, "While outside temporaries would be doing federal work, they would neither be supervised (they would receive technical instructions) nor appointed by federal officials or employees, within the meaning of section 2105." (The statutory criteria for determining whether an individual is a federal employee under 5 U.S.C. 2105 (a) are whether the individual worker is performing an authorized federal function, is supervised by a federal official or employee, and is appointed formally to the civil service.)[133]

In this part of the acquisition, the CO must address the use of small business, small disadvantaged business, and female-owned small business concerns as sources for the product or services. The CO must include actions that will be taken to consider awarding the contract to these firms as prime contractors. The CO must also present in this section the provisions that will flow down from the prime contractor to the subcontractors regarding their use of small businesses, per Part 19 of the FAR. If it is to be a negotiated contract, the CO may include ways the prime contractor will be rewarded for increasing the amount of business awarded to small business and small disadvantaged business.

Also to be included under this section are the extent and results of market research. This would include comments regarding how the results of market research affect various parts of the acquisition plan. This would include a determination regarding the product and:

- If sources are capable of meeting the user's needs
- If commercial items define the extent commercial components of the end item will satisfy the user's needs
- If non-developmental items are available or could be modified to meet the user's needs

- If non-developmental components could be incorporated into the end item and meet the user's needs
- If commercial items or non-developmental items could be incorporated into the end item and meet the user's needs.

Market research can also provide information on the business practices, methods of product distribution, and support services that are available or that could be modified to meet the user's needs. Data about energy conservation and efficiency should be included.

Competition: It is an objective of the federal acquisition system to satisfy the customer's needs in terms of cost, quality, and timeliness by maximizing the use of commercial products and services, using contractors that have successful track records, and promoting competition. In this segment of the acquisition plan, the CO's task is to describe how competition will be pursued, promoted, and sustained. Procedures that are available to meet the requirement for full and open competition include sealed bids, competitive proposals, two-step sealed bidding, and, in the case of selection of sources for architecture and engineering, following the provisions of PL 92-582.[134]

In this section the CO must identify the major components and subsystems and also disclose component breakout plans describing how competitors will be sought for each. The CO also must describe how subcontracting competition will be sought.

If spares and repair parts are involved, the CO should describe how competition will be sought, promoted, and sustained throughout the course of the acquisition. This will include the identification of such logistic milestones that affect competition as development of technical data, acquisition method coding, and spares breakout.

The following are exceptions to the requirement to have full and open competition on all new contracts:

- The existence of only one responsible source
- Unusual and compelling urgency
- Industrial mobilization, developmental or research capability, or expert services
- International agreement
- Authorization by statute
- National security
- Public interest.[135]

If full and open competition is not possible, the CO must initiate a document to justify and obtain approval to award without providing for it. This document, commonly referred to as a Justification and Approval (J&A), must be available for public inspection. Information required in the J&A also meets the FAR requirements for this part of the acquisition plan. It includes the following: (1) a description of the contractor's unique qualifications and why the nature of the acquisition requires such action, (2) a description of efforts made to ensure that offers were solicited from as many potential sources as practicable, (3) an explanation of why the anticipated cost will be fair and reasonable, (4) a description of market surveys conducted, and (5) other factors that will support not using fair and open competition.

Source selection procedures: The objective of this section is for the CO to prove that the source selection procedures are designed to select the contractor whose proposal is most advantageous and realistic and whose performance is expected to meet the user's stated requirements. In addition, the section must show how competition is to be enhanced and the source selection procedures designed to ensure the impartial evaluation of each respondent's proposal.

When making a competitive procurement, government policy stresses that the request for proposal clearly define the evaluation factors and subfactors along with their relative importance. The source selection authority will use this information to evaluate proposals and make the subsequent source selection. The acquisition team is given the latitude to exercise its own discretion when determining which evaluation factors, and their relative importance, will be applied to the procurement. It is important to define these factors clearly in the solicitation because confusion over the award criteria is cited as one of the top four reasons that losing offerors file bid protests.[136]

When using sealed bidding the CO must identify not only the price but also all other price-related factors that may be considered by the source selection authority when making the contract award. Part 14 of the FAR includes the following as possible considerations:

- Foreseeable cost or delays to the government resulting from such factors as differences in inspections, locations of supplies, and transportation
- Transportation cost to the designated point of delivery is to be considered in determining the lowest cost if bids are free on board (f.o.b.) at origin
- When making more than one award, the individual award shall be for items or a combination of items that result in the lowest aggregate cost to the government, including an estimated additional $250 to cover government administrative cost
- Federal, state, and local taxes in accordance with Part 29 of the FAR
- Origin of supplies and, if foreign, the application of the Buy American Act or any other prohibition on foreign purchases.[137]

Evaluation factors for negotiated procurements should also be tailored to each acquisition. Price or cost to the government is to be evaluated in every source selection, as is the quality of the product or service. Other considerations include past performance, compliance with solicitation requirements, technical excellence, management capability, personnel qualifications, and past experience. Here again, the procuring activity is given discretion in selecting which key areas, other than cost, are important and their relative ranking.[138]

Contracting considerations: Here the CO must address whether sealed bidding or a negotiated contract will be used. The CO is expected to include the rationale for this decision in this section of the plan.

Acquisition doctrine requires the maximum use of commercial items. FAR Part 12 covers policies and procedures "unique" to the acquisition of commercial items that have been provided or offered for sale to the general public.[139] Doctrine also calls for efficiency, use of business judgment, and innovation in contracting. Buying agencies are instructed to use simplified acquisition procedures to the maximum extent practicable for all purchases of supplies and services not exceeding the simplified acquisition threshold ($5,000,000), including purchases at or below the micro-purchase threshold ($100,000).[140] The Simplified Acquisition procedures contained in FAR Part 13 best fulfill the intent of acquisition doctrine. The procedures contained in FAR Part 13 allow the CO broad discretion to craft suitable evaluation procedures and to evaluate in a minimally burdensome fashion. Evaluation procedures prescribed in FAR Part 14 (Sealed Bidding) and FAR Part 15 (Contracting by Negotiation) are not mandatory. This emphasis on efficiency gives the CO the discretion not to use formal evaluation plans, nor establish a competitive range or hold, which are mandatory in Parts 14 and 15 of the FAR.[141]

Simplified acquisition procedures do not apply when the agency can meet the requirement by using:

- Sources of supplies outlined in FAR Part 8, i.e., Federal Prison Industries, Federal Supply Schedule Contracts, etc.
- Existing indefinite delivery/indefinite quantity contracts
- Other established contracts.[142]

Simplified acquisition methods include:

- Government commercial purchase card
- Purchase orders
- Blanket purchase agreements
- Imprest funds or third-party drafts
- SF Form 44 Purchase Order/Invoice/Voucher.

When purchasing commercial goods and services, the following four Parts of the FAR are also relevant: Part 14, Sealed Bidding; Part 15, Con-

[handwritten margin note: SAT = $250K   MPT = $10K]

tracting by Negotiations; Part 35, Research and Development Contracting; and Part 36, Construction and Architect-Engineering Contracting. In keeping with the desire for the federal procurement process to become more efficient and innovative, COs are told to make purchases other than commercial items that do not exceed the simplified acquisition threshold in a simplified manner that is suitable, efficient, and economical, based on the circumstances of each acquisition. In the purchase of commercial items exceeding the simplified acquisition threshold, the provisions of FAR Parts 14, 15, 35, or 36 apply.[143]

The type of contract pricing arrangement to be used is also included in this part of the acquisition plan. The final selection of the contract type occurs in one of three ways. First, FAR 16.1 states that the type of contract is generally determined during the negotiation process.[144] Second, the appropriate type of contract is obvious to all concerned and is established in the solicitation. Third, for major DoD acquisitions the agency's acquisition executive, or head of the agency, makes or confirms the decision as part of the acquisition strategy when approval to begin the program is obtained at Milestone I.[145]

A goal of the contract type is to link the profit or fee to the contractor's performance so that the contractor is rewarded for exceptional performance and penalized when it performs poorly. Because total responsibility for the cost of performance is placed on the contractor, the firm-fixed-price contract is judged to best utilize the profit motive as a motivational force. It is used when the uncertainties can be predicted, i.e. priced, with an acceptable degree of accuracy. When a reasonable basis for a firm-fixed-price contract does not exist, other contract types should be considered. The negotiation of contract price and type are related and should be considered together. "The objective is to negotiate a contract type and price (or estimated cost and fee) that will result in reasonable contractor risk and provide the contractor with the greatest incentive for efficient and economical performance."[146]

A primary function of the contract is allocating the risk of failure. This is accomplished by the type of pricing arrangements and through the terms and conditions of the contract. The principal factor in determining the risk is the uncertainty associated with the technical content of the work relative to the current state-of-the-art. The greater the variance between the current state-of-the-art and the technical objectives of the contract, the greater the uncertainty of the estimated performance cost. Pushing the state-of-the-art when combined with technical instability and unclear specifications results in a high probability of technical failure and rework.[147] The greater the uncertainty the larger the amount of risk the government must assume in the contract document. As the uncertainty decreases, the contractor is expected to assume a greater amount of the risk because the contractor has more and more control over the results as the uncertainties decrease.

Table 3-3, Factors in Selecting Contract Types, lists the questions the CO should consider when selecting and negotiating the contract type.[148] During the examination of these questions, the CO can also determine what special clauses and deviations to the FAR may be required.

Budget and funding: Project managers, as part of the acquisition planning process, are required to develop the budget for the project. When approved, and when funds are available, this budget is translated into a spending plan. When a contract is awarded it is either: (1) fully funded and, if it is a fixed-price contract, funds are obligated to cover the price or target price; or (2) incrementally funded, and funds are obligated to cover milestones or periods of performance. If it is a cost-reimbursement contract, the government is obligated to pay only actual allowable and allocable cost incurred in performing the contract. If the evaluation of the cost realism of the offeror's approach is higher than the government's best estimate, the offeror's figure should be used in the evaluation of the proposal as well.

Obligation of funds is equivalent to legally reserving these funds. This is possible because they are tied to a government liability for goods and services. In managing government contracting, one of the most important statutes affecting the obligation of funds is the Anti-Deficiency Act, 31 U.S. Code 665. It has two main provisions:

1. Any officer or employee is prohibited from making or authorizing an obligation in excess of the amount available in an appropriation or in excess of the amount permitted by agency regulations.
2. The government is forbidden from being involved in any contract or obligation to pay money in advance of appropriations.

The government attempts to assist contractors by arranging payments during the period of performance that they can use as working capital. The

---

Table 3-3. Factors in Selecting Contract Type

Extent of Price Competition Establishes the Market Price
Degree of Price Analysis Provides a Realistic Pricing Standard
Extent Offeror and Government Cost Estimates Provide a Basis for Negotiating Contract Pricing Arrangements
Magnitude of the Complexity of the Requirements
Degree of Urgency of the Requirement
Length of Time of the Period of Performance
Degree of the Contractor's Technical Capability and Financial Responsibility
Adequacy of the Contractor's Accounting System
Amount of Concurrent Operations Under Other Contracts
Extent and Nature of Proposed Subcontracting Involved
History of the Acquisition of the Product

government benefits from such a policy because it mitigates the potential financial risk. There are four methods by which the government provides contractors with working capital:

1. Customary progress payments
2. Guaranteed loans
3. Unusual progress payments
4. Advanced payments.

The acquisition plan must specify if any of these methods will be used. Customary progress payments, which are based on a percentage of cost incurred, are the method used most frequently to assist the contractor in obtaining working capital, thereby reducing the risk of non-performance for financial reasons. These are guaranteed loans usually applied to firms involved in national defense and are not often used in peacetime.[149] Unusual progress payments, which permit payments to the contractors in excess of cost incurred, require justification by the contractor prior to being included in the contract. The least preferred method of financing is the advance payment. Under this method, the contractor can draw on funds that have been placed in a bank. Liquidation is through payments due the contractor for performing under the contract.

Customary progress payments are used for production contracts or contracts involving long lead times or a preparatory period of over six months or more (four months for small business concerns) between the start of work and the first delivery. The decision to authorize progress payments to the contractor for this acquisition is a decision that must be made as part of the acquisition plan. The use of progress payments must be coordinated with the contract finance office prior to the solicitation if the planned payment rate exceeds the customary rate. The CO is required to notify potential offerors if progress payments are, or are not, to be part of the final contract.[150]

Product or service descriptions: This part of the acquisition plan includes the description of the product or service being acquired. Information for this part of the plan comes from such documents as the Operational Requirements Document (ORD), Capabilities Required, and System Characteristics.

In 1991 OFPP issued Policy Letter No. 91-2, requiring federal agencies to use performance-based contracting methods to the maximum extent practicable when acquiring services. This policy is especially significant because, as noted in Chapter 1, in 1999 federal government purchase of services represented 41 percent of the total value of government purchases. Performance-based contracting emphasizes the use of objective, measurable performance requirements and quality standards in developing statements of work, selecting contractors, determining contract-type incentives, and performing contract administration.[151]

Market research plays a major role in identifying possible sources that will satisfy the user's needs as well as defining the deliverable to achieve maximum competition. In the past the government has described its requirements in terms that created a product that differed from standard commercial products. This practice in turn created inventories of government-unique items. Using functional descriptions of the needed supplies and equipment to the maximum extent practicable could reduce this problem.[152]

Priorities, allocations, and allotments: In this section the acquisition team defines the urgency of the requirement. In some cases, because of their importance to national security, programs are designated "authorized programs" by the procuring agency. When approved by the Federal Emergency Management Agency (FEMA), authorized programs are eligible for priorities and allocation support under the Defense Production Act of 1950. Under this act, authorized programs are placed on the Defense Priorities and Allocations Systems (DPAS) list. DPAS has been established to promote timely availability of necessary industrial resources to meet current national defense requirements and to provide a framework to facilitate rapid industrial mobilization in case of national emergency. This priority allocation procedure is flowed down to any prime contract and subcontract for any product, service, or material in support of a program on the DPAS list by the CO. The prime contracts for products, services, or material on the DPAS list are referred to as "rated orders."[153]

There are two levels of rated contracts (orders): DO and DX. All DO-rated orders are equal to each other and have priority over DX- and non-rated orders. Often DoD further prioritizes DX- and DO-rated contracts through the use of numeric suffixes. The valid rated order must contain, in addition to the appropriate DX or DO rating, the required delivery date or dates and the signature of the authorizing official.[154]

A rated order is to be accepted by the contractor or supplier. (There are reasons a contractor or supplier can reject an order in CFR 700.13(b), but it is rare that they do.) The prime contractor is required to extend the priority rating to subcontractors or vendors, and they in turn are required to pass the rating to their suppliers.[155]

Contractor versus government performance: Included in this section is an explanation of the considerations used to determine if the work will be performed by a contractor or through the use of government resources. As previously noted, there are certain tasks or duties that are inherently governmental, i.e., policy making, regulation, and investigative decisions. In addition, DoD has maintained a depot-level maintenance capability in-house to be able to surge in time of national emergency.[156]

The decision to perform the work in-house or contract it out is in essence equivalent to the make-or-buy decision that is made by industry and must be answered according to where it would be most economical, all other considerations being equal.

Management information requirements: One of the traditional beliefs that have guided government contracting over the years is the idea that because goods and services are being procured for the benefit of the public, increased surveillance of the contractor's performance is necessary. In this section the acquisition team is charged to discuss, as appropriate, the management information that will be needed to monitor the contractor's effort.

The objective of government surveillance of the contractor's performance is to increase the probability that the product or service will be delivered on time. Over the years the thinking regarding the best way to ensure that deliveries would be on time has evolved from concentrating on site physical verification by government contract administrators to ensuring that the contractor has an adequate management system in place to increase the probability of timely delivery. Under the latter concept the contractor is charged to report status as part of the management information furnished under the contract. The evolution of reporting techniques used to report delivery status is a good illustration of this transition. Early on, Gantt milestone charts portrayed target dates for key events and product deliveries. During World War II the Line-of-Balance technique was also used to report the status of manufacturing line operations. In the late 1950s the Program Evaluation Review Technique (PERT) was introduced. PERT is based on the development of a network of tasks, the portrayal of interrelated events, and the identification of a critical path where management was to focus its attention. The Navy later tied cost to the tasks and events in an attempt to improve the management of cost on the Polaris program.

In the late 1960s the government developed a specification for management of large projects or programs that would require contractors on large cost-reimbursement contracts to develop and enhance their internal management planning and program tracking systems. This change was brought about by the realization that there was not necessarily a direct correlation between what was spent and progress made in completing scheduled work. Resource planning relates to time-phased schedules and technical performance requirements. The value (cost) of planned resources when compared to the earned value (cost) measures the dollar amount of work planned, as opposed to the equivalent dollar volume of work accomplished. The end product, based on this earned value concept, was titled Cost/Schedule Control System Criteria (C/SCSC). The configuration of each contractor's system left it to the prime contractor. The C/SCSC specification permits tailoring a management system to the characteristics of the organization and operation. However, the contractor's system must meet the minimum criteria outlined in the specification.

The integration of project management using the earned value concept is growing in government, industry, and professional organizations. Several major defense contractors are using an earned-value approach on all defense contracts regardless of the contract requirement.[157]

Test and evaluation: In this section the government and contractor test program is described for each major milestone if it is to be a major systems acquisition. The test and evaluation program should be planned so that all developmental and operational evaluation testing is integrated as much as possible. It is important for the acquisition team to show in this section how the test and evaluation strategy is designed to mitigate risk. If concurrency is planned, the extent of testing that will be accomplished prior to production must be addressed.

Logistics considerations: The design of a system or product has tremendous impact on what resources will be required to support it. Logistics support is a major consideration in developing design criteria and in evaluating alternative designs. The objective is to obtain a product that will meet the needs of the user at the lowest life-cycle cost.

The depth of the logistics planning effort is dependent on the type, size, and complexity of the item or services being purchased. For major systems, the key to any logistics support consideration is the planned employment and deployment concept for the equipment. The maintenance concept is also an integral part of all logistics considerations. This section should also address the reliability, maintainability, and quality assurance requirements. If applicable, the relationship of the item being purchased to the standardization requirements should be included so that future purchases can be made from the same manufacturing source.

The CO should also consider using a warranty if the item is being purchased under a fixed-price contract. The principal purposes of a warranty under a government contract are: (1) to delineate the rights and obligations of the contractor and government for defective items and services, and (2) to foster quality services.[158] Some of the considerations involved in any e-tradeoff decision on the advantages and disadvantages of including a warrant provision are:

- Complexity and function of the item
- Degree of development and state-of-the-art
- Difficulty in detecting defects prior to acceptance
- Potential harm to the government if the item is defective
- The contractor's charge for accepting the deferred liability
- The government's ability to enforce the warranty.[159]

Government-furnished property (GFP): The property to be furnished to the contractor, including material and facilities, along with their condition and availability in relation to the need date, is included in this section. The acquisition team should address the risk if the material or facilities are not available at the times needed by the contractor. Quite often the material or facilities are not in the correct configuration or are not serviceable for their intended need. Because the success of the project is often affected by late or unserviceable GFP, this section would be enhanced by including the government's plan to ensure that the GFP is delivered on time and is suitable for its intended use. From a contract performance standpoint, late or unserviceable GFP represents a constructive change to the contract.

Government-furnished information (GFI): The identification and availability of such information as drawings, manuals, and test data to be provided the prospective offerors is another potential problem area. Not only must the ownership of the needed information be resolved prior to the submission of the solicitation, but it also must be suitable and accurate. Late or unsuitable GFI represents the same risk to the buyer as GFP. It therefore behooves the acquisition team to develop a risk mitigation plan for GFI.

Environmental and energy conservation objectives: This area of the acquisition plan addresses such environmental topics as pollution control and clean air and water. Also included in this section are the assurance that items purchased are energy efficient; the identification of hazardous materials, if applicable; provisions to use recovered materials; and requirements of the drug-free workplace.

Security requirements: If the acquisition deals with classified information, Subpart 4.4 of the FAR covers safeguarding this information. It is the responsibility of the CO to review all proposed solicitations to determine whether access to classified information will be required by the offerors in the preparation of their proposals or by the contractor during performance. During the solicitation phase, the CO is responsible for ensuring that the classified acquisition is conducted and that appropriate security requirements provisions are included in the solicitation and resulting contract.[160]

Contract administration: The PCO has the opportunity to describe how the government's acquisition team intends to ensure compliance with the terms and conditions of the contract. FAR Part 42.302 defines 75 contract administration functions to be performed after the award of the contract. The FAR further divides these functions into two categories: (1) the 65 tasks that are normally performed by the cognizant CAO, which are either assigned directly to the contractor's plant or to a contract administration office in the contractor's area; and (2) two functions that are performed by the CAO only when and to the extent specifically authorized by the PCO. The latter category includes negotiations of supplemental agreements, negotiation of prices, negotiation to change contract delivery schedule, issuance of amended shipping instructions, issuance of change orders, and changes to the place of inspections.[161]

Other considerations: Included here are the applicable standardization concepts, the industrial readiness program, the Defense Production Act, the Occupational Safety and Health Act, foreign sales, and any other matters germane to the acquisition plan not covered previously.

Milestones for the acquisition cycle: The acquisition plan concludes with an outline, including milestones, of the tasks and events that must be completed before awarding the contract. These milestones will be discussed in subsequent chapters.

CONCLUSION

Determining what to procure does not begin when the purchase request is written. It begins with the requirements determination process, which identifies and ranks alternative solutions. It represents one of the most critical steps in the acquisition process because it is at this time that the "wants or desires" are translated into goods or services that can be expressed as cost and cost of ownership. Key tasks include market research and analysis as well as functional analysis, where technical requirements are traded off with customer acceptance, manufacturing considerations, and cost of ownership.

The acquisition team approach is organized around the product being purchased, as opposed to the traditional functional approach. This permits consideration of a broad spectrum of technical, functional, and financial issues. The net result is the development of a menu of tradeoffs that lead to an optimum acquisition strategy.

In Chapter Four, The Solicitation, we will discuss how the acquisition plan is converted to a request for bid or how the request for negotiated competitive proposal is developed and forwarded to prospective offerors.

NOTES

[1]Burt, Davis N., and Richard L. Pinkerton. 1995. *A Purchasing Manager's Guide to Strategic Proactive Procurement*. New York: American Management Association, 38.

[2]FAR 4.502.

[3]*Micro-purchase* is defined as the acquisition of supplies or services (except construction), the aggregate amount of which does not exceed $2,500. Nash, Ralph C., Steven L. Schooner, and Karen R. O'Brien. 1998. *The Government Contracts Reference Book: A Comprehensive Guide to the Language of Procurement*. 2d ed. Washington, D.C.: The George Washington University Law School, 345.

[4]Drake, Daniel J. 1997. Electronic Catalog in Government Procurement. *Contract Management* February: 7.

[5]Jacobs, Daniel M. 1997. Wake Up! It's Time to get Back to the Basics in Program/Contract Startup. *Contract Management* July: 20.

[6]"Best Value" is defined in FAR 2.101 to mean the expected outcome of an acquisition that, in the government's estimation, provides the greatest overall benefit in response to the requirement.

[7]FAR 1.102.

[8]Perry, James H. 1990. Procurement Lead Time: The Forgotten Factor. *National Contract Management Journal* 23(2):17.

[9]FAR 1.102-2.

[10]Perry, 20.

[11]Perry, 24.

[12]Perry, 17.

[13]Ibid.

[14]Croom, Simon, 1999. *Restructuring Supply Chain Through Information Channel Innovation.* Operations Management Group, Warwick Business School, University of Warwick, UK: 6.

[15]Croom, 3.

[16]Augustine, Norman R. 1980. *Augustine's Laws and Major System Development Programs.* Reprint compiled by Defense Systems Management Review, 10.

[17]Battershell, A. Lee. 1995. Technology Approach: DoD Versus Boeing (A Comparative Study). *Acquisition Quarterly* (Summer): 213.

[18]Ibid.

[19] Gansler, Jacques S. 1989. Affording Defense. *National Contract Management Journal.* 23(Summer):5.

[20]Battershell, 213.

[21]Smith, Preston G., and Donald G. Reinerson. 1991. *Developing Products in Half the Time.* New York: Van Nostrand Reinhold, 13.

[22]Smith and Reinerson, 13.

[23]Smith and Reinerson, 162.

[24]The intranet is a private Internet network that operates within an organization and which is usually insulated from the outside. The extranet is a close relative of the Internet, the difference being that both specified trading partners and remote organizations can access it via the Internet. Shaw, Jack. 1999. *Surviving the Digital Jungle.* Marietta, GA: Electronic Commerce Strategies, 104.

[25]Smith and Reinerson, 162–164.

[26]Graham, Robert, and Captain Eric Hoffman, USAF. 1999. Acquisition Process: A Quantitative Example of Acquisition Reform Working for the Air Force's Launch Program System Program Office. *Acquisition Quarterly* (Winter), 97.

[27]Graham and Hoffman, 88.

[28]Graham and Hoffman, 97.

[29]FAR 7.102 (b).

[30]FAR 11.02 (a)(2)(i).

[31]Burt, and Pinkerton, 38.

[32]Bergmann, Walter B. III. 1997. Military Specifications Reform: Change Is Underway in the Way We Write and Apply Standards Prescribing Management and Manufacturing Practices. *Program Manager.* (January-February):, 32.

[33]FAR 11.101(a).

[34]FAR 12.102(c).

[35]FAR 12.203.

[36]FAR 12.207.

[37]FAR 12.302.

[38]Burt, and Pinkerton., 107.

[39]Nash, Ralph C., Jr. 1997. Training the Contracting Officer of the Future. *Contract Management* (March): 16.

[40]Garrett, Gregory A. 1995. Performance-Based Contracting Incentives: Myths, Best Practices, and Innovations. *Contract Management.* (February): 6.

[41]FAR 2.101.

[42]Rumbaugh, Margaret G. 1997. *Conducting Market Research: Participant Guide.* Vienna, VA: National Contract Management Association, 43.

[43]Mulhern, John J. 1991. Policy Guidance on Market Research for Contracting Officers. *National Contract Management Journal.* 24(2): 33.

[44]Mulhern, 34.

[45]FAR 11.001, dated May 1, 1990.

[46]FAR 2.101.

[47]FAR 2.101.

[48]FAR 2.101.

[49]Volk, Joseph F. 1997. Market Research: For People Who Have to Do It Today. *Contract Management* (November): 13.

[50]FAR 11.103(a)(1).

[51]Rider, Melissa, Kenneth D. Brody, David B. Dempsey, Bernard L. Weiss. 1997. *Understanding The FAR Part 15 Rewrite.* Vienna, VA: National Contract Management Association, September, 30.

[52]FAR 15.202.

[53]Rumbaugh, 45.

[54]FAR 7.501

[55]Stanley, 155.

[56]FAR 7.501

[57]Stanley, 173.

[58]For the purpose of this section, "contractor intellectual property" includes patents (inventions), technical data, copyrights, and proprietary processes.

[59]FAR 27.104 (g).

[60]Grindley, Peter C., and David Teece. 1997. Managing Intellectual Capitol: Licensing and Cross-Licensing in Semiconductors and Electronics. *California Management Review.* 39(2): 36.

[61]Grindley and Teece, 8.

[62]Grindley and Teece, 10.

[63]Moore, James F. 1997. *The Death of Competition: Leadership & Strategy in the Age of Business Ecosystems.* New York: Harper Collins Publishers, xv.

[64]Gifis, Steven H. 1984. *Law Dictionary, Barron's Legal Guide.* Barron's Educational Series Inc., 337.[AU: city?]

[65]FAR 27.104.

[66]FAR 27.204-3 (c).

[67]Nash, Ralph C., Steven L. Schooner, and Karen R. O'Brien. 1998. *The Government Contracts Reference Book: A Comprehensive Guide to the Language of Procurement.* 2d ed. Washington, D.C.: The George Washington University Law School, 47.

[68]FAR 27.201-1.

[69]Nash, Schooner, and O'Brien, 47.

[70]FAR 52.227-3.

[71]Nash, Schooner, and O'Brien, 388.

[72]Arnavas, Donald P., and William J. Ruberry. 1994. *Government Contracts Guidebook.* Washington, D.C.: Federal Publications Inc., 10-2.

[73]Nash, Schooner, and O'Brien, 327.

[74]DFARS 227.7103-4 (a).

[75]FAR 27.303.

[76]FAR 27.302(b).

[77]The definition of technical data and computer software can be found in FAR 52.227-14 Rights to Data-general. Data means recorded information, regardless of form or media on which it may be recorded; it also includes computer software. It does not include information incidental to contract administration, such as financial, administrative, cost or pricing, or management information. Computer software, as used in reference to rights to data, means computer programs, computed data bases, and documentation thereof.

[78]FAR 27.402 (b).

[79]Gabig, Jerome S., and Roger J. McAvoy. 1985. The DOD's Rights in Technical Data and Computer Software Clause — Part II. *National Contract Management Journal.* (Winter): 50.

[80]DFARS Subpart 227.71.

[81]FAR 27.404 (a) and FAR 52.227-14 (b).

[82]FAR 27.401 and FAR 52.227-14 (a).

[83]FAR 27.401, FAR 52.227-14 (a), and FAR 52.227-14 (g) (3).

[84]FAR 27.404 (b).

[85]FAR 27.401 (b).

[86]FAR 27.401.

[87]Arnavas and Ruberry, 10-8.

[88]FAR 27.302(b).

[89]Duffy, Roberta. 1999.Where Are We Headed? *Business Briefing: Global Purchasing and Supply Chain Management.* London: World Markets Research Center, 102.

[90]Burt and Pinkerton, 218.

[91]Don't Just Survive, Thrive: The Contracting Professional as a Business Manager. 2000 National Educational Seminar. Vienna, VA: National Contract Management Association, 8-5.

[92]Don't Just Survive, Thrive: The Contracting Professional as a Business Manager. 2000 National Educational Seminar. Vienna, VA: National Contract Management Association, 8-4.

[93]Nash, Schooner, and O'Brien, 507.

[94]Conner, William E. 1999. Contractor Teaming Agreements: The Enforceability of 'Agreeing to Agree. *Contract Management*. (April): 20.

[95]FAR 9.603.

[96]FAR 9.602.

[97]Hicks, Herbert G. 1972. *The Management of Organizations: A Systems and Human Resources Approach,* 2d ed. New York: McGraw-Hill Book, 244.

[98]FAR 7.101.

[99]FAR 7.103 .

[100]DOD 5000.2-R, Mandatory Procedures for Major Defense Acquisition Programs (MDAPs) and Major Automated Information Systems (MAIS) Acquisition Programs, paragraph 2.9.3, January 4, 2001.

[101]Nash, Schooner, and O'Brien, 345.

[102]FAR 7.105 contains information on the contents of written acquisition plans. The following material is drawn in large part from that part of the FAR.

[103]FAR 7.101.

[104]Noel, Martin A., Jr. 1998. Controlling Cost and Schedule—A Contractor's Perspective. *Program Manager*(July-August), 79.

[105]FAR 7.101.

[106]Nash, Schooner, and O'Brien, 186.

[107]Carroll, Thomas D. 1994. Cost Realism. *Contract Management* (May): 21.

[108]FAR 15.404-1 (d).

[109]DOD 5000.2-R, paragraph 3.1, January 4, 2001.

[110]Kerzner, Harold. 1992. *Project Management: A Systems Approach to Planning, Scheduling, and Controlling.* New York: Van Nostrand Reinhold, 869.

[111]Kerzner, 857.

[112]Smith, Preston G., and Donald G. Reinertsen, 1991, *Developing Products In Half the Time,* New York: Van Nostrand Reinhold, 22.

[113]Sweeney, John. 1995. Some Homespun Wisdom on Risk Management. *Program Management* (July-August): 78.

[114]Mayer,Kenneth R. 1993. *The Development of the Advanced Medium-Range Air-to-Air Missile: A Case Study of Risk and Reward in Weapon System Acquisition.* Santa Monica, CA: The RAND Corporation , 7.

[115]DOD 5000.2, The Defense Acquisition System, paragraph 4.7.3.2.2.4, 23 October 2000.

[116]DOD Instruction 5000.2, Operation of the Defense Acquisition System, paragraph 3.1, Change 1 January 2001.

[117]Noel, Martin A. 1998. Controlling Cost and Schedule—A Contractor's Perspective. *Program Manager* (July-August): 78.

[118]Sweeney, 23.

[119]Glennan, Thomas K., Jr., Susan J. Bodilly, Frank Camm, Kenneth R. Mayer, and Timothy J. Webb. 1993. *Barriers to Managing Risk in LargeScale Weapon System Development Programs.* Santa Monica, CA: The RAND Corporation, x.

[120]Glennan, xi.

[121]FAR 1.102-4 (e).

[122]Muller, Ed. 1998. One-on-One Preproposal Conferences. *Contract Management.* (January): 29–30.

[123]Drake, , 4-1.

[124]Burns, Anthony P. 1998. "Internet Construction Solicitations. *Contract Management.* (March): 14.

[125]Sherman, 157.

[126]Sherman, 155.

[127]Sherman, p 157.

[128]FAR 8.001 (a).

[129]FAR 8.001 (b).

[130]FAR 8.002.

[131]FAR 37.101.

[132]Cordin, Marilyn. 1999. Personal Services Definition: Need for a Change. *Contract Management* (February): 23.

[133]Cordin, 23.

[134]FAR 6.102.

[135]FAR 6.302.

[136]Roemerman, Steve. 1998. Why Contractors File Protests...And Why Some Don't. *Program Manager.* (March-April): 29.

[137]FAR 14.201-8.

[138]FAR 15.304.

[139]FAR 12.000.

[140]FAR 13.003.

[141]Shariati, Linda. 1999. Bid Protest Decisions Related to Commercial Items: Raising Unanswered Questions. *Contract Management.* (June): 6.

[142]FAR 13.003(a).

[143]FAR 13.003(h).

[144]FAR 16.103 (a).

[145]DOD Instruction 5000.2, Operation of the Defense Acquisition System, paragraph 3.1, Change 1 January 2001, paragraph 2.9.3.2.

[146]FAR 16.103.

[147]Sherman, 324.

[148]FAR 16.104.

[149]Sherman, 217.

[150]FAR 32.502-3 (c).

[151]Nash, Schooner, and O'Brien, 392.

[152]Sherman, 242.

[153]FAR 11.601.

[154]FAR 11.603 (a) and (b).

[155]FAR 11.603.

[156]The author vividly remembers how valuable the Air Force Depot capability to deploy and repair crashed and battle-damaged aircraft onsite in Viet Nam was, and later how responsive the Air Force Depot at Warner-Robbins AFB was in modifying conventional bomb racks for the B-52 when they were suddenly thrust into a tactical air role.

[157]Abba, Wayne F. 1997. Earned Value Management—Reconciling Government and Commercial Practices. *Program Manager* (January-February): 63.

[158]FAR 46.702.

[159]FAR 46.703.

[160]FAR 4.403.

[161]FAR 42.302.

The Solicitation

In Chapter 3 we emphasized the importance of acquisition planning by citing a University of Houston study that concluded the primary cause of program/contract failure was the inadequate definition of the program at the beginning.[1] This chapter will cover the development of the solicitation document. The solicitation, which is the next iteration of the acquisition process, is defined as the document sent to prospective contractors by a government agency requesting submission of offers or information. Methods by which this is done include Invitations for Bids (IFBs), Requests for Proposals (RFPs), and Requests for Quotations (RFQs). The term *solicitation* is used to refer to the process of issuing these documents and obtaining responses.[2] A Request for Information (RFI) is used when the government does not presently intend to award a contract but needs to obtain information for planning purposes.

It serves three purposes: (1) it describes the buyer's requirement, (2) it specifies the proposed conditions of the sale, and (3) it requests that the prospective contractor submit an offer. In government contracting, a potential contractor becomes the offeror if and when it responds to the solicitation.

A successful procurement depends on the quality of the solicitation: "Submitting a high-quality solicitation is vital to the buyer's success. Better solicitations from the buyer generally result in having better bids, quotes, proposals, or tenders submitted by the seller in a more timely manner. Poorly communicated solicitations often result in delays, confusion, fewer bids or proposals, and lower quality responses."[3] The solicitation is one of the most revealing reflections of the procurement and technical professionalism of any agency.[4]

As we saw in Chapter 1, acquisition reform has made sweeping changes to proposal preparation and evaluation processes. The new policy emphasizes increased use of commercial goods and services and makes it easier for a contractor to incorporate its effort into its own processes. On the other hand, potential offerors no longer can quote the government requirements from the RFP. They now must have a more comprehensive understanding of the technology, and planning by the acquisition team will be necessary when preparing the solicitation. A thorough understanding of the government's requirements is needed when developing the proposal.[5]

Beginning early in the acquisition planning phase, an acquisition team is formed composed of experts in the areas of knowledge that will be needed to manage the acquisition during the planning, solicitation, negotiation, and award phases. The acquisition team's initial task during the planning phase is to define the requirements by surveying the market to identify all possible ways to satisfy them. After this has been completed, the team's job evolves to determining the source selection criteria and specifying contracting considerations. During the solicitation phase the government's acquisition team may be small, possibly consisting of only the CO, assisted by an ACO, an industrial specialist, and possibly an engineer. Legal assistance is sometimes needed in the preparation of the IFB. In more complex procurements the acquisition team may be a much larger group of specialists who will prepare the solicitation and also be involved with proposal evaluations, source selection, and contract award.

When the solicitation is released, the government is not only publishing the potential requirement for goods or services, but it is also defining the proposed terms and conditions of the ensuing contract. The government generally structures each procurement so that offers are made by prospective contractors and acceptance of an offer is made by the government.[6] Therefore, it is important to remember that the solicitation creates the power of acceptance by the other party, thereby transforming the contractor's response into a contractual obligation. The contractor's response is a "manifestation of (its) willingness to enter into a bargain, so made as to justify another person (in this case the government) an understanding that his assessment to that bargain is invited and will conclude it."[7] Thus a prospective contractor's response to the solicitation, when the government accepts it, results in a contract that binds the contractor to perform in accordance with the agreement.

The exception to the above practice is a purchase order in which the government sends the prospective contractor an offer that must be accepted by the contractor before it becomes a legally binding agreement.[8] In addition, the government cannot accept the RFI to form a binding contract.[9]

THE SOLICITATION AS BASIS FOR FORMAL CONTRACT AGREEMENT

"Although the federal government's purchasing procedures are governed extensively by statutes and regulations, the creation of a contractual relationship between the government and contractor is, for the most part, determined by the same legal rules applicable to the formation of private contracts. The basic sources of contract law, judicial decisions summarized in the Restatement of Contracts and in the Uniform Commercial Code, embody principles [that] although not totally binding upon the federal government, are useful tools in determining the rights and liabilities or the contracting parties in the formation process."[10]

A government procurement contract is a bilateral agreement. It includes numerous commitments that not only obligate the government to expend appropriated funds in exchange for goods and services, but it also includes promises by the contractor to perform, or refrain from performing, designated acts in accordance with the terms and conditions of the contract. Contracts not only serve as awards or notices of an award, but they also can take the form of job orders, task letters issued under basic ordering agreements, letter contracts, orders and purchase orders under which the contract becomes effective upon written acceptance or actual performance, bilateral contract modifications, and other written instruments.[11]

There are two basic methods of contracting: the sealed bid method and the negotiated procurement method. Under the formal sealed bidding process, when the government issues an IFB, it is not considered an offer. Under the process used by the government, the prospective contractor's bid is intended to be the offer. The award is the acceptance of the contractor's bid. This creates the binding agreement between the bidder and the government. Creating a contractual agreement under a negotiated procurement method is much more complicated. The negotiated procurement method introduces an opportunity for numerous oral and written discussions between the parties in response to the solicitation. This raises the possibility of a series of offers being submitted. This is considered to be part of the negotiation process "until an offer acceptable to the government is made, and accepted, or it becomes apparent that no offer [that] is acceptable will be made."[12]

The Standard Forms SF 33 (Solicitation, Offer, and Award) and SF 1442 (Solicitation, Offer and Award, Construction, Alteration, or Repair) are the forms that have traditionally been used by the government as the first page of a solicitation. The forms contain signature blocks where the contractor signs the resultant agreement as the offeror, and the appropriate CO's signature signifies acceptance and contract award.

The contract instrument has five main functions, each of which must be considered by the acquisition team as it develops the solicitation (see Table 4-1).

COs are instructed to prepare invitations for bids and contracts using the Uniform Contract Format presented in Table 4-2 to the maximum extent possible. Not only does the use of a uniform format facilitate the preparation of the IFB, but it also ensures that there is consistency between the topics covered in the solicitation and those contained in the final contract.

Table 4-1. The Functions of the Contract[13]

Provides a record of an agreement
Facilitates the administration of the agreement
Allocates risk among the parties
Defines payment terms
Provides a performance incentive for the contractor

For firm-fixed-price or fixed-price with economic price adjustment acquisition, the CO may use a simplified contract format. Although the CO has the flexibility to use the simplified contract format, it is suggested to follow the format shown in Table 4-3, Simplified Contract Format, to the maximum extent practical.[14]

Record of an agreement: This is the most obvious function of the contractual instrument because the language in the document is written evidence of the intent of the parties. There is a contract management proverb that says, "what has not been written has not been said." Traditionally, to be enforceable a commercial sale of $500 or more must be supported by some

Table 4-2. Uniform Contract Format

Section	Title
	Part I—The Schedule
A	Solicitation/contract form (SF 33)
B	Supplies or services and prices
C	Description/specifications
D	Packaging and marking
E	Inspection and acceptance
F	Deliveries and performance
G	Contract administration data
H	Special contract requirements
	Part II—Contract Clauses
I	Contract clauses
	Part III—List of Documents, Exhibits, and Other Attachments
J	List of documents, exhibits, and other attachments
	Part IV—Representations and Instructions
K	Representations, certifications, and other statements of bidders
L	Instructions, conditions, and notices to bidders
M	Evaluation factors for award

Table 4-3. Simplified Contract Format

Section	Title
A	Solicitation/contract form (SF 1447)
B	Contract schedule
	1. Contract line-item number
	2. Description of supplies, services, or data sufficient to identify the requirement
	3. Quantity and unit of issue
	4. Unit price and amount
	5. Packaging and marking requirements
	6. Inspection and acceptance, quality assurance, and reliability requirements
	7. Place of delivery, performance and delivery dates, period of performance, and f.o.b. point
	8. Other item-peculiar information as necessary (e.g., individual fund citation)
C	Clauses required by regulation. Other clauses shall be limited to those considered to be absolutely necessary to the acquisition.
D	List of documents and attachments
E	Representations and instructions
	1. Representations and certifications
	2. Instructions, conditions, and notifications
	3. Evaluation factors for award

writing signed by the parties to indicate that a contract sale has been made.[15] This legal rule came from English statutes enacted in the late 17th century to reduce the likelihood of fraud or misrepresentations. There is no similar rule with respect to government contracts; therefore, case law has relied on the normal practice of requiring documentary evidence to an agreement. In addition, the courts have traditionally ruled that a signed written document supporting the agreement between the parties is needed to support the payment of public funds as a protection against fraud.[16]

On June 30, 2000, President Clinton signed the Electronic Signature Act. This new legislation means "electronic signatures and documents have the same legal validity as manual signatures and hard copy." Public Law 106-229, which became effective October 1, 2000, also establishes rules for the retention of electronic records, a procedure for notarization of an electronic record, and procedures for determining who has control of an electronic record secured by a deed of trust.[17]

From a performance perspective, a contract represents the common language for not only the acquisition team but for all participants in the contract effort—the buyer as well as the seller. From the legal perspective, in the event of a dispute, the cardinal rule of contract interpretation used by the courts is to carry out the intent of the parties.[18] The language contained in the contractual agreement defines what both parties intended the contractual requirements to be. The contract should also be used to define the performance measurement baseline (PMB). The PMB is a quantitative sum of the budgets assigned to the scheduled cost accounts for the work to be accomplished.

As noted above, technology advancements in the form of electronic data interchange (EDI) are rapidly changing the way business is transacted. Information and business transaction flows have evolved from physical to virtual. The Department of Defense is pushing to have a paperless procurement environment. The Departments of Agriculture and Interior are likewise turning to EDI and e-commerce as ways to handle both large and small purchases.

This move to a paperless procurement system will not eliminate the requirement that some sort of record—paper or electronic—be maintained to determine the original intent of the parties. Changes in the way information is handled and business transacted are already occurring rapidly. With the increased use of e-commerce and computer-to-computer communications, encryption is now being used to authenticate the agreement reached via buyer and seller Web server.[19] The exchange of encrypted signatures (private passwords) is replacing the handwritten signature as the means of authenticating a purchase electronically. Electronic information technology is also being used extensively to exchange information among automated business management systems without human intervention. Structured information concerning the purchase of goods and services can also be exchanged among people and business management systems across a network. This reduces the cost of maintaining, storing, and disposing of files of contract documentation.

Enhance the administration of the contractual agreement: The objective of contract administration is to be proactive by paying attention to the terms and conditions of the contract up front rather than reacting when there is a problem. Contract administration can be thought of as the effort undertaken by both the buyer and seller to ensure that the terms and conditions of the contract are being complied with. For the government, this includes the duties and responsibilities defined in FAR Part 42, such as monitoring the contractor's progress, inspecting deliverables, evaluating progress payments, and approving invoices. Administrative tasks for the contractor include planning, organizing, and controlling their effort as defined in the contractual document. Both parties benefit from a contractual agreement that defines the performance standards and establishes acceptance criteria.

Key to effective administration of a contract is the ability to answer the often-asked question, "What does the contract say?" The written terms and conditions contained in the contract serve as the common language for all involved in administering the contract. Continuous and open communication among all parties is an essential factor during the contract performance phase. The ability to access documents using EDI permits placing the contract on the Internet, where it can easily be updated and readily referenced by all government and contractor members of the acquisition team. Therefore, the contract agreement should define the kinds of information that will be exchanged electronically.

On many procurements, the terms and conditions of the contract can be expressed quantitatively by extrapolating the budgeted estimates for the work to be performed from the negotiated agreement. By quantifying the contract PMB, both the government and the contractor can track the status of the contract effort using what has been referred to as the "earned value" method. This technique serves as the basis for measuring performance by monitoring the budgeted cost of work performed by the contractor. It enables corrective action to be initiated earlier in the performance phase and increases the probability of completing the contract on time and within budget. Variances from the planned budget might also be a signal that there is a possible change to the method or manner of performance, which might in turn justify modifying the contract.

Allocation of risk among the parties: A contract also addresses the risks accompanying the agreement. In Chapters 1 and 2, we defined risk as a potential problem that could lead to a failure to achieve the desired objective. Contract risk and program risk are different. The latter includes such factors as the loss of funding or a technology advance that changes the requirement. Contractual risk involves the interdependence of the two parties. Examples of risks in a contract situation include such things as the availability of the work site, unforeseen performance problems, incorrect language in specifications, delay in the receipt of government-furnished equipment, acts of God, and delivery schedules. The terms and conditions of the contract are the means by which the parties allocate and mitigate the risk associated with potential problems.

A fundamental fact of every government procurement contract is that the buyer and seller cannot satisfy the user's needs independently. Therefore, the two parties must collaborate to meet the procurement objective. Each party has different fundamental interests, some of which are occasionally in conflict. Performance often fails when one party imposes contractual provisions that prevent the other party from realizing its interests. This act fails to motivate one of the parties from the real purpose of the contract. Therefore, it is in the best interests of both parties to understand the interests associated with the proposed contract at the outset. Doing so should enable the parties to share common objectives, thereby avoiding or minimizing the impact of conflicting interests.

The allocation of risk function of a contract has to do with the risk-sharing or risk-mitigating agreements that are included as part of the terms and conditions. The process of identifying the interests of the parties includes the following steps:

- Determining the buyer's objectives that must be achieved—One study determined that in most government contracts, the primary objectives are to meet specifications, ensure that the delivery schedule is met, and keep to the agreed price.[20]
- Ascertaining the key objectives of the prospective contractors—It is generally believed that contractors are motivated to increase sales to earn a long-term profit, improve their cash flow, and earn a high return on invested capital. A study of defense contractors by the Logistics Management Institute (LMI) concluded that contractors rarely seek to maximize profit during a short-run single contract. Industry is primarily interested in growing the company's operations, increasing future business, enhancing the company's image and reputation, benefiting its non-defense business, or relieving such immediate problems as loss of skilled personnel and a narrow base for fixed cost.[21]
- Determining which of the factors identified in the acquisition plan will add risk to the objectives for both parties.
- Determining the impact these potential problems will have on the objectives.
- Estimating the probability these problems will occur.
- Ranking these risks by multiplying the magnitude of the risk by its probability of occurrence.
- Developing contract provisions that will minimize or share the risk between the parties. When total avoidance of the risk is sought, a cost/benefit tradeoff should be conducted to determine if the benefits realized from the preventive actions are worth their cost.

Identifying the risk associated with the effort involved as well as the objectives of prospective contractors is not enough. It is also important to evaluate the attitude potential contractors have toward the risk associated with their investment if they are awarded the contract. Is the potential contractor willing to expose its investment in labor and capital to accomplish contract goals? When developing the terms and conditions of the contract, the acquisition team must consider how potential contractors will look at the risk exposure their investment has under the contract terms and conditions. Will they be likely to make an unbiased decision regarding the contractual terms, conditions, and contract type?

Companies, like people, have different levels of tolerance to the amount of risk they will assume. Their level of tolerance affects their quantification of the probability and magnitude of risk they will take on. Below are three possible attitudes potential contractors may have toward risk.

- *Risk seeker*: Some contractors will gamble. Given two contract opportunities with the same rates of return, the contractor will accept a higher level of risk to gain the contract.
- *Risk neutral*: Some contractors are indifferent to risk. Given two contract opportunities with the same rates of return, the contractor will not consider the level of risk.
- *Risk averse*: Some contractors look at risk unfavorably. Given two contract opportunities with the same rates of return, the contractor will choose the project with the lower level of risk. This does not necessarily mean that the contractor will not tolerate risk of any kind. It means it will require compensation in the form of higher returns if it pursues the effort having higher levels of exposure to risk.
- *The contract as a performance incentive for the contractor*: Another primary function of a contract is to motivate the contractor.[22] It is widely believed that a properly structured contract pricing agreement will serve as a motivational tool, rewarding the contractor for exceeding performance expectations or reducing its profits when targets are not met. The government generally looks to fulfill contractual requirements at a fair and reasonable price while maintaining the delivery schedule and avoiding cost growth.

Given that the principle financial objective of the contractor is to maximize the shareholders' wealth, a risk-averse contractor will expect a higher rate of return when it is bidding on a contract it perceives to be risky. There is a tradeoff between risk and return. The higher the level of risk associated with the contract, the larger the expected rate of return. The relationship between risk and the rate of return is illustrated in Figure 4-1, Relationship between Risk and Return. A risk-free rate of return is shown at point A on the y-axis. It represents the amount of return available from a risk-free investment and is equivalent to an alternative contract or investment. For example, if the contractor were to make a financial investment, the rate of return could be equated to that of a long-term government loan. In negotiation, it is the amount where the seller may break off bargaining because of an alternative solution available, i.e., the Best Alternative to a Negotiated Agreement (BATNA).[23] As the level of risk increases along the x-axis, the larger the rate of return premium the contractor will expect to earn for successfully performing the work. The slope of the AC line depicts this risk premium. For example, at a level of exposure to risk shown as point D, a risk-averse contractor would consider a risk premium equal to point G as the amount of compensation needed for assuming the risk. This amount is equal to the risk-free rate, line DE, plus the risk premium rate of EF.

When structuring contract incentives, the CO must understand what motivates the contractor. This is important because during negotiations,

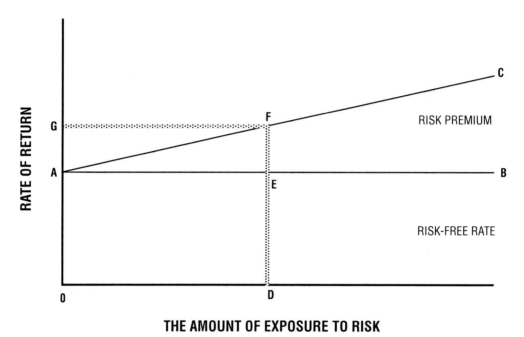

THE AMOUNT OF EXPOSURE TO RISK

Figure 4-1 Relationship between Risk and Return

---

incentives should be tailored to address the interests of the applicable contractor. To the average contractor, the rate of sales, earned profit, and the rate of return on the invested resources are important motivational factors, especially with company's management.

As we discussed above, there are motivational factors in addition to profit. These other factors include growing the company's operations, improving the company's image, applying the technology to other business areas, and employing resources during slack periods. However, the CO also must understand that these factors sometimes do not provide a strong incentive. Contractors are reluctant to sacrifice performance to attain profit because of the importance they place on company image and future business. A large profit or fee on a contract arouses suspicion of cost padding and profiteering, making future negotiations more difficult and possibly damaging the contractor's reputation.[24] This is even more important under an acquisition doctrine that stresses the contractor's past performance record as a source selection factor.

For many contractors the fact that the federal government has the right to cancel, in whole or in part, work being performed under the termination for convenience clause represents an additional risk to contracting with the government. Although the terminated contractor will be reimbursed for cost incurred, it will not be paid potential profit on terminated work.

Define terms of payment: All contracts should include written terms of how, when, and where the contractor will receive payments for goods and services delivered. In addition, the government will consider providing financing to the extent of actual need for prompt and efficient performance, considering the availability of private financing. The CO plays a key role in contract financing and payment. Government policy has traditionally emphasized using the private sector as the primary source of capital. Because interest paid on loans is not an allowable cost on a government contract, contractors often seek alternative ways to minimize their capital needs.

Government contracts either pay upon completion of all the work, or they may authorize partial payments as a designated quantity of the work is completed, delivered, and accepted. The standard payment clause used in fixed-price contracts stipulates that the contractor will be paid "for supplies delivered or services rendered and accepted upon the submission of proper invoices and vouchers."[25] This method of payment requires the contractor to finance all of its working capital needs until the entire effort is completed. This means the contractor could be using its own capital to pay employees, subcontractors, and suppliers for a significant period of time. For contracts involving long material production lead times, this represents a significant amount of financial risk exposure to the contractor. Under the partial payment method, the contractor is authorized to receive payment for partial deliveries if the amount delivered justifies and the contractor requests partial payments.[26]

The government has also adopted a policy of providing financial assistance to contractors as part of the effort to maximize competition, ensure a large competitive basis for contract award, and aid small business. The government can use four methods to provide contractors with working capital, thereby reducing their financial risk. In order of preference, these methods are: making progress payments, authorizing guaranteed loans, making unusual progress payments, and making advanced payments.[27] Solicitations frequently include provisions to pay progress payments if the CO believes it will maximize competition and assist small business while benefiting the government by aiding performance and delivery. Thus financial assistance in the form of progress payments is paid to the contractor based on costs incurred as work progresses.[28] Progress payments are normally authorized when the production lead time is six months or more, or four months for small business. For construction or shipbuilding, the payment schedule is based on the percentage of completion rather than cost incurred.[29] This policy benefits the government because it reduces the risk of a lack of working capital being an impediment to the contractor's performance.

The availability of funds is a prerequisite to awarding a contract. Under the Anti-Deficiency Act, 31 U.S.C. 1341, no officer or employee of the government may create or authorize an obligation in excess of the funds available or in advance of appropriations.[30]

If contracts are fully funded, funds are obligated to cover the price or target price of a fixed-price contract or the estimated cost and any fee of a cost-reimbursement contract. Most fixed-price contracts for work to be completed within a year are fully funded at the time of contract award. If the contract is incrementally funded, funds are obligated to cover the amount allotted and any corresponding increment of fee.[31] With incrementally funded contracts both the CO and the contractor must be aware of the funding status of the contract because there is a limit to the government's legal obligation, the cost for work incurred by the contractor, and the potential liability if the effort is terminated for convenience.

THE SOLICITATION AS BASIS FOR THE RFP

Federal procurement policy assumes that a competitive solicitation will guarantee that the government realizes the full benefit of competition. There are two categories of acquisitions: (1) sealed bids and (2) competitive negotiations. Under the sealed bid method, contracts are awarded to the bidder with the lowest price. When making an award following the competitive negotiation process, any one or a combination of evaluation factors and subfactors can be used in selecting the source. It is referred to in the Part 15 of the FAR as the best value continuum approach, meaning that the relative importance of price can vary.[32] When making the source selection decision, the buying agency can use as part of the tradeoff any one or a combination of approaches, depending on the characteristics of the acquisition.

During this process cost or price and non-monetary factors and subfactors are traded off among each other, using various weighting schemes to select the proposal that best meets the needs of the government. For example, the "relative importance" of cost or price may vary. When the requirement is definable and there is relatively low risk, cost/price could be the dominate source selection factor. Where there is greater risk because the requirement is less definitive, the greater weight may be given to technical and past performance factors in selecting the source.

The public has historically preferred the sealed bidding method to the negotiated procurement because it promotes competition and because the award of the contract is based entirely on the offeror's price, which is drawn from a sealed envelope and announced at a public bid opening. On the other hand, contracting by negotiation is often distrusted because it is perceived to be too complex to be accurately priced. Therefore, arriving at a price through bargaining easily leads to excessive profits, which are paid by the taxpayer.

COs are expected to exercise good judgment when selecting the method of contracting. Sealed bids, which are often referred to as contracting through formal advertising, have historically been the favored method of procurement. Laws and regulations dating back to 1798 "required supplies be purchased on the open market or through formal advertising for competitive bids and contracts awarded to the lowest bidder."[33] Using formal advertising and obtaining competitive sealed bids often forces the buying agency to prepare detailed specifications to secure competitive bids on identical products.[34] During World War II the pressure to speed up the acquisition process introduced contracting by negotiation. In 1942 the War Production Board abandoned the use of formal advertising altogether. The process used during World War II included the practice of soliciting formal bids from as many qualified suppliers as possible and then making awards to the lowest bidders.[35] As far as practical, competition remained a fundamental acquisition principle throughout the war. Because it had greater flexibility and more easily lent itself to the increased technical aspects of the users' needs, the use of negotiated procurements continued after the end of World War II and throughout the remainder of the 20th century.

One must not lose sight that the objective of each procurement is the timely delivery of a best-value product or service to the customer while maintaining the public's trust and fulfilling policy objectives. The method of procurement is important and the principal subject of many government regulations, but the goal is nevertheless the paramount consideration. Whenever there is a good reason for the government to deviate from normal contracting practice to meet the objective, courts and boards generally will not interfere when the price is arrived at independently and legally.[36]

The Use of Sealed Bidding

The sealed bidding process is much more structured than the negotiated procurement. The key event in the process is the public opening of the bids. All actions by both parties are directed toward the time and date of the opening and public reading of all the bids. When diligently followed, the process ensures that the price of each bid will be arrived at independently. The sealed bidding process has traditionally enjoyed a greater degree of public acceptance because of the openness of the process itself and the belief that competition reduces the fear of excessive profits.[37]

The sealed bid method is primarily used when price is the primary consideration in making the source selection. This is based on the fundamental philosophy that it is in the government's best interest to take advantage of the competitive forces in the marketplace. In theory, when there are numerous independent contractors, each having an opportunity to compete for the government's business, the lowest bidder will be awarded the contract. The philosophy underlying the use of the sealed bidding method was expressed in an opinion by the United States Supreme Court in the case of the United States of America vs. Brookridge Farm, 111 F. 2d.461 (1940):

"The purpose of statutes requiring the award of contracts to the lowest responsible bidder, after advertising, is to give all persons equal right to compete for government contracts, to prevent unjust favoritism, collusion or fraud in awarding government contracts, and to secure for the government the benefits which flow from free and unrestricted competition."[38]

The sealed bidding process is highly structured, with each step controlled to ensure that each bidder will arrive at the bid independently and that only the bidders know the bid price until all bids are disclosed at the public opening (see Figure 4-2, Invitation for Bid Process, Sealed Bid Method). Preparation of bids and contract award under the sealed bidding process will be covered in Chapters 5 and 6, respectively.

The following are criteria for the CO to consider when deciding if the sealed bid method is the most appropriate: (1) there must be sufficient time to permit preparation of the solicitation, (2) there are at least two prospective contractors, (3) there must be sufficient time for offerors to submit the bids, and (4) there will not be a requirement to conduct discussions with responding offerors prior to the award.[39] Whether the award will be made based on the price or on something other than a price-related factor is another consideration.[40] If the choice is to use the competitive proposal method rather than sealed bidding, the CO is required to explain briefly which of the four conditions enumerated above had not been met.[41]

Under the sealed bidding process, award of the contract without discussion is the norm. This necessitates that the definition of the goods or services to be purchased be as precise as possible so that offerors can respond with satisfactory bids. If the CO determines that discussion is needed, he or she is expected to furnish a reasonable explanation as to why. In addition, the CO also must have sufficient information on the adequacy of competition before issuing the solicitation to determine that the sealed bid method is appropriate. These prerequisites to using the sealed bidding method underscore the importance of doing a thorough job of market research before developing the RFB.

Because of the character of the sealed bidding process, the offeror assumes the risk of performance and delivery. Therefore, firm-fixed-price arrangements are almost always used.[42] In situations such as inflation, which affects an entire industry, the playing field can be kept level by using a fixed-price contract with an economic price adjustment.[43]

Preparing the Invitation for Bid

The Invitation for Bid (IFB) must describe the government's requirements clearly, accurately, and completely.[44] It must not include unnecessary restrictive specifications or requirements that will limit the number of bidders. The IFB should follow the uniform contract format to the maximum extent practicable.[45] This includes the terms and conditions of the proposed contract so that all offerors can develop and submit their bids on

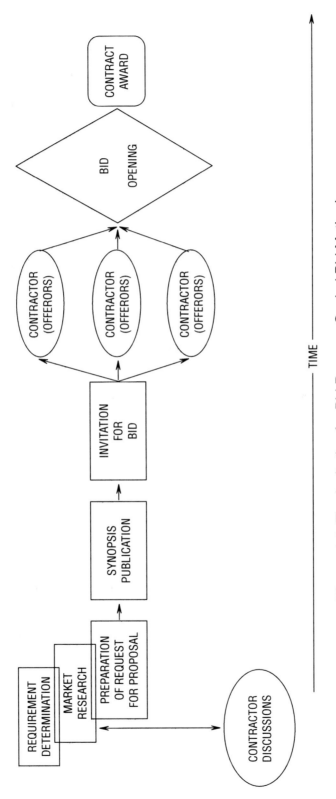

Figure 4-2 The Invitation for Bid Process, Sealed Bid Method

the same basis. It also must incorporate or reference all supporting documents that will be needed to prepare the bid. Uniformity is necessary so the contract can be awarded entirely on the price, or other price-related factors, without any discussion that would be prejudicial to other prospective offerors.

When developing the IFB, the acquisition team must remember that it must be distributed sufficiently prior to bid opening so that prospective bidders are able to prepare and submit bids.[46] It is publicized and distributed to prospective bidders by posting in public places, advertising through the publication of a synopsis in the *Commerce Business Daily,* and through any other appropriate means.[47] The CO must comply with the applicable synopsis requirements in FAR Part 5. When acquiring commercial items, the CO may use a combined synopsis/solicitation. The key is that there is enough information to permit potential suppliers or offerors to develop quotations.

With the increased use of EDI, a larger number of solicitations are: (1) being publicized using an electronic format via disk/CD-ROM, (2) posted electronically on a dial-up bulletin board system, (3) posted electronically on a specified Internet File Transfer Protocol (FTP) address, and (4) posted electronically on appropriate organizational home pages. To receive the IFB, prospective offerors should be requested to respond and provide the CO their Internet address, point of contact, mailing address, telephone number, and any other desired data. The CO can then use this information to build the bidders list, provide status of the solicitation, or announce amendments to the solicitation.[48]

Electronic data interchange also may be used to submit bids when it has been specifically approved, in which case the solicitation shall specify the EC method the bidders may use.[49] Telegraphic bids are authorized only if prices are subject to frequent change or if the date for the bid opening does not permit bidders sufficient time to submit bids in the prescribed format.[50]

With the rewrite in 1996 of FAR Part 15, Contracting by Negotiation, the prohibition against auctioning was eliminated from government procurement because there was no statutory prohibition against it.[51] This act increases the possibility of using auctioning techniques to obtain supplies. The availability of EDI also introduces the possibility of government buying offices aggregating their requirements and using the Internet to obtain price advantages using reverse auctioning via a site collector.[52]

The Two-Step Sealed Bid Procurement Process

When adequate specifications are not available, a two-step sealed bidding process may be used. The object of the two-step process is to develop a sufficiently descriptive technical data package rather than use restrictive statements of government requirements. The goal is to have a satisfactory data package for subsequent acquisitions that normally follow the conventional sealed bidding process.[53]

The initial step of this process is the issuance of a request for a technical proposal (RTP), in which no pricing is involved. Included in the contractor's technical proposal can be such technical products as the engineering approach, special manufacturing processes, and special testing techniques. The first step often also includes a discussion between the acquisition team and prospective offerors as part of the government's technical review. The second step utilizes the technical information gained from all the respondents, following established sealed bidding procedures, with the exception that the IFB is sent only to the sources that submitted acceptable technical proposals.

The release of an RTP must be synopsized in the *Commerce Business Daily*, and the names of the firms to which IFBs were sent are subsequently published there. This publication informs prospective subcontractors of the business opportunity.

CONTRACTING BY COMPETITIVE NEGOTIATION

FAR Part 15 classifies any contract awarded using other than sealed bidding procedures as a competitive negotiated contract.[54] As opposed to the sealed bidding method of procurement, the negotiated procurement method can be made using a wide variety of considerations, such as price, technical excellence, management capability, personnel qualifications, prior experience, past performance, and factors bearing on quality.[55] Figure 4-3, The Contracting by Negotiation Process, illustrates this process. The negotiation process usually includes such steps as discussing deficiencies or weaknesses in the offeror's proposal as well as providing the prospective contractors an opportunity to revise their offers before the award of the contract. These acts are not possible under the sealed bidding method.

The development of technology, with its multiple alternative products and services, has greatly increased the requirement to exchange information between the buyer and seller before contract award. The sealed bidding method, with the prerequisite for the buyer to describe the needed product or service in great detail, does not always fit the bill. The sealed bidding method does not provide the flexibility and close buyer-seller relationship needed for many of the products and services purchased by the federal government. Sealed bidding is inflexible not only because it is limited to fixed-price contracts, but also because it is restricted to solving the user's needs with similar products or services rather than describing the requirements in broad and unrestrictive terms.[56]

Competitive negotiation is the principal method the federal government used to purchase goods and services. In 1990, for example, negotiated competitive procurements equaled 85 percent of the competitive contracting

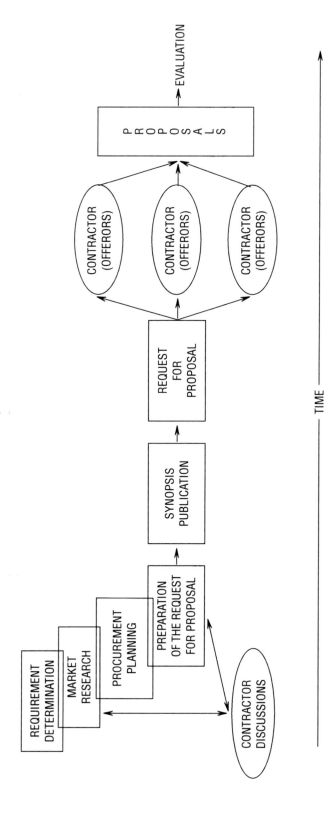

Figure 4-3 The Request for Proposal Process—Contracting by Negotiating Method

actions, with a dollar value of $178 billion, or 93.1 percent of the total.[57] As illustrated in Table 4-4, for fiscal year 1999, 87 percent of total contract actions and 95 percent of the acquisition dollars were for contracts awarded under the provisions of the Competition in Contracting Act (CICA).

In 1947 Congress first gave the Department of Defense the authority to negotiate contracts in peacetime as part of the Armed Services Procurement Act. Civilian agencies were provided similar authority in 1949 under the Federal Property and Administration Act. However, to avoid using the sealed bidding method, the CO had first to obtain authorization to use the competitive negotiation process by describing the characteristics of the acquisition and the circumstances that prevented using the sealed bidding method. Congress had historically preferred the "formal advertising" method of procurement. However, with the passage of Competition in Contracting Act (CICA) in 1984, Congress' position changed regarding the two methods of contracting. In this act, the procurement technique referred to as "formal advertising" was changed to sealed bidding. Contracting by competitive negotiation became as accepted as sealed bidding. No longer would the criteria used to judge whether a procurement was competitive or not be limited to only those awards made as the result of formal advertising.[58] To evaluate the degree of competitiveness, it became necessary to ask if there was full and open competition.

When adequate competition is not present and the proposed contract price exceeds $500,000, the Truth in Negotiation Act (TINA) of 1963 requires, as a condition of receiving the contract, that the prospective contractor submit cost or pricing data in support of negotiation proposals.[60] The prospective contractor also must certify that the cost or pricing data furnished the government is current, accurate, and complete as of the time of the negotiated agreement. This policy is an example in which statutes assist the government negotiator in determining the validity of the offeror's proposal by providing the seller's cost or pricing data. This requirement for cost or pricing data also flows down to the subcontractors if

Table 4-4. Federal Government Procurement Solicitation Summary Fiscal Year 1999[59]

	Actions	Dollars (000,000)
Pre-CICA	3,546	$4.9
CICA Awards	408,202	166.7
Simplified Acquisitions	49,717	2.3
Statutes Other Than CICA	8,927	1.5
Total	470,392	$175.4

the value of their contract with the prime contractor is also expected to exceed the $500,000 threshold. Certified cost or pricing data are also required for modifications to negotiated contracts, as well as contracts awarded under the sealed bid method, when the benefit of competition is not realized. An exception is that cost or pricing data need not be furnished if the price is set by law or regulation or when the price of a commercial item sold in substantial quantities to the public is based on an established catalog price.

As discussed in Chapter 3, acquisition doctrine stresses long-range planning and the use of market research early in the process of determining requirements and planning the acquisition. Recent revisions to FAR Part 15, covering Contracting by Negotiation, emphasize one-on-one exchanges of information among "all interested parties." These begin before the receipt of proposals, i.e., with the initial identification of a requirement, and should continue through the receipt of proposals.[61] The primary purpose of exchanging information is for the acquisition team to acquire an understanding of the capabilities of industry and to improve the efficiency of the source selection process by gaining data on the capabilities, quality, and price of supplies and services that are currently available. Another benefit of exchanging information is insight acquired by the prospective offerors of the users' needs. Diligent market research will provide the acquisition team information that can be used to:

- Define performance requirements
- Finalize the acquisition strategy
- Determine the proposed contract type
- Develop proposed terms and conditions
- Finalize the source selection schedule
- Determine the appropriateness of the proposal preparation instructions
- Finalize the evaluation criteria
- Confirm the availability of reference documents.

A part of every discussion is a fear on the part of prospective contractors that the government may either directly or indirectly disclose business-sensitive information to their competitors. General information about the buyer's needs may be disclosed at any time; but when specific information about a specific procurement, or element thereof, is disclosed to one or more offerors, that information must be made available to all offerors as soon as possible.[62] The only restriction is that the parties' exchange of information must be consistent with the Procurement Integrity (FAR 3.104) or the Freedom of Information Act.[63] Therefore, both parties should be advised that during all discussions prior to contract award they must not disclose contractor bid and proposal or source selection information.[64]

Other methods used by the government to enhance the early exchange of information include:

- Industry small business conferences
- Public hearings
- Site visits
- Pre-solicitation notices
- Draft Requests for Proposals (RFPs)
- Requests for Information (RFI) if the buyer does not presently intend to award a contract
- Pre-solicitation or pre-proposal conferences
- One-on-one meeting with potential offerors.[65]

In any of the above methods, exchanges of data about the government's needs and future requirements may be explained to prospective offerors at any time. In the general release of information to potential offerors, all information obtained during these exchanges that is judged to be necessary for preparing a proposal is also divulged to all potential offerors, whether or not they participate in the discussions.[66]

After the release of the solicitation, the CO becomes the focal point for all exchanges of information between the government and potential offerors.[67]

Preparing the Request for Proposal

The CO has the authority to tailor the Request for Proposal (RFP) to fit the circumstance of each acquisition. Paper-based and electronic solicitations are treated equally. However, facsimile RFPs are subject to more restrictions because they require human intervention to get the solicitation, along with the attachments and exhibits, to the right individuals in the government contracting office and at the contractor's office.[68]

There are numerous alternative means to solicit competitive proposals, such as the standard written RFP solicitation in the standard contract format. In addition, oral solicitations are permitted if there is an urgent need for them. Oral solicitations are also used for perishable subsistence or when it is determined that the time required to develop and process a written solicitation would be detrimental to the public good. Letter RFPs can also be used when something other than full and open competition is authorized.[69] Broad Proposal Agency Announcements (BAA) can be used to secure basic research proposals.[70] Public announcements can be used to secure design concepts for architectural and engineering work and for surveying and mapping work.[71] Unsolicited proposals can sometimes be accepted as the basis for sole-source federal contracts.[72]

With the increased use of EDI, the Internet is now a primary medium by which the government widely discriminates procurement opportunities. It is also fast becoming the predominant method by which RFPs are quickly and easily distributed to businesses throughout the country. However, the CO must be sensitive to the fact that although the use of EDI for the purchase of goods and services is growing exponentially, the Uniform Commercial Code and contract law have not kept pace with the speed of this growth. Today there is not an existing body of law that applies specifically or exclusively to the exchange of contract data electronically.[73]

Web-based Internet services, similar to the one initiated by the National Aeronautics and Space Administration (NASA), are available to potential sellers via their personal computers. The NASA Acquisition Internet Service provides "immediate access to advanced procurement notices, solicitations, a host of related acquisition information, i.e., a library of all competitive acquisitions over $25,000, a user-defined e-mail service notifying industry of new acquisition releases, access to NASA's database of active contract summaries, and an online reference library of regulations, procedures, and forms."[74]

With the improvements in information technology and the growing acceptance of EDI, the traditional administrative tasks, which have been sequentially performed during the acquisition process, can easily be overlapped. Time or location that has previously constrained communications among members of the acquisition team is fast becoming a non-factor. Completion of essential designated steps during the process is becoming more concurrent. All members of the acquisition team can now obtain data simultaneously from a common-use database, i.e., a common electronic bulletin board, and convert it to information before distribution of the solicitation. At the appropriate time a draft RFP can also be uploaded to an electronic bulletin board that is accessible by potential offerors as the final solicitation is being finalized. This means that potential contractors are given an opportunity to have meaningful discussions with the acquisition team before issuance of the formal solicitation. The net result is a more in-depth understanding of the requirements on the part of the government as well as the potential contractors. Figure 4-4 illustrates this concurrent process.

RFPs are used to disseminate the government's requirements to prospective contractors in order to elicit proposals. It is believed that using a uniform format facilitates not only the preparation of the RFP but also the ensuing contract. Therefore, COs are instructed to prepare solicitations and resulting contracts using the contract format outlined in Table 15-1, found in FAR Part 15.204-1.[75] Exceptions to using the uniform format are permitted in the case of construction and architect-engineer contracts, subsistence contracts, designated supply and service contracts, letter contracts, and contracts exempted by the agency head or designee.[76] Public Law 103-355 establishes special requirements for acquiring commercial items so that the process closely resembles the commercial marketplace.

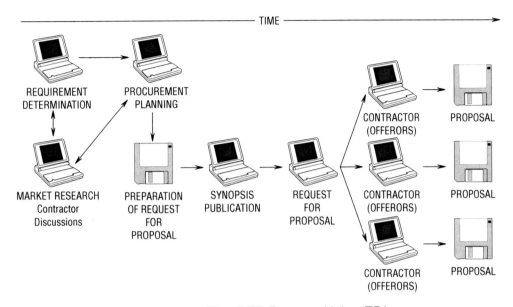

Figure 4-4 The RFP Process Using EDI

FAR Part 12 prescribes policies and procedures that are unique to the acquisition of commercial items.[77]

The Uniform Contract Format

The Uniform Contract Format specifies several parts that must be included in a proposal and the ensuing contract (see Table 4-2 on page 144).

Part I: The Schedule

Section A, Solicitation/Contract Form: Traditionally, Optional Form (OF) 308 or Standard Form (SF) 33 have been the authorized forms that act as cover sheets and provide fundamental data regarding the solicitation and the ensuing contract. In addition to the solicitation number, information on the issuing office, and table of contents, these forms have provided instructions on submitting the proposal and information on whether the ensuing contract will be a rated order under the Defense Priorities Authorization System (DPAS). To facilitate the use of EDI, these forms are no longer mandatory as long as such information as the solicitation number, the date the solicitation was issued, the closing date, the number of pages, the registration and purchase authority, a description of items or services, the offer expiration date, and the name and address of the CO are included.[78] In addition, it is now policy that "if EC is employed in the solicitation process, availability of the RFP may be limited to the electronic medium."[79]

Section B, Supplies or Services and Prices/Costs: This part includes a brief description of supplies or services to be furnished by the contractor; the item number, national stock number/part number, nouns, nomenclature, and quantities are provided to the prospective contractors.[80] Offerors are permitted to use alternative contract line-item structures in their proposals.

Section C, Description/Specifications/Statement of Work: The government uses three basic ways to describe the goods or services to be purchased: (1) specifying the design; (2) defining the performance, or operational characteristics, of the desired item; and (3) describing the functional purpose, or intended use of the product. Descriptions or specifications serve the following functions:

- Notifying the CO what to purchase
- Informing prospective contractors and their subcontractors what is required and what they are obligated to deliver
- Affecting the price and cost of ownership
- Influencing the amount of competition
- Serving as the standard for measuring the contractor's overall performance
- Establishing the standards against which inspections, tests, and quality checks are made.[81]

Traditionally, the government has included significant amounts of detail in its specifications in order to obtain standardization, avoid duplication of cost of design, ensure fair competition, and create a firm baseline for measuring performance.[82] All offerors then are able to use these detailed descriptions to develop and price their response to the government's solicitation. Although this method facilitated communication and proposal evaluation, it was expensive to prepare and limited the use of alternative solutions. Use of detailed government-directed specifications and standards also often resulted in the contractors using outmoded manufacturing processes and outdated standards.

Acquisition doctrine calls for maximum use of commercial products and services as well as minimalization of administrative cost.[83] Previously in the Competition in Contracting Act (CICA), Congress mandated increased competition and maximum use of functional and performance specifications for commercial procurements.[84] Consequently, users are being advised to describe their requirements using performance or functional objectives rather than providing the design and telling the prospective offeror the manner in which the work is to be performed.

The desired tradeoff among performance, high quality, reliability, suitability, and cost must be included in what DoD refers to as the Operational

Requirements Document (ORD). The ORD, which is initially developed by the using agency, is a quantifiable definition of requirements establishing measurable thresholds that are then integrated into the solicitation. For competitive negotiated procurements, early interchanges with potential contractors on the government's needs, including reviews of draft solicitations, are an effective way to refine performance requirements documentation and increase the utility of the final solicitation. Using performance specifications can result in a "competition of concepts," resulting in great savings for the buyer.[85]

The acquisition team may select from existing requirements documents, combine existing documents, or create new documents to describe the user's needs. The FAR establishes the following order of precedence for this task:

- Documents mandated for use by law
- Performance-oriented documents
- Detailed design-oriented documents
- Standards, specifications, and related publications issued by the government outside the Defense or Federal series for the non-repetitive acquisition items.[86]

The final content of the documents defining the requirements is a product of the design and development process. Under acquisition reform, acquisition teams are instructed to use specifications, standards, and related documents for initial guidance only. Detailed design specifications are not to be established prematurely. Needs are to be described in terms of the performance. This enables prospective prime contractors and subcontractors to use commercial or non-developmental items. In addition, acquisition activities are instructed to define requirements and prepare plans, drawings, specifications containing products incorporating recoverable and environmentally-friendly material, and energy-efficient products and services.[87]

When purchasing goods or services from the commercial marketplace, customary practices of the appropriate industry should be followed. The description should detail the type of product or services to be acquired and how the user intends to use the product or service in terms of functions to be performed, performance requirements, or essential physical characteristics.[88] To avoid restricting competition, requirements documents also must be written so that they will not restrict the purchase to a specific brand name, product, or feature of a product peculiar to one manufacturer unless it is essential to the needs of the government. If this is not possible, the contract file also must include an explanation of the necessity for this action and documentation of appropriate approvals.[89]

The ability of the RFP to describe the goods and services to be delivered has a direct effect on determining which type of contract pricing arrangement best fits the circumstances of the acquisition. The ability of the potential offeror to understand and quantify the buyer's requirements and scope of work has a direct relationship to the risk assumed by the contractor because the contractor cannot accurately quantify the cost, and the potential for cost growth increases when the government and contractor must explore alternative solutions. It is only when the performance requirements are clearly understood and the Technology Readiness Level (TRL) is at an acceptable stage that a firm-fixed-price contract can be used. This point cannot be over-emphasized because when either party fails to understand the requirements, a fixed-price contract is easily transformed into what in reality is a cost-reimbursement contract via the contract change process. Cost-reimbursement contracts are appropriate when the requirements are not well defined or when the government wants more control over the contractor's activities.[90]

In describing requirements for services, the acquisition team is charged with ensuring that such inherently government functions as protecting the public interest are performed by a government employee and not assigned to a contractor.[91] Examples of functions that fall under the act of governing include determining program priorities for budget requests; directing and controlling federal employees; conducting foreign relations; commanding military forces; determining what government property is to be disposed of; awarding and terminating contracts; collecting, controlling, and disbursing fees and royalties; and administering public funds.[92]

When it is necessary for a contractor to prepare requirements documents, the CO must remember that the same contractor is not normally allowed to act as a supplier, either as a prime contractor or subcontractor, for a reasonable period of time or for the duration of the initial production contract.[93] The reason behind this policy is that these contractors can be expected to design and develop the specifications or work statements based on their corporate knowledge, thereby giving them a competitive advantage in obtaining follow-on contracts. Additional information on policies regarding the protection of the competitive process is outlined later in this chapter in the section titled "Organizational and Consultant Conflicts or Interest."

Section D, Packaging and Marking: Packaging, packing, preserving, and marking requirements that apply to the deliverable are defined in this section. Of primary importance are the product's characteristics and their intended long-term or short-term use. Questions to be considered include:

- Is the item perishable?
- What is its shelf life?
- What is its method of shipment? Storage?
- What is its breakability?
- What are the safety and environmental considerations?

Section E, Inspection and Acceptance: The primary goal of each acquisition is the timely completion of the work as described in the contract. "A secondary goal in requiring contractor compliance with contract specifications is to preserve the integrity of the competitive procurement system."[94] In Section E the buyer establishes the inspection, acceptance, quality assurance, and reliability requirements that apply to the contractor. This section should explain the criteria for accepting the goods or services contracted for. Of primary importance is the fundamental rule that the government is entitled to enforce strict compliance with the terms and conditions of the contract. The strict compliance standard not only ensures that deliverables will satisfy the user's needs, but it also ensures that public funds are properly expended and the integrity of the acquisition process maintained. Holding the contractor to the letter of the contract discourages the contractor from submitting low bids while intending to use less expensive materials or methods than those specified in the contract.[95]

Also important when purchasing goods and services is the fact that the act of acceptance can also acknowledge that the supplies or services conform with applicable contract and quantity requirements.[96] For example, for fixed-priced contracts the standard government inspection clauses for supplies and services include the following statement: "acceptance is conclusive, except for latent defects, fraud, gross mistakes amounting to fraud, or as otherwise specified in the contract."[97] This means that the government's right to correct defects after acceptance is limited. On the other hand, commercial items delivered under the terms and conditions of the UCC have an implied warranty of merchantability, trade usage, and fitness for particular purposes that does not apply to most government contracts after the item has been accepted.[98] Consequently, it is important to all concerned that the criteria for acceptance should be spelled out in each contract.

The concept behind the proverb "You can't inspect quality into the product" is a practice that places the obligation on the contractor to fulfill the contract requirements and to facilitate government inspections. W. Edwards Deming believed that relying on mass inspections of completed products just before delivery as the means of ensuring delivery of a quality product in effect pays workers to produce defects and then pays the worker to correct them.[99] Under this philosophy it is the role of the government to ensure that the contractor has a quality system that is adequate for the product being produced.

Government contracting quality assurance can be defined as "a planned, systematic pattern of actions taken to provide adequate confidence that sufficient technical requirements are established, that products and services conform to those requirements, and that satisfactory performance is achieved."[100] The government fulfills its quality assurance responsibilities either by physically inspecting the work, witnessing tests, or surveillance of the contractor's inspections system. "The trend in government contracts has been to place greater responsibility for contractor inspections on the contractor."[101] Quality assurance places greater importance on defining the extent of the contractor's inspection obligations.[102] The government then evaluates the contractor's quality system to determine if it is adequate and is being complied with as part of its contractor surveillance tasks.

The range and scope of contract quality requirements are based on the classification of the items being delivered. For example, complex items having quality characteristics not entirely visible in the end item would require the application of more stringent quality requirements than simpler items. Higher-quality requirements are appropriate for items where failure could injure personnel or jeopardize a vital mission.[103]

Quality assurance plans should be prepared in conjunction with the statement of work and should specify all the work requiring surveillance and the method of surveillance. Government inspection is to be performed by or under the direct supervision of government personnel. The government inspection is to be documented on a receiving report or a commercial bill of lading/packing list. The contract should designate all locations where the government reserves the right to perform quality assurance. Locations may not be changed without CO authorization.[104] When a higher level of quality is required and government inspection during contract performance will be carried out, quality assurance is to be performed at the source.[105] When supplies are perishable or purchased off the shelf, government quality assurance is to be performed at the destination.[106] Quality assurance at destination is used for small purchases and services or when the test equipment needed to perform the test is located at the point of delivery.[107]

When defining inspection and testing requirements in the contract, the acquisition team should consider the following factors in the context of the overall quality assurance strategy:

- Type of inspection or test to be performed
- Place of the inspection or test
- Time of the inspection or test
- Quantity of the inspections or tests
- Method of the inspection or test
- Pass or fail criteria for the inspection or test
- Criteria for acceptance of deliverables.

The type and extent of a product's contract quality requirements should be based on the risk of the deliverable not meeting the performance objectives defined in the contract.

Contract quality assurance requirements and plans need to be tailored to the risk involved. Overall risk can be prioritized by determining the probability of occurrence and the consequences, e.g., jeopardizing the mission, risking personal safety, or creating an environmental hazard if the item fails. Because of its form, fit, and functional characteristics, each deliverable has a varying probability of failure related to each step in the manufacturing or assembly process. The extent of contractual quality requirements is determined by the risk associated with the general product classifications listed below.

1. The technical description of the supplies or services
    a. Commercial items sold, leased, or licensed to the general public
    b. Military-Federal
2. The complexity of the supplies or services
    a. Complex items that have quality characteristics that are not wholly visible and for which contractual conformance must be established progressively through precise measurements, tests, and controls applied during purchasing, manufacturing, performance, assembly, and functional operation, either as stand-alone items or components of an end item
    b. Non-complex items that have quality characteristics for which simple measurements and test of the end item are sufficient to determine conformance to contract requirements
3. The criticality of the supply or service (impact of failure)
    a. A critical application of an item, in which the failure of the item could result in injury or jeopardize a vital mission
    b. A non-critical application of an item.

Using these classifications as a guide, the acquisition team would assign a higher probability of failure to a military-federal item that is more complex in nature than a commercial, off-the-shelf, non-complex item. Adding the criticality, or impact, dimension permits further ranking of deliverable products by their risk.

Contract quality requirements for federal contracts fall into four general categories. The relationship between product classification and the categories of contract quality requirements is shown in Figure 4-5, Categories of Contract Quality Requirements.

Reliance on inspection by the contractor:[108] Policies for acceptance of commercial items and noncommercial items are the same, that is, they rely on the contractor to accomplish all inspections and testing needed to ensure that supplies and services meet contract requirements. Clauses requiring the inspection and testing of non-complex and non-critical commercial supplies and services in a manner inconsistent with customary commercial practices is not permitted without approval of a waiver to do so.[109]

Acceptance of commercial items is based on the assumption that the government will rely on the contractor's assurances that the item tendered

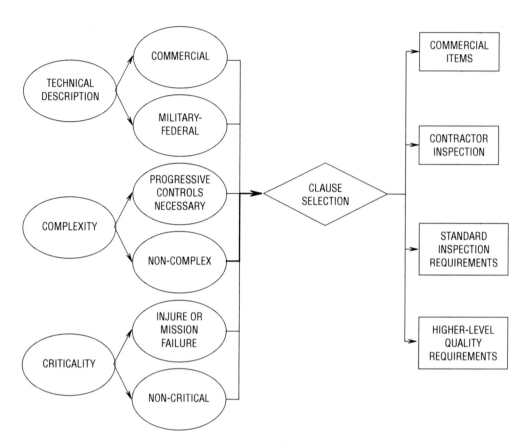

Figure 4-5 Categories of Contract Quality Requirements

for acceptance conforms to the contractual requirements. This is consistent with the implied warranty of "merchantability" and "fitness for a particular purpose," which are provisions under the Uniform Commercial Code.[110] When commercial items are to be used, the critical applications under the criteria outlined in FAR 46.204 are applicable. The government inspection of commercial items does not prejudice its other rights under the acceptance clause. The government always has the right to refuse nonconforming items. The CO must also carefully examine the terms and conditions of any express warranty with regard to the effect it may have on the post-acceptance rights of the government.[111]

Government reliance on inspection by the contractor: The government shall rely on the contractor to accomplish all inspections and testing at or below the simplified acquisition threshold before supplies or services are tendered for acceptance. The exemption to this rule occurs when the CO determines that the government has a need to inspect or test supplies or services before they are tendered for acceptance to determine the adequacy of the contractor's internal work process. In making this decision the CO should consider: (1) the nature of the supplies or services being purchased and their intended use, (2) the potential losses in the event of defects, (3) the likelihood of uncontested replacement or correction of defective work, and (4) the cost of detailed government inspection.[112]

Standard inspection requirements: These are required under fixed-price supply contracts, cost-reimbursement research and development contracts, and facility contracts when: (1) the contractor is required to maintain an inspection system that is acceptable to the government, (2) the government requires the right to make inspections and tests while work is in process, and (3) the contractor is required to complete and make records of its inspection work available to the government.[113] Standard FAR inspection clauses give the government broad comprehensive rights to inspect the contractor's work, but they do not impose a contractual duty on the government to inspect.[114] Government quality assurance must be performed at such time and place as are necessary to determine that the supplies or services conform to the requirements of the contract. This can be done during the manufacturing process, as services are being performed, and at subcontractor's plants. It is based upon the belief that: (1) a system that delivers 100 percent conforming material is the least costly, and (2) delivery of a quality product is ensured when the manufacturing processes are under control.[115]

Higher-level contract quality requirements: These are appropriate in solicitations and contracts for complex or critical items when the technical requirements of the contract require: (1) control of such things as work operations, in-process controls, and inspections; or (2) attention to such factors as organization, planning, work instructions, documentation control, and advanced meteorology. Examples of higher-level quality standards are ISO 9001, 9002, or 9003; ANSI/ASQC Q9001, Q9002, or Q9003; QS-9000; AS-9000; ANSI/ASQC E4; and ANSI/ASME NQA.[116]

As the DoD increases its reliance on an integration of the civil-military industrial base, the government's business practices must also incorporate best commercial practices. In the area of product quality, the primary best practice is the ISO 9000 Quality Management System. ISO 9000 was developed by the International Organization for Standardization (ISO), an organization based in Switzerland with a membership of over 100 countries. ISO's quality management guidelines, which were created through international consensus, include a variety of standards for products, processes, and information technology. The set of requirements describes what must be accomplished; the method is left up to the individual organization. These guidelines are generic and can be applied to many types of businesses, e.g., manufacturing, software, and services.[117]

Section F, Deliveries or Performance: The establishment of a performance schedule that meets the customer's needs is a key element of every contract. The acquisition team is also called upon to ensure that delivery schedules are realistic and attainable. An understanding of the norms for the industry gained through market research can provide insight into probable delivery schedules.

Delivery or performance dates may be expressed in terms of specific calendar dates, specific periods of time from date of contract award, or a specific period of time after the notice to proceed from the government. The CO is instructed not to specify a delivery time that places an unjust burden to perform on the contractor because of a delay by the government, e.g., delay in the notice of award or late delivery of government-furnished property.[118]

When establishing contract delivery schedules, consideration will be given to:

- Need date of the ultimate user
- Industry practice
- Market conditions
- Transportation time
- Production time
- Capabilities of small business
- Administration time for the evaluating offerors and awarding the contract
- Time required for the contractor to comply with any conditions precedent to contract performance
- Time for the government to perform its obligations under the contract, i.e., furnishing government property.[119]

Sometimes when timely delivery is critical to the government because it is key to another event or contract, the CO may include a liquidated damages clause as an additional motivational factor. This clause establishes a sum for which the contractor will be liable upon breach of the contract's delivery schedule. The requirement for using this clause is that the government may expect to suffer damage if delivery or performance is delinquent. This clause would be appropriate, for example, if failure by the contractor to complete renovation causes the government to incur unplanned facility rental cost because a new facility is not available for occupancy. When establishing the rate of damages, the CO is instructed to be reasonable because liquidated damages should not be viewed as a penalty solely for not meeting the schedule. The amount should be fixed without referring to probable actual damages, which may be held to be a penalty and therefore render the clause unenforceable.[120]

Section G, Contract Administration Data: Appropriate accounting, fund appropriation data, and contract administration information is to be included here. The section is usually limited to information that is not included on the solicitation form discussed under Section A of the Uniform Contract Format.

The contract administration information that is often embodied in Section G is:

1. The organization that has been delegated the cognizant Contract Administrative Officer (CAO), along with responsibilities that will be performed
   a. The contract administration functions listed in FAR 42.302(a) to the extent they apply to the contract, functions specifically authorized by the PCO
   b. The contract administration functions listed in FAR 42.302(b) when and to the extent authorized by the PCO
   c. Any added contract administration functions not listed in FAR 42. 302 (a) and FAR 42.302 (b) or not otherwise delegated by the PCO.[121]
2. Designation of the government paying office.
3. Instructions on the submission of invoices and applicable accounting codes.
4. Instructions regarding the assignment of claims.
5. Instructions regarding contract financing if the contract provides for progress payments.

With the increased reliance on electronic means to procure goods and services, there is a requirement to define the kinds of information that will be exchanged electronically. There must be a contractual understanding regarding:

- Transfer of messages and which Computer-Aided Acquisition Standards and Logistics Support Standards (CALS) should be used
- Access to data
- Intellectual property and rights to use data files
- Responsibility for imperfect data.[122]

Section H, Special Contract Requirements: This section includes unique agreements or nonstandard contract requirements that are not contained in Part I, Sections A through G, or other sections of the Uniform Contract Format. Topics included under Special Contract Requirements include issuance of contract changes, limitation of the government's liability, exercise of options, identification of the sources of supply, use of Data Item Descriptions (DIDs), listing of government property to be furnished for the performance of the contract, government installations or facilities that will be made available under the contract, government property that will be mailed to the contractor under the contract, special performance incentives, acceptance of technical data, ground and flight risk clauses, warranty of supplies, acquisition of unlimited technical data/computer software, and allotment of funds.

This section also can be used to reduce the risk by sharing it with other parties if future events do not materialize. A good example is a contract for indefinite quantities, in which the buyer can moderate the risk that consumption will be less than anticipated by including a contingent provision whereby the government commits to purchase a defined quantity of items over a designated period of time. If consumption does not materialize, the buyer can cancel the undelivered quantities and pay an agree-upon price.

Under acquisition reform, DoD is now limiting only deliverable data to that truly needed to manage the acquisition or support the product in the field after delivery. This is a significant change, as data were previously required to be developed and delivered to the government as proof the contractor was complying with the letter of the contract.[123]

As noted in Chapter 1, acquisition doctrine encourages COs to take the initiative and develop business strategies that are tailored to the acquisition, as long as they are not specifically prohibited by law or regulation. These special provisions would be included in Section H.

Part II: Contract Clauses

Section I, Contract Clauses: This section includes clauses required by law or regulation or additional clauses expected to be included in the contract and not contained in any other section. The Provision and Clause Matrix contained in FAR Subpart 52-300 includes a list of over 700 FAR Standard Clauses. This list is displayed in a matrix that is cross-referenced to the various types of contract pricing arrangements. The matrix also states whether the use of the clause is required by law or regulation, when it is applicable, or if its use is optional. In applying these standard clauses, the CO is expected to exercise sound business judgment and to determine if the benefits received by the government justify any added cost.

In Chapter 1 we covered the fact that some government procurement regulations and clauses may have the force and effect of law, providing they can be incorporated into the contract by "operation of law" as if they had been there all the time. The prerequisite is "express or implement significant or deeply ingrained strand of public procurement policy" if incorporation is sought by the party that would not benefit from its presence.[124] To eliminate any later confusion, the CO must ensure that all clauses applying to this acquisition have been incorporated into the contract initially.

In government contracts risk is specifically allocated between the parties by using contract clauses. The government uses standard clauses to provide for time extensions or price adjustments should various contingencies occur. Some of these clauses allocate risk regarding conditions encountered during performance that were not as expected or represented in the solicitation, e.g., access to the work site or availability of government-furnished equipment. In the absence of any specific government contract clauses that allocate risk, common law principles would apply to the allocation of risk.[125]

Due to the risk associated with defects after acceptance, the applicability of FAR warranty clauses in government contracts deserves special mention. Because of the "conclusiveness" of the language of the fixed-price inspection clause, the government does not generally enjoy the benefit of the implied warranties as does the private sector, subject to the UCC. In the private sector the implied warranty of "merchantability" means that the consumer is guaranteed that the goods purchased are "reasonably fit for ordinary purpose for which such goods are used."[126] Until 1984 the use of warranties in government contracts was optional. However, in the Defense Procurement Reform Act of 1984 (Public Law 98-525), Congress passed what was then referred to as the Weapon System Warranty Act (WSWA). This statute required the government to obtain warranties before entering into weapon system production contracts having a unit cost of over $100,000.[127] The use of warranties on other government contracts remained optional. After operating under this statute for almost 10 years, it was determined that the benefits of mandatory warranties on weapon systems production contracts were not worth the cost of implementation and administration. Therefore, warranties are no longer mandatory in weapon system production contracts.

Under FAR clauses covering the Inspection of Supplies—Cost Reimbursement (52.246-3) and Inspection of Research and Development—Cost Reimbursement (52.246-8), the CO is not to include warranties in cost-reimbursement contracts unless specifically authorized[128] because the government has generally participated in the design and development of goods and services being purchased under these types of contracts, and it is therefore difficult to conclude that the defect is entirely the fault of the contractor.

When determining if a warranty is appropriate for other acquisitions, the CO must consider the following factors:

- The nature and use of the supplies or services
- Their complexity and function
- The degree of development
- The state of the art
- The end use
- The difficulty in detecting defects before acceptance
- The potential harm to the government if the item is defective
- The cost of the warranty arising from contractor charges for accepting the deferred liability created by the warranty, as well as the cost of administering and enforcing the warranty.[129]

When it is determined that a warranty is appropriate, the terms and conditions to be included in the solicitation should clearly state the information listed below to facilitate pricing and enforcement of the warranty:

- The exact nature of the item, components, and characteristics that the contractor warrants
- The extent of the contractor's warranty, including all of the contractor's obligations to the government for breach of warranty
- The specific remedies available to the government
- The scope and duration of the warranty.[130]

Part III: Lists of Documents, Exhibits, and Other Attachments

Section J, List of Attachments: In this section the CO lists the title, date, and number of pages for each attachment (e.g., documents or exhibits). It is important that this list is current and complete and that the referenced documents themselves are consistent in content with other provisions in the contract. One of the basic common-law rules for interpretation of a contract is that it is "interpreted as a whole (document), and all writings that are part of the same transaction are interpreted together."[131] This rule is coupled with the fact that the government may be liable if the data that are included in the document create problems for the contractors that could have been foreseen, as would be the case where a contractor is required to supply a component that is shown on the drawing but omitted from the specifications.

Part IV: Representations and Instruments

Section K, Representations, Certifications, and Notices: In this section the CO includes the representations, certifications, and notices that the prospective contractor is required to furnish. Most often these are based on legal requirements or implement socioeconomic policies of the government.

Section L, Instructions, Conditions, and Notices: This section should be compatible "on a one-for-one basis with Section M, 'Evaluation Factors for Award.'" Section L specifies the format and content of proposals, and Section M tells offerors how the government will evaluate what is required by Section L.[132]

This section also contains boilerplate provisions that must be included in RFPs and information or proposal preparation instructions that are not included elsewhere in the solicitation. It does not become part of any subsequent written contract.

FAR 52.215, Instructions to Offerors—Competitive Acquisitions, is an "omnibus" provision to be used in all solicitations. It should be considered when developing the content of Section L. By inclusion of FAR 52.215-1, it presumes that the government intends to award the contract without discussion. If Alternative II of FAR 51.215-1 is inserted in the solicitation, it allows prospective offerors to submit alternative proposals.[133] Alternative II is also used in the case of cost-reimbursement contracts with educational institutions or other non-profit organizations. Alternative III omits the examination of records by the Comptroller General and is considered when the solicitation applies to negotiated contracts with foreign contractors and is deemed by the agency head and Comptroller General to be in the public interest.

Other subjects that are included under this omnibus provision are Audit of Records (FAR 52.215-2), Requests for Information or Solicitations for Planning Purposes (FAR 52.215-3), Type of Business Organizations (FAR 52.215-4), Facsimile Proposals (FAR 52.214-5), Place of Performance (FOE 52.215-6), Annual Representations and Certifications (FAR 52.215-7), and Order of Precedence (FAR 52.215-8).

The prospective offerors often are instructed to submit proposals in a specific topical format to facilitate evaluation. Page limitations are sometimes included. A typical format includes the following sections:

- Administration
- Management
- Technical
- Past performance
- Cost or pricing data.

Instructions for submitting cost/price proposals when cost or pricing data is required is covered extensively in FAR 15.408, FAR 52.215, and Table 15-2, "Instructions for Submitting Cost/Price Proposals When Cost or Pricing Data Are Required."

For negotiated procurements, the government often furnishes a work breakdown structure (WBS) as part of the RFP. The WBS subdivides the work to be performed under the contract into logical segments for reporting purposes. This is a method whereby the contract scope of work is delineated, tabulated, segregated, and organized in a hierarchical manner. It provides a logical method for summarizing cost of contract deliverables from the lowest-level components to the highest level. The solicitation often contains instructions to the prospective contractors to organize and submit their proposed costs in WBS framework. By having the contractor organize the proposed work into smaller work packages, the government can ensure that all work activities are accounted for. Providing a common framework for accomplishing all work to be done also provides the government a method to compare common segments by different contractors during proposal evaluation. Figure 4-6 depicts a partial WBS tree diagram for the design, manufacture, and test of a hypothetical aircraft.

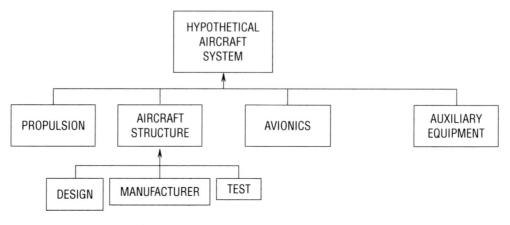

Figure 4-6 Work Breakdown Structure

This tree diagram is divided into three levels of work packages. The top level is the prime objective of the aircraft. The work breakdown structure is developed downward by proceeding from the aircraft end item to the next level, which consists of the four major components: the propulsion sub-system, the aircraft structure, the avionics package, and the auxiliary equipment. The top two levels are product oriented. The third, which is shown in Figure 4-6 only for the aircraft structure, includes the major tasks, i.e., design, manufacture, and testing. Each of these tasks have subtasks. How many levels a WBS should have depends on the complexity of the product and the extent to which manageable levels can be defined.

The work breakdown structure also can be used to provide the basis for development of the:

- Master integrated program matrix
- Master integrated scheduling
- Segregating costing
- Organizational structure
- Coordinating objectives
- Contract administration.

Section M, Evaluation Factors for Award: As was the case in Section L, the instructions in Section M apply only to the solicitation and do not become part of the contract. In this section the acquisition team describes how it will evaluate the factors included in Section L. Here the acquisition team describes the relationship between cost or price and the non-cost factors and subfactors and how they will be used as the basis for source selection. The objective is to inform prospective offerors of the factors and significant subfactors that will be used when making the source selection decision as well as their relative importance.[134] The comptroller general has ruled that if no evaluation factors are identified, award should be made to the lowest-priced technically acceptable quotation.[135]

The relative importance of cost or price to other factors, such as technical performance, may vary depending on the characteristic of acquisitions.[136] The "best value" method of evaluating negotiated proposals has evolved from what once was referred to as the lowest-price, technically acceptable source selection method. It can be tailored to the situation because it may be in the best interest of the buyer to consider awarding the contract based on a factor other than lowest price or the highest-ranked technical proposal.[137] Evaluation factors and significant subfactors must: (1) represent the key areas of importance in the source selection decision, and (2) support meaningful comparison and discrimination among competitive proposals.[138]

In conjunction with a comprehensive rewrite of FAR Part 15, Contracting by Negotiations, published in September 1997, FAR 2.101 included a definition of "best value": "Best value is the expected outcome of an acquisition that, in the government's estimation, provides the greatest overall benefit in response to the requirement."[139]

It is appropriate to note that this definition has been questioned because it is not explicitly related to the source selection process.[140] When related to the source selection process, the term "best value continuum" is used. An agency can obtain "best value" by using any one or a combination of source selection approaches; the relative importance of cost may vary.[141] The FAR goes on to describe a tradeoff process that requires the use of three statutorily mandated categories of factors and significant subfactors: cost or price; quality (technical merit and other measures of the proposal's "goodness"); and past performance (unless the contracting officer has made a written determination that past performance is not applicable to the instant contract).[142]

The Comptroller General noted that each offeror has a right to know whether the procurement is intended to achieve minimum standard at the lowest cost or whether cost is secondary to quality. This statement is based on the principle of maximum competition; to achieve competition, the offerors must be provided the relative values of technical excellence and price.[143] Therefore, all evaluation factors and significant subfactors that will affect contract award are to be clearly stated in Section M of the solicitation. The rating method may also be disclosed in Section M, although the FAR states that the government need not do so. At a minimum, the acquisition team is instructed to state in the solicitation when all evaluation factors other than price or cost are combined if they are: (1) significantly more important than cost or price, (2) approximately equal to cost or price, or (3) significantly less important than cost or price.[144]

For competitive negotiated procurements, Section M must specify which source selection approaches or combination of approaches will be used. The "best value continuum" of source selection process and techniques are addressed in FAR Part 15. At one end of the continuum is the tradeoff process. The term *tradeoff* is used to describe trading off cost or price factors with non-cost or non-price factors, using varying weighting schemes to select the proposal that best fits the government's needs. At the other end of the spectrum is the lowest-price technically acceptable offer. This method is one step above sealed bidding and is used on technical acquisitions. Using this method permits the government to hold discussions with prospective contractors, if required.[145]

The evaluation factors differ with each acquisition. The acquisition team's tailoring of the factors and subfactors is subject to the following:

- Price or cost to the government is to be evaluated in every source selection
- Quality of the product or service is to be addressed in every source selection through consideration of:
  –past performance
  –compliance with solicitation requirements
  –technical excellence
  –management capability
  –personnel qualifications
  –prior experience.

Past performance must be evaluated in all source selections that are expected to exceed $100,000, unless the CO documents the reason that it is not a fitting evaluation factor.[146]

The rewrite of FAR Part 15, Contracting by Negotiations, now calls the best value process the tradeoff process, and it states: "The less definitive the requirement, the more development work required, or the greater the procurement risk, the more technical or past performance considerations may play a dominant role in the source selection."[147]

As noted previously, an underlying principle of the procurement process is "fairness." Award of a contract is easier to defend when it can be shown that it was based on objective criteria and that the decision was made fairly. The principle of fairness as it is now stated in FAR 1.102-2(c) has been cited by industry as being ambiguous. The September 1997 revision to the FAR 1.1029(c) states: "The Government shall exercise discretion, use sound business judgment, and comply with applicable laws and regulations in dealing with contractors and prospective contractors. *All contractors and prospective contractors shall be treat fairly and impartially but need not be treated the same.*" (Emphasis added.) Under what circumstances will this treatment be in violation of law as opposed to a "different" but nevertheless "fair and impartial" treatment of contractors and prospective contractors? Industry asked if it is "fair" and "impartial" to allow incumbents to have exclusive access to competitive information regarding a procurement by virtue of their status as an incumbent.[148]

This policy statement that "all contractors and prospective contractors shall be treated fairly and impartially but need not be treated the same" has been explained as merely acknowledging that all proposals are different and should be treated differently based on their individual merits.[149] This policy may allow incumbent contractors exclusive access to competitive information. One obvious concern, particularly in light of exchanges under FAR 15.201 and 15.306, is that FAR 1.102(c)(3) may be used to rationalize or justify arbitrary, unreasonable, or questionable business behavior by COs during the proposal evaluation stage.[150]

ORGANIZATIONAL AND CONSULTANT CONFLICTS OF INTEREST

Former Assistant Secretary of the Army Dr. Ronald J. Fox observes in his book *Arming of America*, "A contractor who waits until an RFP is issued or a notice of a planned procurement appears in the *Commerce Business Daily* rarely, if ever, wins a major procurement contract."[151]

An organizational conflict of interest is said to exist when, "because of other activities or relationships with other persons, a person is unable or potentially unable to render impartial assistance or advice to the government or a person's objectivity in performing the contract work is or might be able to be otherwise impaired, or a person has an unfair competitive advantage.[152] This situation most likely will occur in the initial phases of a product's life cycle in design and development contracts. The types of effort open to conflict of interests are most prevalent when a contractor does not have overall contractual responsibility for development or production of a product. Examples of where potential conflict could exist are contracts with the government for: (1) management support services, (2) consultant or other professional services, (3) contractor performance of technical evaluations, or (4) systems engineering or technical direction work.[153] These situations can create the potential for giving preferential treatment in future acquisitions. Not only does this treatment raise ethical questions, but it also undermines the integrity of the competitive procurement process.

The CO is responsible for identifying and resolving potential conflicts of interest.[154] Each contracting situation must be analyzed on the basis of facts as they apply to the proposed contract. The CO must evaluate each planned contracting situation, using technical and legal assistance if needed, to identify and evaluate the potential for conflicts so they can be avoided. When there is a potential conflict of interest, the CO is responsible for recommending a course of action to resolve it to the head of the procurement agency before issuing the solicitation. General rules that prescribe limits to be placed on organizations and consultants to avoid a conflict of interest are contained in the FAR 9.5. The CO should use common sense, good judgment, and discretion in developing appropriate means to resolve the potential conflict while upholding the following underlying principles:

- Preventing the existence of conflicting roles that might bias the contractor's judgment
- Preventing unfair competitive advantage, such as when a contractor competing for a government contract possesses:
  - Proprietary information that was obtained from a government official without proper authorization
  - Source selection information relevant to the contract but not available to competitors that would assist the contractor in obtaining the contract.[155]

If the CO determines that awarding the contract to an apparent successful offeror creates a conflict of interest, the contractor should be notified and given an opportunity to respond to the allegation. When it is judged to be in the best interest of the United States to award a contract, notwithstanding the conflict of interest, a waiver must be obtained from the agency prior to the award.[156]

PRE-QUALIFICATION OF OFFERORS

An essential act in every procurement is the determination that the offeror is qualified to serve as a government contractor. This is part of managing risk. To mitigate risk of poor performance on contracts, government policy limits the award of contracts to "responsible" contractors whose bid or proposal conforms to the solicitation and will be the most advantageous to the government. If the acquisition team wants to determine which of the potential contractors are responsible prior to issuing the solicitation, it must satisfy certain conditions prior to taking this action. Caution is important because any pre-qualifying of contractors has generally been considered to be a restriction on full and open competition.[157]

Before establishing pre-qualification requirements the agency must justify the necessity for such action, specifying all the requirements that must be satisfied to become qualified and estimating the likely cost for the necessary testing and evaluation.[158] Pre-qualification procedures have been approved when competition is enhanced or when it is necessary to ensure a continuous supply of items that are under stringent quality requirement.[159] Comptroller general decisions over the years have judged pre-qualification actions to be restrictive when they are used to ease the administrative burden of evaluating a large number of prospective offerors.

Qualification and listing in a Qualified Products List (QPL), Qualified Manufacturers List (QML), and Qualified Bidders List (QBL) is the process by which products are obtained, examined, and tested for compliance with the standards specified for qualification. These qualifications are generally performed in advance and are independent of any specific solicitation.[160]

PUBLICIZING CONTRACT ACTIONS

Government policy has traditionally emphasized wide dissemination of proposed contracting opportunities to enhance competition, broaden industry participation, and promote participation in government contracts by small business. For contracts that are expected to exceed $25,000, a synopsis is required to be published in the *Commerce Business Daily* (CBD) at least 15 days before the issuance of the solicitation. The *CBD*, which is published daily by the Department of Commerce, lists solicitations, contract awards, subcontracting opportunities, sales of surplus government property, and foreign business opportunities. The *CBD* does not, however, cover a significant number of procurements. For contract actions between $10,000 and $25,000, synopses are disseminated by being displayed on purchasing office bulletin boards, electronic bulletin boards, or electronic means in the contracting office that will issue the solicitation. Paid advertisements in newspapers are used only when it is anticipated that adequate competition cannot otherwise be obtained.[161]

In support of the DoD mandate of paperless acquisition, there is an increase in the use of personal computers, and buying offices are now using electronic bulletin boards to advertise contracting possibilities. This means that all managers anywhere in the United States, regardless of the size and location of their business, can easily access information on what government business opportunities are available.

Pre-solicitation notices may also be mailed to business concerns at least 15 days prior to the issuance of the solicitation. In sealed bidding, the purpose of the pre-solicitation notice is to determine if there is an interest in receiving the IFB on the part of the recipient. Plans or drawings are not provided as part of any pre-solicitation notice. If it will be a negotiated procurement, either the pre-solicitation notice or a pre-solicitation conference may be used to identify potential contractors. They are also used to develop an interest and to explain complicated specifications. In a complex acquisition, the pre-solicitation notice may be used to request information on the firm's management, engineering, and production capabilities. Synopsizing in the CBD is still required prior to the issuance of any resulting solicitation.[162]

TYPES OF CONTRACT PRICING ARRANGEMENTS (CONTRACT TYPES)

As noted earlier, a primary function of the contract pricing arrangement is to motivate the contractor. The contract should be structured so that it rewards the contractor if it exceeds contractual expectations or penalizes it if it fails. There are two basic categories of pricing arrangements: fixed-price contracts and cost-reimbursement contracts. Figure 4-7, The Contract Risk Continuum, illustrates the range of the risk spectrum. At one end of the spectrum is the fixed-price contract, in which the contractor is totally accountable for performance costs and the percentage of profit or loss they will realize. Here the contractor assumes the total risk of the cost of its performance, no matter what actions the government takes that are within the original scope or intent of the contract. At the other end is the cost-reimbursement contract, in which the government assumes the risk. The contractor has minimal responsibility for performance cost, and the fee is fixed at a negotiated amount. (In government contracting, *fee* is the term for the amount paid to the contractor above allowable cost under a cost reimbursement contract.[163]) There is a large variety of contract types between these two extremes. These are variations of the two basic contract types, and each allocates the cost performance risk differently. In every contract negotiation, both the buyer and seller will try to promote their own interests by advocating favorable contract conditions.

The firm-fixed-price contract is the preferred and most commonly used contract type. Table 4-5, Contract Types Used in Federal Procurement, is a breakout of contract types used by the government in FY 1999.[164] It shows that the number of fixed-price actions exceeds the number of cost-reimbursement actions by a factor of five. The contract value of fixed-price contracts is 40 percent greater than the value of cost-reimbursement contracts. This is because fixed-price contracts fit the conditions prevalent in most routine purchases, which can clearly be described, and because there is a

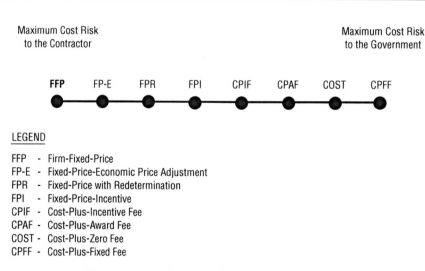

Figure 4-7 The Contract Risk Continuum

Table 4-5. Contract Types Used in Federal Procurement, 1999

Type of Contract	Actions		Value of Award	
	Number	*Percentage*	*Dollars (000)*	*Percentage*
Fixed price	384,154	79.8	99,231,602	56.1
Cost reimbursement	71,384	14.8	70,644,094	39.9
Time & material	19,557	4.1	5,659,808	3.2
Labor hours	6,238	1.3	1,294,757	0.8
Totals	481,333	100.0	176,830,261	100.0

minimum amount of uncertainty associated with the acquisition. Fixed-price contracts are also preferred by government buyers because they believe they force the contractor to be more efficient and because the opportunity for unreasonable profits is minimal.

As increases in technological content of government requirements have taught us, the traditional firm-fixed-price pricing arrangement has not fit every situation, and it has not prevented cost growth on many projects. This is because it has not always been possible for the government to prepare precise specifications and work statements prior to the award. Contractors, therefore, would not accept the risk. In addition, as part of the negotiation process both parties had different views concerning the appropriate contract type, and variations on the basic two types were developed to achieve a compromise.

We are entering an era calling for strategic alliances between the supplier and customer because of expected major shifts in contractual relationships. Buyer and supplier relationships will last for longer periods of time; there are expected to be fewer suppliers, especially of high-tech military requirements. Specialized investments in time and money can be high for both parties, and more firms will be interdependent. This makes joint strategic decisions necessary.[165] This environment calls for more flexible contract pricing arrangements. More flexibility in contract types becomes especially critical when:

- The effort is risky because of technical and other uncertainties, and some sharing of the risk between the government and the contractor is necessary
- The buyer desires nonstandard supplies or services, and a long-term period of performance is likely
- The proposed undertaking involves a large monetary investment, and there is a high degree of complexity in the required technical effort
- The immediate contract effort leads toward substantial follow-on contractual opportunities for which the buyer desires to seek competition

- The circumstances of the purchase are such that the buyer seeks performance cost data from the supplier
- The government's objective in entering into a contractual relationship includes the reduction of inventory, the simplification of ordering procedures, the reduction in the cost of repetitive purchasing processes, and other logistics goals.[166]

Acquisition policy states that the final decision regarding the contract type is an appropriate part of the negotiation process and should be determined at the same time an agreement on price/cost is reached.[167] This is because at the end of the proposal evaluation and contract negotiation process, the CO should have additional information upon which to base an opinion on the type of contract that would best motivate the contractor's performance.

The Firm-Price Group of Pricing Arrangements

The fixed-price group of contract pricing arrangements allocates the majority, if not all, of the performance risk to the contractor. However, from the contractor's point of view it provides the maximum incentive to perform efficiently, thereby rewarding the contractor with the highest profit potential. It also should impose fewer administrative requirements for the government. The criteria for using fixed-price contracts are that: (1) it is possible to describe accurately the quality and quantity of the work or service desired prior to the beginning of the contractual effort, (2) detailed specifications and statements of work can be prepared, and (3) a detailed bid package can then be provided to each prospective contractor so that each bids on the same specifications and each has an accurate understanding of the requirements. There is a high probability that both parties will be able to quantify an agreed-on price. The buyer-seller relationship after contract award is relatively straightforward, with each party working independently. There also will be a minimum of government intervention during contract performance.

Fixed-price contracts provide for a firm price or, in appropriate cases, an adjusted price. The contract ceiling price or target price can be adjusted only through exercise of contract clauses providing for equitable adjustment or other revisions to the contract price under stated circumstances, e.g., inflation.[168]

On the down side, the contractor may try to cut cost by reducing quality, thereby requiring the buyer to add staff to increase inspections of the contractor's work. There is also a potential for claims for work the contractor considers out of its scope, thereby increasing the government's administrative cost. The buyer also has little control over the quantity and skill level of the contractor's manpower. It is also more difficult for the buyer to change delivery schedules as the situation warrants. In addition, there is a temptation for the contractor to build in contingencies and add additional profit during the biding process. The contractor's startup investment is exposed to a loss if the contract is terminated for the convenience of the government.

The potential pricing arrangements that are available to the CO under the fixed-price group are: (1) firm-fixed-price contracts; (2) fixed-price-incentive contracts; (3) fixed-price-redeterminable contracts; (4) fixed-price contracts with a provision for an economic price adjustment; (5) fixed-price, level-of-effort term contracts; and (6) fixed-price-incentive contracts with multiple incentives.

The Firm-Fixed-Price (FFP) Contract: This is the standard on which all other types of pricing arrangements are compared. The price, including profit, is determined prior to awarding the contract. Figure 4-8, The FFP Arrangement, illustrates that under the fixed-price contract the government is obligated to pay the contractor the contract price regardless of the actual cost of performance, i.e., the 0/100 sharing arrangement. The only exception is if the cost is revised pursuant to the Changes clause in the contract. Without changes to the contract being made under provisions of

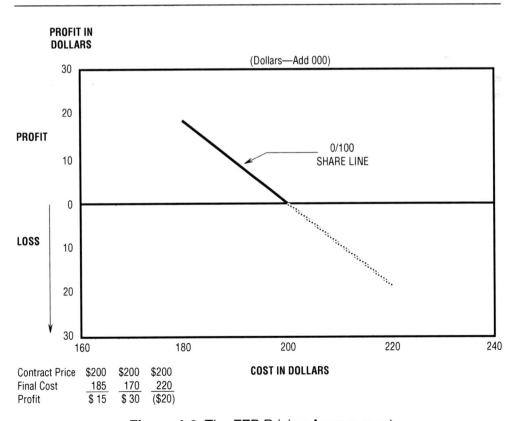

Figure 4-8 The FFP Pricing Arrangement

the Changes clause, mistakes made during performance are absorbed by the contractor and corrections are made at no additional cost. The contractor loses money when incurred costs exceed the pre-established price.

FFP contracts are not to be awarded for development programs unless a written determination can prove that the risk permits realistic pricing and the Under Secretary of Defense concurs.[169]

The Fixed-Price-Incentive (FPI) Contract: This type of contract is characterized by the inclusion of a sharing formula that establishes the final price. The important points of the FPI contract are that target cost, target price, ceiling price, and the sharing arrangement are established as part of the negotiated agreement. The pricing arrangement is based on the relationship between the total cost incurred and the total target cost. It also establishes sharing arrangements between the buyer and seller for all cost over- or underruns. The ceiling price limits the buyer's obligation regardless of the contractor's cost. The FPI contract is used when a fixed-price contract is not suitable because the government desires to have additional leverage on the contractor's management. This type can be used to protect the government from excessive profits when the contractor will not agree to an FFP contract at a price the government feels is appropriate for the cost performance risk.[170]

In structuring the performance incentive, the term *performance* refers not only to the performance of goods and services delivered under the contract, but also to the performance of the contractor. Performance that meets the minimum level the government will accept will warrant only the minimum profit. Performance that meets the stated targets will warrant the "target" profit. Performance that exceeds the targets should be rewarded by additional profit.

The Fixed-Price-Redeterminable (FPR) Contract: There are two types of FPR arrangements. The first provides for negotiation of prospective fixed prices to be paid in the future. This method leaves the determination of the final total price until the work has progressed to a point where both parties understand the cost of performance so that each can estimate the cost with a greater degree of accuracy and negotiate the final price. The contractor's books and accounts are thus subject to government audit. Often this method includes a series of two or more FPR arrangements negotiated at stated times during the period of performance. The FPR pricing arrangement should cover the longest period that it is possible to negotiate a fair and reasonable price. Subsequent periods should be at least 12 months long.[171] This method has been used primarily in procuring aircraft propulsion units when the nature of manufacture and the resulting methods of accounting for cost have lent themselves to periodic, plant-wide pricing on a prospective basis.[172]

The retroactive FPR is the other type of re-determinable pricing arrangement. It provides for adjusting contract price after performance has been completed. It is similar to an FPI contract in that a ceiling price is negotiated initially and actual, suited contract costs are used to revise the price. The significant difference is that there is no sharing formula written into the contract because the degree of cost responsibility is negotiated at the time of redetermination. This requires a subjective evaluation of how well the contractor performed overall after performance is completed. For this reason, the use of this arrangement is limited to small-dollar, short-term contracts for research and development.[173]

Fixed-Price Contract with a Provision for an Economic Price Adjustment: This type of fixed-price contract is designed to cope with economic uncertainties. To protect both parties, it provides for an upward or downward revision to the contract price when the contingencies specified in the contract occur. The contingency factors should be events that management cannot control. The FAR cites three types of adjustments: (1) adjustments based on established prices of specified items or the contract end item, (2) adjustments based on actual cost of labor or material during the period of contract performance, and (3) adjustments based on cost indexes of labor or material defined in the contract.[174] One reason for its use is to avoid contingency allowances being included in the contract pricing policy to reduce its risk.

Fixed-Price, Level-of-Effort Term (FILET) Contract: This contract type is used for investigation or study in a specific research and development area. It covers a limited period of time, and payment is based on the effort expended rather than on results.[175]

Fixed-Price-Incentive Contract with Multiple Incentives (FPI): Where the FPI contract uses cost as a single independent variable to determine the profit to be paid, the FPI contract includes several variables, such as cost and schedule. A multiple incentive contract is the most complex type to negotiate and administer because of the intricacy of the tradeoff decisions. It is an attempt to motivate the supplier to achieve maximum performance. It does require that the contractor submit its accounting records to government audit. Although it is not used very often because of its complexity, it can be useful in the purchase of the first or second production quantity of a newly developed item.[176]

The Cost-Reimbursement Group of Pricing Arrangements

The first large-scale use of cost-reimbursement contracts came during World War I, when over 200 builders, faced with the gigantic task of constructing new military camps and cantonments, met with the General Munitions Board in Washington, D.C. Both parties "...concluded the best way to get the job done would be on the basis of contracts allowing for payment of costs plus a percentage of cost as profit." This was because the normal peacetime form of contracting, the lump-sum or fixed-price contract, was not practical because it involved unknown cost, frequent changes in specifications, and other conditions of this type. "While the cost-plus principle overcame the disadvantages of the lump-sum contract, no one was blind to the inherent serious possibilities for waste and extravagance, and policies were soon introduced in order to minimize the cost. The Army was given the right to audit the contractor's expenditures. The contract type was soon changed to cost-plus-with-limited fee."[177]

Use of contracts within the cost-reimbursement group is based on two factors. First, the uncertainty associated with the nature of the work and length of the period of performance makes it impossible to estimate the cost without adding an amount for contingency. Second, a willingness on the part of the buyer to share the financial risk with the supplier makes it desirable.

A cost-reimbursement contract provides for payment of allowable cost incurred up to the amount prescribed in the contract. It establishes the total cost for the purpose of obligating funds and establishing a ceiling that the contractor may not exceed, except at its own risk, without approval of the CO.[178] This type of pricing arrangement places the majority of the risk related to the cost of performance, delays in performing the work, and nonperformance on the government rather than the contractor. However, the ultimate allocation of risk between the buyer and seller is determined by numerous possible terms and conditions, warranties, and incentives that may or may not be included in the contract.[179] Contractors are not contractually responsible for performing at the estimated cost level. However, the contractor is responsible for ensuring that the incurred costs are allowable and allocable.

An understanding of the criteria for determining when a cost is allowable is very important when performing cost analysis, fact finding, and evaluating invoices submitted by the contractor under cost-reimbursement contracts. Costs that are unallowable must be identified and excluded by the contractor from any billing, claim, or proposal. For a cost to be allowable it must pass the following tests:

- Test for reasonableness—An incurred cost is judged to be reasonable if, in its nature and amount, it does not exceed that which would be incurred by a prudent person in the conduct of competitive business.[180]
- Test for allocability—An incurred cost is judged to be allocable if it is incurred specifically for the contract, benefits both the contract and other work, can be distributed in a reasonable proportion to the benefits received, and is necessary to the overall operation of the business.[181]
- Test to determine if it conforms to the standards set by the Cost Accounting Standards Board, which are designed to achieve uniformity and consistency in measuring, assigning, and allocating cost to contracts.[182]

- Test to determine if it follows the General Accepted Accounting Principles (GAAP). The GAAP address the broad and general problems of accounting and are not always specific when it comes to giving guidance or establishing a standard way to handle or distribute a specific cost.[183]
- Test to determine if it conforms to the terms and conditions of the contract.
- Test to determine if it is covered as a "selected cost" that is addressed in the detailed guidance on the allowability of 52 categories of cost in FAR 31.205.[184]

The cost-reimbursement contract is best suited for an ill-defined effort or research and development project, where the cost estimates are so unreliable it is necessary for the buyer to assume the cost risk. In a cost-reimbursement contract the contractor is subject to an increased amount of supervision by the government because there is little or no incentive for the contractor to simplify the design, shorten the delivery time, or control cost after contract award. Some even feel that the cost-reimbursement contract goes so far as to make the contractor a de facto civil servant with the fiduciary responsibility to help the government complete the contract most expeditiously and efficiently, relying on increased supervisory responsibility of the government to do so.[185]

The major reason a cost-reimbursement contract is attractive is that it enables the government to obtain goods and services when there is a great deal of technical uncertainty or poorly defined specifications and statements of work. This has been especially true in the case of highly complex technical requirements. Other reasons for selecting cost-reimbursement contracts are: (1) work can begin without having a complete engineering package, (2) the design package can be developed outside the contractor's standard process, (3) the contractor is paid to favor quality over cost if a tradeoff between the two is necessary, (4) the contractor can more easily adjust schedules, and (5) the government has greater say over selection and location of contractor personnel. Under this type of pricing arrangement the cost risk associated with contract cancellation is borne by the government.

Disadvantages that should be considered prior to selecting from this contract group include the fact that the contractor has little incentive to keep cost at a minimum. Therefore, it has historically been the government's practice to manage the contractor's effort closely by having government employees perform contract administration tasks at the contractor's facilities. To be effective these government employees should have a high degree of training experience to ensure that the buyer only pays for labor, materials, and equipment actually used on the job and to determine that the items are needed for the job and that quantities are appropriate. Government employees also must expend effort determining if payments are made according to the terms and conditions of the contract. Cost-reimbursement contracts are not always awarded using competitive procedures. One criterion that is a prerequisite to a contractor being awarded a cost-reimbursement contract is that the contractor's accounting system must be able to segregate cost applicable to the contract.

Cost-Plus-Fixed-Fee (CPFF) Contracts: The CPFF contract is the standard cost-reimbursement contract and is the direct opposite of the FFP pricing arrangement. As illustrated in Figure 4-9, The CPFF Pricing Arrangement, the fee is fixed during negotiations at an amount above reimbursed cost. The fixed fee can only be changed if the negotiated work package is changed pursuant to the Changes clause in the contract. The contractor bears the risk that the fee is adequate. The allowability of cost is governed by the cost principles outlined in Part 31 of the FAR and specific terms of the contract.

A CPFF contract is most often used when performing research, exploration, and study work when the level of effort is unknown. It is also recommended for development and efforts for which it is not practicable to use a cost-plus-incentive contract.

There are two basic forms of CPFF contracts. The first is the *completion form*, in which the contractor is to complete and deliver a specified end

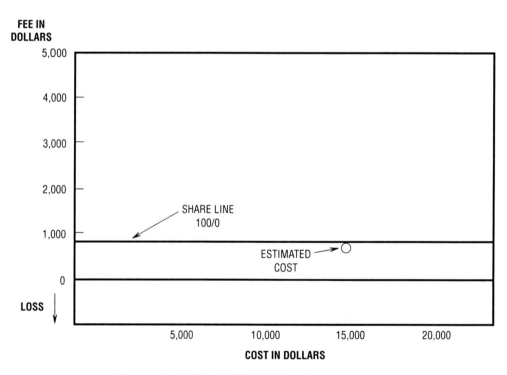

Figure 4-9 The CPFF Pricing Arrangement

product as a condition of payment of the entire fixed fee. The other form, which requires the contractor to devote a specific level of effort for a specified period of time, is referred to as a *level of effort* contract.

Cost-Plus-Percentage-of-Cost: Because there is no incentive for the contractor to work efficiently—in fact, one could argue that there is an incentive to work inefficiently—the use of a contract with a fee based on a percentage of incurred cost is prohibited by 10 U.S.C. § 2306(a) and 41 U.S.C. § 254(b).

Cost-Sharing Contract: This type of contract is used when it is clear the performing contractor will gain a commercial advantage from the work performed under the contract. It is not used often.[186]

Cost-Plus-Incentive-Fee (CPIF) Contract: This type of cost-reimbursement contract provides for the contractor's fee to be determined by a pre-established sharing arrangement. A cost-incentive formula that determines the fee is based on the relationship of total allowable cost to the total target cost. The significance of the cost-incentive formula is that the contractor's earned fee varies inversely with the amount of cost incurred as long as the actual cost incurred falls within the range of the sharing arrangement. Elements of the contract formula are: target cost, target fee, maximum fee, minimum fee, and the Range of Incentive Effectiveness (RIE). The contract is structured so that the contractor's fee might fall above or below the target amount, depending on performance. Figure 4-10, Key Elements of a Cost-Plus-Incentive-Fee Contract, is a graphic presentation of these elements and their relationship to each other.

- *Target cost* serves as the baseline for adjusting the contractor's target fee.
- *Target fee* is the amount of fee a contractor will receive if its total allowable cost is equal to the target cost.
- *Maximum fee* is the dollar amount negotiated at the inception of the CPIF contract as the maximum amount of fee a contractor is entitled to receive. This is also referred to as the *fee ceiling*.
- *Minimum fee* is the dollar amount negotiated at the inception of a CPIF contract as the minimum amount of fee the contractor is entitled to receive. This is also called the *fee floor*.
- The *sharing arrangement* is defined as the range of costs between the maximum fee and the minimum fee. It is the dollar range of possible cost outcomes under which the contractor has a monetary incentive to control costs through sound management. It is expressed in a ratio of government share/contractor share.

The CPIF contract differs from the FPI because a ceiling is not established at the time of contract award. Instead, limits are placed on the amount of increases or decreases allowed by the cost incentive formula, which is the ratio of the target fee to the maximum fee.

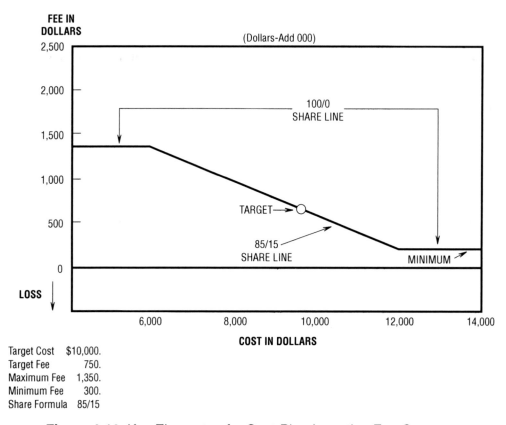

Figure 4-10 Key Elements of a Cost-Plus-Incentive Fee Contract

The Cost-Plus-Award-Fee (CPAF) Contract: This type of pricing arrangement provides a monetary base fee plus an additional fee based on a periodic subjective assessment of the contractor's performance. Because of the type of incentives used in this kind of contract, there is no quantitative formula. CPAF contracts are very effective when applied to services or where the mission is defined. They are also used when it is not possible to write specifications or when specifications and statements of work do not contain precise descriptions of the job the contractor is expected to perform.

The fee in a CPAF contract consists of two elements. First, the fixed fee amount is not affected by the contractor's performance. The fixed fee portion of the total fee is generally a low amount. Second is the award fee pool, which is the award portion that may be earned by the contractor in whole or in part. The amount earned depends on a periodic subjective appraisal of predetermined evaluation factors by the acquisition team. The contractor's performance in such areas as responsiveness, quality, timeliness, risk management, ingenuity, and cost management are examples of possible evaluation factors.

It is common for the government to change its evaluation criteria at designated milestones during the period of performance.

One of the major advantages to this type of contract is that it improves communications between the buyer and seller. This is because during the periodic evaluation of the contractor's performance, the government provides the contractor a detailed critique of its performance. Thus the contractor can improve its performance or convince the government that the evaluation is incorrect. A disadvantage to both parties is the substantial administrative effort needed to evaluate and process the award fee information. In addition, the fact that the evaluators are normally the government personnel who monitor the contractor performance may also cause the contractor to follow government direction and perform out-of-scope work without challenge.

Selecting the Type of Contract Pricing Arrangement

As part of the acquisition planning process, the CO must determine the most appropriate contract type that will be included in the solicitation. This decision has been compared to the game of golf, in which the location of the ball determines the type of club that should be used.[187] There is a "best" contract type for a given amount of risk. You don't want to over-club or under-club, and the CO should make sure the situation fits the contract type.

The type of contract pricing arrangement selected should be linked to the cost risk associated with the contractor's performance. Factors that FAR Part 16 lists as considerations in selecting the appropriate contract type pricing arrangement are outlined below.

- *Price competition*: The degree to which effective price competition produces realistic prices.
- *Price analysis*: The degree to which price analysis can provide a realistic pricing standard.
- *Cost analysis*: The degree to which the uncertainties involved in performance and their possible impact on costs can be evaluated so that the amount of cost responsibility that can be placed on the contractor can be negotiated.
- *Type and complexity of the requirement*: The uniqueness of the requirement. Often with complex, unique government requirements, there is a high probability of performance uncertainties or changes that make it extremely difficult to estimate performance in advance.
- *Urgency of the requirement*: If expedited delivery is a factor, the government may offer an incentive or assume a larger portion of the risk to meet the user's requirements.

- *Period of performance or length of production run*: In times of economic uncertainty, the length of the period of performance may place a high degree of cost risk on the contractor.
- *Contractor's technical capability and financial responsibility*: A factor that is determined through market research and record of past performance.
- *Concurrent contracts*: The impact of other contracts, and their pricing arrangements, that are being performed concurrently.
- *Extent and nature of proposed subcontracting*: If extensive subcontracting is involved, as in the case of a contractor that is a systems integrator, the proposed contract should reflect the actual risks to the prime contractor.
- *Acquisition history*: The product can be defined more clearly, the degree of risk diminishes, and economies are realized in the production process as the product is repeatedly acquired.[188]

The acquisition plan should define which of the two major types of contracting agreements will be most suitable for the acquisition. The government and its contractor counterparts will be affected by the conditions set up by the type of contract. For example, a cost-reimbursement contract requires the expenditure of much more effort performing the surveillance tasks of contract administration. Stanley N. Sherman, who conducted a series of interviews of key government and contractor personnel, concluded that the contract type "is not a major issue in most acquisitions, yet it remains crucial to the interests of the parties" (see Table 4-6). Sherman reported that "the decision on contract type is normally made prior to formal involvement of the potential contractor."[189]

As outlined above, FAR Part 16.104 offers a list of factors that can be applied when making the contract type decision. The negotiators have an unlimited set of choices of ways to allocate the risk between the parties within the umbrella of the fixed-price or cost-reimbursement contract. These include the selection of cost-sharing formulas, award fee concepts, multiple independent variables, ceiling levels, warrants, and risk-modifying clauses. From his interviews with government and contractor acquisition personnel, Sherman developed the criteria that can be considered to select the contract type.[190]

The initial consideration is the technical uncertainty related to performance requirements and the risk related to the state-of-the-art with respect to proven or unproven technology. Sources of technical uncertainty include such items as physical and material properties, systems integration, product testing, software and firmware design, and operational environment. As the required performance dictates advances beyond the current state of the art, the amount of uncertainty from knowns and unknowns

Table 4-6. Additional Considerations in Selecting Contract Pricing Arrangements, Contract Terms, and Conditions

Current State-of-the-Art as Determiner of Uncertainty
Current Stability of Technology
Nature and Clarity of the Contract Specifications
Program Cost, Schedule, and Performance Objectives
Level of Political Interest
Phase of the Product's Life Cycle
Duration of the Performance Period
Motivational Factors
Contractor's Past Performance
Legal and Policy Constraints
Production Potential
Complexity of Contract Management
Buyer Involvement During Performance
Administration Cost of Involvement
Use of Government-Furnished Property
Availability of Cost and Pricing Data
Adequacy of the Contractor's Accounting System

---

can be great, and the resulting risk increases. The higher the probability of failure, the greater the risk that should be assumed by the government.

The stability of technology refers to the existing state of knowledge in the field. Rapidly evolving technology leads to a moving baseline and a high potential for changes to the contract. This situation creates uncertainty related to the cost and delivery schedule and an increased risk of failure. Unstable technology equates to a high level of risk. Stable technology means minimum uncertainty and low risk.

The ability to define the government's requirements in precise terms has a direct effect on the potential offeror's ability to quantify the cost accurately. As the uncertainty resulting from unproven technology and incomplete technical knowledge increases, it becomes more difficult to delineate what is required, who is responsible for what part of the effort, and the criteria for the inspection and acceptance of work performed.

Each program has its cost, schedule, and performance and supportability objectives. Each of these in turn influences the type of contract selected. If the objective is to control cost, a fixed-price type of contract is most appropriate. This act may restrain the level of technological achievement, impair meeting the delivery schedule, or reduce supportability rate. Consequently, an alternative contract type that places more emphasis on the other factors can be used. For example, more weight can be placed on performance through a CPAF contract, level of effort, or risk-modifying clauses.

The greater the interest in the program by the legislative branch or other high-level governmental decision makers, the greater will be the requirement to provide them technical and financial data. Top-level involvement often leads to disagreements over program plans and the qualitative or quantitative requirements. This practice threatens program stability and increases the probability of contract changes. It also means that the selection of the contract type may be the subject of controversy. In these situations fixed-price contracts are often favored over the cost-reimbursement type. Incentives can also be included as terms and conditions to compensate the contractor for frequent reporting requirements and program instability.

Every project goes through an acquisition process. For the purpose of complying with applicable laws, the DoD revised its acquisition process in DoD Instruction 5000.1, issued on January 2, 2001. DoDI 5000.2, which implements an Evolutionary Acquisition strategy, establishes the following milestone events as the new acquisition process and management structure. The DoD Acquisition Management Framework is defined as follows: "Milestone A will serve as Milestone O; Program Initiation, when it occurs at or during Component Advanced Development Milestone A, will serve as Milestone I. Milestone B will serve as Milestone II. Milestone C will serve as the Low-Rate Initial Production Decision Point. Full-Rate Production Decision Review will serve as Milestone III. In addition, Systems Development and Demonstration will serve as Engineering and Manufacturing Development."[191] (Programs planned in accordance with the 1996 versions of DoD Directive 5000.1 and 5000.2R are to continue to be executed in accordance with approved program documentation.[192]

Figure 4-11, Technical Unknowns Related to the Life Cycle of a Product, illustrates the relationship of technical knowledge of a product to the technical known/unknowns and unknown/unknowns during the milestones established by DoD in the 5000 Model (Acquisition Management Framework) described above. There are a significantly greater number of unknowns during Concept and Technical Development than when the product is being produced and fielded. Over the life cycle of every product there is technical uncertainty in the form of what is known and unknown. The uncertainty of the outcome of future events can further be categorized as originating from known questions as well as the unknowns that arise during development. The latter is referred to as unknown/unknowns. For example, government-furnished equipment (GFE) that needs to be supplied and integrated into the product may be technically compatible, or integration may result in the discovery of a technical incompatibility that affects interoperability. In addition, the GFE may require repairs and upgrade before it is suitable for integration. All these questions represent risk that needs to be addressed in the Risk Handling Plan.

Figure 4-12, Contract Selection as Related to the Life Cycle of the Product, shows the relationship of the life cycle of the product to the type of

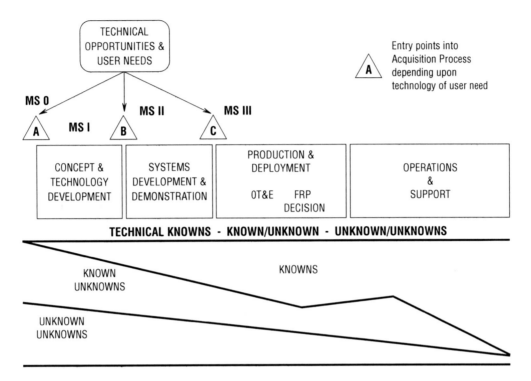

Figure 4-11 Technical Unknowns Related to the Life Cycle of a Product[193]

contract and allocation of risk. Technical unknowns associated with the product decrease as it progresses through the life cycle. In addition, competing suppliers may come on the scene. Consequently, contractors are more willing to accept a larger portion of risk.

Sherman's interviews with government concluded that the types of contracts most frequently selected at the key stages of the acquisition program are:

- Conceptual Phase—Fixed-price because this effort is a conceptual design study as to how to meet the needs of the mission. There is limited risk, and contractors often make the business decisions to participate in order to be ready for the validation phase.
- Validation Phase—Cost-reimbursement contracts with some sort of incentive provision to encourage cost reduction are the most often-used contract types.
- Full-scale Development—Cost-reimbursement contract that identifies the incentives a contractor can earn for superior performance is the preferred method in areas where performance can be measured, such as cost. Cost-Plus-Award-Fee contracts are used because they permit

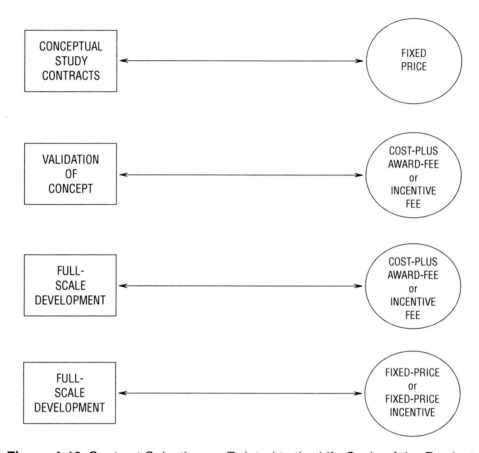

Figure 4-12 Contract Selection as Related to the Life Cycle of the Product

the buyer to highlight such areas as program management, planning, and customer service, where performance evaluations are subjective in nature.

• Production Phase—A fixed-price contract is judged to be most appropriate during this phase. Award fee provisions are included when the government feels identifying areas of importance in order to stimulate the contractor's performance is worth the administrative burden of an award fee contract.[194]

Risk is also prevalent when the period of performance is lengthy. Known/unknowns are are: (1) possible contract termination for convenience of the government; (2) inflation, especially in future years; (3) cuts in funding; and (4) potential liability for warranties as the number of deliveries increases. Fixed-price-incentive or fixed-price with an economic price adjustment clause are two types of contracts that share these risks.

As we have seen earlier, one of the primary functions of a contract is to provide a performance incentive for the contractor. The opportunity to earn a profit is the obvious incentive.

The award-fee report card is a powerful motivational tool that makes the cost-plus-award-fee contract an attractive contract type if contractor motivation is important. The cost-sharing provisions of the value-engineering clause also provide the contractor an opportunity to earn additional profit. Noncontractual motivational factors include an opportunity for follow-on contracts, development of a technical capability that makes the contractor more competitive, and a chance to earn a record of positive performance.

The contractor's past performance record is a key consideration when selecting the appropriate contract type. The greater the procurement risk because the requirement is not explicit or because development work is required, the more past performance considerations may play a dominant role in the source selection process.[195] A contractor's record of past performance also plays a role in the selection of the ultimate type of contract pricing arrangement. The CO may select a cost-plus-fixed-fee contract for a contractor with a proven track record because additional motivation is not required and the government would avoid the increased administrative cost of a cost-plus-award-fee contract. On the other hand, if the contractor has an unproven performance history, the additional administrative cost of the cost-plus-award-fee contract might be worthwhile.

Legal and policy constraints place limits on the CO's ability to craft certain types of contract pricing arrangements. The Anti-Deficiency Act, which prohibits expenditures or contract obligations in excess of the actual appropriation of funds, does not prohibit conditional contracts in which the government's liability is contingent on future appropriations. The practice of annual appropriations also means that the government cannot benefit from long interrupted production runs commonplace in the private sector. Therefore, government must also demonstrate that long-term, fixed-price options do not hinder competition. (In the private sector long-term production runs enable a contractor to spread start-up costs over more work.) The uncertainty that additional funding will be available when needed places added business risk on contractors. The policy that promotes "full and open competition," which is flowed down to subcontractors, is a constraint against long-term contractual agreements. The government contractor also faces the uncertainty of program termination for the convenience of the government, which prevents the contractor from receiving damages for lost potential profits. Limitations, for example, that the contractor's accounting system be capable of segregating cost applicable to a cost-reimbursement contract, restrict the use of that type of contract. Use of any contractual arrangement whereby the contract assures itself of greater fees by incurring additional cost will be held illegal.[196]

Statutory limitations are imposed on the amount of fixed fee a CO can negotiate. For experimental, developmental, or research work, the fee cannot exceed 15 percent of the contractor's estimated cost excluding fee. For architect-engineer services for public works or utilities, the cap on the amount of fixed fee is 6 percent. The statutory limit on all other cost-plus-fixed-fee contracts is 10 percent.[197]

In the 1980s many defense contractors accepted FFP research and development (R&D) contracts, feeling that if they did so there was a high probability they would be awarded the follow-on production contract. This type of pricing arrangement ignored the nature of the engineering development process and placed the risk of cost growth directly on the contractor. Consequently, many contractors suffered financial losses on these programs, causing the DoD to change its policy. Current DoD policy recognizes that there are several categories of R&D contracts, i.e., research, exploratory development, advanced development, engineering development, and operational systems development. Therefore, the contract type must fit the work required rather than the classification of the overall program. In the DoD, COs are instructed to use fixed-price type contracts when risk has been reduced to the extent that realistic pricing can occur, e.g., when a program has reached the final stages of development and technical risks are minimal.[198]

The complexity of the contractor's management task is not determined entirely by the nature of the technology, the duration of the contract, and the magnitude of the program. The number of different government agencies involved in the acquisition and magnitude of the subcontractor effort also determines the complexity of the contractor's management task. Acquisition management today requires open and continuous communication with all members of the acquisition team. Project status and required actions must be reported to all levels of management, including those between subcontractors and major primes/major team contractors, between major primes/major team contractors and government program offices, and between program offices and their leadership. A structured approach to communicating in both verbal and written form is vital to the success of the acquisition. The complexity of the management task is also driven by the characteristics and criticality of goods or services being supplied by subcontractors and vendors. For the past few years, at least 50 percent of the contract value could be subcontracted to others. Today the trend is toward the formation of longer-term strategic alliances between corporations and their suppliers.[199] Prime contractors are responsible for the performance of their subcontractors. The right of the government to deal directly with subcontractors is limited because it is not a party to the contractual agreement. (In legal terms it is said that there is no privity of contract.) Consequently, how well prime contractors manage their subcontractors has become more and more significant.

After contract award, the nature of the interrelationship between government and contractor representatives on the acquisition team is directly determined by the type of contract. An important matter to consider when selecting the type of contract is the desired roles of the two parties. Fixed-price contracts or contracts with tight ceilings and steep incentive slopes place management responsibility directly on the contractor while restricting involvement by government personnel in the contractor's decision process. On the other hand, a cost-plus-fixed-fee contract increases the participation by government personnel in day-to-day decisions while reducing the independence of the contractor's management.[200] Often government officials feel controls through government surveillance are necessary because fixed-price contracts were written for programs in which the element of uncertainty was too high.[201] The key question that should be answered is how much government involvement in the day-to-day workings of the contractor in this acquisition is necessary. The answer relates to the amount of uncertainty associated with the effort and the direction the leadership of the acquisition team wishes to take. These two elements can be mutually exclusive.

The administrative cost associated with the different types of contracts also plays a part in the selection of the type of contract used. The firm-fixed-price contract requires the least amount of administrative cost because a minimum amount of oversight is required. In contrast, cost-reimbursement contracts require cost and technical reviews as well as audits to determine the allowability of the cost incurred. When making the decision as to which type of contract will best serve the acquisition, the CO must determine if the government has the capability to perform the oversight tasks at the appropriate locations.

The use of government-furnished property (GFP) and government-furnished equipment (GFE) increases the contractor's risk of possible delays in receipt of the GFP/GFE and the possible need to repair or modify the items furnished. Availability and adequacy of government-furnished information (GFI) is also a concern. The contract may insist that appropriate special provisions place the responsibility on the government to meet the delivery schedule and ensure that the items furnished by the government are appropriate, accurate, and usable.

When the government requires detailed information on performance costs, the contract type that permits the government to audit contractor cost during performance must be selected. Firm-fixed-price contracts only permit the government to audit for the purpose of verifying cost or pricing data at the time of negotiation. Earned-value cost and management reporting are used primarily on cost-reimbursement contracts.

A contractor performing work under a cost-reimbursement contract must have a cost accounting system that meets government needs. This system must have the capability of recording and accumulating costs by contract so the cost specifically incurred for government business is segregated from the commercial work. Because of the requirement to audit cost-reimbursement contracts, the contractor's accounting system must also record direct transactions so they can be identified to a specific government contract. When allocating indirect cost to government contracts, the specific rules set out in the Cost Accounting Standards (CAS) apply to most contracts. (The most notable exceptions are contracts under $500,000 and designated small businesses.[202]) "A contractor's accounting system must provide: (1) traceability of every transaction, from its origin to its final posting in the books of account, including ledger summarizing cost by contracts; (2) that every posting, including ledger summarizing contract cost, be susceptible to breakdown into identifiable transactions; and (3) adequate documentation (e.g., time cards, vendor's invoices) is available and accessible to support the accuracy and validity of individual transaction."[203]

CONTRACT TYPES FOR THE 21st CENTURY

In 1993 the Acquisition Law Advisory Panel reported to Congress that the "many government requirements would be unnecessarily delayed unless agencies have the clear flexibility to enter into delivery order contracts for goods and task order contracts for services where detailed requirements, definite dollar value, and the timing of work are left to individual orders issued as needs arise during the life of the contract." This led to Congress codifying the use of task and delivery-order contracting in the Federal Acquisition Streamlining Act (FASA) in 1994. Government agencies are now able to continue competition while avoiding the delays and work associated with conducting new procurements by using indefinite-delivery and umbrella contracts, which FASA refers to as "delivery order" and "task order" contracts.[204]

A task order contract is a contract for services that does not procure or specify a firm quantity. It provides for the issuance of orders for performing tasks during the period of the contract. Like delivery order contracts, a task order contract must include: (1) the period of the contract, including options; (2) maximum quantity or dollar value of services that may be procured; and (3) a statement of work that reasonably describes the general scope, nature, complexity, and purpose of the services to be procured under the contract. Policy also encourages the award of these orders be issued under multiple award contracts. Failure to receive "fair" consideration is not subject to protest but may be referred to the agency ombudsman.[205]

Delivery orders are orders for supplies or services placed against an established contract or with government sources of supply. A delivery order contract does not procure or specify a firm quantity of supplies, other than minimum or maximum quantity, and provides for the issuance of orders for the delivery of supplies during the period of the contract. These contracts must state: (1) the period of performance, (2) maximum quantity or dollar value for the supplies being procured, and (3) a statement of work that reasonably describes the scope, nature, complexity, and purposes of the supplies being procured. To enhance competition, directives require that delivery order contracts be issued to multiple contractors whenever practicable. Delivery order contracts are generally issued as indefinite-quantity contracts.[206]

As noted earlier, the DoD has established the goal of having a paperless contracting infrastructure. One of the major advantages of automating the process using EDI is that electronic forms can be in multiple places at the same time rather than only one place at a time, as is the case with paper forms. The infrastructure of the acquisition system must adapt to EDI. Figure 4-13, A Distributive Electronic Order Processing System, depicts how a purchase order can be submitted electronically and digital signatures used to speed up the administrative portion of procurement lead time and improve productivity.[207] (Note that approval of the purchase order and the resultant invoice occur on electronic forms that are available to all concurrently.) Selection of the most appropriate contract type that will enable the acquisition process to be conducted electronically is vital to achieving the acquisition objectives.

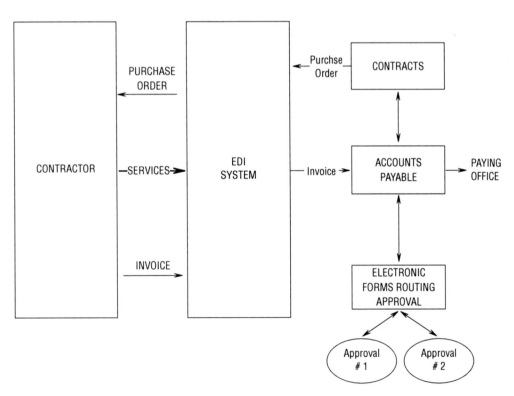

Figure 4-13 A Distributive Electronic Order Processing System

Indefinite-Delivery Contracts

An indefinite-delivery contract is defined as a type of contract in which the time of delivery is unspecified in the original contract but is established by the CO during the period of performance.[208] Having a delivery or task-order contract in place permits the buying agency to satisfy its requirements without issuing separate contracts with a narrower scope of work. Indefinite-delivery contracts can be used rather than individual purchase contracts when the government wishes to obtain a contractual commitment for suppliers of goods and services but the buyer is not able to forecast quantities and delivery dates precisely.

As Figure 4-13 illustrates, this method of procurement is especially appropriate in today's e-commerce environment because it is flexible and avoids repetitive individual contractual transactions. By using this type of contract, the government can maintain inventories at minimum levels because reduced administrative lead times enable inventories to be replenished faster and cheaper. It encourages longer-term relationships with vendors and is an appropriate contracting method for replenishing inventories using paperless computer-to-computer exchange.

When using the indefinite-delivery contract method, the government is obligated to purchase a stated minimum quantity, and the contract terms and conditions define a fixed period of time during which deliveries will be scheduled. The contract also limits the contractor's obligation by establishing a maximum value beyond which the contractor is not liable to deliver.[209] Cost and pricing arrangements may be FFP, cost-reimbursement, time-and-material, labor-hour, or a combination thereof.[210]

One of the most significant factors in an indefinite-delivery contract is that the solicitation provides a general statement of work, specifications, or description. It is also possible to make multiple awards from the same solicitation for the same or similar supplies or services. To ensure that potential offerors can make a decision on responding to the RFP, the ground rules for solicitation and contract shall:

- Specify the period of the contract, including the number of options and the period for which the options may be extended, usually limited to three years, including options
- Specify the total minimum and maximum quantity of supplies and services to be acquired
- Include a statement that reasonably describes the scope, nature, complexity, and purpose of the goods or services
- Notify the prospective offeror if multiple awards may be made.[211]

The FAR lists three types of indefinite-delivery contracts: (1) definite-quantity contracts, (2) requirements contracts, and (3) indefinite-quantity contracts.[212]

Definite-quantity contracts permit the buyer the opportunity to order supplies or services after contract award when the quantities and delivery schedules come together. The definite-quantity contract provides for delivery of a definite quantity of specific supplies or services for a fixed period, with deliveries to be scheduled at designated locations upon order. It provides the government a means to maintain minimum inventories and to direct shipments to the ultimate user. The FAR states that this method is most applicable when: (1) a definite quantity of supplies or services can be determined in advance, and (2) the supplies and services are regularly available or will be available after a short period of time.[213]

Requirements contracts can be used to fill all of a procurement activity's needs from a single supplier during a specified contract period. The key is that the government has a legal obligation to order all of its needs rather than fixed quantities of work, as in the case of the indefinite-quantity contract. This form is also used when it is impossible, prior to contract award, to quantify precisely the total requirements during a designated period of time. Deliveries are scheduled as orders are placed with the contractor. Funds are also obligated with each delivery order. Requirements contracts are most efficient in situations in which quantities are large and the suppliers are motivated to maintain optimum inventory levels. This method permits the buyer to eliminate individual purchase orders and minimize inventories. It can be done through continuous inventory replenishment using direct computer-to-computer exchange of daily usage data, shipping information, submission of invoices, and payments.

The buyer must guard against unbalanced bidding when using this method. This is when the supplier bids higher than it normally would on some line items and lower on others than if it were bidding in a competitive environment on each line item individually. In this situation the contractor is gambling that it is able to estimate more accurately the user's requirements on all line items over the designated period than is the government. Safeguards that can be used against unbalanced bidding include requiring bidders to bid a single discount against a schedule of unit prices included in the solicitation and government audit of previous prices.[214]

Indefinite quantity contracts are used when: (1) the government cannot determine the precise quantities of supplies or services, above the minimum, that will be required during the contracting period; (2) it is inadvisable for the government to commit to the maximum quantity; and (3) the goods and services are commercial products or commercial-type products that have been modified to meet some government-peculiar requirement. To be binding on the contractor, a definite-quantity contract must be for a "meaningful" minimum quantity that is more than the "normal" amount of an individual order.[215] The CO may place orders when it is most advantageous to the government, as long as they are received within the time specified in the contract. Indefinite-delivery contracts may be used for commercial items, where the prices are established based on a firm-fixed-price or fixed-price with economic price adjustment. (The use of any other contract type to acquire commercial items is prohibited.[216]) Funds for other than the stated minimum quantity are obligated by each delivery order, not by the contract itself.[217] This type of contract is to be used when a recurring need is anticipated and the government is unable to estimate its requirements precisely, above a specified minimum level, during the contract period. Another prerequisite is that it is not advisable to commit to more than the minimum quantity.[218]

Modular Contracting

In July 1996 Executive Order 13011 was issued, requiring: "where appropriate...(agencies are to) structure major information system investments into manageable projects as narrow in scope and brief duration as practicable...to reduce risk, promote flexibility and interoperability, increase accountability, and better correlate mission need with current technology and market conditions."[219] This action was taken to permit the use of modular contracting during the system development and demonstrations as well as in the information technology area in order to reduce the risk exposure of the government.

Evolutionary acquisition and the building block strategy, advocated in DoD 5000.1, 5000.2, and 5000.2R, deal with the realities of systems development and the information technology environment, where performance advances occur rapidly. Historically, the purchase of large-scale information systems has been fraught with the risk inherent in the "grand design mode" that has been traditionally followed when developing information systems. Because of the rapid change in computing power and communications technology, the acquisition of large information systems has often resulted in less-than-advertised capabilities, cost growth, delivery delays, and even the delivery of outdated systems.

For the purpose of acquiring information technology, a module is defined as an economically and programmatically separable segment that has a substantial programmatic use, even if no additional segments are acquired.[220]

Breaking the acquisition into increments, i.e., modules, the government benefits by:

- Having easier increments for managing than a comprehensive information system
- Increasing the likelihood of achieving workable solutions by addressing complex technology issues incrementally
- Testing and delivering discrete increments of the information system that are not dependent on subsequent increments to perform its principle functions

- Providing the opportunity for subsequent increments of the acquisition to benefit from any evolution in technology or needs that occur during the conduct of earlier increments.[221]

Modular contracting is accomplished when an "agency's need for a system is satisfied in successive acquisitions of interoperable increments. Each increment complies with common or commercially accepted standards applicable to information technology so that the increments are compatible with other increments of information technology comprising the system." Under the modular approach, modules are incrementally awarded and managed rather than having a contractor price and managing the entire effort concurrently. The three contracting methods that can be used are: (1) indefinite-delivery/indefinite-quantity contracts, (2) single contracts with options, and (3) successive competitive contracts.[222]

Although by using modular contracting, the cost, schedule, and performance risk inherent in the traditional all-inclusive method is addressed, the risk associated with the integration of the modules is introduced. This can be even more significant if different contractors are responsible for developing different modules.

Basic Agreements, Basic Ordering Agreements, and Blanket Purchase Agreements

Basic agreements, basic ordering agreements, and blanket purchase orders are written understandings between the government and a contractor used to expedite the procurement process when anticipated needs for specific items, quantities, and prices are not known. Simplified Acquisition Procedures contained in FAR 13.3 apply to these acquisition methods. These agreements are useful when there is a repetitive need for small quantities of supplies and services. Although agreements are not contracts until exercised, they: (1) contain renegotiated contract clauses that would apply to future purchases and (2) contemplate separate future contracts that will incorporate these pre-negotiated clauses. These orders can result in economies in ordering parts for equipment by reducing administrative purchasing agreements. As in the case of the indefinite-quantity method of contracting, agreements can be used to facilitate purchases via e-commerce.

A Basic Agreement (BA) can be used with negotiated fixed-price or cost-reimbursement contracts. It should be used when a substantial number of separate contracts may be awarded to a single contractor during a particular period and significant recurring negotiation problems have been experienced with the contractor. One of the provisions of the agreement is that either party can discontinue it on 30 days' written notice. BAs are also to be reviewed and modified, as necessary, to conform to the requirements of the FAR.[223]

Each contract incorporating a BA shall include a scope of work and price, delivery, and other terms and conditions. BAs shall not: (1) cite appropriations or obligate funds, (2) state or imply an agreement by the government to place future contracts or orders with the contractor, and (3) be used to restrict competition.

A Basic Ordering Agreement (BOA), like a BA, contains terms and clauses that will apply to future contracts between the government and a specific contractor. It also contains: (1) a description of the supplies or services to be provided; (2) delivery terms and conditions or specifications regarding how they will be determined, such as the point at which each order becomes a binding contract; and (3) a statement of the method for pricing, issuing, and delivering future orders under the BOA. Each BOA needs to be reviewed annually to ensure that it conforms to the FAR. Before issuing an order under a BOA, the CO must obtain competition and ensure that the agreement does not prejudice other offerors. Prices must be established prior to the contractor being authorized to begin work on an order unless a ceiling limiting the government's liability is established.[224]

Blanket Purchase Agreements (BPA) are also designed to reduce administrative costs and simplify acquisitions by eliminating the need to prepare, negotiate, and award individual purchase contracts. The BPA is an efficient method of purchasing such items as hardware, electrical supplies, and office supplies. It establishes "charge accounts" with qualified firms where individual purchases will probably be made during a given period of time. BPAs may also be established with Federal Supply Schedule contractors.

BPAs must contain the following:

- Description of the agreement in general terms, including method of request and period of the agreement
- Statement of the limitations of the government's obligation
- Statement that the prices to the government shall be low or lower than those charged to the supplier's most favored customer
- Statement specifying the dollar limitation of each individual purchase
- List of individuals authorized to purchase under the BPA
- Description of the information to be included on each delivery ticket
- Description of billing procedures. (Common billing procedures used under a BPA include summary monthly invoice, itemized monthly invoice, and individual invoice for each delivery.)[225]

The existence of a BPA does not justify a sole source purchase, and COs are encouraged to place BPAs concurrently with more than one supplier. The dollar value of individual purchases under a BPA cannot exceed the dollar limitation established for simplified acquisitions.[226]

The Federal Supply Schedule Program

The Federal Supply Schedule (FSS) program is fundamentally a cooperative purchasing agreement managed by the General Services Administration (GSA). The basis of the cooperative purchasing concept is simple. By purchasing in bulk, the government purchasing entity has the leverage to negotiate quantity discounts that translate to a lower per-unit cost, which is then passed on to the government user. Cooperative purchasing is used in the commercial sector by such corporations as ACE Hardware, Dunkin' Donuts, Kentucky Fried Chicken, and Popeye's Chicken and Biscuits.[227] It must be pointed out that FSS has been used by federal government organizations, government agencies, and even some contractors under cost-reimbursement contracts for the past 30 years as one of their sources for commonly used supplies and services.

GSA establishes indefinite delivery or requirements contracts with commercial firms to provide these supplies and services for a stated period of time. The GSA provides potential users the information necessary for placing delivery orders with contractors on the schedule by issuing Federal Supply Schedule Catalogs. (The DoD manages a similar contracting arrangement for military items.[228])

The ordering office need not synopsize the requirement, seek further competition, make a determination of fair and reasonable pricing, nor consider small business when placing orders against FSS. By placing an order against the schedule under the provisions of FAR 8.4, the ordering office has also concluded that the order also represents the best value and results in the lowest overall cost alternative (considering price, special features, administrative cost, etc.) to meet the government's needs. Order can also be placed with any FSS contractor at or below the micro-purchase threshold. Orders exceeding the micro-purchase threshold but not exceeding the maximum order threshold also can be placed with the schedule contractor after determining that the supply or service represents the best value. With orders exceeding the maximum order threshold, the ordering office should seek a price reduction before placing the order. If a further price reduction is not offered, the order may still be placed if determined appropriate.[229]

The ordering office is responsible for order placement, inspection and acceptance, and handling of delinquent performance. The latter includes termination of individual orders for default or convenience of the government in accordance with Part 49 of the FAR. Unresolved disputes are to be referred to the schedule contracting office for resolution under the Disputes clause of the contract.[230]

An outgrowth of the National Partnership for Reinventing Government was the promotion of cooperative purchasing that would benefit not only the federal government but state governments as well. Although the FASA expanded the use of the GSA to departments, agencies, or political subdivisions of the state, the concept has not been fully supported by Congress, which repealed the cooperative purchasing authority of FASA in Public Law 105-61 § 413,11.Sat.1272 (1998).

Congress without doubt was influenced by a study by the General Accounting Office (GAO), which cited 16 factors that inhibited expected benefits. Four of these shortcomings were: (1) state or local laws or ordinances, (2) the unavailability of certain items or products through the FSS program, (3) the availability of lower prices or better terms and conditions on items obtained from other sources, and (4) the likelihood that non-federal governments would need to maintain the procurement capability using their supply sources for items they do not purchase using FSS schedules.[231]

Time-and-Materials and Labor-Hour Contracts

The Time-and-Material (T&M) method of contracting is used to acquire supplies and services on the basis of: (1) direct labor hours at specified fixed hourly rates that include wages, overhead, general and administrative expenses, and profit; and (2) material at cost, including indirect material handling cost, if appropriate. This method of contracting is to be used only when it is not possible to estimate accurately the extent or duration of the effort involved or to anticipate costs with a reasonable degree of confidence. A T&M contract provides no profit incentive for the contractor to control cost or efficiently utilize its work force. Consequently, before initiating a T&M contract, the CO must make a determination that no other method of contracting is suitable and establish a ceiling price at which the contractor will assume the risk.[232]

The labor-hour method of contracting is a variation of a T&M contract. As the name implies, the contractor does not supply material. As in the case of the T&M contract, this method of contracting is to be used only when it is not possible to estimate accurately the extent or duration of the effort involved or to anticipate costs with a reasonable degree of confidence. Contract terms provide no profit incentive for the contractor to control cost or efficiently utilize its work force. Therefore, prior to initiating a labor-hour contract, the CO must determine that no other method of contracting is suitable and establish a ceiling price where the contractor assumes the risk if the cost exceeds the ceiling.[233]

Letter Contracts

A letter contract is a written preliminary instrument authorizing a contractor to commence work under its conditions immediately pending the definition of a pricing arrangement for the work performed. Because of the potential liability the government assumes under this method, use of letter contracts is discouraged. The situation must be such that a definitive contract cannot be negotiated in sufficient time to meet the requirement date and government interests "demand" that the work start immediately.

A letter contract may not be used unless the head of the contracting activity determines that no other contracting instrument is suitable. Other conditions placed on the use of letter contracts include the requirement to specify the following in the letter authorizing the contractor to begin work:

- The maximum liability of the government, which is not to exceed 50 percent of the estimated cost of the definitive contract unless approved in advance by the official authorizing the letter contract
- The definitive schedule, including the date the contractor's price proposal is to be submitted, date negotiations will begin, and the target date for completing defining
- The government cannot be committed to a definitive contract in excess of the funds available at the time the letter contract is executed
- The letter contract cannot be amended unless the requirement is inseparable from the existing letter contract. The limitations that apply to the initial written instrument also apply as a new letter contract.[234]

CONCLUSION

The solicitation is more than a formal invitation for a bid or proposal. It represents the genesis of what will become the documented agreement between the parties, i.e., the contract that defines the scope of work and compensation. Thoughtful planning preparation of the solicitation and subsequent adjustments to include decisions reached during discussions and negotiations in the later phases of the acquisition process are important to attainment of the acquisition objective. The final contract represents the common language across the acquisition team. The buyer must not lose sight of the fact that the intended purpose of a contract is to communicate clearly the requirements and obligations of the parties. A document that withstands litigation is a subordinate goal.

In Chapter 5 we will turn our review of the acquisition process to the preparation of the contractor's response to the government solicitation.

NOTES

[1]Jacobs, Daniel M. 1997. Wake Up! It's Time to Get Back to the Basics in Program/Contract Startup. *Contract Management* (July): 20.

[2]Nash, Ralph C., Jr., Steven L. Schooner, and Karen R. O'Brien. 1998. *The Government Contracts Reference Book*, 2d ed. Washington D.C.: The George Washington University Law School, 481.

[3]Garrett, Gregory A. 1997. *World-Class Contracting: 100+ Best Practices for Building Successful Business Relationships*. Arlington, VA: ESI International, 8.

[4]Wilson, Hugh H. 1996. RFPs—Let's Make Them Better. *Contract Management* (September): 18.

[5]Talbot, Terry R. 1997. Source Selection After Acquisition Reform: How Does It Stack Up Now? *Contract Management* (December): 44.

[6]Nash, Jr., Schooner, and O'Brien, 3.

[7]Schaber, Gordon D., and Claude D. Rohwer. 1990. *Contracts in a Nut Shell.* St. Paul, MN: West Publishing Co., 9.

[8]FAR 13.004(a).

[9]Nash, Jr., Schooner, and O'Brien, 442.

[10]Cibinic, John, Jr., and Ralph C. Nash, Jr. 1982. *Formation of Government Contracts.* Washington D.C.: Government Contracts Program, George Washington University, 77.

[11]Nash, Jr., Schooner, and O'Brien, 121.

[12]Cibinic, Jr., and Nash, Jr., *Formation of Government Contracts,* 79.

[13]Sherman, Stanley N. 1991. *Government Procurement Management.* Germantown, PA: Wordcrafters, 321.

[14]FAR 14.201-1.

[15]UCC § 2-201.

[16]Cibinic, Jr., and Nash, Jr., *Formation of Government Contracts,* 96.

[17]Final Edition. 2000. *Contract Management* (September): 31.

[18]Cibinic, John, Jr., and Ralph C. Nash, Jr. 1985. *Administration of Government Contracts,* 2 ed. Washington, D.C.: George Washington University, 103.

[19]Ghosh, Anup K. 1998. *E-Commerce Security: Weak Links, Best Defenses.* New York: John Wiley & Sons, Inc., 114.

[20]Williams, Robert F. 1987. Contract Risk Sharing. *Contract Management* (June): 9.

[21]Fox, J. Ronald. 1974. *Arming of America.* Cambridge, MA: Harvard University Press, 241.

[22]Sherman, 313.

[23]Fisher, Roger, and William Ury. 1983. *Getting to Yes: Negotiating Agreement Without Giving In.* New York: Penguin Books, 100.

[24]Fox, 241.

[25]FAR 52.232-1.

[26]FAR 52.232-1 (a) and (b).

[27]Sherman, 219.

[28]FAR 32.102 (b).

[29]Sherman, 219.

[30]FAR 32.702.

[31]FAR 32.703-1.

[32]Rider, Melissa, Kenneth D. Broody, David B. Dempsey, and Bernard L. Weiss, ed. Margaret G. Rumbaugh. 1997. Vienna, VA:18–19.

[33]Huston, James A. 1996. The Sinews of War: Army Logistics 1775–1953. Washington, D.C.: Army Historical Series, Office of the Chief of Military History, United States Army, 468.

[34]Sherman, 256.

[35]Huston, 469.

[36]Witte, Robert D. 1998. Bid Improprieties. *Contract Management* (April): 41.

[37]Sherman, 260.

[38]Sherman, 239.

[39]FAR 6.401 (a).

[40]Ibid.

[41]FAR 6.401.

[42]FAR 14.104.

[43]Sherman, 245.

[44]FAR 14.101.

[45]FAR 14.201-1.

[46]FAR 14.101.

[47]FAR 14.203.

[48]Drake, Daniel J. 1996. Electronic Procurement: Recommendations to Improve the Process. *Procurement Manager's Guide to EC/EDI*. Vienna, VA: Holbrook and Kellogg Inc., Appendix 17.

[49]FAR 14.202-8.

[50]FAR 14.202.

[51]Rider, Melissa, Kenneth D. Brody, David B. Dempsey, and Bernard L. Weiss. 1997. *Understanding the FAR Part 15 Rewrite*. Vienna, VA: National Contract Management Association (September): 75.

[52]Dean, Joshua. 2000. Procurement Execs Consider Reverse Auctions. Government Executive, jdean@govexec.com, August 4, 2000.

[53]FAR 14.501.

[54]FAR 15.000.

[55]Nash, Jr., Schooner, and O'Brien, 363.

[56]Sherman, 257.

[57]Sherman, 257.

[58]Sherman, 123.

[59]Total Federal Snapshot Report, Federal Procurement Report, Fiscal Year 1999.

[60]FAR 15.403-4.

[61]FAR 15.201 (f).

[62]Roberts, William A., III, Lee P. Curtis, and Andrew D. Irwin. 1998. Opportunities and Risks Associated with Preproposal One-on-One Exchanges. *Contract Management* (July): 14.

[63]FAR 3. 104.

[64]FAR 15.201 (c).

[65]Rider, Broody, Dempsey, Weiss, 31.

[66]FAR 15.201 (f).

[67]Rider, Broody, Dempsey, Weiss, 35.

[68]FAR 6.302.

[69]FAR 6.102.

[70]FAR 15.203.

[71]FAR 36.601-1.

[72]FAR 15.607(b).

[73]Gabbard, Ernest. 1998. Terms and Conditions for Electronic Commerce. *Contract Management* (September): 17.

[74]Bradford, Jim. 1998. NASA Demonstrates Electronic RFP Savings. *Contract Management* (July): 21.

[75]FAR 15.204-1.

[76]FAR 15.204.

[77]FAR 12.000.

[78]FAR 15.204-2.

[79]FAR 5.102 (a)(7).

[80]FAR 15.204-2 (b).

[81]Burt, David N., and Richard L. Pinkerton. 1996. *A Purchasing Manager's Guide to Strategic Proactive Procurement.* New York: American Management Association, 40.

[82]Cibinic, Jr., and Nash, Jr., *Formation of Government Contracts,* 188.

[83]FAR 1.02 (b).

[84]Sherman, 123.

[85]Burt and Pinkerton, 40.

[86]FAR 11.101.

[87]FAR 11.002.

[88]FAR 12.202 (b).

[89]FAR 11.104.

[90]Lucas, Raymond C. 1997. The Owner's Perspective of Contract Types Relative to Commercial Contracting. *Contract Management* (November): 9.

[91]FAR 11.105.

[92]FAR 7.500.

[93]FAR 9.505.

[94]Cibinic, Jr., and Nash, Jr., *Administration of Government Contracts,* 601.

[95]Ibid.

[96]FAR 46.501.

[97]FAR.52.246-2 (k).

[98]Uniform Commercial Code §2-314 and §2-315.

[99]Walton, Mary. 1986. *The Deming Method.* New York: Perigee Books, 35.

[100]Nash, Jr., Schooner, and O'Brien, 428.

[101]Cibinic, Jr., and Nash, Jr., *Administration of Government Contracts,* 583.

[102]Cibinic, Jr., and Nash, Jr., *Administration of Government Contracts,* 584.

[103]FAR 46.203(c).

[104]FAR 46.401.

[105]FAR 46.402.

[106]FAR 46.403.

[107]Ibid.

[108]FAR 12-208.

[109]FAR 12.402 (b).

[110]Uniform Commercial Code § 2-314 and § 2-315.

[111]FAR 46.706(b)(1).

[112]FAR 46.202-2(b).

[113]FAR 46.202-3.

[114]Cibinic, Jr., and Nash, Jr., *Administration of Government Contracts,* 569.

[115]Sherman, 249.

[116]FAR 46.201-4.

[117]Executive Overview—ISO 9000 Quality Management System, September 10, 2000.

[118]FAR 11.402(1)(a)(9).

[119]FAR 11.402(1)(a).

[120]Nash, Jr., Schooner, and O'Brien, 330.

[121]FAR 42.202.

[122]Roth, Rudolf. 1999. Legal Aspects of Electronic Tendering and Procurement. *World Market Research Center, Proceedings of the 11th World Congress of International Federation of Purchasing and Materials Management,* 17–19 November 1999, Milton Qld, Australia, 88–91.

[123]Talbot, Terry R. 1997. Source Selection After Acquisition Reform: How Does It Stack Up Now? *Contract Management* (December): 44.

[124]Wyatt John B., III. 1993. The Christian Doctrine: Born Again But Sinfully Confusing. *Contract Management* (November): 65.

[125]Cibinic, Jr., and Nash, Jr., *Administration of Government Contracts,* 178.

[126]Summerill, Joseph, and Todd Bailey. 1998. The Use of UCC-Implied Warranties in Public Contracts. *Contract Management* (November): 13.

[127]Engelbeck, R. Marshall. 1988. Weapon System Warranties: Are We Creating a Monster? *Contract Management* (March): 16.

[128]FAR 46.705.

[129]FAR 46.703(a).

[130]FAR 46.706.

[131]Cibinic, Jr., and Nash, Jr., *Administration of Government Contracts,* 110.

[132]Wilson, 20.

[133]Rider, Broody, Dempsey, and Weiss, 42.

[134]FAR 15.304.

[135]Shariati, Linda. 1999. Bid Protest Decisions Related to Commercial Items: Raising Unanswered Questions. *Contract Management* (June): 7.

[136]FAR 15.101.

[137]FAR 15.304.

[138]FAR 15.304(b).

[139]Nash, Jr., Schooner, and O'Brien, 58.

[140]Dempsey, David B. 1999. The FAR 15 Rewrite—Two Years Later, a Section by Section Rewrite. *National Contract Mangement Journal* 29(2):9.

[141]Rider, Broody, Dempsey, and Weiss, 19.

[142]FAR 15.304(c).

[143]Arnavas, Donald P., and William J. Ruberry. 1994. *Government Contract Guidebook.* Washington, D.C.: Federal Publications, Inc., 4–6.

[144]FAR 15.304(e).

[145]Rider, Broody, Dempsey, and Weiss, 22.

[146]FAR 15.304(c).

[147]Solloway, Charles D. Jr. 1997. The New FAR Part 15—Is it a Step Backward in Acquisition Reform? *Contract Management* (December): 45.

[148]Rider, Broody, Dempsey, and Weiss, 8.

[149]Ibid.

[150]Dempsey, 40.

[151]Fox, J. Ronald. 1974. *Arming of America.* Cambridge, MA: Harvard University Press, 293.

[152]FAR 9.501.

[153]FAR 9.502(b).

[154]FAR 9.504.

[155]FAR 9.505.

[156]FAR 9.504(e).

[157]Cibinic, Jr., and Nash, Jr., *Formation of Government Contracts,* 146.

[158]FAR 9.202.

[159]Cibinic, Jr., and Nash, Jr., *Formation of Government Contracts,* 146.

[160]FAR 9.203.

[161]FAR 5.101.

[162]FAR 5.204.

[163]Nash, Jr., Schooner, and O'Brien, 245.

[164]Total Federal Snapshot Report, SF279. Actions Reported Individually on SF279. Fiscal Year 1999 Through Fourth Quarter. www.FPDS.GSA.gov.

[165]Bowersox, Donald J., Patricia J. Daugherty, Cornelia L. Dröge, Richard N. Germain, and Dale S. Rogers. 1992. *Logistical Excellence: It is Not Business as Usual.* Burlington, MA: Digital Press of Digital Equipment Corporation, 33.

[166]Sherman, 314.

[167]FAR 16.103.

[168]FAR 16.201.

[169]DFARS Part 235.006 (Contracting Methods and Contract Type).

[170]Cibinic, Jr., and Nash, Jr., *Formation of Government Contracts,* 506.

[171]FAR 16.205-2.

[172]Armed Services Pricing Manual. 1986. Chicago, IL: Commerce Clearing House, Inc., 1–21.

[173]Ibid.

[174]FAR 16.203-1.

[175]FAR 16.207-2.

[176]Armed Services Pricing Manual, 1–18.

[177]Huston, James A. 1965. *The Sinews of War: Army Historical Series.* Washington D.C.: U.S. Government Printing Office, 319.

[178]FAR 16.301-1.

[179]Sherman, 319.

[180]Nash, Jr., Schooner, and O'Brien, 434.

[181]Nash, Jr., Schooner, and O'Brien, 23.

[182]Nash, Jr., Schooner, and O'Brien, 137.

[183]Gallimore, Carl G. 1982. *Accounting for Contracts.* 2d ed. Chelsea, MI: Bookcrafters, Inc., 1.

[184]Nash, Jr., Schooner, and O'Brien, 25.

[185]Hills, Jeffrey W. 1997. Cost Type Contracts—The Right Way To Do HTRW Contracts. *Contract Management* (September): 26.

[186]Sherman, 320.

[187]Crawford, Robert. 1985. For Beginners Only: Selecting the Right Contract Type. *Contract Management* (August): 22.

[188]FAR 16.104.

[189]Sherman, 322–323.

[190]Sherman, 324–329.

[191]DODI 5000.2, Operation of the Defense Acquisition System, dated January 4, 2001.

[192]Ibid.

[193]Shaw, T.E. 1990. An Overview of Risk Management Techniques, Methods and Application. Huntsville, AL: AIAA Space Programs and Technologies Conference, Sept. 25–29, 12.

[194]Sherman, 326.

[195]Solloway, Jr., 45.

[196]Cibinic, Jr., and Nash, Jr., *Formation of Government Contracts,* 462.

[197]FAR 15.404-4(c)(4)(i).

[198]DFARS, Part 216.104-70.

[199]Bowersox, Daugherty, Dröge, Germain, and Rogers, 33.

[200]Sherman, 328.

[201]Fox, 237.

[202]FAR 30.201-4.

[203]Alston, Frank M., Franklin R. Johnson, Margaret M. Worthington, Louis P. Goldsman, Frank J. DeVito. 1984. *Contracting with the Federal Government.* New York: John Wiley & Sons, Inc., 114.

[204]Williams, Linda G., and Matthew Blum. 1996. Task Order and Delivery Order Contracting under FASA. *Contract Management* (January): 18.

[205]Nash, Jr., Schooner, and O'Brien, 506.

[206]Nash, Jr., Schooner, and O'Brien, 175.

[207]Shaw, Jack. 1999. *Surviving the Digital Jungle.* Marietta, GA: Electronic Commerce Strategies, 48.

[208]Nash, Jr., Schooner, and O'Brien, p. 295.

[209]FAR 16.504.

[210]FAR 16.501-2(c).

[211]FAR 16.504-(a) (4).

[212]FAR 16.501-2.

[213]FAR 16.502.

[214]Cibinic, Jr., and Nash, Jr., *Formation of Government Contracts,* 514.

[215]Cibinic, Jr., and Nash, Jr., *Formation of Government Contracts,* 540.

[216]FAR 12.207.

[217]FAR 16.505.

[218]FAR 16.504.

[219]Clark, John O. 1999. Innovative Acquisition Procedures: Modular Contracting. Topical Issues in Procurement Series. *Contract Management* (June): 2.

[220]Clark, 1.

[221]Ibid.

[222]Clark, 5.

[223]FAR 702(b).

[224]FAR 16.703(d).

[225]FAR 13.303-3.

[226]FAR 13.305-5(b).

[227]Fisher, Brian T. 1999. FSS and Cooperative Purchasing: Friend or Foe? *Contract Management* (February): 5.

[228]FAR 8.401(b).

[229]FAR 8.404(a)(3).

[230]FAR 8.405-7.

[231]Fisher, 6.

[232]FAR 16.601(b)(3).

[233]FAR 16.602.

[234]FAR 16.603-2(d).

Bid and Proposal Preparation

The primary objective of this chapter is not only to provide information about preparing bids and competitive proposals, but also to expose the reader to some of the techniques used in developing responses to government solicitations. To do this we will review the process of preparing and submitting bids and preparing proposals in response to a solicitation. A secondary goal of the chapter is to emphasize the obligation potential contractors have to clarify any ambiguities before receiving the solicitation. Seeking clarification of ambiguities is part of the potential contractor's sales campaign and is a way to mitigate risk prior to responding to the solicitation.

With the passage of the Competition in Contracting Act (CICA) in 1984, Congress dropped its traditional preference for using the amount of formal advertising to judge the amount of contract awarded competitively. Although the CO was required to hold discussion with all offerors in the competitive range, negotiated procurements were considered as being noncompetitive. This was because negotiated proposals were not subject to a public opening, which demonstrated to all that responsible bidders had been allowed to compete. On the other hand, the openness of formal advertising and public opening of sealed bids was widely accepted as a confirmation of the fairness of the federal acquisition process. There are two major reasons why the use of negotiated procurement procedures is now favored by the government over sealed bidding. First, negotiated procurement is more flexible and accommodating to purchasing the user's "unique" needs. Second, it enables the buyer to realize a "best value" acquisition by considering evaluation factors and subfactors that have been tailored to the government's needs. Both methods are now recognized in the Competition in Contracting Act of 1984 as ways of obtaining free and open competition.

It is widely recognized that the federal government, to ensure that both parties understand the requirements, places a great deal of emphasis on the bid and proposal process. Compared to a commercial solicitation, responding to a government request is much more comprehensive and complicated. This is changing, however, with the increased emphasis being placed on strategic procurement in the private sector.

Government procurement operates within a political environment that places a premium on the public interest as well as on the integrity of the process and accountability. The objectives of acquisition regulations that address this area are to:

- Implement policies established by statute
- Implement executive orders issued pursuing a mandate or delegation of authority from Congress
- Implement regulations pursuing specific statutory requirements or to implement a fundamental procurement policy
- Preserve the integrity of the competitive acquisition process[1]
- Mitigate risk by ensuring that the prospective contractor understands the government's requirement.

The contractor's marketing arm is responsible for identifying and pursuing new business opportunities. Companies have two basic marketing concepts. One is to introduce new products and then persuade the customers to purchase them, such as the American automobile manufacturers of the 1960s–1980s did. The other is to ask what the ultimate user needs rather than to produce goods and then tell salesmen to go out and sell them. In other words, tailor the technology to meet the needs of the users. Gaining information about the current needs of potential buyers and their future requirements is a function of company sales representatives.

There are six steps prospective offerors (sellers) follow in developing the response to a solicitation (see Figure 5-1, Six Steps in Responding to a Solicitation). As you would expect, the scope of the prospective contractor's effort in each phase is driven by the proposed method of procurement, i.e., sealed bidding and competitive procurement. Responding to a Request For Bid (RFB) does not require the in-depth analysis under the negotiated procurement process necessary when preparing a response to a Request for Proposal (RFP). Therefore, the following description of the process should be used as more of a guide to responding to an RFP. The steps are:

1. *Strategic marketing*: Prior to the receipt of the solicitation, a marketing representative of the prospective offeror must contact prospective customers and perform sufficient research to identify needs and plans of the ultimate customer. The prospective offeror must define the specific business opportunity it wants to pursue. This includes enter-

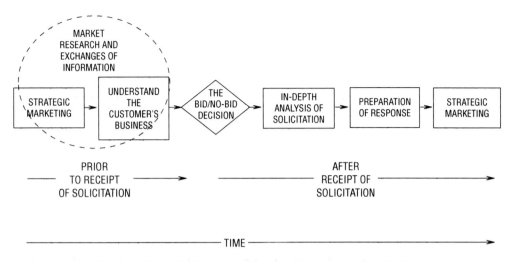

Figure 5-1 Six Steps in Responding to a Solicitation

ing into strategic alliances with possible subcontractors or with firms that have unique capabilities that will enhance the potential offeror's competitiveness. With these pieces in place, the potential offeror can determine if the probability of winning that piece of the business warrants expenditure of additional time and money. If the answer is yes, the prospective offeror moves to the second step.

2. *Understanding the customer's business*: Participating in this step helps the potential seller understand what information the buyer expects in a future proposal. It is a two-way communication process because a constant objective of all potential sellers is to increase the customer's confidence in its products and capabilities. Sometime a pre-bidders conference occurs during this step. Tasks performed by the potential seller include an in-depth analysis of the ultimate user's requirements to gain a full understanding of their needs, interests, and attitudes. This process is designed to find out who buys what and how much. Is it the buyer's desire to establish a strategic alliance? With the increased use of EDI, there is also a need to determine the customer's long- and short-term goals for buying over the Internet.

3. *The "bid/no bid decision"*: After examining the solicitation and preparation instructions, including submission data, the business opportunity is presented to management for the purpose of making a bid/no-bid decision. The goal is to determine if it is the worth the risk of not being selected. Continuing to the next step is contingent on receiving a positive bid decision from an appropriate level of company management. Topics reviewed include information on the potential customer's need, company strategic plans and objectives, capabilities

of the competition, and an opportunity and risk assessment. This data is considered, along with forecasting the potential long- and short-term payoffs and the administrative cost of preparing the response to the solicitation. An initial discussion of the proposed capture strategy is another subject covered when making the bid/no-bid decision. "High-performing companies reject 40 percent of their potential business. The Consulting & Systems Integration Group, a unit of CSC, one of the largest global software services companies in the world, asks four basic questions: Is there an opportunity? Can we compete? Can we win? Is it worth winning?"[2]

If the decision is to proceed, a "capture team" is selected to develop the response. At this time management draws up, reviews, and approves the budget for submitting the proposal.

4. *In-depth analysis of the solicitation*: The goals of this step are to understand thoroughly the performance requirements and terms and conditions of the proposed contract. It is vital that the prospective seller understands the buyer's source selection criteria, allocation of risk, and preparation instructions. During this step all patent ambiguities must be identified and addressed with the buyer, assumptions delineated, and provisions developed to mitigate the risk. The output of this process is a preparation plan that includes assumptions and ways risk can be mitigated, along with the organizational outline of the proposed response.

5. *Preparation of the response*: This is a mutual effort by a multi-functional team. The response must be consistent with the seller's capture strategy and must demonstrate that the respondent understands the user's requirements. Key to meeting the submission schedule with a quality product is continuous coordination among members of the response team. Most firms have general standardized procedures and practices that are to be followed to avoid misunderstandings, remain focused, or avoid wasting time because someone takes a misdirected path.

6. *Review and submission*: The final step includes the review of the draft response, revisions to the draft, review by management, final revision, and submission. An important element included in this step is the performance commitment by the response team with company management prior to the submission of the final document. This performance commitment includes such factors as projected sales, profit, and return on investment (ROI).

MARKET RESEARCH AND EXCHANGES PRIOR TO RECEIPT OF SOLICITATION

During the first two steps, the potential offeror has an opportunity to gain insight into possible business opportunities and to begin to posture itself to win the contract. Government policy now encourages earlier interchange between the buyer and seller so the potential offeror can gain an understanding of government requirements. The emerging practice to post drafts of the solicitation and the requirements documents on the buying agency's bulletin boards enables the potential offeror to review and exchange information with the buyer on these documents.

Addressing Ambiguities and Other Significant Discrepancies

As noted earlier, the solicitation as amended during the proposal and award phases becomes the contractual document, i.e., the "common language" that will govern the performance of the parties. At the time of contract award it is unrealistic to think everything will go without a hitch. Case law is full of examples of the government benefiting from lower prices at the expense of unwary contractors and from ambiguous, inaccurate, or incomplete descriptions. Contractors should be alert to the fact that one of the risks of government contracting is the absorption of the cost of an ambiguous requirement that occurs after contract award.[3] Inquiring when there is a patent ambiguity is a way for the offeror to address this risk.

Availability of draft contractual documents, prior to issuance of the solicitation, gives a contractor's acquisition team insight into the proposed terms and conditions and details regarding requirements. Potential offerors should not overlook this opportunity to analyze the entire draft solicitation and offer comments to the government's acquisition team prior to receipt of the solicitation. Having the ability to identify ambiguities and gaining an understanding of how the proposed contract document allocates risk early in the process furnishes a potential offeror: (1) an opportunity to influence the document before it is issued, (2) removal of uncertainty that would be present if ambiguities had not been addressed before beginning the response to the proposal, and (3) the opportunity to seek clarification of all significant ambiguities before submitting its bid or proposal.

The potential contractor's CM, along with technical and functional representatives from the potential buyer, should examine the draft solicitation and supporting documents for ambiguities in the terms and conditions as well as major discrepancies or errors in the description of requirements or drawings. The purpose would be to initiate a discussion with the government's CO and eliminate any ambiguities before issuance of the solicitation and preparation of the response. When making the inquiry after the solicitation has been issued, the offeror must understand if the answer will result in a material change to the solicitation, of which the government is obligated to notify all prospective offerors. This may benefit another firm more than it does the one raising the question. For this reason, after the solicitation has been issued most firms consider the seriousness of the ambiguity and handle inquiries carefully, often approaching the subject indirectly.

A key rule of contract writing, i.e., *contra proferentem*, places responsibility on the drafter of contractual documents to use language that permits only one meaning.[4] An ambiguity is defined as contract language that is capable of being misunderstood, by a reasonable person, to have more than one meaning. There are patent ambiguities (obvious ambiguities) that arise from defective, contradictory, obscure, or senseless language. There are also latent ambiguities that appear to be clear and intelligible but offer a choice between two or more possible meanings because of some extraneous evidence.[5] Case law has ruled that a potential contractor has a duty to seek clarification and attempt to have the government resolve a patent ambiguity before bidding in order to put all bidders on an equal plane and deter a bidder who knows (or should know) of a serious problem in interpretation from consciously taking the award with a lower bid by taking the less costly reading.[6]

The pre-bid or pre-proposal conference, a common source of discussion before contract award, is a primary source of evidence that the prospective offerors did or did not seek clarification of ambiguities. It represents an excellent opportunity to obtain clarification on ambiguous provisions in the solicitation. In the absence of written agreements to the solicitation, oral statements made by knowledgeable government officials representing the CO at the pre-bid conference, which appear to be consistent with the plans, specifications, and contract, can be taken into account when preparing the response to the solicitation.[7]

Granting the contractor contractual relief under the rule of *contra proferentem* will not be applied if the non-drafting party fails before bidding to seek clarification of an ambiguity of which it was or should have been aware.[8]

Risk Allocation and Management

In government contracts risks are allocated primarily by the selection of the contract pricing arrangement, i.e., contract type. Under fixed-price contracts the contractor is exposed to cost growth from non-performance and delays, whereas under cost-reimbursement contracts, the government accepts these risks.

The contract clauses and special contract requirements are often included in the terms and conditions that also allocate risk. They are in the form of standard clauses that expressly provide for time extensions or price adjustments should various contingencies materialize or unexpected conditions occur. These clauses are examples of how risks are allocated. Other examples include the Changes, Differing Site Conditions, Suspension of Work, and Default clauses.[9]

Fundamental rules of risk allocation have evolved over the years from common law principles. These may provide for a remedy in the absence of any specific contract clauses granting remedies, such as constructive changes and constructive suspensions of work. These rules cover such situations as late delivery of government-furnished equipment (GFE), furnishing of drawings that are not of the current model, unavailability of the work site, impossibility or impracticality of attaining performance requirements, and government failure to respond to requests for information in a timely manner.

These risks fall into the six categories of contingencies described below:

- Performance may vary from the plan based on the occurrence of events outside of the contractor's control.
- Performance may vary from the plan because the contractor was misled by the government's incorrect statements or failure to disclose facts or knowledge.
- Performance may vary from the plan under theories of the government's implied warranties of specifications.
- Performance may vary from the plan because it was interfered with by the government's action or inaction.
- Performance may vary from the plan because it is found to be greatly different than expected.[10]

Concurrent with the analysis the contractor's team should examine the solicitation and determine: (1) what could go wrong, (2) what would cause the potential problem, and (3) what action could be taken to reduce the likely effects. These contingencies often are addressed by the offeror in its proposal as a means to illustrate the contractor's ability to identify and manage risk.

FORMING THE BID OR PROPOSAL TEAM

Writing the response to the solicitation is a team effort. Most companies do not have a permanent department that specializes in writing proposals. At best, there may be an "expert" who has extensive experience writing proposals and a group of administrative personnel available to work on the larger proposals. The offeror must assemble a team that has the knowledge needed to develop the proposal. A single person may be able to perform all the functions necessary to prepare the proposal, but, as the requirement gets bigger and more complicated, specialists must be added. For larger efforts, a team built around a proposal manager, a contract manager, and a technical expertise core is quite common. This team is supported by other functional experts on a full- or part-time basis. Of course, the offeror's marketing representatives play a very significant role in developing the proposal.

Managing proposal preparation requires someone who understands the proposal process as well as business management, contractual issues, and the government customer and its needs. The management functions of planning, organizing, communicating, and controlling all come into play.

Although actual proposal writing is a relatively short-term undertaking, in reality members of the proposal team work either full- or part-time during the pre-sales phase, often concurrent with the government's market research effort. Quite often the specialized skills in the contractor's team mirror that of the government's acquisition team. The ideal candidate must be experienced and able to look beyond functional boundaries to develop solutions that best meet all the customer's objectives and help the team identify potential suppliers.[11] If the team is instrumental in gaining the contract award, many members of the proposal preparation team are often rewarded with positions on the contractor's operational team.

Cost is a major consideration in staffing the team. Selecting experienced people is not only key to a winning proposal, but it also helps keep down the cost of preparation. This is a critical factor in any corporation because the cost of proposal preparation comes out of the current year's proposal budget for the entire firm or division or from profit. Consequently, offerors are always performing tradeoffs between incurring proposal cost on Opportunity A versus Opportunity B and any possible impact on short-term profit.

THE BID/NO-BID DECISION

One of the toughest decisions facing a company's management is determining if it wants to respond to a solicitation. The question they must answer is if the payoff, in potential profit, is worth the administrative support cost and risk of not winning the bid.[12] It is the task of the contractor's proposal team to assemble and present the data needed to make this decision.

The bid/no-bid decision requires an analysis of the business opportunities the potential contract brings to the firm as well as the risk associated with the proposed effort. Initially, there must be an assessment of probability of winning the competition. If the probability of winning is low, then only special circumstances would warrant proceeding with the bid/no-bid decision process (see Figure 5-2, The Bid/No-Bid Decision Process).

Data needed to make this analysis include information gathered by the company's marketing function prior to the issuance of the solicitation. It is the job of marketing to provide details on the long- and short-term needs and desires of the user, characteristics of the product or service being procured, an estimate of the buyer's budget, an analysis of the characteristic and competitiveness of the competitor's product, and an estimate of the target price for the product. All these elements are important in making the bid/no-bid decision.

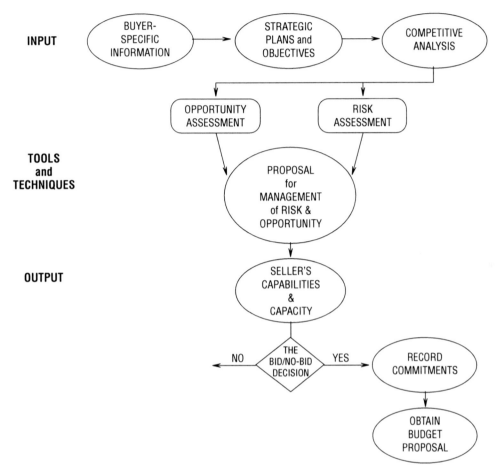

Figure 5-2 The Bid/No-Bid Decision Process

Internal company data that will be studied include details on the firm's core competencies, sales and investment plans, experience with similar products, and manpower and facilities required and available at the times needed to perform the work to meet the schedule. One question is if there are any similar programs under contract that the company can latch onto to minimize start-up cost and take advantage of increased quantities, learning curves, and the ability to the spread cost over additional units.

An analysis of the solicitation is vital to an understanding of the risks associated with the proposed effort by the decision makers. Some things that must be assessed are the risk associated with the technical requirements as defined in the specifications, scope of the software effort, and the proposed terms and conditions. Does the solicitation clearly establish the criteria for completion? Another crucial question has to do with the proposed delivery schedule, i.e., is it realistic or success oriented?

Financial considerations are very important to making any bid/no-bid decision. Are the potential short-term revenue and longer-term income opportunities worth the cost of submitting the proposal? Is the estimated cost of producing the proposal worth the potential revenue and long-term income potential of the new program?

Many contractors have defined their central values and objectives and only enter into contracts that have a high probability of achieving these goals. Financial ratios shown in Table 5-1 are most often keys to this decision.

PRICING OF THE PRODUCT

Before going further into the two methods of procurement, it is appropriate to examine briefly trends in contractor pricing methodology.

As we discussed in Chapter One, the federal government market does not behave as a competitive market because there is not a widespread demand for many products and services purchased by the government. Many of the characteristics of the private marketplace that help drive down the prices paid by the user are not present in government purchasing.

To compensate for this disadvantage, Congress has implemented statutes that in turn foster policies and procedures that make up for the lack of the forces of the marketplace. The most obvious examples are the guiding principles of "promoting competition" and "maximum use of commercial products and services in meeting government requirements."[13] In addition, the statutes call for the potential contractor to provide cost or pricing data when there is not adequate competition on negotiated procurement contracts of over $500,000 to ensure that the price paid by the government is "fair and reasonable." This cost or pricing data must also be certified as being current, accurate, and complete as of the date negotiations were concluded and price agreement was reached.[14] Failing to comply with this re-

---

Table 5-1. Financial Ratios

Efficiency Ratios

Inventory Turnover _____	Sales/Inventory
Total Asset Turnover _____	Sales/Total Assets

Profitability Ratios

Profit Margin on Sales _____	Net Profit on Sales/Sales
Return on Total Assets _____	Net Profit after Taxes/Total Assets
Return on Net Worth _____	Net Profit after Taxes/Net Worth

quirement or certifying falsely to the accuracy of the cost-related information can result in penalties up to and including being charged with a felony.

When evaluating proposals, the Rewrite of FAR Part 15.404-1 emphasizes the use of cost analysis to evaluate the separate cost elements and profit in the proposal. this includes cost or pricing data submitted by the offeror. It also includes the application of judgment to determine how well the proposed cost represents what the cost should be, assuming reasonable economy and efficiency.[15] Some feel that cost analysis and cost realism analysis are being promoted as substitutes for price analysis.[16]

These policies and procedures, along with audits, have placed the spotlight on the contractor and subcontractor cost and have cultivated cost-driven pricing by the government customer. Writing in *The Wall Street Journal*, Peter Drucker cites cost-driven pricing as one of the avoidable mistakes that harm a business. He goes on to say, "The only thing that works is price-driven costing....The only sound way to price is to price out what the market is willing to pay...and design to that price specification." Dr. Drucker concludes: "cost-based pricing is the reason there is no American consumer electronics industry anymore."[17]

Information on the probable cost of the product gathered early in a product's life cycle can be used to establish a target price for the potential contractor's product. Priced-based pricing means the design engineer must focus on target price when considering the product's performance and schedule. This requires engineers, purchasing, manufacturing, and suppliers to form strategic partnerships to identify target prices for components and subassemblies. Strategic partnerships are relatively few in numbers, frequently accounting for 50–80 percent of a firm's purchasing expenditures.[18] The strategic partners are then able to develop processes and procedures to acquire the required materials at the target prices. Writing in *The Wall Street Journal* in January 1999, Dr. Drucker credits the change to price-based pricing by many U.S. firms as the primary reason inflation had remained low.

BID PREPARATION UNDER THE SEALED BIDDING METHOD

The FAR defines a sealed bid as an offer submitted to the government in response to an invitation for bids (IFB). The bidder must be given a reasonable time (generally at least 30 days) to prepare and submit bids that are consistent with the needs of the government.[19] The purpose of this method is to secure the most advantageous contract for the government by giving potential offerors an opportunity to compete for a government contract, thereby maximizing free and open competition. Allocation of risk under the firm-fixed-price type of pricing arrangement best lends itself to the sealed bid method of procurement.

Today's sealed bidding process is based on congressional preferences dating back to 1809.[20] The procedure, referenced in Table 5-2, The Sealed Bidding Method, consists of the following steps:

- Advertisement of the requirement shall be made in sufficient time before the purchase or contract to permit free and open competition.
- Bids shall be opened publicly at the time and place stated in the advertisement.
- Awards shall be made to the responsible bidder, with reasonable promptness, whose bid conforms to the invitation and will be the most advantageous to the United States, price and other factors considered.
- A bid may be rejected if the head of the agency determines that rejection is in the public interest.[21]

A key element of this process is that all bidders must bid on the same effort and make a public bid opening to the offeror "whose bid conforms to the invitation."[22] The thought behind this criterion for award is to promote objectivity and fairness in the procurement system by ensuring that a bidder cannot win a contract by offering to perform the work in a less expensive way—a way that other bidders could have proposed if they had known that the government was willing to accept a similar standard of work.[23] Therefore, one of the most significant policies with respect to the sealed bidding is that the CO is required to reject bids as being non-responsive when they vary from the requirements in the IFB.

Responsiveness

The responsiveness criterion is embodied in the federal statutes in the statement that an award may only be made to a bidder "whose bid conforms to the invitation." In other words, a responsive bid is an unqualified offer to perform the exact work called for in the solicitation.[24]

The CO has little latitude in making the award to an offeror other than the low bidder. Considering bids on varying levels of effort would inevitably involve the CO in further discussions with the bidders to determine the precise nature of their offerors. This would lead to a discretionary decision

---

Table 5-2. The Sealed Bidding Method

Advertisement of the Requirement
Bid Preparation
Public Bid Opening
Award to the Lowest Responsive Responsible Bidder

as to which offer was low, taking into consideration both price and level of performance offered, which is contrary to the conceptual nature of the sealed bidding process. This method could also provide other bidders the opportunity to withdraw their bids after the disclosure of their competitors' bids and possibly resubmitting their offers in a way that would meet the government's revised requirement. Such a process is synonymous to negotiated procurement, with neither the safeguards from unequal treatment of the bidders nor lack of favoritism considered to be essential in sealed bidding. Nor does it have the protection from open disclosure of competitive price, all of which is thought to be a necessary part of the procurement process.[25]

Examples of circumstances that cause a bid to be rejected as being non-responsive include:

- An offer to deliver products or services that differ from those solicited
- An offer that fails to agree to the delivery schedule in the solicitation
- An offer that imposes conditions that alter the requirements of the solicitation or limit the rights of the government
- An offer that is indefinite, uncertain, or ambiguous
- An offer that fails to furnish the required items of information
- An offer that includes accompanying documents that are not completed accurately
- An offer that fails to acknowledge the receipt of all amendments containing material requirements
- An offer in which cover letters and additional information furnished create an ambiguity
- An offer that is received at the designated office after the exact time specified in the solicitation.[26] (FAR 14.304(a) establishes rules for special circumstances whereby bids received after the exact time for bid opening can be considered.)

A claim of mistake can be considered only when the bid is responsive to the solicitation. Whatever mistake is made on a bid must not affect the price, delivery time, quality, or quantity rule to have it reinstated.[27]

Responsibility

Responsibility involves the question of whether the contractor can or will perform as promised in the bid. The CO has a great deal of discretion in determining if a potential contractor is responsible. The evaluation is based on all information submitted with the bid and other facts available up to the time of award. This flexibility is in contrast with the CO's judgment regarding the responsiveness of the potential contractor. An evaluation of the bidder's responsiveness deals only with the question of whether the potential contractor has promised to do exactly what the IFB requested. More information on determining if a potential contractor meets the tests of responsibility will be provided in Chapter 6.

The Purchase of Supplies and Services

The purchase of supplies: Orders for spares and repair parts represent a significant amount of the government's IFB activity each year. Spare and repair parts fall into two categories: (1) those that are ordered so they can be produced concurrently with the major components or assemblies, and (2) those that are ordered at a time when they cannot be produced concurrently with production assemblies and subassemblies.

Spares and repair parts purchased concurrent with production: When component spares and repair parts are assembled, tested, and delivered concurrently with major components, they will be in the same configuration as those being used in the higher components. Therefore, an active bill of material is available, and the same drawings, tooling, test equipment/facilities, and work force would be applicable to produce these added spares and repair parts. Quantities can be inserted into the production line, and the learning curve can usually be applied to the assembly and test hours. Additional engineering development cost should not be required. However, a collateral engineering factor would apply to cover production, inspection, and test issues. As for material cost, quantity purchase benefits may also be realized for some of the components.

Non-concurrent spares and repair parts: These are normally part of the replenishment process not ordered concurrently with a product run. They are sometimes referred to as out-of-production spares and repair parts. They are usually ordered by the government using a request for quotation (RFQ), purchase request (PR), basic ordering agreement (BOA), or an indefinite quantity purchase agreement. The type of item lends itself to ordering over the Internet using EDI. The length of time the items have been out of production is key to determining if an up-to-date bill of material is available as well as availability of drawings, production planning, tooling, test equipment, test facilities, and component parts. This can potentially be a very costly way to obtain replenishment spare parts because the price is so sensitive to volume and timeliness of the order. When price competition is not present, the government often uses formula pricing, which is based on an average of the contractor's estimated cost.

The purchase of services: The range of services used by the government is very broad. Service contracts are generally less capital intensive. Therefore, because of the ease of entering into the market, service contracting is highly competitive. Services are task related and include engineering design, research and development, maintenance and repair, operation of facilities, and utilities. The Office of Federal Procurement Policy defines services as being "identifiable tasks to be performed, rather than the delivery of an end item of supply. The term 'services' also includes tasks that are delivered under a contract where the primary purpose of the contract is to provide supplies."[28]

The process of purchasing services is lengthy and complex and has traditionally required extensive documentation. Service contracts often have tailored statements of work and are subject to extensive administrative oversight of the quality of work completed and compliance with labor laws. The terms of a performance contract often span several fiscal years and often have renewable options. The contractor is usually able to invoice frequently, thus enhancing its cash flow.

Although various types of pricing arrangements are used when purchasing services, fixed-price contracts are suitable for acquiring services when the buyer has a reasonably definitive statement of work. The following type of pricing arrangements are often applied to the bidding process:

- Fixed-price with Economic Price Adjustment of Escalation
- Fixed-price Indefinite-Quantity/Indefinite-Delivery
- Fixed-price Requirements Contracts.

Preparation of the bid: After making the bid/no bid decision to respond to an IFB, and before the initiation of any bid activity, most companies have a procedure whereby a bid authorization and planning document must be issued by the Bid Manager (see Table 5-3, Steps in the Preparation of the Bid). This document contains more than bid preparation instructions—it also represents the authority to expend company funds in preparing the bid. In most cases company cost accounting systems preclude direct-charge employees from working any task without budget authorization.

Solicitation analysis: Analysis of the solicitation must be completed prior to beginning bid planning and preparation. Ambiguities in the solicitation should be identified and resolved early in the process. Analysis of the bid also includes a thorough understanding of the terms, conditions, and requirements. The bidder's capability to meet the proposed delivery schedule must be assessed in view of the availability of skills, personnel, and facilities. Analysis of risk and cost drivers as they may affect profit potential should also be part of the analysis. Often the offeror's sales representative has technical and market information, gained during market research, that can add to the bidder's understanding of the requirement.

In the Uniform Contract Format, other key areas of the solicitation, in addition to Part I of the Schedule, are Part II, Section I, Contract Clauses; Part III, Section K, Representations, certifications, and other statements of bidders; and Part IV, Section L, Instructions, conditions, and notices to bidders; and Section M, Evaluation factors for award.

Table 5-3. Steps in the Preparation of the Bid

Make the Bid Decision
Analyze Solicitation
Prepare Bid Preparation Plan
Prepare Sealed Bid
Review, Approve, and Submit Bid

Bid preparation plan: The purpose of the bid plan is to coordinate the activities of the contributors to the bid (see Table 5-4, Outline of the Bid Preparation Plan). The instructions to the bid preparation team should include such information as: (1) key assumptions and conditions, (2) documents to be prepared in support of the bid, (3) method used to disseminate information on amendments as well as changes, (4) bid responsibility matrix, (5) contractual matters, (6) flow-down requirements for contractual specifications, (7) instructions on handling corrections to the bid prior to submission, (8) cost estimating instructions, (9) pricing the bid, and (10) schedules for the review and submission of the formal bid. The data available and complexity of the bid activity are functions of the size and characteristics of the business opportunity. An example of a responsibility matrix is shown in Table 5-5, Sample Responsibility Matrix.

As was pointed out in Chapter 3, often at least 60 percent of the prime contractor's cost is in the form of purchased supplies, equipment, materials, and services.[29] The Bid Manager must ensure that a make-or-buy (outsourcing) tradeoff is completed early in the bid preparation process to determine if: (1) teaming agreements are appropriate, (2) the requirement can best be satisfied through the use of subcontractors or vendors, or (3) the organization will develop an organic capability. (More detail on team-

---

Table 5-4. Outline of the Bid Preparation Plan

Key Assumptions and Conditions
Supporting Documentation
Discrimination Process for Solicitation Amendments and Changes
Flow-down Requirements for Contractual Specifications
Assignment of Bid Responsibility
Special Contractual Terms and Conditions
Procedures on How to Handle Corrections to Bid
Instructions on Cost Estimating Methods
Pricing the Bid
Schedule for Review and Submission of Formal Bid

Table 5-5. Sample Responsibility Matrix

Reference	WBS	Responsible	Instructions
3.2 SOW	1.3.2	Engineering	Engineering #6
3.3 SOW	1.3.3	Material Mgt	Purchasing #3
3.4 SOW	1.3.4	Shipping	Packaging #6
3.5 SOW	1.3.5	Shipping	Transportation #2
3.7 SOW	1.3.7	Logistics	Logistics #1

ing arrangements and subcontract/vendor bids will be included later in this chapter when we discuss the preparation of proposals under the competitive negotiation process.)

The make-or-buy decision is a strategic one, requiring the firm to reexamine its core competencies to determine if the product or service in question should be outsourced. Top management has the ultimate responsibility for this decision because it answers the question as to what kind of company it wants to be. Often the decision is made by following operating procedures. The firm's CM should identify candidates for the make-or-buy analysis. If an item or service near or at the heart of the firm's core competencies is outsourced, it should be supplied by a carefully selected supplier under a "tightly woven strategic alliance."[30]

Preparation of the sealed bid: The purpose of the proposal is to convert specific requirements into a quantitative offer that is competitive. This is because under the sealed bidding method, the CO's award decision will be based on an objective determination of which bid is responsive and provides the lowest overall cost to the government. The bid must specifically address all the requirements set out in the solicitation. The CO does not have the authority to enter into a contract that incorporates interpretations that are clearly contrary to the terms in the IFB.[31]

Elements of the work defined in the solicitation will fall into two categories: tasks to be performed directly by the prime contractor and tasks to be performed outside the prime contractor's organization. Each can be further partitioned into labor hours, material requirements, travel, and other direct costs. The responsibility for the preparation of detailed cost estimates of the work to be performed is specified in the bid responsibility matrix in the bid plan. The PM is responsible for handling bid estimates and completing contractual arrangements with subcontractors for the tasks outsourced. The CM is usually the focal point for development and negotiation of teaming agreements.

Direct labor hour estimates are developed by subdividing each of the tasks. The goal is to use established engineered standards or to compare the proposed task to the known cost history of a similar task and extrapolate to estimate the cost. Another method includes making a direct estimate based on individual experience.

Material cost estimates can be based on a bill of material, which is submitted to the purchasing department for a review of past purchasing history or obtaining vendor quotes.

Travel estimates are developed by identifying the number of trips, number of persons participating, length of time, auto rental, and airfare.

The cost of capital equipment and similar investments needed to complete the work are stipulated in the solicitation.

Bid review and submission: The Bid Manager is responsible for conducting a review of the bid with the appropriate level of management after it has been consolidated. This review also includes the examination of cost estimates for each of the functions participating in the bid. The CM is responsible for verifying that all elements of the bid responsibility matrix have been accounted for.

To ensure that the bid is responsive, the review should focus on answering the following questions:

- Does the bid accurately contain the cost of all work defined in the solicitation?
- Are all amendments to the IFB accounted for and considered in the bid?
- Is the delivery schedule proposed in compliance with the solicitation?
- Is the bid responsive to the instructions contained in the IFB?
- Are provisions in place to ensure that the bid is delivered to the address listed in the solicitation prior to the time and date specified?

After the review process has been completed and adjustments made, the bid is signed off on by the level of management designated in company policy. As part of this review functional managers are often required to make presentations to company management assessing the risks as well as anticipated opportunities associated with the effort. Projections of sales value and return on assets and an assessment of cash flow are also included for most significant bids.

THE TWO-STEP SEALED BIDDING METHOD

The Two-Step Sealed Bidding Method was introduced in an attempt to obtain more competition in military procurements. In 1957 the House Armed Services Subcommittee for Special Investigations recommended that the Air Force attempt a two-step procurement procedure. In the first step the government obtains proposals on a technical solution to their requirement, enabling the buyer to discuss the requirement with the potential contractor. A down selection process is then followed, and the successful contractors are requested to submit a sealed bid. The service test was successful, and the two-step method was incorporated into the procurement regulations in 1963.[32]

The Two-Step is a hybrid method of acquisition that is well suited to the procurement of technical and complex requirements. It combines competitive procedures (first step) to obtain the benefits of sealed bidding (second step) when adequate specifications are not available. The buyer's objective when using this method is to develop a technical data package in the first step that sufficiently describes the government's needs but is not unduly restrictive so the subsequent acquisition can be made following the conventional sealed bidding method[33] (see Figure 5-3, The Two-Step Sealed Bidding Method).

A request for a technical proposal is made in the first step. The government buying office is required to publicize its plans to issue a request for a technical proposal (RFTP) via publication of a synopsis of the solicitation. At a minimum, the solicitation for a technical proposal should include: (1) a description of the supplies or services needed, (2) a statement of intended use, (3) the evaluation criteria for selecting the winning proposal, (4) a statement that technical proposals shall not include prices or pricing information, (5) a statement of the intent to use the Two-Step method, and (6) a statement that only bids based on technical proposals determined to be acceptable will be accepted and will be considered for award in step two.

Proposals received in response to the RFTP are evaluated and categorized as: (1) acceptable, (2) reasonably qualified but capable of being made acceptable, and (3) unacceptable if they modify or fail to conform to the essential requirements of the specifications. The CO may, if additional proposals are needed to ensure adequate price competition, request additional clarifying or supplemental information from the offerors with reasonably susceptible proposals. When received, the additional information is incorporated as part of the offeror's proposal, and the proposal is evaluated as acceptable or unacceptable.[34]

In the second step, two IFBs are sent only to potential contractors whose proposals were judged to be acceptable.[35] These potential contractors are then requested to submit an offer in the form of a sealed bid, using its own technical proposal. (It is not necessary to publish a synopsis.) The award process follows the procedures applicable to sealed bids, i.e., no discussion, modification, or negotiation with the offeror submitting the lowest price on the acceptable technical proposals.

PROPOSAL PREPARATION UNDER THE CONTRACTING BY NEGOTIATION METHOD

The term "proposal" is generally used in FAR Part 15 to mean the offer submitted by the offeror in a negotiated procurement plus all information

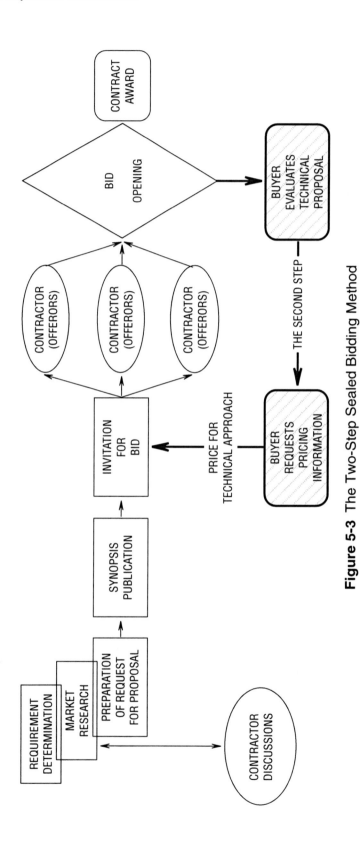

Figure 5-3 The Two-Step Sealed Bidding Method

in the invitation for proposal required to be submitted with the offer.[36] An offer also may take the form of an unsolicited proposal submitted on the initiative of the submitter.[37] Figure 5-4, The Request for Proposal Process, represents an overview of the RFP process.

Proposals are submitted to the government to gain new business or to modify contracts in force. They are submitted in response to a request for proposal (RFP) or a Broad Agency Announcement. This segment of the chapter will concentrate on responding to an RFP. Broad Agency Announcements are used by a procuring agency to solicit proposals in areas of basic research and development when varying scientific and technical approaches can reasonably be expected.[38] Both meet the criteria for full and open competition as defined in the Competition Act.

The federal government requires a great deal of supporting information when making a source selection. The proposal is used to eliminate contractors who are not qualified to perform the work defined in the government's RFP. It must be viewed as an element of the risk management process. Therefore, the federal government places a great deal of emphasis on the proposal process. The goal is that after evaluating the proposal, the government's acquisition team should be able to answer questions regarding the offeror's:

- Experience with the supplies or services being procured
- Technical capabilities
- Soundness of their total quality control program
- Management capabilities
- Caliber of the purchasing process
- Performance history.

In the commercial sector, with an increase in the use of strategic procurements to form long-term supplier alliances, there is an increased need for information from potential suppliers to minimize the risk of making a poor source selection. Therefore, there is expected to be an increased use of more detailed proposals to support making the contract award in private industry.

Changes implemented as part of acquisition reform have made the offeror's job no easier. In fact, some argue that the government's policy to state requirements in broad terms and give the prospective contractor the latitude to innovate has done just the opposite. "No longer can offerors parrot back the details of the government requirement—the buying office must now thoroughly understand the requirement and the lay of its plan to accomplish it."[39]

The proposal is a sales document. It must tell the buyer that the offeror understands the requirements, knows what is important to the buyer, has the capability to satisfy the government's requirements, and has a unique

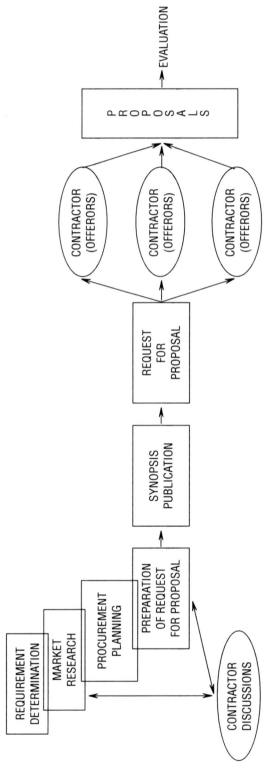

Figure 5-4 The Request for Proposal Process

plan to do so. The proposal must convince the buyer why it is better qualified than the competition's. How this is expressed in the proposal is commonly referred to as the *theme*. The theme is derived from the capture strategy that is developed after the offeror's proposal team has completed a comprehensive examination of the solicitation package and considered information gained while performing market research. In other words, the capture strategy is the key reason why the government should purchase from the firm rather than from a competitor. The capture strategy is translated into an idea or theme that threads its way throughout the proposal. Its goal is to remind the buyer continuously that this is the best solution.

Preparing a proposal requires a great deal of teamwork to integrate a massive amount of information in a relatively short period of time. Contractors must minimize their cost in pursuing business by carefully managing their proposal budgets because it cuts directly into the organization's short-term profit margin. Therefore, as part of the bid/no-bid decision, the potential offeror first decides which proposals it is going to pursue and then how much money it is going to take to win the procurement. The final decision is based on a cost-benefit tradeoff between money it will take to win and the potential long- and short-term revenue benefits.

Analysis of the RFP: The RFP is the formal source of information on the buyer's requirements. However, information gained through the market research process plays a significant role in the preparation of the response to the solicitation. This is because market research not only provides the respondent insight into the critical factors behind the statements of requirements, but it is also the principal source of information on who buys what, when, and how. It is also the origin of data on the competitors and their products.

The first step in analyzing the solicitation is to examine the instructions outlined in Section L, Instructions, Conditions, and Notices to Offerors or Quoters. Section L contains three types of information:

1. Boilerplate solicitation provisions that must be included as amendments to solicitations, modifications, and withdrawals of proposals as required by the FAR or the buying activity
2. Specific instructions for the offerors to follow in developing and submitting their proposals. They should address proposal content and format. They should also reflect the evaluation factors that will be identified and explained in section M. (This is a good source of information on the philosophy of the activity.)
3. Background information that should assist offerors in developing meaningful proposals. The objective is to provide, quantify, or qualify information that will assist the offeror in scoping out the resources required.[40]

Next, the analysis needs to examine Section C, Description/Specifications/Work Statement, because this is where the buyer tells the offeror what it needs. By definition, the negotiated procurement method is used when requirements cannot be precisely described. If the need could be satisfied by a standard or well-defined product or service, the sealed bidding process would be used. Consequently, the potential offer must make a concerted effort to determine what the customer really needs. This leads to ambiguities and the need to make assumptions. Data gathered through market research is important in defining the tasks to be performed.

As noted earlier, acquisition doctrine emphasizes the use of statements of requirements or performance specifications that tell the potential offeror what the buyer wants. It does not specify in great detail how the work is to be done.

The objectives of analyzing the specification are to: (1) understand what attributes the delivered product must have, (2) classify and address ambiguities, and (3) partition the total requirement in a way that ensures that all specified and implied tasks are identified and their interrelationship established.

The third step is to review Section M, Evaluation Factors for Award, to determine how the evaluation team will rank the proposals. After reviewing the proposal, the government buyer wants to have a great deal of confidence that the offeror will do everything that was promised in the proposal. FAR 15.204-5(c) requires Section M of the solicitation to identify all significant factors and subfactors that will be considered in awarding the contract, as well as their relative importance.[41] These factors and subfactors are to be stated clearly in the solicitation.[42] The source selection is to be made after evaluating all proposals, first rating them solely on the evaluation factors and subfactors, and then comparing them against each other to establish the competitive range. (The rating method that will be used by the source selection authority need not be disclosed in the solicitation.[43])

The 1997 rewrite of FAR Part 15 incorporates the acquisition principle of using contractors who have "a track record of successful past performance" as a specific evaluation factor.[44] The solicitation is required to "describe the approach for evaluating past performance, including evaluating an offeror with no relevant performance history." Offerors are "authorized to provide information on problems encountered on the identified contracts and the offeror's corrective actions." Offerors must also realize the government will survey other government agencies to obtain past performance information. The government is to consider this information, including any information received from other sources, in the evaluation of the offeror' past performance.[45]

This rewrite of FAR Part 15 also focuses on the use of cost analysis to establish price reasonableness and cost realism to determine what the government should pay as an apparent function of price reasonableness. The rewrite also explicitly authorizes providing the technical evaluation team with cost information during the evaluation of the technical portion of the proposal. This practice was not permitted in the past.[46]

Last but not least, the offeror must review the solicitation for the purpose of identifying ambiguities. This includes examining the clauses that are included in the solicitation. "Any government contract includes requirements which are expressed, incorporated by reference, or made a part of drawings, specifications, and subspecifications, but it also includes mandatory clauses incorporated by operation of the law."[47] As noted earlier in this chapter, potential offerors have the duty to inquire and receive clarification prior to submission of the proposal if there are obvious ambiguities.

The proposal preparation plan: Preliminary steps to develop the proposal preparation plan should begin long before the release of the RFP. The possible offeror needs to gather information on the requirements of the ultimate user, business practices of the buying office, probable contents of the solicitation, issue date of the solicitation, and target date for contract award. It has been written that "more proposals lose through failure to comply with requirements than are ever beaten by competitors."[48]

The content, complexity, and size of the final plan are a function of the magnitude of the government's requirement. The plan should be tailored to the acquisition (see Table 5-6, Suggested Topics for the Proposal Preparation Plan). Some suggested topics to consider include:

- Description of the product or services to be delivered under the proposed contract from Section C, Description/Specifications/Work Statements, of the solicitation.
- Related experience.
- Expected contract type and value and date of expected contract award.
- Period of performance.
- Key milestones in the proposed contract from Section F, Deliveries or Performance.
- Assumptions that are to be made about the schedule, technology involved, industry trends, resource availability, follow-on contracts, etc.
- Potential risks associated with this acquisition and business practices of the buying office.
- Potential opportunities, including annual sales, return on assets, follow-on business, inventory turns, and profit.
- Terms and conditions that have a financial impact.
- Contractual considerations such as the requirement for government furnished equipment, facilities, information. Is there a requirement for a warranty? What are the special terms and conditions?
- Requirements for capital equipment or facilities. Do capabilities or capacity of facilities need to be expanded?
- Identification of functions that will be involved in the preparation of the proposal.

Table 5-6. Suggested Topics for the Proposal Preparation Plan

Description of the Product or Services To Be Delivered
Key Performance Milestones
Assumptions
Potential Risks
Potential Opportunities
Terms and Conditions with Financial Impact
Contractual Considerations
Requirements for Capital Equipment or Facilities
Functions Involved in Preparation of Proposal
Proposal Preparation Instructions
Competitive Strategy and Evaluation Factors
Anticipated Funding Profile
Planned Contract Award Schedule
Capture Strategy and Theme To Be Used
Information on Competitors
Proposal Preparation Milestones and Critical Path
Proposal Preparation Budget
Supporting Elements to the Proposal Plan
Technical Solutions
Logistics Requirements
Process That Will Be Used
Make-or-buy Tradeoffs
Subcontracting Plan

- Proposal preparation instructions from Section L, Instructions, Conditions, and Other Statements of Offerors or Quoters.
- The competitive strategy that can be used in addressing evaluation factors used in Section M of the solicitation, Evaluation Factors for Award.
- Anticipated funding profile and a summary of the planned schedule to award contract.
- Capture strategy that will be employed to win the contract and theme to be used throughout the proposal.
- Who are the competitors, what is their most likely course of action, and how does their product compare to the companies offering?
- What milestones must be completed to meet the proposal due date, and who is responsible for each? Identification of the critical path.
- Proposal preparation budget and how it will be allocated and controlled.

Supporting elements to the proposal plan include short descriptions of the:

- Technical solution to the customer's needs
- Logistics requirements, i.e., spares, technical data, training, maintenance or overhaul services, and logistics support analysis

- Process that will be used to fabricate, assemble, and test items to be delivered, including facility needs and capital needs
- Make-or-buy tradeoffs and subcontracting plan.

Early in the process the potential offeror must determine what portions of the effort it will make or what it will purchase from outside sources. This make-or-buy decision is critical because it determines the kind of business the offeror wants to continue or pursue. Chief executives realize that the make-or-buy decision is a strategic one and therefore must not be made at too low a level in the organization.[49]

Make-or-buy analysis should concentrate on comparing advantages and disadvantages between making the item and purchasing it from outside sources. The prime contractor is responsible for having mandatory make-or-buy programs when the anticipated contract value is $10 million. In contracts of this value or greater, the government reserves the right to review and agree on a contractor's make-or-buy program when it is necessary to ensure the negotiation of a reasonable price.[50]

Table 5-7, Considerations in the Make-or-Buy Decision, illustrates considerations that are used to determine if the item or service is to be made or purchased.

- The difference between the fixed and variable cost of performing the work in-house versus contracting it out. All relevant costs, both direct and indirect, including realistic estimates of in-house production costs, rework, anticipated facility, and capital needs, must be considered.
- The difference in quality between items purchased and items produced in-house, as compared to the quality standards required to meet provisions of the solicitation.
- Quantity of items required. Frequently the decision to make the item is based on the quantity of the requirement, which is too small to interest suppliers. Large quantities that can be produced on a repeti-

---

Table 5-7. Considerations in the Make-or-Buy Decision

Difference in Cost Between In-house and Outside Sources
Difference in In-house Capacity and Quantity Required
Difference Between Total Capacity and Quantity Required
Reliability of Service Record Between In-house and Outside Sources
Differences in Capabilities Between In-house and Outside Sources
Differences in Knowledge Between In-house and Outside Sources
Requirement to Maintain Core Competency
Urgency of the Requirement
Risk of Labor Unrest Between Sources
Need to Employ Idle Resources

tive basis over long periods of time are more cost effective to produce because the allocation of start-up cost over short production runs may be exorbitant. Some companies maintain the capability to store minimum quantities and purchase additional quantities from outside suppliers as leverage against price, quality, and performance problems from the suppliers.

- Comparison of the reliability of the service record between the sources. Service includes meeting schedules by delivering conforming products on time. It also encompasses such intangible factors as dependability and product reliability, which lead to customer satisfaction.
- Comparison of specialized knowledge, abilities, and production know-how of the potential supplier.
- Requirements to protect an in-house proprietary design or process.
- Which source has the capability to supply urgently needed items to prevent a work stoppage or to provide just-in-time support to the production line?
- Is there a need to maintain a core competency or develop specialized skills for new technology?
- What is the risk of labor unrest between the sources?
- Capacity limitations of the offeror's plant or test facility without making a competent capital investment.
- Employment of idle resources during off-season or business slowdown.[51]

With the end of the Cold War, this country has entered into the era of innovation fueled by introduction of EDI, along with more efficient communications and transportation systems. This is transforming the way the private sector is thinking about business relationships. Businesses are learning there is an alternative to head-to-head combat with other companies to achieve their goals.

As noted earlier, the practice of forming strategic alliances with key suppliers is becoming more prevalent because it is seen as a way to become more efficient and hence more competitive. Efficiency is gained through horizontal integration of functions enabling joint participation in forecasting, marketing, product design, cost estimation, production planning, purchasing, quality assurance, inventory control, and distribution. As companies compete in the international marketplace, they are finding they have to share research and development expenses and results, sometimes with their principal competitors. This alternative includes elimination of middle management and increased teaming with customers, suppliers, distributors, investors, and others with resources that can be used to achieve common objectives.

Formalized Cooperative (teaming) Agreements are drawn up "where partners pool or exchange resources, while remaining separate business entities, with the purpose of achieving their goals and interests."[52] Teaming agreements are not contracts for the purchase of goods or services. A teaming agreement provides the umbrella arrangement for the working relationship and is used to enhance an organization's capabilities, protect proprietary data, and preserve the firm's competitive position by establishing duties, responsibilities, and obligations of the parties.

Strategic alliances have three attributes (see Table 5-8, Attributes of Strategic Alliances). They include:

- Commitment to sharing database information on a routine basis
- Quick response to requests for tailored information
- Development of an inter-organizational culture based on a formalized operating agreement. This operating agreement includes inter-firm rules and procedures and may facilitate the spinoff or absorption of functional responsibilities by one member of the alliance.[53]

Teaming agreements are specific contractual agreements, tailored to specific contracts, and are tendered when the prime contract is awarded. The contents of teaming agreements usually include:

- A Statement of Purpose that defines the scope of the agreement and the technology each member contributes to the alliance.
- Identification of the prime team member and specific rights, duties, and obligations of each member in areas such as forecasting, marketing, product design, cost estimation, production planning, purchasing, quality assurance, inventory control, and distribution. Acknowledgement that each party is an independent contractor.
- An "exclusivity" provision saying potential subcontractors will not propose to work as a prime or subcontractor with any other corporation in the sale of goods or services within the scope of the agreement.
- Provisions covering the exchange and use of proprietary information
- Events that would cause the agreement to be terminated.

As an offshoot of these teaming agreements, formed contractual type agreements are negotiated and awarded during the proposal preparation phase. The main sources for work outside the firm include:

Inter-departmental work agreement: This is work obtained from another group, division, plant, location, or subsidiary of the offeror's company that

---

Table 5-8. Attributes of a Strategic Alliance

- Sharing of information
- Quick response to request for information
- Development of an inter-organization culture
  –Formalized operating agreements
  –Inter-firm procedures
  –Absorption of functional responsibilities

reports its financial data separately. Usually these components have core competencies, facilities, or capabilities not possessed by the offeror.

Subcontractors and vendors: With at least 60 percent of the effort performed outside the firm, subcontractors and vendors are major participants in most efforts. The support required is performed under a contractual agreement that goes into effect when the contract is awarded. Under this agreement the offeror acts as the prime contractor. A subcontractor that holds a contract with a prime contractor is referred to as the first-tier subcontractor. Second or third-tier subcontractors are companies that hold subcontracts with a subcontractor. It is important to remember that the legal responsibilities among parties to the same contract, i.e., privity of contract, are limited to the government and the prime contract. "Generally there is no privity of contract between the government and subcontractors."[54]

Proposal Preparation Instructions

The proposal preparation instructions provide detailed information on all aspects of the bidding effort. They are issued prior to the initiation of the bid and preparation of a written proposal (see Table 5-9, Elements of the Proposal Preparation Instructions). Often the instructions are reviewed with the proposal team at the initial proposal "kick-off" meeting. Key elements of the proposal preparation instructions include:

- Part 1. Major Milestone Events: Along with the time frame in which each event is to be accomplished, these are presented in the form of a master program schedule. Often this includes the Integrated Master Schedule (IMS), which can be traced back to the key events included in the IMP and the related Work Breakdown Structure (WBS). The level of detail included in the proposal must be able to convince the evaluator that the prospective contractor understands the requirement and its related risk. Deliverables are portrayed on a time-phased chart showing production requirements on a month-by-month basis by line items listed in Section B, Supplies or services and prices/cost, of the solicitation.

Table 5-9. Key Elements of the Proposal Preparation Instructions

Major Milestone Events
The Integrated Master Plan
The Work Breakdown Structure
The Bid Responsibility Matrix
Contract Considerations
Technical Considerations
Cost Estimating Instructions

- Part 2. The Integrated Master Plan (IMP): The government will want to evaluate how the cross-functional tasks of the contractor's acquisition team fit together. The IMP is an event-based plan that defines all the major contract tasks gleaned from the RFP and its Statement of Work (SOW) or Operational Requirement Document (ORD) and includes such functions as design engineering, manufacturing engineering, production operations, reliability and logistics support, quality control, testing and evaluation, packaging, and management of suppliers.
- Part 3. A Work Breakdown Structure (WBS): A government-recommended WBS is often included with the proposal preparation instruction. (This sometimes leads to a negotiated agreement with the buying office that requires the development of a revised WBS and the publication of a description of each task.) The WBS is a method of organizing the contractual tasks and sub-tasks into the manageable components of end products to be produced or performed, e.g., hardware, software, technical data, repairs, or services. The entire scope of work to be performed under the proposed contract must be accounted for within the WBS. The WBS represents the framework for the IMP and IMS.

  The government uses this breakdown to compare the amount of resources needed with the amounts proposed by other offerors. Use of the WBS also permits assigning responsibility for proposal preparation. The WBS becomes the basis of funding profiles and projection of personnel needs. After contract award the WBS also becomes a key management tool because it is used to develop budgets, accumulate costs, schedule interrelated tasks, and monitor progress under the earned value concept. This additional actual cost history can be used to support future cost estimates.
- Part 4. A Bid Responsibility Matrix: This is also provided with the proposal instructions. The bid matrix is a listing of WBS elements cross-referenced to the tasks delineated in the solicitation and to functional areas responsible for preparation of the proposal. The matrix also indentifies the person responsible for preparing each WBS and shows the interrelationship of the functions, ensuring that all are given an opportunity to define their needs.
- Part 5. Contractual Considerations: This includes information on the probable type of pricing arrangement, warranty provisions, and data and reporting requirements. The CM's role is to determine how risk is being allocated and to define the obligations being undertaken by both parties. The results of this analysis become part of the proposal preparation instructions in the proposal file. Topics of special interest include payment provisions, inspection and acceptance criteria, contract incentives, patent and data rights, rights in technical data and computer software, and the contractor's liability for damage to government furnished property, such as details on government-furnished

equipment (GFE) and customer-furnished information (CFI), indemnification for unusual hazards, hidden warranties, and warranty clauses.

- Part 6. Technical Considerations: Includes a description of the technical baseline as defined in the ORD or SOW. These include top-level acquisition objectives. The system and subsystems, as well as systems engineering and software requirements, are defined. Documentation includes preliminary identification of configuration items (CI): "A CI is an aggregation of hardware, firmware, computer software, or any of their discrete portions, that satisfies an end use function....Any item required for logistics support and designated for separate procurement is a configuration item."[55] Also included is a definition of the testing and acceptance criteria. Information on reliability, maintainability, and configuration management requirements is described. The need for corporate capital to improve or expand plant equipment and facilities is also expressed here, if appropriate.

- Part 7. Cost Estimating Instructions: With the passage of the Truth in Negotiation Act (TINA) in 1962, Congress changed the way proposals were prepared, evaluated, and negotiated. The objective of TINA was to ensure that the government had an opportunity to review all significant and relevant cost or pricing data available to the contractor in order to arrive at the contract price. Provisions of the act require contractors to submit current, accurate, and complete cost or pricing data in negotiating "certain contracts" with the government. The government is entitled to an adjustment of the negotiated price, including profit or fee, providing the government relied on the defective data submitted by the contractor, or a prospective or actual subcontractor. It is crucial that all members of the offeror's proposal preparation team understand the legal rules that apply—not just the few individuals who put the pricing package together and submit the proposal. All cost estimates must be explained and supported with the understanding they will be read and analyzed by the government's acquisition team, fact finders as well as auditors.

The government's solicitation usually mandates the format for presenting cost data for government evaluation. An exception is that any acquisition that meets the definition of a commercial item or any modification that does not change the item into a noncommercial item is exempt from the requirement for cost or pricing data.[56] This does not relieve the CO from the duty to purchase from responsible sources at a fair and reasonable price and not to obtain any more information than is necessary to make this determination.[57] The CO is instructed to use every available means and has the freedom to ascertain whether this can be done before requesting cost or pricing data. When certified price and pricing data are required, the solicitation must so specify. Then the solicitation must state: (1) that an offeror may request an exception to the requirement, (2) whether any information other than cost or pricing data is required, and (3) whether there is any necessary pre-award or post-award access to offeror's records.[58]

To reduce the workload cost, cost or pricing data is to be obtained only if the CO concludes that none of the following applies:

- The CO determines there is adequate price competition. This is defined as two or more responsible offerors competing independently.[59]
- The CO determines that prices agreed on are based on prices set by law or regulation.[60]
- An item meets the description of a commercial item in FAR 2.101. This includes a modification to a commercial item that does not change it to a noncommercial item.[61]
- A contract is modified for commercial items.[62]
- The acquisition is below the simplified acquisition threshold.[63]

ESTIMATING THE COST OF THE PROPOSED EFFORT

The term *cost* can have two meanings. First, it refers to the amount of money the government incurs to purchase an item. It also can mean the amount paid for the item plus the cost of operating and maintaining the item once it is acquired. The latter meaning is often referred to as the cost of ownership or life-cycle cost. The former meaning refers to the total cost a contractor incurs in meeting the terms and conditions of a contract. It is the amount of money the government spends to purchase an item or service, which will be discussed below.

Most companies price on a cost-plus basis. The cost-plus theory of pricing is a direct function of the cost to perform, and a fair price is a combination of: (1) an accurate representation of cost and (2) a fair profit. The emphasis the government places on audit, detailed cost principles, and cost accounting standards is believed to be a logical extension of the belief that maintenance of the public trust demands accurate cost representations.

The degree of accuracy of the cost estimate varies with the approach being employed by the contractor and subcontractors. The degree of realism or likely accuracy required of the estimate is a function of the stage of the design process, number of alternatives available, and the likely cost magnitude of the item whose cost is being estimated.[64]

There are two approaches to estimating cost: preliminary and detailed. The preliminary approach is used during the formative stages of the project when there is a lack of verifiable information. Preliminary estimates are used during the early planning stage of a project to evaluate design tradeoffs and to aid in the formation of the budget. Detailed estimating techniques are used when the data on which they are based can be verified.

As the item moves through its life cycle, verifiable cost history becomes increasingly available, and cost history should be used to estimate the labor and material requirements. To substantiate the proposal, the method used to develop all cost estimates should be documented by a description of the task and an explanation of the estimating methodology used and the reason for its use.

The following are brief descriptions of some representative estimating techniques:

- The *historic cost method* is used when cost history is available and relevant to the item or services being estimated. This is a very creditable method when the cost history is used that is representative of the anticipated effort.
- The *bottom-up estimating* starts with the lowest level in the process and follows the item or service being delivered from the start of the process to the end. It requires the effort to be broken down into tasks and sub-tasks, to which time factors such as engineered and material time standards are applied. History also can be used when engineering standards are not available. Accurate bottom-up estimates require a considerable amount of data on:
  - –Product specifications
  - –Delivery quantities and rates
  - –Bill of material
  - –Cost of delivered purchased parts and material
  - –Detailed drawings of parts to be manufactured
  - –Parts routing
  - –Manufacturing equipment requirements
  - –Testing and inspection requirements
  - –Packing and shipping requirements.[65]
- *Modular pricing* depends on developing and retaining a database of cost information of the modules or components of the end item. Experienced personnel use this historic database to develop cost estimates using a "similar to" method. This method is based on the historic cost of one component and then extrapolating the cost of the proposed item, judging its complexity. For example, the item being proposed is 1.3 times more complex as item X. Therefore, the estimated cost would be 1.3 times the historic cost of item X.
- The *improvement curve*[66] should be used when developing estimates when there are repetitive operations. Improvements in repetitive tasks take place in two areas: the individual and the organization itself. It is a concept that takes into consideration that the time workers take to perform repetitive tasks is reduced over a period of time. Worker experience and changes made to the workflow process, working environment, and work simplification also result in changes to the hours

needed to produce a given quantity of items. The theory as it is practiced today was introduced in 1936 and validated by the Stanford Research Institute after studying input data from all World War II direct airframe labor hours. The improvement curve theory can be stated: "As the total quantity of units produced doubles, the cost per unit decreases by some constant percentage."[67]

The improvement concept was initially used in estimating hours needed for airframe production. It also has been used to estimate requirements for electronics systems, machine tools, shipbuilding, missile systems, and depot level equipment maintenance.

- *Parametric estimating* is a method of estimating costs by using the mathematical relationship of the item to one or more of its functions or characteristics. The most elementary example is taking the historic cost per pound of an aircraft and extrapolating it to estimate the cost of another aircraft. Another example is using the cost per pound of engine thrust to project the cost of an advanced engine model.

- *Roundtable estimating* is a technique that brings functional representatives together to develop costs estimates using their experience, knowledge of the product, and the market.

- *Expert estimates* rely on the judgment of an individual who is able to combine experience and instinct to estimate the hours required to perform the task. Quite often this method is used to estimate the cost of tasks. This requires knowledge of the tasks to be performed and skill levels that will be available.

FORWARD PRICING RATE AGREEMENTS

Any cost that does not directly benefit a single final cost objective but is incurred for two or more cost objectives is commonly referred to as "indirect cost," "overhead," or "burden." When pricing contracts or contract modifications, this situation can be handled by negotiating indirect cost rates that are to be used in pricing during specified periods of time. When a contractor has a significant volume of government business, the CO may request that the cognizant ACO initiate action to negotiate a Forward Pricing Rate Agreement (FPRA).[68] An FPRA is a written record of negotiations between the contractor and the government of reasonable projections of indirect costs prior to their occurrence. The purpose of an FPRA is to make certain rates are developed for such indirect costs as labor hours, material and labor variances, material handling, efficiency factors, and allowances for obsolescences.

The ACO is responsible for determining if the benefits to be derived from the agreement are commensurate with the effort of developing the rates and negotiating the agreement. When making this decision the ACO must determine: (1) the volume of future pricing actions, (2) the reliability of the contractor's cost accounting data and cost estimating practices, (3) if the period of time the rates will be in effect justifies the administrative effort needed to monitor the rates, (4) if the period of time the rates will be in effect represents an unacceptable risk, and (5) the effect the nature of the contractor's operations and product mix will have on the agreement. If the evaluation is positive, this information can then be used to gain agreement from all government agencies doing business with the contractor on the conditions under which the rates will be used.

The process for developing rates is for the contractor to submit a proposal, along with appropriate cost of pricing data current at the date of submission, to the ACO. The ACO, in conjunction with the cognizant contract auditor and CO, has a significant interest in developing a government objective for rate negotiations. Headquarters of large contractors are required to account for home office expenses in one pool and allocate them to divisions to the maximum extent possible.[69] The FPRAs, which are negotiated by the cognizant CACO, are incorporated into the subordinate corporation's rate. The ACO prepares a price negotiation memorandum and forwards it, along with the negotiated FPRA, to the cognizant auditor and all COs affected by the agreement.

The FPRA contains specific terms and conditions covering expiration, application, and data requirements for systematic monitoring to ensure the validity of the rates. It also contains a provision that either party may cancel the agreement and a requirement that the contractor will notify the cognizant auditor if there are any significant changes to cost or pricing data. When an FPRA is invalid, the contractor should submit a new proposal that reflects the changed conditions. Until a revised FPRA is negotiated, the ACO issues a forward pricing rate recommendation (FPRR) to the buying activities. The FPRR is used to assist negotiators.[70]

In the absence of an FPRA or FPRR, the ACO shall include support for rates utilized.[71]

THE SUBCONTRACT ESTIMATING PROCESS

On average, 60 percent of a company's expenditures are for procuring goods and services from external sources.[72] There are six conditions by which these companies usually establish the cost of items furnished by their suppliers:

1. They request quotes from vendors. This approach is limited to homogeneous products manufactured by multiple producers.
2. They use established catalog or market price.
3. The prime contractor and supplier enter into a cooperative agreement to form a strategic alliance and to work closely together to design to cost or target price of the required item. Value-added analysis is then used to establish a price. The buyer seeks out high-quality, low-priced

suppliers and remains with them as long as it is beneficial to do so. Use of this method is growing in the private sector under the supply-chain management or value-chain management concept.

4. A customer goes to the supplier with an offer to purchase a product with these performance and quality attributes at a price not to exceed $X. If this ceiling price is not met, the customer approaches another supplier until one is found at the required price.

5. The supplier goes to a leader in the industry that offers the needed product at what amounts to a "take-it-or-leave-it" price. This happens with state-of-the-art products or products that have features not found in other products of the producer and represents the best price available. The buyer accepts this price because there is no alternative and because its competitor will be required to do the same.

6. A buyer begins with an established market or catalog price and combines this information with other available information to establish a base price. Using price analysis, the buyer then changes this base price to compensate for technical differences.[73]

The government CO has the responsibility of analyzing the subcontractor's cost or pricing data. The prime contractor or subcontractor shall establish the reasonableness of the proposed subcontractors' prices and include the results of these analyses in the price proposal of either $10,000,000 or 10 percent of the prime contractor's proposed price.[74]

HOW MUCH COST OR PRICING DATA IS ENOUGH?

For negotiated procurements, the FAR's pricing policy is founded on the need for the CO to establish the reasonableness of the offered price, including subcontract cost.[75] The CO is obligated to request no more cost or pricing data than necessary because it increases proposal preparation cost and often delays contract award. The FAR presents three ways to ensure that the proposed price is reasonable. In order of preference, these are:

1. Determining that there has been adequate price competition.
2. Obtaining information other than cost or pricing data. This includes established catalog prices, market prices, or previous contract prices. Sources of this information are from within the government itself or from the offeror if it is necessary. At a minimum, the CO may base the determination on prices of the same or similar items sold previously that have been obtained from the offeror. The FAR does not require this category of data to be certified. (This source may be used when the proposal is below the $500,000 threshold, where cost or pricing data is not requested.[76])

3. Obtaining certified cost or pricing data.[77] Cost or pricing data is defined as "including all *facts* that, as the date of price agreement or, if applicable, an earlier date agreed upon between the parties that is close as practicable to the date of the agreement on price, prudent buyers and sellers would reasonably expect to affect price negotiations significantly...*Cost or pricing data are factual, not judgmental; and are verifiable ...* they are all the facts that can be reasonably expected to contribute to the soundness of estimates of future cost and to the validity of determinations of cost already incurred."[78] (Emphasis added.)

When cost or pricing data are provided, an officer of the corporation is required to execute a Certificate of Current Cost or Pricing Data saying that the cost or pricing data furnished the government are current, accurate, and complete as of the date indicated in the certificate. It is important to understand that this certification does not address the accuracy of the contractor's judgment on the estimation of future costs or projections. It applies only to the verifiable facts on which the judgment was based.[79]

Instructions for submitting cost or pricing data are outlined in Table 15.2 of the FAR. The table instructs the offeror to provide the following information as it is applicable:

- Material and services: A consolidated price summary of individual material quantities included for the effort proposed and the basis for pricing the material, e.g., vendor quotes, invoice prices, or catalog prices. Raw materials, parts, components, assemblies, and services that will be produced or performed by the offeror must also be included. The prime contractor is expected to complete and provide the government the results of its cost analysis of subcontractor and vendor's cost or pricing data. (When the government is ordering spares and repair parts not concurrent with production, the offeror must notify the buying office which items can be ordered directly from the vendors.)
- Direct labor: A time-phased summary of labor hours, rates, and cost of labor by category, as well as the basis for estimate, must be provided.
- Indirect costs: The computed and applied indirect costs, including cost breakdowns. A summary of the forward price rate agreements or interim forward pricing rate agreement used must also be provided.
- Other costs: Costs not included above, such as travel, must be provided.
- Royalties: If royalties exceed $1,500, detailed information must be provided.
- Facilities capital cost of money: If the offeror feels facilities capital cost of money is an allowable cost, it must be measured and calculated in accordance with FAR 30.414-40.

PROPOSAL REVIEW AND SUBMISSION

Prior to submitting a proposal, it is common practice for the proposal preparation team to review the submission with an appropriate level of management to obtain approval. The level of management that is required to approve submission of each proposal is a matter of company policy, which usually takes into consideration the proposal size, the customer, the types of financial and contractual commitments, and the amount of company funds involved. The goals of this review are to ensure that the appropriate level of management:

- Agrees that the proposed effort is consistent with the firm's strategic plan and will effectively employ the company's core competencies
- Understands commitments made by each of the functions involved in performing the work
- Will provide the labor, facilities, equipment, and capital investment required to perform the proposed tasks
- Approves of the financial agreements or commitments included in the proposal
- Reviews special provisions and contractual aspects of the proposed contract
- Evaluates the methodology used in developing the cost, along with supporting justification
- Addresses the risks and opportunities associated with the proposed contract.

ALPHA CONTRACTING—GOVERNMENT AND SUPPLIER INTEGRATION

The statement of guiding acquisition principles states that the acquisition team consists of all participants in the acquisition process, i.e., technical, supply, procurement community, customers (ultimate users), and contractors, working together as a team to deliver the best value product on a timely basis.[80] The Alpha Contracting process, introduced in 1996, is an example of how the acquisition team concept can be used to streamline the acquisition process. An integrated acquisition team following the Alpha Contracting Process is able to convert the traditionally consecutive contracting process into a concurrent exchange of information and agreements, reducing the time and cost required to award a contract. Described as integrative partnering, it changes the competitive paradigm to a cooperative one. It is an attempt to improve the customer-supplier relationships that in the past have often been distrustful, zero-sum games where one party gains at the expense of the other.[81]

The concept followed by an Alpha Contracting team is described as follows:

> Together, this team develops the scope of work and other contract requirements which form the baseline from which the team can jointly develop the technical and cost details that are the basis of the contract agreement. During the process, the team may identify the need to change the baseline to provide better performance or lower risk or to reduce the cost. Rather than have a proposal submitted with numerous exceptions or at a price that is not affordable, the team jointly develops an approach that all parties find acceptable and affordable. Instead of an RFP, the team's output is essentially the draft contract....The model contract developed initially is revised and adjusted as the technical and price details are worked out, and becomes the contract document executed.[82]

The most obvious benefit of Alpha Contracting is that it reduces proposal preparation time, thus cutting administrative lead time. The government benefits by having the contractor's expertise available to help define the requirements when the paper is essentially blank. Rather than representatives from the various functional specialties working separately and making decisions sequentially, team members meet to develop collectively the statement of objectives, project plan, and schedule as part of a draft contract. During these meetings the team often identifies areas that need to be changed to meet performance objectives, lower risk, or reduce cost. The team's final product is essentially a draft contract—a draft that is better understood by both parties.

There are some restrictions to the use of Alpha Contracting. Because the process assumes the contractor has already been selected, it lends itself more to sole-source procurements or modifications to active contracts. Alpha Contracting is labor intensive and therefore should be used on acquisitions that are long-range and have a high payoff.[83] In the case of R&D requirements, a majority of the effort is placed on the contractor's technical staff, which may lead the contractor to perform a cost-benefit tradeoff analysis before participating.

ORAL PRESENTATIONS

Rather than depending entirely on written material to make the award, buyers have used oral presentations by the offeror for many years. With emphasis being placed on reducing administrative lead times, however, there has been a renewed interest in using oral presentation to augment or substitute for written proposals. Oral presentations are subject to the same restrictions as written proposals regarding the contractor submitting modifications and revisions, withdrawal of proposals, and all exchanges with offerors after the receipt of proposals. Oral presentations may be held at any time in the acquisition process.[84] Exchanges between the parties during oral presentations are also subject to the same rules of discussions as if it were a conventional negotiated procurement.

When oral presentations are used, the solicitation must provide the types of information required. The FAR's examples of suitable information include details on the prospective contractor's capabilities, past performance, work plans or approaches, staffing, transitional plans, sample tasks, or types of tests. Other ground rules for offerors include required qualifications of the personnel making the presentation, time restrictions, and information on time, date, and location.[85]

The Treasury Department recently reported examples in which oral presentations clearly demonstrated the ability to evaluate technically offers from five offerors while significantly reducing administrative lead time and administrative cost.

In one example, they were able to award an indefinite delivery/indefinite quantity contract to conduct a worldwide education program for users of U.S. currency 55 days after the solicitation was issued, as opposed to the six to eight months it usually took. The technical evaluation was broken down into two phases. The first was a Written Technical Proposal that was evaluated on a pass/fail basis. In the second phase, the remaining offerors gave two-hour oral presentations describing a representative public education campaign, followed by questions seeking clarification.[86]

In another example, Financial Management Services (FMS) of the Treasury used oral presentations to award task orders. The goal was to save time and money. Vendors were instructed to bring an outline of the oral technical proposal, résumés of key personnel, a price proposal, and a representative with the authority to commit the firm to its original proposal and any subsequent changes. The team realized significant savings of time and resources compared with the traditional paper-intensive method. They also indicated that being able to have a face-to-face with the prospective supervisor of the offeror's team was very useful. The only downside reported was the requirement to devote eight employees full time for three days to participate in the evaluation.[87]

UNSOLICITED PROPOSALS

If a contractor has a new product or an innovative idea, it can initiate an unsolicited proposal. An unsolicited proposal is defined as "a written proposal for a new or innovative idea that is submitted to the agency on the initiative of the offeror for the purpose of obtaining a contract with the government. It is not submitted in response to an RFP, Broad Agency Announcement, Small Business Innovation Research topic, Program Research and Development Announcement, or any other government-initiated solicitation or program."[88]

The unsolicited proposal is not substantially different from the one submitted competitively. To be acceptable, an unsolicited proposal must: (1) be innovative and unique; (2) be independently developed and originated by the offeror; (3) be prepared without direct government involvement or supervision, endorsement, or direction; (4) include sufficient detail to permit determination that government support could be worthwhile; and (5) not be submitted in advance of a known agency requirement that could be acquired by competitive means. Proposals that are submitted in response to a publicized general statement of agency needs are considered to be independently originated.[89]

At face value, the unsolicited proposal process appears to be a way for a company to sell its good idea to the government without going through the RFP process. There are many examples in which the government and offeror have mutually benefited from the new ideas that have been placed on contract after the receipt of an unsolicited proposal. However, there are hurdles each unsolicited proposal must overcome before it is accepted. First, the unsolicited proposal bypasses the competitive process and must be scrutinized by the competition advocate as if it were a non-competitive procurement. Another obstacle is the lack of budget support. Because it has not been included in the agency's plan, it will not have a sponsor in the agency; therefore, it must compete at a disadvantage with all other projects for budget dollars. The rules in the FAR require the agency to perform a prompt, comprehensive analysis of the unsolicited proposal. To do this, the agency must divert expertise from other projects to make the evaluation and submit the report.

CONCLUSION

It has been said that proposal preparation is an art. A written or oral proposal must convince the buyer that the offeror will deliver the best value to the government. This can best be accomplished by demonstrating that it: (1) fully understands the requirement, (2) has a technically sound approach, (3) has an approach that is achievable within schedule and cost constraints, and (4) has the capability and capacity to carry out the proposed effort successfully.

Chapter 6 will cover awarding contracts under the competitive bidding process and the source selection process. Source selection is defined as the process of selecting a contractor through competitive negotiations.[90] Factors of the source selection process that will be covered in Chapter 6 include evaluating proposals, determining the competitive range, conducting the written and oral discussions, requesting proposal revisions, selecting the source, and awarding the contract.

NOTES

[1]Cibinic, Jr., John and Ralph C. Nash, Jr. 1982. *Formation of Government Contracts*. Washington, D.C: Government Contracts Program, George Washington University, 18–21.

[2]Hoch, Detlev J., Cyriac R. Roeding, Gert Purkert, and Sandro K Linder. 1999. *Secrets of Software Success*. Boston, MA: Harvard Business School Press, 168.

[3]Witte, Robert D. 1994. Ambiguities. *Contract Management* (February): 30.

[4]Nash, Jr., Ralph C., Steven L. Schooner, and Karen R. O'Brien. 1998. *The Government Contracts Reference Book: A Comprehensive Guide to the Language of Procurement*, 2d ed. Washington, D.C.: The George Washington University, 120.

[5]Nash, Jr., Schooner, and O'Brien, 27.

[6]Cibinic, Jr., John, and Ralph C. Nash, Jr. 1986. *Administration of Government Contracts*, 2d ed. Washington D.C.: Government Contracts Program, George Washington University, 170.

[7]Cibinic, Jr., and Nash, Jr., *Administration of Government Contracts*, 123.

[8]Cibinic, Jr., and Nash, Jr., *Administration of Government Contracts*, 170.

[9]Cibinic, Jr., and Nash, Jr., *Administration of Government Contracts*, 178.

[10]Cibinic, Jr., and Nash, Jr., *Administration of Government Contracts*, 178–252.

[11]Wangemann, Mary Ann P. 1996. Managing Cost on a Proposal Effort: How to Stay Within Budget While Pursuing Contract Awards. *Contract Management* (February): 22.

[12]Hartman, George M. 1990. To Bid or Not To Bid—That Is the Question. *Contract Management*. (July): 26.

[13]FAR 1.102.

[14]FAR 15.406-2(a).

[15]FAR 15.404-1(c)(1).

[16]Dempsey, Davis B. 1999. The FAR 15 Rewrite—Two Years Later: A Section-by-Section Review. *Contract Management*. 29(2): 49.

[17]Drucker, Peter F. 1993. The Five Deadly Business Sins. *Wall Street Journal* Oct. 21, 1993.

[18]Burt, David N., and Richard L. Pinkerton. 1996. *A Purchasing Manager's Guide to Strategic Proactive Procurement*. New York: American Management Association, 152.

[19]FAR 14.202-1.

[20]Cibinic, Jr., and Nash, Jr., *Formation of Government Contracts*, 216.

[21]Cibinic, Jr., and Nash, Jr., *Formation of Government Contracts*, 217.

[22]10 U.S.C. § 2305(c) and 41 U.S.C. §253(b).

[23]Cibinic, Jr., and Nash, Jr., *Formation of Government Contracts*, 217.

[24]Borden, Russell J. 1988. Bidder Beware! A Look at Some of the Contract Pitfalls of Government Contracting. *Contract Management* (March): 13.

[25]Cibinic, Jr., and Nash, Jr., *Formation of Government Contracts*, 252.

[26]Cibinic, Jr., and Nash Jr., *Formation of Government Contracts*, 262–281.

[27]Borden, 14.

[28]*Federal Register.* 1991. Washington D.C.: Government Printing Office, 56FR66091.

[29]Burt and Pinkerton, xi.

[30]Burt and Pinkerton, 98.

[31]Cibinic, Jr., and Nash Jr., *Formation of Government Contracts,* 282.

[32]Cibinic, Jr., and Nash, Jr., *Formation of Government Contracts,* 303.

[33]Nash, Jr., Schooner, and O'Brien, 524.

[34]FAR 14.503-1.

[35]FAR 14.503-2.

[36]Nash, Jr., Schooner, and O'Brien, 419.

[37]Cibinic, Jr., and Nash, Jr., *Formation of Government Contracts,* 371.

[38]Nash, Jr., Schooner, and O'Brien, 70.

[39]Talbot, Terry R. 1997. Source Selection After Acquisition Reform. *Contract Management* (December): 44.

[40]Wilson, Hugh (Hamp) H. 1996. RFPs—Let's Make Them Better. *Contract Management* (September): 20.

[41]FAR 15.204-5(c).

[42]FAR 15.304(d).

[43]FAR 15.304(d).

[44]FAR 1.102(b)(1)(ii).

[45]FAR 15.305(a)(2)(ii).

[46]Dempsey, 45.

[47]Witte, Robert D. 1997. Contract Clauses—In or Not. *Contract Management* (October): 54.

[48]Bishoff, William K. Review of Edmunds, Don L. 1993. Source Selection: A Seller's Perspective. *Contract Management* (June): 63.

[49]Burt and Pinkerton, 98.

[50]FAR 15.407-2 (a).

[51]Burt and Pinkerton, 99–102.

[52]Don't Just Survive, Thrive. 2000. *The Contract Manager as a Business Manager: 2000 National Education Seminar.* Vienna, VA: National Contract Management Association, 8-1–8-2.

[53]Bowersox, Donald J., Patricia J. Daugherty, Cornelia Droge, Richard N. Germain, and Dale S. Rogers. 1992. *Logistics Excellence: It is NOT Business as Usual.* Burlington MA: Digital Press, 155.

[54]Nash, Jr., Schooner, and O'Brien, 408.

[55]Nash, Jr., Schooner, and O'Brien, 114.

[56]FAR 15.403-1(c)(3).

[57]FAR 15.403-3.

[58]FAR 15.403-5.

[59]FAR 15.403-1(c)(1).

[60]FAR 15.403-1(b)(2).

[61]FAR 15.403-1(b)(3).

[62]FAR 15.403-1(c)(3).

[63]FAR 15.403-1(a).

[64]Burt and Pinkerton, 282.

[65] Burt and Pinkerton, 285.

[66]Also known as the learning curve, Boeing curve, cost- or time-reduction curve, experience curve, and unit curve.

[67]1986. *Armed Services Pricing Manual.* Chicago, IL: Commerce Clearing House, Inc., 3–28.

[68]FAR 42.1701(a).

[69]FAR 30.403, Cost Accounting Standard 403—Allocation of Home Office Expenses to Segments.

[70]FAR 42.1701(d).

[71]FAR 42.1701(d).

[72]Burt and Pinkerton, xi.

[73]Nanzer, R. Michael, Michael E. Hebering, Jane E. Dillon, and Mary E. Kinsella. 1998. Pricing: A Major Hurdle in Acquisition Reform. *Contract Management* (April): 27.

[74]FAR 15.404-3(b).

[75]FAR 15.404-3(a).

[76]Sauls, Christine G. 1998. How Much Cost or Pricing Data is Enough? *Contract Management* (November): 54.

[77]FAR 15.402.

[78]FAR 15.401.

[79]FAR 15.406-2(b).

[80]FAR 1.102.

[81]Bounds, Gregory M., and Albert J. Cole. 2000. Enhanced Alpha Contracting through Integrative Partnering. *Contract Management* (January): 8–9.

[82]2000 National Education Seminar (2000 NES). *Don't Just Survive, Thrive: The Contract Professional as a Business Manager.* Vienna, VA: National Contract Management Association, 7-6.

[83]2000 National Education Seminar (2000 NES), 7-5.

[84]FAR 15.102(a).

[85]FAR 15.102(c).

[86]Seegars, Carol L. 1996. Oral Presentations—BEP's Success Story. *Contract Management* (February): 26.

[87]Connors, John M. 1996. Oral Proposals Streamline Task Awards at Treasury's FMS. *Contract Management* (January): 20.

[88]FAR 15.601.

[89]FAR 15.603(c).

[90]Nash, Jr., Schooner, and O'Brien, 483.

6

Source Selection, Negotiations, and Contract Award

The overarching goal of the Federal Acquisition System is to "deliver on a timely basis the best-value product or service to the customer, while maintaining the public's trust and fulfilling public policy objectives."[1] Attainment of this goal culminates with source selection and negotiations, which result in the award of the contract. Awarding a contract with the right source is a key factor in the user's ability to fulfill its mission. During the acquisition process it has been the job of the acquisition team to provide qualified candidates, i.e., contractors that can provide the right quality of goods and services on time, at a reasonable price, and then to award a contract to the right source. This chapter will cover source selection, negotiations, and contract award.

Source selection in our capitalistic system has been described by Robert D. Witte as being accomplished in an environment in which "the customers generally have unlimited discretion to select from whom they shall procure, acquire, or buy. The government appears to be more constricted by rules, but generally enjoys the same status. It merely does this with more formalities and at much greater expense to itself and its suppliers."[2]

From the government's point of view, the nature of the source selection process that is followed is determined by the complexity of the requirements, the risks related to delivering a quality product on time, and the resources available to the government to conduct the acquisition.[3] This process includes an evaluation methodology to determine if the prospective contractor has the capability, tenacity, and perseverance to perform the contract and to ensure that the government is paying a fair and reasonable price.

For products that will more than likely be purchased following the rules of a negotiated competitive procurement, acquisition reform brought with it a significant policy change. The acquisition team has been instructed to communicate its requirements as soon as possible in the form of overall purpose and performance requirements rather than specific design-like specifications. This is referred to as performance-based contracting. It leaves determining the form of the product and the processes that will be followed during contract performance up to the contractor. For technically complex requirements, the long list of specifications and standards that had previously been included in the requests for proposals (RFPs) were reduced to a very few performance-oriented specifications or standards, or maybe none at all. This policy direction has turned the "how to" over to the contractor.[4]

This means that potential offerors must now increase their effort to understand thoroughly the customer's requirements and develop the plan to accomplish the tasks. "Gone are the days when the prospective contractor could merely 'parrot back' the detailed government requirements and specifications furnished as part of the RFP."[5] This change in policy has not made it any easier for the government buyer. As stated earlier, one of the goals of the federal acquisition system is to foster maximum use of commercial products and to encourage innovation. No longer can members of the acquisition team, or Source Selection Authority (SSA), refer to the checklist as they determine if the prospective contractor met the defined criteria. They must now act as true functional experts and not rely primarily on what is spelled out in the MIL-STDs.[6]

Acquisition reform also has elevated the importance of the prospective contractor's record of past performance. The Federal Acquisition Streamlining Act (FASA) states that "past contract performance of an offeror is one of the relevant factors that a CO should consider in awarding a contract."[7] Past performance is to be used as a mandatory evaluation factor on most procurements, and a prospective contractor is responsible for demonstrating to the government that previous contractor performance problems have been eliminated.[8]

CONTRACTOR QUALIFICATIONS: PART OF THE PROCESS OF MANAGING RISK

It is in the public interest to award contracts only to responsible contractors. An essential step in every procurement is determining that the potential offeror has the qualifications needed to serve as a government contractor. Gathering the data needed to make this determination is an integral part of market research that is initiated by the CO early in the planning phase. Sources of data include Dun & Bradstreet reports, trade publications, references from users (internal and external), knowledgeable persons in the industry, annual reports, filing with the Securities and Exchange Commission, and financial statements.

To determine if the prospective contractor is qualified, the CO must determine if the contractor is:

- Capable of completing the contract work in a satisfactory manner
- Organized in such a way that doing business will promote various social and economic goals
- Able to satisfy other special standards of eligibility imposed by statute and regulations.[9]

To minimize the risk of awarding contracts to contractors who later prove they are unable to perform, the government first determines if the prospective contractor is "responsible." The government also has the power to debar and suspend contractors, thereby preventing them from being awarded a government contract.

Determining the Contractor's Responsibility

Determining that the prospective contractor is responsible is a prerequisite to the award of each government contract. The concept of determining a contractor's responsibility was not formally a part of the procurement process until 1948. At that time the Armed Services Procurement Act included the following statement of policy: "Awards shall be made with reasonable promptness by giving written notice to the responsible bidder whose bid conforms to the invitation and will be the most advantageous to the United States, price and other factors considered."[10] The responsibility of the CO to determine the prime contractor's responsibility has been extended to making a similar determination of the critical subcontractors as well.

The Comptroller General has recognized the discretionary nature of the CO's determination of responsibility to make final judgment regarding the qualifications of the prospective contractors, unless they are a small business. The Comptroller General has stated that:

> Deciding a prospective contractor's probable ability to perform a contract to be awarded involves a forecast which must of necessity be a matter of judgment. Such judgment should be of course based on fact and reached in good faith; however, it is only proper that it be left largely to the sound administrative discretion of contracting officers involved who should be in the best position to assess responsibility, who must bear the major brunt of any difficulties experienced in obtaining required performance, and who must maintain day-to-day relations with the contractor on the Government's behalf.[11]

The CO's discretion has proved to be so broad that once a positive determination of responsibility has been rendered, the CO is bound by that determination and may not cancel the contract based on a subsequent discovery of information that leads him to believe it was incorrectly made.[12] In the case of a small business, a Certificate of Competency and Determination of Eligibility stating that the holder is responsible for the purpose of receiving a government contract is to be obtained from the Small Business Administration.[13]

As noted by the Comptroller General, when making this responsibility determination the CO is required to have acceptable evidence of the prospective contractor's resources, current capabilities or commitments, and what arrangements must be made to obtain the required resources at the time of contract award. To be judged responsible, the prospective contractor, as well as critical subcontractors, must have or will be able to meet the standards defined in FAR 9.104. They must have:

- Adequate financial resources or the ability to obtain them.
- A capability to comply with the required or proposed delivery or performance schedule, taking into consideration all existing commercial and government business commitments.
- A satisfactory performance standard.
- A satisfactory record of integrity and business ethics.
- The necessary organization, experience, accounting, operational controls, and technical skills, or the ability to obtain them. (This includes such elements as production control procedures, property control systems, and quality assurance measures applicable to materials to be produced or services to be performed by the prospective contractor and subcontractors.)
- The necessary production construction and technical equipment and facilities or the ability to obtain them.
- The eligibility to receive an award under applicable laws and regulations.[14]

Debarment Actions

Debarment is a civil sanction that excludes a contractor from receiving all contracts, as well as government-approved subcontracts, for a reasonable period of time that is commensurate with the seriousness of the offense, but not for more than three years.[15] The purpose of debarment is to avoid business risk and to motivate contractors to conduct themselves in ways that will further national social and economic goals.[16] Debarment differs from responsibility determination in that it does not apply to a specific contract but to all contracts applicable to the debarred contractor.

The procedural requirements for debarment have their foundation in statutes, executive orders, and regulations. Causes for debarment include:

- Conviction of or civil judgment for a commission of fraud or criminal offense related to obtaining or performing a government contract
- Antitrust violation
- Commission of embezzlement, theft, forgery, bribery, making false statements, etc.
- Commission of any other offense indicating lack of business integrity or business honesty that affects the contractor's present responsibility
- Intentionally affixing a label bearing a "Made in America" inscription to a product not made in the United States
- Willful failure to perform a government contract or history of unsatisfactory performance
- Violation of the Drug-Free Workplace Act of 1988 (may be debarred for five years)
- Commission of unfair trade practice
- Any other practice so serious or compelling in nature that it affects the present responsibility of a government contractor or subcontractor.[17]

Suspension Actions

Like debarment, suspension is a civil action, taken by an individual authorized by the head of an agency, to disqualify a contractor from government contracting and government-approved subcontracting. A firm is suspended from receiving government contracts for a temporary period of time, e.g., 18 months, unless legal proceedings are initiated within that time. Causes for suspension are the same as those for debarment. Suspension is generally used only when firms are suspected of criminal misconduct that might serve as the basis for debarment. It is used where debarment proceedings might prejudice the government's investigation of the case as well as affect the firm's ability to defend itself against a criminal charge in court.[18]

COMPETITIVE SEALED BIDDING

The key factor in the sealed bidding method of procurement is that all bidders must bid on the same exact effort, and the subsequent contract award is made at a public opening to the offeror whose bid conforms (is responsive) to the invitation for bid (IFB).[19] The CO is to reject bids if they are not responsive to the IFB, i.e., if the offer does not propose to perform the work exactly as it is called out in the solicitation.

Mistakes in Bids prior to Award

One of the objectives of FAR, Subpart 14.406-3, is to minimize delays in contract award while preserving the integrity of the competitive bid process. Therefore, the CO is given the authority to make administrative determinations to correct alleged mistakes in responsive bids. However, an administrative determination cannot be used to make the bids responsive or more competitive.[20]

As part of the risk management process prior to contract award, the CO must verify all bids. The targets of this examination are mistakes on the part of the offeror. This is because there is always a risk of mistakes in one or more bids received from the offerors. In some cases mutual mistakes or mistakes made by the government buyer are also discovered. If a CO fails to seek verification, the government may be subject to claims for price adjustment, or the contractor may claim a mistake as a basis for avoiding contract performance.[21]

When there is an obvious or apparent mistake, the CO must call attention to it and request verification from the offeror of the alleged mistake in its bid. Some of the most common indicators of mistakes are: (1) the bid is much lower than other bids received, (2) government's "should-cost" analysis suggests there is a possible error, (3) there is a deviation from a previous purchase of similar items, and (4) other data suggest a possible mistake. If the offeror fails to provide evidence to support a suspected mistake, the CO is instructed to accept the bid unless it is so far out of line that it would be unfair to the bidder or other bona fide bidders. The CO is required to reject an obvious erroneous bid, even if the offeror confirms it is correct.[22]

The FAR categorizes mistakes at this point in the bid process into two areas, i.e., clerical (apparent) and other disclosed mistakes.

A clerical or apparent mistake may be corrected prior to award. Examples of clerical mistakes include misplacement of a decimal, incorrect discount, obvious reversal of a free-on-board (f.o.b.) destination with f.o.b. origin, and a mistake in the designation of the unit.[23]

When the offeror discloses a mistake, corrections are permitted only if it is a responsive bid. Corrections may not be made that will make the bid more responsive. Correction of mistakes disclosed by the offeror is limited to persons who have been delegated the authority to do so by the head of the agency.[24]

Rules governing a determination of mistakes for common situations are outlined below. Each proposed determination shall also have the concurrence of legal council before being made.[25]

The following are provided to illustrate possible situations that can arise:

- *Situation*: The bidder requests permission to withdraw the bid because of a mistake, and there is clear and convincing evidence that shows a mistake was actually made in the bid. *Rule*: The agency head may allow the bidder to correct the mistake if it would result in displacing one or more lower bidders.[26]

- *Situation*: The bidder requests permission to withdraw the bid because of the mistake rather than correct it, and the evidence is clear and convincing of a mistake in the bid. In addition, both the corrected and uncorrected bids are the lowest bids. The agency head may make the determination to correct the bid and not permit its withdrawal.[27]

- *Situation*: The bidder requests permission to withdraw the bid because of the mistake if there is clear and convincing evidence that a mistake was made and if the evidence is not clear to the intended bid or does not warrant a determination under the two situations described above. *Rule*: The agency head may make a determination that the bid be neither withdrawn nor accepted.[28]

Cancellation of Invitations for Bids after Opening

To protect the integrity of the competitive bidding process, after bids have been opened award must be made to the responsible bidder who submitted the lowest responsive bid, unless there is a compelling reason to reject all bids and cancel the invitation.[29]

If there are changes in the requirement or administrative difficulties preventing award before the bidder's acceptance period, the FAR describes appropriate actions for the CO to take.

If there is a change in the requirement after bid opening, the IFB should not be canceled, but a resolicitation must be issued to increase the requirement. In anticipation of a possible change in requirements occurring before bid opening, the solicitation should be written so that bidders are permitted to change their bids. This act will prevent exposure to increases in the bid price on the part of the potential contractors. If this action is not possible, the CO is instructed to continue with the initial award and initiate a new IFB for the added requirement as if it were a new acquisition.[30]

When administrative difficulties are encountered after bid opening that may delay contract award beyond the bidders' acceptance dates, there are actions the CO is instructed to take to avoid adding time to the acquisition process. This can be accomplished by requesting that several of the lowest bidders provide written extensions to the bid acceptance period prior to the bidder's expiration dates.[31]

Nevertheless, compelling circumstances can dictate that all bids can be rejected and the IFB canceled. For example, when it is determined after bid opening, but before the award, that the requirement to cite specifications listed in the GSA Index of Federal Specifications, Standards, and Commercial Item Descriptions, the DoD Index of Specifications and Standards

(DoDISS), or other agency indexes was not provided in the IFB, the offeror's invitation shall be canceled.[32]

Invitations also can be canceled and all bids rejected after opening but before award when the agency head makes a written determination that:

- Inadequate or ambiguous specifications were cited in the invitation.
- Specifications have been revised.
- The supplies or services are no longer required.
- The IFB did not provide for consideration of all the factors of cost to the government, such as the cost of transporting government-furnished property (GFP) to the bidder's plant.
- Bids received indicate that the governments' needs can be satisfied by a less expensive article that differs from the one for which bids were solicited.
- Bids were not independently arrived at in open competition, were collusive, or were submitted in bad faith. (Selective cases should be referred to the Justice Department.)
- Cost comparison as prescribed in OMB Circular A-76, *Policies for Acquiring Commercial or Industrial Products and Services Needed by the Government*, and Subpart 7.3 of the FAR shows that performance of the desired effort by the government is more economical.
- For other reasons, cancellation is clearly in the public's interest.[33]

There are also situations where it may be appropriate to complete the award even after cancellation of the IFB, for example, when bids are received at unreasonable prices or when bids were not independently arrived at. Under these circumstances the agency head can authorize cancellation of the IFB and declare that negotiating is in the government's best interest. The CO may then negotiate and make an award to the responsible bidder offering the lowest negotiated price, without issuing a new solicitation.[34]

Discussion of Bids prior to Contract Award

Fundamental to the sealed bidding procedure is the requirement that the bids be evaluated without discussion. When discussions are held after bid opening and prior to contract award, it becomes a negotiated procurement. Alterations or corrections to the bid are permitted only if doing so is not prejudicial other bidders and when they pertain to a matter of form rather than substance, i.e., no effect or merely a negligible effect on price, quantity, quality, or delivery of the item bid upon.[35]

Almost without exception the CO has little latitude in making the award to any party except the low bidder. No evaluation criteria may be used to make an award that is not defined in the IFB. The evaluation criteria may include such elements as inspection, testing, quality, workmanship, delivery, and suitability for a particular purpose. An objectively measurable standard is the best way the bid price should be evaluated. Examples of such standards are transportation costs and total cost of ownership.

Bid Opening and Contract Award

The CO conducts a public bid opening, usually reading aloud the amount of each bid, other relevant information, and, if practical, the name of each bidder. All bids are then recorded and safeguarded until the completion of a certification of an abstract of all bids received in response to the solicitation.

Prior to the award the CO is responsible for determining if the prices are reasonable in light of the circumstances. Prompt payment discounts are not considered when evaluating bids. However, when payment is made within the discount period specified by the bidder, it is to be taken by the paying center.

There can be advantages to the government in making more than one award if it represents an economic advantage to the buyer. The CO must include in the IFB a notice that multiple awards might be possible.[36]

If fewer than three bids have been received, the CO has the duty to determine why there were not more participants. If appropriate, corrective action to increase competition in future solicitations may be initiated. However, an award will be made regardless of the limited number of bids.[37]

As noted earlier, contracts awarded under the sealed bidding process are usually firm-fixed-price. The amount is fixed by the competitive forces of the market. In this type of contracting arrangement, there is no formula or technique for varying the price in light of unforeseen circumstances. Under the pure firm-fixed-price contract, the cost risk is placed entirely on the contractor. However, there is a variation that provides for adjustment of some elements of the price. The firm-fixed-price with an economic price adjustment provides for adjustment to the price if pre-designated cost elements—most frequently material cost or labor rates—increase or decrease during the period of performance. The basic purpose of the economic price adjustment is to protect the contractor from economic price adjustments that are outside the contractor's control while continuing to motivate the contractor to control costs. The economic price adjustment clauses need to be tailored to the specific procurement in which they are used.[38]

If the bidder proposes an economic price adjustment with a ceiling price that cannot be exceeded, even though the IFB does not contain an economic price adjustment clause, the CO is instructed to reject the bid unless a ceiling price is proposed. In this case the bid will be evaluated on the basis of the maximum possible economic price adjustment of the quoted price.[39]

After proper approvals are obtained, the contract is then awarded to the responsible bidder whose bid conforms to the IFB and will be most advantageous to the government, considering the standards and price and the price-related factors included in the IFB. Price-related factors include such considerations as:

- Cost or delay to the government resulting from differences in inspections, location of supplies, and transportation (costs)
- Changes made at the request of the bidder in any of the provisions of the IFB if they do not represent a cause for rejection.[40]

Mistakes after Award

A mistake is defined is "an act or omission arising from ignorance or misconception."[41] When addressing alleged mistakes after award, the CO not only must consider the contractor's obligation to perform the contractual effort, but he or she must also evaluate fairness to the other bidders and the integrity of the acquisition process. By carefully verifying the bids prior to contract award, the CO can minimize the number of contract claims attributed to mistakes.

Mistakes after contract award fall into three categories: (1) mutual mistakes on the part of both the seller and buyer, (2) unilateral mistakes on the part of the contractor, or (3) unilateral mistakes on the part of the government.

A mutual mistake can occur when: (1) the parties include terms in a contract that do not conform to or express their actual intent or agreement, or (2) both parties labor under the same misconception about the fundamental fact upon which the contract is based.[42]

A unilateral mistake is one made by only one party. A mistake of this kind can never justify reformation or alteration of the contract, although a mistake may be the basis for rescission if parties can be restored to their original positions and one party is seeking an unconscionable advantage over the other.[43] In government contracts no relief is granted after award unless the CO knew or should have known of the mistake before award or failed to ask for verification.[44]

Two-Step Sealed Bidding

In Chapter 4 we discussed the two-step sealed bidding process and learned that it was introduced by the DoD in the late 1950s as a means of enhancing price competition. The two-step process is designed to be used when an adequate data package is not available. A technical data package is developed in the first step. This information then enables the government to use the conventional sealed bidding process in the second step to acquire the best value product.

During Step One, technical proposals are obtained and evaluated, revised, and modified during discussions between the offerors and the acquisition team. At their conclusion the acquisition team then determines which technical proposals are "acceptable," and the applicable offerors are then invited to participate in Step Two. The requirement is only advertised in the *Commerce Business Daily* prior to initiating the Step One RFP.

Step Two follows the conventional sealed bidding process. At this time IFBs are sent to the potential contractors whose proposals were judged to be acceptable. These potential contractors them submit a sealed bid based on the requirements defined in its approved technical proposal. Contract award is then made, without further discussion or negotiations, to the offeror that submits the lowest price on its technical proposal.

The CO is expected to handle Step Two of the bidding process as if it were a conventional sealed bid.

COMPETITIVE NEGOTIATED PROCUREMENTS

The objective of a negotiated competitive procurement is to select the proposal that represents the best value to the government. In a negotiated procurement there can be multiple source selection factors. This is in contrast to competitive sealed bidding, which is focused only on price.[45] The negotiated procurement process is used when the critical requirement variables include quality, technical innovation, cost of ownership, and schedule in addition to a fair and reasonable price.

Part 15.1 of the FAR describes two categories of negotiated procurements. These are the tradeoff between designated critical factors and the technique using the lowest price that is technically acceptable. Each represents the two end points on the "best value continuum."[46]

The Tradeoff Process

The 1997 rewrite of FAR Part 15 speaks of a tradeoff process that is similar to what many agencies have previously called "best value." The FAR rewrite team explained, "This term (tradeoff) was selected because it is an accurate reflection of what occurs as cost or price and non-cost or non-price factors and subfactors are traded off among each other, various weighting schemes, to select the proposal that best meets the needs of the ultimate user. They also found that there was not a standard definition of a 'best value' procurement. Therefore, rather than adopting one of the existing schemes or developing a hybrid of existing schemes, the team decided a new term should be applied, in the interest of minimizing confusion."[47]

This category permits tradeoffs among cost or price and non-cost factors that are designated in Section L of the solicitation. It also allows the government to accept something other than the lowest-priced proposal. (The benefits of a higher-priced proposal that justifies the added cost, as well as the rationale for the tradeoff, must be documented in the negotiation file.[48] The FAR does not provide any guidance as to the scope of documentation nor rationale needed to support the tradeoff.[49])

The Lowest-Price Technically Acceptable Offer

This category is a step above the sealed bid method. However, with the inclusion of the best-value continuum in the 1997 rewrite of FAR Part 15, it has not been officially recognized.[50] It lends itself to complex acquisitions in which discussions between the government and the offerors may be necessary. This method is appropriate when the government will benefit from the selection of the technically acceptable proposal with the lowest price.[51] When using the lowest-price technically acceptable method, the following procedures apply:

- Evaluation factors and subfactors are to be specified in the solicitation.
- The solicitation shall specify that the award will be made on the basis of the lowest-priced proposals meeting or exceeding the acceptability standards for non-cost factors.
- When past performance is a factor, then the offeror's record of performance will be evaluated in accordance with FAR 15.305(a)(2). Past performance need not be an evaluation factor if the acquisition is not expected to exceed $1,000,000 or if it will be awarded to a small business. The CO must document the file by citing the reasons that past performance is not an evaluation factor. Tradeoffs are not permitted.
- Proposals will not be ranked using non-cost/price factors, but will be evaluated for acceptability.
- Exchanges with offerors may occur after receipt of the offer.[52]

Giving the CO the authority not to always consider past performance as an evaluation factor gives small business and other commercial firms a greater opportunity to compete for government contracts.

The Source Selection Participants

The head of the government's procuring agency, or his or her designees, are responsible for source selection. The CO is designated responsible for selecting the source on most acquisitions. When someone other than the CO is given the source selection authority, the title given that official is the Source Selection Authority (SSA). Duties of the SSA are to:

- Establish an evaluation team tailored for the particular acquisition, ensuring a comprehensive team by including members with contracting, legal, logistics, technical, and other skills as needed
- Approve the source selection strategy or acquisition plan

- Ensure consistency among the solicitation requirements, notices to offerors, proposal preparation instructions, evaluation factors and subfactors, solicitation provisions or contract clauses, and data requirements
- Ensure that proposals are evaluated based entirely on factors and subfactors contained in the solicitation
- Consider the recommendations of advisory boards and panels
- Select the source or sources whose proposal provides the best value to the government.[53]

When someone other than the CO is designated the SSA, it is important that the CO is involved in all business aspects of the acquisition. Specifically, the CO's responsibilities are:

- After release of a solicitation, to act as the focal point for all inquiries from actual and prospective offerors
- After receipt of proposals, to control exchanges with offerors by acting as the focal point for communications between the government and the prospective contractor
- To award the contract or contracts.[54]

THE EVALUATION PROCESS

Proposal evaluation is the assessment of the offeror's offer and its ability to meet the requirements set forth in the proposed contract. There are two categories of rules pertaining to the evaluation of offers. The first applies to offers submitted under the Simplified Acquisition procedures outlined in FAR Part 13. This pertains to: (1) supplies and services, construction, research and development, and commercial items, the aggregate amount of which does not exceed the simplified acquisition threshold of $100,000, or $200,000 for purchases made outside the United States in support of a contingency, humanitarian, or peacekeeping operation; or (2) commercial items exceeding the simplified acquisition threshold but not more than $5,000,000, including options.[55] In the second set of rules are competitive and noncompetitive negotiated acquisitions covered under FAR Part 15. As noted earlier, FAR Part 13 calls for efficiency, economy, and innovation in contracting. FAR Part 15, which is more formal, does not contain these objectives.

The simplified acquisition procedures outlined in FAR Part 13 give the CO broad discretion in "fashioning suitable evaluating procedures." The CO must ensure that the offerors are evaluated in an "efficient and less burdensome fashion." Not required are formal evaluation plans and establishing a competitive range, conducting discussions, and scoring quotations or offerors. In addition, a formal database need not be created. "[The]

CO may conduct comparative evaluation of offerors." Evaluation may be based on such information as the CO's knowledge of previous experience with the goods or services being procured, customer surveys, or any other reasonable basis.[56] On the other hand, in the case of goods and services being acquired following FAR Part 15, a critical factor is that the CO's evaluation must be consistent with evaluation factors contained in the solicitation. If no evaluation factors are identified, award should be made to the lowest-priced technically acceptable quotation.[57]

For proposals processed under FAR Part 15, evaluation factors and subfactors must be assessed in the same manner as they are presented in the RFP. Ranking of potential contractors may be accomplished using any rating method or combination of rating methods. These include color or adjectival rating, assigning numerical weights, or ordinal rankings.[58] Proposals are then graded using the evaluation criteria set forth in the RFP. These are then compared to the other proposals, and a competitive range is established.

The competitive range includes only the proposals that are most highly rated. The CO is responsible for determining which proposals are selected to be in the competitive range on the basis of the ratings of each proposal. To permit conducting an efficient competition, the CO may also limit the number of proposals in the competitive range. This can only be done if the IFB contains a notice that the competitive range may be limited.

For procurements that are governed by simplified acquisition procedures, acquisition reform has made proposal evaluation a much more challenging task. This is because emphasis has been placed on expressing requirements in the form of overall objectives and performance requirements as much as possible. This policy is designed to give potential contractors flexibility in determining how the job will be done. To understand the various approaches, functional representatives of the SSA must have extensive technical knowledge of the product and its employment to determine if the proposed product is a viable solution to the government's requirement, as well as understand the product's strengths and weaknesses.[59] In addition, offerors can no longer rely on standard phrases or use buzzwords taken from specifications or standards to assure the buyer that the requirements are understood.

Cost or Price Evaluation

The objective to keep in mind when evaluating the proposal cost or price is to determine if the supplies or services are purchased at a price that is fair and reasonable to both parties. A fair and reasonable price is defined as "a price that is fair to both parties, considering the agreed-upon conditions, promised quality, and timeliness of contract performance." Some say this definition implies that there is a precise price that both parties can agree is "fair and reasonable." Burt and Pinkerton, authors of *A Purchasing Manager's Guide to*

Strategic Proactive Procurement, point out that in every acquisition there are several perspectives as to what is a fair and reasonable price. Examples are:

- Market price is thought to be fair and reasonable when there is competition among potential buyers for available products and competition among potential sellers for the available demand.
- From the seller's point of view, a fair and reasonable price is one that covers the seller's cost plus a reasonable profit. This price may change with market conditions, e.g., the degree and effect of competition.
- From the buyer's point of view, a fair and reasonable price is one that must be paid to purchase the needed item. How much the buyer may pay is influenced by the urgency of need, the item's quality, its utility, its cost of ownership, and the availability of alternatives.[60]

There is a fundamental belief that competition, by its nature, establishes the reasonableness of the price to be paid for goods and services. Consequently, when contracting on a fixed-price, economic price adjustment basis, the comparison of proposed prices will fulfill the need to do a price analysis. The buying activity is also instructed to analyze the cost in order to establish the reasonableness of the successful offeror's price. If it is a cost-reimbursement contract, the evaluation should include cost realism analysis to determine what the government should realistically pay for the stated requirement. Cost realism analysis is a technique that can also be used to assess the risk associated with the proposal because it is a gauge of a potential contractor's understanding of the effort and its ability to perform the contract.[61]

"The purpose of performing cost or price analysis is to develop a negotiation position that permits the CO and offeror an opportunity to reach agreement on a fair and reasonable price."[62] Price analysis may be used to verify that the price offered is fair and reasonable and that cost or pricing data are not required.[63] Price analysis is the process of examining and evaluating a prospective price without performing cost analysis, that is, without evaluating the separate cost elements and offeror's profit included in the price.[64] Price analysis can be described as a process of comparisons. However, when procuring nonstandard goods or services, cost analysis is more useful than price analysis because: (1) it is difficult to identify useful comparisons, and (2) cost analysis includes the review and evaluation of separate cost elements and proposed profit contained in an offeror's or contractor's proposal.[65]

When performing cost analysis, actual and anticipated costs are reviewed. It requires the application of experience, knowledge, and judgment to estimate reasonable contract costs. Cost analysis also may be employed to evaluate information other than cost or pricing data to determine cost reasonableness or cost realism.[66] During proposal evaluation the FAR emphasizes the use of cost analysis to determine what the government should pay, i.e., whether the price is too high. Cost analysis can also be used to determine if the contractor's proposal is realistic and reflects a clear understanding of the requirements as well as being consistent with the other elements of the technical proposal.[67]

Writing in the *Contract Management Journal*, David Dempsey contends:

> It appears that the Rewrite (FAR Part 15) encourages a cost analysis to determine price reasonableness rather than price analysis technique under FAR 15.404-1(d). Consistent with the "cost approach" to price reasonableness, the Rewrite also explicitly authorizes what was not traditionally done in the past during proposal evaluation—providing cost information to the technical evaluation team "in accordance with agency procedures."[68]

The Evaluation Factors and Subfactors

The contract award decision is to be based on evaluation factors and significant subfactors tailored to the acquisition. The evaluation factors must delineate key areas of importance to the government and must enhance a meaningful comparison and enable discrimination between competing proposals. Defining the relative importance of the factors and subfactors is within the broad discretion of the buying activity.[69] However, there are requirements to:

- Evaluate price or cost to the government in every source selection
- Evaluate quality in every source selection by examining such non-cost factors as past performance, responsiveness, technical excellence, management capability, personnel qualifications, and prior experience.

Factors and subfactors and their relative importance to the acquisition at hand are to be detailed in Section M, Evaluation Factors for Award. The solicitation must also state whether all evaluation factors, other than price, when combined are: (1) significantly more important than cost or price, (2) approximately equal to cost or price, or (3) significantly less important than cost or price.[70] This policy statement is consistent with the ruling by the Comptroller General that "each offeror has a right to know whether the procurement is intended to achieve a minimum standard at the lowest cost or whether cost is secondary to quality."[71]

There are three statutory mandated categories of factors and significant subfactors (see Table 6-1, Mandated Factors and Significant Subfactors to be Used in Source Selection) that are to be used in source selection.

- Price or cost
- Quality of the product through consideration of one or more non-cost consideration factors, such as past performance, compliance with so-

Table 6-1. Mandated Factors and Significant Subfactors to be Used in Source Selection

- Price or cost
- Quality of the product as determined by
  - Past performance
  - Compliance with solicitation requirements
  - Technical excellence
  - Management capability
  - Personnel qualifications
  - Prior experience
- Past performance

---

licitation requirements, technical excellence, management capability, personnel qualifications, and prior experience
- Past performance (unless the value of the acquisition is less than $1,000,000 or the CO has made a written determination that past performance is not applicable to the instant acquisition).[72]

There has been a great deal of discussion regarding the disclosure of the rating method to potential offerors in the solicitation. However, the language used in the Rewrite of FAR Part 15 states the rating method need *not* be disclosed in the solicitation (emphasis added).[73] However, for an acquisition that calls for a tradeoff between evaluation factors and subfactors, it does seem that details on the rating method should be disclosed.

Technical Evaluation

When technical tradeoffs are performed, the source selection file shall include an assessment of each offeror's ability to accomplish the technical requirements and a summary matrix, or quantitative ranking along with appropriate supporting narrative, of each technical proposal using the evaluation factors.[74]

Past Performance As an Evaluation Standard

Past performance has always been a de facto consideration in source selection. However, it was not until it was formally included in Armed Services Procurement Regulation 1-903.3 in 1947 that it was officially sanctioned in determining a contractor's responsibility. In 1963 DoD policy formally institutionalized the consideration of contractor past performance when evaluating proposals. Implementing this policy required establishing a mandated reporting process, databases, and standards for the performance review; retention standards for records; and procedures for the release of past performance data. This initiative was abandoned in 1971 "because the benefits derived from [the contractor performance record system] were judged not sufficient to warrant the cost involved." Notwithstanding, past performance did survive in areas of construction and architect-engineering contracting.[75]

There was a resurgence of the use of the past performance process by the Air Force in the early 1980s. It became a significant cornerstone of acquisition reform when in the mid-1990s the Federal Acquisition Streamlining Act established past performance as a mandatory factor to be considered in the evaluation process. It was felt that past performance is an important risk mitigation technique to determine the likelihood that the offeror will successfully perform the contract after it is awarded.[76]

The Rewrite of FAR Part 15 included past performance as an evaluation consideration in all competitive negotiated acquisitions expected to exceed $1 million. However, its use may be waived if the CO issues a written statement explaining why past performance should not be considered.[77]

Past performance is more than a way to ensure that a contractor is responsible. Beginning in 1993 OFPP issued policy statements and guidelines regarding the use of past performance and an evaluation factor in source selection. In May 1995 OFPP issued an interim version of *A Guide to Best Practices for Past Performance*, which provides extensive guidance regarding the evaluation of past performance.[78] The guide included five areas for evaluation, listed below. The OFPP guide advised against using past performance as the "minimum mandatory requirement," i.e., "go/no-go factor." Instead, past performance should be an evaluation factor against which offerors' relative rankings are compared. The guide recommends that it represent a major factor with a weight equal to the most significant noncost factor in the evaluation criteria.[79]

- Management responsiveness: Is the contractor cooperative, businesslike, and concerned with the interests of the government customer?
- Contract change proposals: What is the contractor's history regarding contract proposals?
- Substitution of key personnel: What is the contractor's history of changing the key personnel it has offered?
- Emergency responsiveness: Has the contractor responded in a credible manner to emergency service requirements?
- Overall satisfaction: Would former customers do business with the contractor again if they had a choice?

If an offeror does not have a past performance history, it is to be given an opportunity to identify past or current contracts, including federal, state, local government, and private industry, for efforts similar to the government's requirement. Judgment as to the relevance of these efforts is the responsibility of the SSA. Offerors without relevant past performance information cannot be evaluated either favorably or unfavorably on the matter of past performance.[80] Industry has asked if this policy represents a barrier to small business from entering into the government marketplace.[81]

Negative past performance must be confirmed, and actions by all parties must be fully confirmed. The CO must provide information to the offerors on the content of their past performance reports that are being used in the evaluation. The offeror then must be given an opportunity to respond to that information as to its relevancy and corrective actions that have or will be taken to improve performance or correct the performance shortfall. What is especially troublesome to potential contractors when award is to be made without discussions is that the offeror *may* have the opportunity to comment on new past performance information that had not been available previously (emphasis added).[82]

The Comptroller General sustained a protest involving a case in which an agency failed during discussions to mention its concerns about the past performance problems of an offeror's major subcontractor. Consequently, the source selection may be invalidated if the agency has past performance information in its possession but ignores it.[83]

If past performance is going to be an effective method for the CO to use in making the source selection decision, the information made available must be relevant. Irrelevant data on a contractor's past performance makes source selection decisions even more difficult.[84]

Other lessons that have been learned since the OFPP past performance guide was issued are: (1) the number of past performance references that should be requested should range from five to 10, and (2) past performance evaluations rendered during contract administration must be standardized among agencies by identifying major business areas and the requirements under business areas for evaluation.[85]

COMMUNICATIONS EXCHANGES AFTER RECEIPT OF THE PROPOSAL

Exchanges of data between the potential contractor and the CO prior to the establishment of the competitive range are held for the purpose of determining if the proposal will or will not become part of the competitive range.[86] (The competitive range is defined as the range of most highly rated proposals as determined by the CO. The CO can further reduce the number of proposals within the range for the purpose of efficiency.[87]) The act of exchanging information between the CO and the offeror to establish the competitive range is referred to in the FAR as "communications." Communications are not to be conducted with offerors whose proposals are definitely in, or definitely out, of the competitive range—only those in question.[88] The purpose of communication is: (1) to improve the government's understanding of the proposal, (2) to allow reasonable interpretation of the proposal, (3) to provide information related to past performance, or (4) to facilitate the evaluation process. These communication exchanges can be described as being similar to fact finding. The data obtained by the government result may not be used to correct deficiencies, materially alter the technical or cost elements of the proposal, or otherwise improve the proposal.[89]

When past performance becomes a matter of concern, communications must also address "adverse" past performance issues to which the offeror has not previously had an opportunity to respond. What constitutes an "adverse" past performance issue is left to the judgment of the CO, as the FAR Rewrite does not provide any guidance on the subject.[90]

ESTABLISHING THE COMPETITIVE RANGE

The competitive range is a concept that was introduced in the Truth in Negotiation Act in 1962 as a way to include more competitors in the process because Congress perceived that many offerors in competitive negotiated procurements were not being fully considered, even though they responded to the RFP. The law also required the CO to hold discussions with all offerors within the competitive range. This legal requirement changed the entire communications and negotiations process leading up to negotiation and pricing or negotiated procurement. Prior to requirement, the government was permitted to carry out the negotiation process without any detailed, congressionally imposed guidelines.[91]

Incorporated into most solicitations is FAR 52.215-1, Instructions to Offerors—Competitive Acquisition. It contains not only information on the competitive range but also a warning to offerors that their initial proposal should contain the best terms from a cost and technical standpoint. It also states that:

- The government reserves the right to award the contract without discussion, except for clarification purposes, with the offerors.
- The government reserves the right to conduct discussions if the CO determines them to be necessary.
- The government has the right to limit the number of proposals if the CO determines that the number of proposals that would otherwise be in the competitive range exceeds the number at which an efficient competition can be conducted.[92]

The competitive range includes only those proposals that were the most highly rated, based on an evaluation of each using the criteria described in Section M of the solicitation.[93] The CO is responsible for determining the number of proposals that are to be included in the competitive range. The drafters of the Rewrite intentionally declined to define the terms *highly rated* and *efficiency*. Apparently these terms were considered to depend on the unique facts of each solicitation, and, by remaining undefined, it provided the CO a greater opportunity to exercise discretion. The decision and supporting rationale must be documented in the contract file.[94] The policy established in the FAR Rewrite has the potential of being more restrictive than previous FAR policy. Previously the competitive range included proposals that had a reasonable chance of being selected for award, and the proposal was to be included if there was a doubt.[95] The "reasonable chance of being selected" standard was interpreted by the GAO to consist of and include proposals that, although deemed unacceptable, could be acceptable through discussions.[96]

It is clear that under the new FAR Part 15 Rewrite, the CO has a great deal more discretion in limiting the size of the competitive range than previously permitted. The comments in the preamble to the Rewrite of competitive range policy in FAR Part 15 stated that the new rule "ensures that offerors with little probability of success...are advised early that their competitive position does not merit additional expense in a largely futile attempt to secure the contract."[97]

Deciding which proposals belong in the competitive range is a two-step process. The first step is an evaluation of all proposals received in accordance with the evaluation factors and subfactors listed in Section M of the solicitation to determine the ones that are highly rated and efficient. The second step includes communications with offerors, which are limited to prospective contractors whose past performance information is the determining factor preventing them from being in the competitive range and those on the line of inclusion or exclusion.[98]

NOTIFICATION TO UNSUCCESSFUL OFFERORS

Unsuccessful offerors have traditionally had a right to request and receive a post-award debriefing. However, during congressional hearings on acquisition reform, it became clear that industry was frustrated because of the lack of a meaningful explanation of the basis of the award decision. They contended this uncertainty led many firms to file protests. Consequently, the Rewrite of FAR Part 15 required that offerors eliminated from the competitive range be so notified.[99] Offerors not awarded the contract can request either a pre-award or a post-award debriefing, but not both.[100] The primary purpose in giving these debriefings to unsuccessful offerors is to eliminate the filing of protests as a means to discover the propriety of an award decision.[101]

Offerors requesting a pre-award debriefing must do so within three calendar days of receipt of notification of exclusion from the competition.[102] The CO is instructed to make every effort to brief the unsuccessful offeror as soon as practicable. However, after submitting its request the unsuccessful offeror also has the right to request to delay the debriefing until after contract award. The advantage to the unsuccessful offeror to delay debriefing is that significantly more information is available at a post-award debriefing than at a pre-award debriefing. However, the probability of the unsuccessful offeror's gaining a favorable judgment diminishes over time. For the government, the agency has a better and earlier opportunity to correct pre-award deficiencies, and there is less risk of disrupting contract performance due to a protest when a pre-award debriefing is provided.[103]

The debriefing may be done orally, in writing, or by any other method acceptable to the CO. A summary of the debriefing is to be included in the contract file. At a minimum, the debriefing provides the unsuccessful offeror:

- An evaluation of significant elements in the offeror's proposal
- A summary of the rationale for eliminating the offeror from the competition
- A reasonable response to relevant questions about whether source selection procedures contained in the solicitation, applicable regulations, and other applicable authorities were followed in the process of eliminating the unsuccessful offeror from the competition.

Not to be disclosed is such information as:

- The number of offerors
- The identity of the other offerors
- The content of the other offerors' proposals
- The ranking of the other offerors' proposals
- The evaluation of other offerors
- Other information, such as trade secrets, confidential manufacturing processes, and names of individuals providing reference information about the offerors' past performance.[104]

PROPOSAL ANALYSIS

The objective of proposal analysis is to ensure that the final agreed-to price is fair and reasonable.[105] The CO should not become preoccupied with any single element and should balance the contract type, cost, and profit or fee negotiated to achieve the total result—a price that is fair and reasonable to both the government and the contractor.

Fundamental to the analysis of proposals are the cost principles that are contained in FAR Part 31, Contract Cost Principles and Procedures. These cost principles pertain to the allocability of cost rather than its allowability. Efforts to develop cost accounting principles for government contracts dates back to the Revolutionary War; however, a formal set of cost principles were never documented until September 1916, when Congress included them in the Revenue Bill. In the closing days of World War II, Joint Termination Regulations were issued that contained cost principles for determining costs upon termination of contracts. In the years since World War II, the cost principles have evolved to those contained in FAR Part 31. These principles are to be used when cost analysis is performed when pricing government contracts and modifications to contracts.[106] These cost principles are also to be used when pricing fixed-price contracts, subcontracts, and modifications to contracts and subcontracts whenever: (1) cost analysis is performed, or (2) a fixed-price contract clause requires the determination or negotiation of cost. When pricing contracts with commercial firms, the cost principle and procedures contained in FAR Part 31.2 are to be used for:

- Determining reimbursement cost rates under cost-reimbursement contracts and subcontracts and the cost-reimbursement portion of time-and-material contracts, except when material is priced on a basis other than cost
- Negotiating indirect cost rates
- Proposing, negotiating, or determining costs under terminated contracts
- Price revisions of fixed-price incentive contracts
- Price re-determination of price re-determination contracts
- Price changes and other contract modifications.[107]

Evaluating the reasonableness of the prime contract, including subcontracting cost, is the responsibility of the CO.[108] Proposal analysis consists of both quantitative and qualitative techniques. The complexity and circumstances surrounding each acquisition determine the level and detail to be analyzed. The government has a fairly extensive selection of analytical techniques and procedures to use to determine reasonableness[109] (see Table 6-2, Analytical Techniques and Procedures Used to Determine Reasonableness).

Price Analysis

Price analysis is defined as the process of examining and evaluating the proposed price in the aggregate rather than separate cost elements and

---

Table 6-2. Proposal Analysis Techniques

- Price Analysis
- Cost Analysis
- Cost Realism Analysis
- Technical Analysis
- Unit Prices
- Unbalanced Pricing

profit.[110] When using price analysis, the buyer is looking for comparisons of what the proposed price should be with market prices, past purchases, catalog prices, prices of similar items, independent government estimates, and comparable yardsticks as price per pound, as in the case of parametric estimating methods. Much of the data used in price analysis is gained through market research.

Cost Analysis

Cost analysis is the review and evaluation of separate cost elements and profit in an offeror's proposal.[111] Sources analyzed include cost or pricing data, make-or-buy tradeoffs, bills of material, blueprints, labor standards, and direct and indirect costs. This data is provided by the offeror or gained through market research. To ensure that past inefficiencies are not built into the proposal, cost trends for direct labor and material are analyzed, and the learning curve is applied if length of the production run is sufficient. In government contracts is it important to verify that the offeror's proposed costs are allowable in accordance with contract cost principles and procedures included in Part 31 of the FAR. The allocability, i.e., the assignable or chargeable portion of proposed costs, also must be consistent with the offeror's disclosure statement, if applicable (reference the application of the Cost Accounting Standards in FAR Part 30, Cost Accounting Standards Administration).

Cost Realism Analysis

The cost realism analysis process is an independent review and evaluation of specific elements of each offeror to determine if: (1) they are realistic for the work to be performed, (2) they reflect a clear understanding of the requirements, and (3) they are consistent with unique methods of performance and materials described in the offeror's technical proposal. Cost realism analysis is to be performed on cost-reimbursement contracts to determine the probable cost of performance for each offeror's technical proposal. The offeror's proposed cost is then compared to the government's best-cost estimate for the effort and variances addressed. If the government's best estimate of the most probable cost is lower than the offeror's proposed figure, then the offeror's proposed figure should be used for evaluation. If the government's best estimate of the most probable cost is higher than the contractor's proposed cost, then the offeror must prove the proposed costs are consistent with the proposed technical approach. Cost realism analysis also may be used on competitive fixed-price incentive contracts or on competitive fixed-price contracts when there is a question that the competing offerors did not understand the requirement, when there are quality concerns, or when the offeror has a proposed cost history of shortfalls in quality or service.[112]

Case law, the General Accounting Office, and the courts have consistently held that a contracting agency's method of evaluating a particular cost proposal and adjusting it for "realism" involves exercising informed business judgment and that the agency's cost realism determination will not be disturbed without showing that it lacks a reasonable basis.[113]

Technical Analysis

Technical analysis is performed by personnel (from the acquisition team or SSA) who have specialized knowledge, skills, experience, or capability in engineering, science, or management performance. Their objective is to determine the reasonableness of the proposed resources delineated in the offeror's proposal. Technical analysis is accomplished on the proposed types and quantities of material, labor, processes, special tooling, facilities, reasonableness of scrap and spoilage, and other factors included in the proposal.[114]

Unit Prices

Unless the offeror's proposal is based on catalog, market, or adequate price completion, unit prices shall reflect the intrinsic value of the item or service and shall be in proportion to the item's manufacturing or acquisition cost (base cost). The objective is not to distort the unit price, as would be the case if costs were only distributed equally among line items. In addition, for non-commercial items the solicitation shall require that the offerors' proposals list the items of supply that they will not manufacture or that they will not "contribute significant value, unless there is adequate price competition." This is to determine if the intrinsic value of an item has been distorted through the application of overhead and if the items should be considered for breakout and purchased directly from the original manufacturer. If it is appropriate, this information may be requested in all other negotiated contracts.[115] The latter policy applies to spares and repair parts that are not purchased concurrently with the production of the end item or its components.

Unbalanced Pricing

Unbalanced pricing exists when, despite an acceptable total evaluated price, the price of one or more contract line items is significantly over- or understated. Unbalanced prices represent increased performance risk and could result in payment of unreasonably high prices. Examples of when this can occur are: (1) when startup work, mobilization, or the first article test are separate line items; (2) when base quantities and option quantities are separate line items; or (3) when the evaluated price is the aggregate of estimated quantities to be ordered under separate line items of an indefinite-delivery contract. An offer may be rejected if the CO determines that the lack of balance poses an unacceptable risk to the government, e.g., if it establishes the competitive range or if award of the contract means the government will pay unreasonably high prices for the contract effort.[116]

Because the cost of any contract is negotiated prior to contract award, it behooves the buyer to determine the amount of the cost risk involved along with the probability of occurrence. The degree of cost risk associated with any proposal depends on how accurately the cost can be estimated prior to performance. Cost risk associated with off-the-shelf commercial items, products ordered from a catalog, or items sold on the commercial market is usually minimal. However, when the buyer requires a product with distinctive characteristics, the uncertainty associated with determining cost reasonableness must be measured prior to negotiations. The accuracy of the cost estimate and the risk associated with the proposal are usually functions of both the technical and contract schedule risks.[117]

Subcontracting Pricing Considerations

As noted earlier, 60 percent of the cost incurred for products or services by a typical prime contractor is purchased from suppliers.[118] Between 50 percent and 80 percent of this amount is concentrated with a few key strategic suppliers.[119] Therefore, COs often concentrate the examination of the subcontract price on these suppliers.

The CO is responsible for determining the price reasonableness for the prime contract. This includes subcontracting cost. In fulfilling this responsibility, the CO should also obtain answers to such questions as:

- Does the contractor or subcontractor have an approved purchasing system?
- Did the prime contractor perform cost or price analysis of the proposed subcontract prices?
- Did the prime contractor negotiate the subcontract price before negotiation of the prime contract?[120]

Field Pricing Assistance

The CO also has the authority to request field pricing assistance when data available at the buying activity are inadequate to determine if the price is fair and reasonable. The request for field pricing assistance should be tailored to obtain the minimum essential supplementary information needed to conduct technical, cost, or pricing analysis. Field pricing assistance can be obtained to gather needed data from both prime and subcontractors.

When field pricing assistance is requested, the CO is encouraged to team with appropriate experts in the field throughout the acquisition, including negotiations.[121] Principal sources of expertise from the field are the Administrative Contracting Officers (ACOs) and other government personnel, such as pricing specialists, quality assurance, industrial specialists, engineers, and property managers, assigned to significant government contractors as plant representatives. Auditors, under the Defense Contract Audit Agency, are additional resources that can be called on to assist the CO in making the "fair and reasonable" assessment.

The information obtained from the field is to become part of the contract file.

Deficient Proposals

If the data the offeror provides for government review are so deficient that they prevent review or audit, or if access to any records has been denied, the CO is to take the necessary action to obtain the required data. If the offeror again denies access to the data, the CO shall withhold the award and notify a higher authority.[122] Failure to provide the required information renders the proposal non-responsive when the required data or information is identified in the solicitation.

MAKING THE SOURCE SELECTION DECISION

Source selection is defined as the process of selecting a contractor through competitive negotiations.[123] When making the source selection decision, the Source Selection Authority (SSA) is to perform a comparative assessment of proposals using all source selection criteria in the solicitation. The SSA is supported by a Source Selection Board (SSB), which oversees the evaluations submitted in competitive negotiations. The SSB is generally responsible for ensuring that the evaluations submitted to the SSA are consistent and represent a fair evaluation of the proposal submitted.[124] Although reports and analyses may be received from others, the source selection decision represents the independent judgment of the SSA.[125] The SSA's decision is to be based on a comparative assessment of proposals against all source selection criteria contained in the solicitation. Although the SSA uses information and analysis from other sources, their final decision represents their independent judgment. The source selection decision is required to be documented, and the documentation is to include the rationale for any business judgments and tradeoffs made or relied on by the SSA. The documentation need not quantify the tradeoffs that led to the decision. However, if there is an additional cost associated with the selected approach, the benefits from this added cost are also to be included in the documentation.[126]

This lack of specifics in the documentation, i.e., quantitative analysis of tradeoffs leading to selecting the source, has been criticized by industry.

They look at the requirement to document the benefits while not requiring any detailed analysis or explanation supporting the conclusion as a way to eliminate protests by other offerors of a source selection decision that involved tradeoffs.[127]

Source selection officials have a great deal of discretion in making their selection. The primary rule is that the SSA must have a rational basis for making the selection decision and must not act in an arbitrary and capricious manner.[128]

DISCUSSIONS AND NEGOTIATIONS

Discussions are defined as "exchanges between the government and the offerors in the competitive proposal process undertaken with the intent of allowing the offeror to revise its proposal."[129] On the other hand, negotiation is seen as a method of contracting that uses either competitive or other procedures that permit bargaining with offerors after receipt of proposals.[130] A negotiation also has been described as a full-circle feedback system in which the buyer and seller set the goals. The feedback comes from the effect every demand, concession, threat, delay, fact, deadline, authority limit, and good/bad-guy remark has on the other side's expectations.[131]

As related earlier in this chapter, the requirement in the Truth in Negotiation Act of 1962 for the CO to establish a competitive range and then hold discussions with all potential contractors within the competitive range was a radical change to the way the government negotiated and awarded contracts. The Act also required the CO to change the evaluation process to demonstrate that all offerors within the competitive range had been considered.[132] The practice of implementing this requirement was varied among the agencies. For example:

> National Aeronautics and Space Administration (NASA) considered discussions and negotiations as two different processes. Upon receipt of the proposals they were evaluated in order to determine an initial competitive range. After conducting written and oral discussions the competitive range was narrowed for the purpose of requesting a best and final offeror (BAFO). Upon the receipt of the BAFOs NASA selected one or more offerors to negotiate. The result of negotiations would determine which contractor would be awarded the contract.[133]

Historically, the DoD has considered discussions as being equivalent to negotiations. When proposals were received, they were evaluated for inclusion in the competitive range and for both source selection and negotiation purposes. During discussions some proposals could be dropped from the competitive range because they were considered unacceptable. Written and oral discussions, including negotiation of contract terms and conditions, would continue with the CO requesting a BAFO from the remaining offerors. Source selection and award would follow without further negotiation.[134]

In an apparent attempt to minimize this variance, the FAR Rewrite now describes negotiations as "exchanges ... between the government and offerors that are undertaken with the intent of allowing the offeror to revise the proposal."[135] In Part 15 of the FAR, negotiations and discussions are interchangeable. In FAR 52.215-1 discussions are defined as negotiations that occur after establishment of the competitive range that may, at the CO's discretion, result in the offeror being allowed to revise its proposal.[136]

After the competitive range has been established, the CO is to hold discussions with all of the offerors whose proposals are judged to be within the competitive range. It is important to emphasize that when the parties seek clarification of the terms and conditions of a proposal, the asking of a question can easily be transformed into a discussion if the offeror is given the right to change the proposal.

The concept of dual negotiations was also introduced with the Truth in Negotiation Act of 1962. Because the objective was to foster more competition, the federal government began conducting discussions with the contractors in the competitive range sequentially until all were provided the opportunity to change their proposals.[137] The changes included in the Rewrite of Part 15 probably were introduced because bargaining between too many competitors is impracticable in terms of time, especially when BAFOs are requested.

Dual negotiations not only increase the administrative complexity of the acquisition, but there is also a danger that there will be a transfer of technical information among contractors during negotiations. This can occur when the acquisition team attempts to facilitate the comparison of technical or management proposals encouraging technical transfusion. This can violate the intellectual property rights of the contractors.[138] With a policy that encourages independent ideas and commercial industry to compete for government business, the risk of transfusion of proprietary information is even greater than before.

Pre-Negotiation Objectives

Negotiation must not be viewed as being merely an event. As the above FAR references imply, it is a process that begins with market research, which takes place long before the competitive range is established. You must prepare for negotiations because the more you know before the give-and-take of bargaining, the better your position and the more confident you feel. Data needed include details on the product specifications, prices, costs, extent of the competition, and characteristics of the industry and are useful in defining a negotiation strategy and plan to provide input to the government's pre-negotiation objectives. At the same time the seller's marketing personnel are actively seeking information about how their product will or will not satisfy the ultimate user's needs and assessing the competition.

To succeed in negotiations the buyer must establish pre-negotiation objectives and then do all the necessary planning as well as taking the actions necessary to attain the ultimate goals. Objectives that are common to all negotiations are obtaining the goods or services at a fair and reasonable price, obtaining the required quality and quantity, and getting the supplier to deliver on time. Sometimes there are other benefits a buyer seeks to gain during the negotiations, such as:

- The ability to exercise some control over the manner in which the contract is performed
- The development of a sound and continuing relationship or partnership with competent suppliers
- The commitment by the supplier to give maximum cooperation to the buyer.

The Negotiation Process

There are six steps in the negotiation process: (1) defining the desired results, (2) gathering data, (3) analyzing the situation, (4) planning, (5) bargaining, and (6) documenting the agreement.

Defining the desired results to be achieved: Formulation of the desired results to be achieved begins as the acquisition team defines the requirement. Performance of market research during the requirement determination phase of the acquisition process represents the beginning. It is not entirely concentrated on defining purchase descriptions or statements of work. Market research also includes determining and prioritizing the government's long-term, intermediate, and immediate interests. These can be both tangible and intangible interests. The acquisition team begins formulating the criteria for success and determining future buyer-seller relationships at this time. Alternative courses of action are also examined in case a suitable agreement cannot be negotiated.

Gathering of data: Costs often vary significantly among contractors. Many factors affect why some firms are high-cost producers and others are low-cost producers and why a firm can be a low-cost producer on one item and a high-cost producer on another. Some of the most important factors affecting cost are the: (1) capabilities of management, (2) efficiency of labor, (3) amount and quality of subcontracting, and (4) plant capacity and continuity of output.[139] Insight into the prospective contractor cost is obtained by gathering data early in the process. Sources of data include:

- Published reference material as reports available from the Securities and Exchange Commission
- Material obtained from the Internet
- Dun and Bradstreet reports, research services (LEXIS-NEXIS), trade journals, association information, newspaper and magazine articles, networking, and the potential offerors themselves.

The best source is asking questions of the potential contractor itself. This can be accomplished during fact finding. The CO initiates fact finding after receiving reports on the respective proposals from the acquisition team, price analysis, field pricing analysis, and the auditor. The purpose of fact finding is to obtain clarification and resolve inconsistencies between the proposal and buyer's information on both technical and cost subjects before entering into bargaining. One objective of fact finding is to understand the potential contractor's interests behind the positions they are taking. "It is much easier to satisfy interests than it is to move one's opposite off their positions."[140]

Analysis of the situation: Gathering facts on the proposal preparation includes determining the business interests of the potential offerors. Relevant subjects to pursue include answering such questions as: Is it in their long-term interests to commit to continuing with this product line? Is their management looking at opportunities in other product lines? What are the unique characteristics of the industry, and how do each of the potential offerors line up relating to industry practices? What interests are underlying the positions taken by the potential contractor?

No two negotiations are the same, but the outcome usually depends on three factors: (1) the bargaining power of the parties, (2) information each party has, and (3) the time available to reach an agreement.

Bargaining power: Bargaining power or leverage is defined as the ability of a negotiator to influence the behavior of an opponent. Power is always relative and limited because its range depends on government regulations, ethical standards, and present or future competition.[141] The buyer's bargaining strength depends on the extent of competition, adequacy of the cost or price analysis, and the thoroughness with which the SSA has prepared for the negotiation.

Information each party has: The greater the amount of cost, price, or financial data available to the CO, the greater the buyer's chance for successful negotiations.[142] Another source of power is the information one party has on the other party's interests. Knowledge of the other party's financial goals, long- and short-term priorities, deadlines, and intra-organizational pressures enables one party to create a negotiating option that will satisfy its interests.

Time: The party most constrained by time provides the other party a source of power. Resulting time maneuvers, such as establishing deadlines, can be a factor, e.g., the price goes up the next week, or the only person authorized to sign a contract of this size is going out of the country on a long business trip. Inventory replenishment time is money because the time required to negotiate the contract must be compensated for with added inventory.

The pre-negotiation objectives as to what is a fair and equitable price to both parties are based on cost analysis, cost realism analysis, or price analysis. Other elements of the RFP are also subject to negotiation. These include the statement of work, delivery schedule, warranties, payment terms, terms and conditions, and reporting requirements.

Sources of data that can be used to develop the pre-negotiation agreement include:

- Analysis of the offeror's proposal
- Field pricing assistance
- Audit reports
- Technical analysis
- Fact-finding results
- Independent government cost estimates (this can include cost realism analysis)
- Price histories.[143]

The pre-negotiation objectives also should tie back to Part One of the Acquisition Plan, which was discussed in Chapter 3. They must be consistent with the mission needs, financial constraints, technical parameters, cost-schedule-performance tradeoffs, and life cycle cost constraints, as originally defined in the acquisition plan. Reasons for variances should be examined in detail to ensure that they are substantiated, consistent with the current requirements and the financial environment, and can be met by the offers received.

Planning: Many consider planning the most important step in negotiations.[144] "The more prepared you are—the more you know about your goals and their goals, your absolutes and theirs, amount of flexibility, time limits, creative alternatives, pressures—the greater the opportunity to make a good deal."[145] At this time pre-negotiation objectives are redefined for all topics to be discussed during negotiations because the contract type and price are also related to risk and uncertainty to the contractor and government. The CO must not concentrate on any single element. To achieve total results there must be harmony among the contract type, cost, and profit/fee negotiated.[146]

When defining your pre-negotiation objectives, the initial question to ask should not be about the terms and conditions of the deal but should be, "What future relationship do you desire to have with the other party?" If one side approaches the negotiations with the objective of winning—the classic win-lose strategy—negotiations can easily become a one-time event with a short-term follow-on relationship. When bridges have been burned or one side is destroyed in making the deal, it will be very difficult to have a close and positive working relationship during contract performance. Follow-on business probably will not be possible.

At this time bargaining positions are established and contingency plans formed. The buyer uses cost or price analysis to set up various pricing positions. The CO should establish three specific positions: (1) the objective, (2) the minimum position, and (3) the maximum position. For the government the objective is the best estimate of what is expected to be a fair and reasonable price. The seller's maximum position is the offer on the table at the time discussions are initiated.

In their book *Getting to Yes: Negotiating an Agreement Without Giving In*, Roger Fisher and William Ury recommend the development of a Best Alternative to a Negotiated Agreement, or BATNA. The BATNA serves as a "protection from entering into an agreement that should be rejected, and to help make the most of the assets you do have so any agreement you reach will satisfy your interests as well as possible."[147] An economist refers to a BATNA as an opportunity cost. It is the alternative you give up when entering into the contract. The better your BATNA, the greater your ability to improve the terms of any negotiation. It is also easier to break off negotiations when you, along with your management, have an alternative course of action.[148]

Developing the BATNA requires three operations:

- Developing a list of actions to take if no agreement is made
- Improving some of the more promising ideas and converting them into realistic options
- Tentatively selecting the one option that seems best.[149]

In establishing your negotiation objectives, you should set a range for each objective rather than a fixed position. This provides you negotiation flexibility and adds tradeables. Areas that lend themselves to the establishment of ranges of objectives are identified in Table 6-3, Establishment of Negotiation Objectives. The more thoroughly a range of alternatives is prepared within these objectives, the more confident you will be in the negotiations.

Bargaining (discussions): In government contracting there is a distinction between discussions and bargaining as they are related to the give and take of negotiations. Under a sole-source contract, discussions that include the give and take of bargaining may occur any time after receipt of the proposal. However, under the negotiated competitive procurement process, bargaining does not occur until after the establishment of the competitive range. As noted earlier, prior to the establishment of the competitive range

Table 6-3. Establishment of Negotiation Objectives

- Cost
    - Negotiation objective
    - BATNA
    - Maximum (seller)
    - Minimum (buyer)
- Other topics
    - Technical characteristics
    - Delivery information
    - General terms and conditions
    - Patents and data rights
    - Warranty terms and conditions
    - Types of material and substitutes
    - Government-furnished material and facilities
    - Payment terms
    - Liability for claims or damages
    - Packaging
    - Type and frequency of reporting
- Contract type
    - Pricing arrangement
    - Incentives

---

the CO must discuss the weaknesses or deficiencies of their proposal with each and every offeror being considered for award. After this is completed and the competitive range solidified, the CO may begin bargaining. This is referred to in the FAR as exchanges between the government and the offeror with the intent of allowing the offeror to revise its proposal.[150] When discussions are conducted after the establishment of the competitive range, all deficiencies must be identified.[151] Communications with offerors after receipt of proposals and before establishment of the competitive range are referred to as exchanges.[152] Consequently, discussions are considered to be synonymous with bargaining. Bargaining is defined as getting something you value highly for something you value less.[153]

The primary concern of the CO is the overall price the government will actually pay for the goods or services. More specifically, the CO is to negotiate a contract with a price that provides the contractor the greatest incentive for efficient and economical performance. The CO should seek a balance among contract type, cost, and profit that is fair and reasonable to both the government and the contractor.[154]

The scope and intensity of discussions are a matter of the CO's discretion. Bargaining includes persuasion, altering assumptions and positions, and give-and-take, and may apply to price, schedule, technical requirements, type of contract, or other terms of a proposed contract.[155] Discussions are to be tailored to a specific proposal.[156]

Limitations placed on government personnel in their dealings with offerors are defined in FAR 15.306(e). There are unclear policy statements included in the rewrite of FAR Part 15 having to do with the dealings with the potential contractors that have created some ambiguities. FAR 15.306(d)(4) states that government personnel are not to engage in conduct in which one offeror is favored over another offeror.[157] However, this statement must be evaluated in the context of policy statements contained in other parts of the FAR. The two most significant examples are:

- All contractors and prospective contractors shall be treated fairly and impartially but need not be treated the same [FAR 1.103-2(c)(3)].
- When communicating with offerors before establishing the competitive range, government communications are limited to: (1) offerors whose past performance information is the determining factor that could prevent being placed within the competitive range, and (2) offerors whose inclusion or exclusion from the competitive range is uncertain.

Discussions must address significant weaknesses or deficiencies that could "be altered or explained to materially enhance the proposal's potential for award."[158] When a solicitation states that evaluation credit will be given for technical solutions that exceed any mandatory minimums, then the government may negotiate with the offeror to increase its performance beyond the mandatory minimums. In situations in which the proposed performance is already beyond any mandatory minimums, the CO also may suggest that the offeror's proposal would be more competitive if excesses were removed.[159] A CO has discretion to conduct "discussions as he or she sees fit" but may not identify technical weaknesses in order to put an offeror in a better competitive position than it otherwise occupied. This amounts to technical leveling.[160]

If during discussions the proposal of the contractor is no longer considered to be among the "most highly rated offer being considered for award," the potential contractor may then be eliminated from the competitive range. This can occur even if all material aspects have not been covered and the offeror has or has not been given the opportunity to submit a revised proposal.[161] After an offerors' proposal has been eliminated, no further revisions to the proposal can be accepted or considered.[162]

Proposal revisions are allowed only during discussions, and each offeror is allowed to submit proposal revisions to clarify and document understanding reached during negotiations. There is no limit to the number of proposal revisions that can be submitted during the period of discussions.

At the conclusion of discussions, the following events occur. First, each offeror still in the competitive range is given the opportunity to submit a final proposal revision (FPR) in writing. This permits an award being made without obtaining any further revisions. Next, the CO establishes a common cutoff date for receipt of final proposal revisions.[163]

From a historic perspective the interesting point of this Rewrite is that the "time-honored practice" of Best and Final Offers (BAFOs), Best and Really Final Offers (BARFOs), and Best and Really, Really Final Offers (BARRFOs) have been replaced by Final Proposal Revisions (FPRs), with a common cutoff date for receipt of common proposals.

Auctioning: Previously the government representatives were specifically prohibited from becoming involved in auctioning. *The Government Contracts Reference Book* includes the following examples of auctioning: (1) indicating to an offeror the cost or price that it must meet to obtain further consideration, and (2) advising an offeror of its price standing relative to another offeror.[164] The Rewrite of Part 15 omitted this prohibition. The reason cited by the Rewrite team was that there is no statutory prohibition on auctioning, and the team had discovered an Attorney General decision in the early 1800s emphasizing that government contracting should use the same methods employed in the commercial marketplace.[165] Stanley Sherman points out that most government contracts involve contracting for future work to produce a material end item, component, or service. When the circumstance involves effort that has not been performed at the time of contract award, the use of the auctioning technique could create an unconscionable contract relationship.[166] Industry believes that auctioning is not fair to the contractor because it is based solely on price, which is inconsistent with the "best value" concept. In addition, because the offeror must meet the price or leave the competition, it does not meet the give-and-take concept of bargaining.[167]

Award without discussions: FAR Part 52 includes an omnibus clause (52.215-1) to be included in all solicitations, warning the offeror that a contract award may be "made without discussion." These instructions go on to recommend that the offeror's initial proposal should contain the offeror's best terms from a cost or price and technical standpoint.[168] Some feel that with the elimination of the prohibition on auctioning, awarding can become "real-time unsealed bidding," assuming the CO has permission from the offeror to post its prices publicly.[169] In fact, the structure of FAR 52.215-1 (f) leads one to believe that it is government's preference to award contracts without discussion. When this clause is included in the solicitation and the CO later elects to engage in discussions (negotiations), the CO is now required to provide a written statement as to why it was necessary to do so.[170]

Despite a policy that is friendly to the award of a contract without discussion, it is difficult to believe that COs will significantly increase the number of negotiated purchases awarded in that manner. This conclusion is based on such realities as:

- History has shown that "best-value" procurements awarded to a higher-priced offeror without discussion are more likely to be overturned when challenged.[171]

- The number of noncommercial items purchased by the federal government using custom ordering procedures lends itself to cost analysis, or a determination of its cost realism calls for discussions.
- It is also difficult to negotiate for services to be awarded without discussion because of their unique dimensions and characteristics that must be individually tailored.
- Decisions by the Comptroller General on bid protests state that the goal of competitive bargaining is to persuade the offeror to improve its proposal, especially with respect to price.[172] These decisions have been incorporated into the detailed guidance on bargaining.[173]

Profit or fee: Profit is the amount realized by a contractor after the direct and indirect costs of performance are deducted from the amount to be paid under the contract.[174] With cost-reimbursement contracts, the amount paid to a contractor beyond allowable costs is referred to as the fee. The fee amount reflects a variety of factors, including the amount of cost risk assumed by the contractor.[175]

When negotiating a contract, it is not in the best interest of the government to enter into discussions with potential contractors with the objective of reducing the price by reducing profit or without recognition of the function profit plays in motivating the contractor's performance.[176] The potential for profit provides the incentive that attracts the best industrial and technical capabilities to work on government contracts and to maintain a viable industrial base. A primary concern of the CO is to negotiate a contract of a type and price that provide the contractor with the greatest incentive for efficient and economical performance. In doing this the CO should consider contract type as well as price because both are determined by the degree of exposure to risk and uncertainty on the part of the contractor as well as the government.[177]

When competition establishes the price, it has been government policy not to be too concerned about the amount of profit the contractor realizes. This is because the amount of profit depends on the contractor's ability to control its cost.

When competition does not establish the price, the CO is instructed to use a structured approach to analyze profit. When price negotiations are based on cost analysis, the COs are instructed to use a structured approach—referred to in the DoD as weighted guidelines—to analyze profit and calculate a pre-negotiation profit objective. The DoD utilizes this model to calculate the profit objective for use as a guide during conduct negotiations. The objective of using a model is that it brings a uniform structure that is based on an established profit policy. This leads to improved consistency for the same work. In the 1970s the DoD implemented a weighted guidelines model. In a recent iteration of the DoD, model profit policy shifted emphasis away from cost and toward investment. As an incentive not to let general and administrative (G&A) expenses grow, the DoD model excludes G&A expense from the calculation of the profit objective. No other agency prohibits profit on G&A expenses.[178]

In preparing for negotiations, the FAR requires buying agencies, when making noncompetitive contract awards over $100,000 totaling $50 million or more a year, to determine what would be an appropriate profit or fee to negotiate for the procurement.[179] The relevant factors to consider when making what the FAR describes as a structured approach include:

- **Contractor effort:** This includes an evaluation of the material and skills needed to perform the contract, such as the complexity of the task and the technical skill of the resources needed, the degree of professional and management skills needed, and the technical facilities and assets that will be used. This can be accomplished by breaking down the contractor's cost estimate to determine cost realism. The contractor that is doing a good job in controlling and managing cost should be rewarded.
- **Material acquisition:** Included in this category are the managerial and technical effort involved in obtaining the required purchased parts and materials, the magnitude of the subcontract effort, and the complexity of the items purchased. Significance of material in determining the amount of profit has traditionally been lower when compared to other costs because it usually represents the lowest investment of resources per dollar of cost. The amount of commercial off-the-shelf purchases normally represents a limited amount of technical or management effort unless multiple contractors are involved or there is a significant systems engineering task to ensure that components interface with each other.
- **Conversion of direct labor:** This category measures the contribution of direct engineering, manufacturing, and other labor categories needed to convert the raw materials, data, and subcontracted items into deliverables. Added weight is given when top management and distinguished scientific talent are to be applied to research and development contracts. When determining profit, a greater amount of weight is given to engineering labor over manufacturing labor, and manufacturing labor is given more weight than services labor.
- **Conversion-related indirect costs:** This subfactor measures the amount of indirect costs contributing to contract performance. Limited profit consideration is given where the contribution is routine. On the other hand, indirect elements making a significant contribution should be recognized for the contribution they make. For example, the contribution of depreciation of modern production equipment, which reduces contract cost by increased efficiency, should be assigned a higher profit rate than older, less efficient equipment. Fa-

cilities' capital cost of money is not allowable cost in any contract, and therefore is not included in the cost objectives amounts.

- **General management:** This is the contribution other indirect costs and G&A expenses make to contract performance.[180] Included in this category is the contribution management and support personnel make to contract performance.

- **Contract cost risk:** Cost risk has two considerations. The first is, who is responsible for cost overruns? Second, what is the probability of a cost overrun? The former is determined by the pricing arrangement, the sharing ratio, fee swing, or ceiling price. The latter is determined by the difficulty of the overall contract and the confidence in the accuracy of the cost estimates.

  Determine the degree of cost responsibility and associated risk that the proposed contractor will assume under the contemplated contract type. The greater the risk, the greater the reward. The reliability of the cost estimate in relation to the complexity and duration of the contract is also a factor. The government's incentive is to encourage the contractor to assume greater responsibility for controlling and reducing cost as well as avoiding unnecessary costs.

  Contractors that assume the greatest cost risk are those that have agreed to a firm-fixed-price contract for a complex activity. Except in unusual circumstances, time-and-material, labor-hour, and firm-fixed-price level-of-effort contracts should be treated as cost-plus-fixed-fee contracts.

- **Federal socioeconomic programs:** Contractors that give unusual support to federal socioeconomic programs should be rewarded. This includes support given to small businesses that are owned and controlled by socially and economically disadvantaged individuals, women-owned small business, handicapped sheltered workshops, and energy conservation programs.

COs are not to negotiate a price or fee that exceeds the statutory limitations of 15 percent on experimental and developmental contracts or 6 percent on architect-engineering services contracts for public works contracts or utilities.[181]

Documenting the agreement: It is important to document the agreement in order to keep a record of all significant considerations and agreements for the purpose of facilitating their recovery if the need arises. The CO should immediately prepare a record at the conclusion of each negotiation of an initial or revised price. This record should include enough detail to allow someone other than the buyer or seller to understand what was agreed to, how it was agreed to, and why.[182]

Pre-negotiation objectives: The CO is required to establish pre-negotiation objectives before negotiating any pricing action. These objectives are to be based on the CO's analysis of the offeror's proposal. The scope and depth of the analysis supporting these objectives are to be directly related to the dollar value, importance, and complexity of the pricing action. This includes information provided from the field, audit reports, results of fact-finding, independent government estimates, and price histories.[183]

Certificate of current cost or pricing data: When there is inadequate competition, the selling party must furnish copies of the cost or pricing data used by the contractor during negotiations. The CO must include the requirement that the winning contractor execute a Certificate of Current Cost or Pricing Data under the terms of the Truth in Negotiation Act. The certificate is now to be dated when the data were used in the negotiations. This means that "sweeps" are no longer required after the price is negotiated and later adjustments made to the contract price.[184] Certification is not required when the prices are set by law, are for commercial items, or are not based on adequate price competition. Certification is required when the price of the procurement is expected to exceed $500,000.[185]

Price negotiation memorandum (PNM): The PNM is the document that has historically recorded the decisions made during negotiations and delineated the details of negotiation. However, the Rewrite of FAR Part 15 emphasizes including appropriate information throughout the contract file. This suggestion has been interpreted to downplay the requirement for the use of the PNM.[186] The information the CO must include in the contract file includes:

- Documentation of the purpose of the negotiation
- Description of the acquisition
- Names and positions of those participating in the negotiations
- Provision of the status of the contractor's purchasing system
- Reason for exemption if cost or pricing data are not required
- A statement as to the extent cost or pricing data, if required, were relied upon
- A summary of the contractor's proposal and summary recommendations from field pricing assistance and the reasons for varying from them
- A statement of the most significant facts and considerations that controlled the pre-negotiation objectives
- The quantification and impact of direction given by Congress
- The basis for the profit or fee
- Documentation of fair and reasonable pricing.[187]

NEGOTIATIONS IN THE FEDERAL GOVERNMENT

Acquisition reform emphasizes the award of negotiated competitive procurement contracts without discussion. It has also dropped the prohibition against auctioning. The wholesale use of Electronic Data Interchange (EDI) has been mandated to take advantage of its capability to place orders quickly and accurately, confirm prices, direct shipments, and transfer funds online. "With business-to-business (B2B) networking, commercial companies can tap into online auctions and eliminate truckloads of paperwork."[188] In addition, the increased use of government-wide commercial purchase cards for the purchase of supplies, services, and construction is introducing "on-the-spot" purchasing and receiving, shifting the purchasing duties away from a CO to the end user. Each of these acquisition initiatives minimizes the CO's involvement in the process. It also begs the question, does it change the need for the CO to have negotiating skills?

To answer this question we must look at practices being followed by the private sector, which the federal sector is trying to emulate. The underlying theme of acquisition reform is to commercialize the federal acquisition process as much as possible. This calls for the participants in the acquisition process to work together as a team, adopt practices that promote competition, and maximize the use of commercial products and services.[189] Michael F. Miller, writing in *Contract Management*, concludes that industry still values negotiations because:[190]

> A majority of products that are outsourced are uniquely designed for custom-crafted parts which are similar to the federal government's noncommercial classification. The commercial world is turning more and more to setting target prices and then entering into strategic partnerships to improve the quality at a bargained price based upon cost-analysis. This has resulted in manufacturing prices going down at a rate of 1% a year compounded, which is one of the main reasons why we have no inflation.[191]

Online auctioning may work well for commercially available supplies but cannot work well for services. As the FAR acknowledges, statements of work for services must be individually tailored to the period of performance, deliverable items, and desired degree of performance. Performance-based services contracts are also awarded through competitive negotiations, when appropriate, to ensure selection of services that offer the best value to the government.[192]

Even when buying commercial items, it often pays to use a negotiator skilled in structuring alternative agreements to achieve the best value to the government. When the CO enters into discussions to inform the offeror of deficiencies, resolve uncertainties involving technical or other terms and conditions, and resolve suspected mistakes in its proposal, he or she is expected to allow the offeror to revise its proposal. Comptroller decisions on bid protests encourage the COs to bargain.

The need for contract negotiating skills is not vanishing with the introduction of B2B. As we will see in the next chapter, modifications of ongoing contracts will still represent a significant workload. It is the CO's responsibility to negotiate these amounts of equitable compensation the contractor is entitled to for implementing these modifications. In FY 1999 the total number of contracting actions by the federal government was 487,264. Contract modifications represented approximately 30 percent of that total (144,419). However, what is most significant is the fact that the dollar value of contract modification represented approximately 55 percent of the total dollar value of all contract actions ($100,533,589,000/ $183,199,003,000).[193]

Approaches to Negotiating

There are two primary approaches to negotiating. A study performed in 1986 of the different negotiation styles used in industrial buyer-seller relations concluded that the cooperative and competitive approaches were used the most. The cooperative approach, sometimes referred to as interest-based bargaining, is often the basis for a win/win style of negotiation that has been found to lead to more positive long-term relationships between negotiating parties.[194] The key to win/win negotiations is the parties' seeking ways to reap joint gains, i.e., improvement from each party's point of view. In this situation, value has been created. On the other hand, the competitive approach, which is sometimes called *positional bargaining,* is seen as a win/lose style in which one side seeks to claim value at the expense of the other. The objective of win/lose negotiations is to convince the other party that what they want from you is much more valuable than what you want from them. This style most often leads to hard, tough bargaining in which "winning" results in the other party "losing."[195]

In every bargaining situation each party has two kinds of interests. The first is to gain something they did not have before from the pending agreement. The second is to determine the possibility for a future working relationship.[196]

Bargaining for gain: Each party's interests motivate them to benefit from each situation. In win/win negotiation (interest-based bargaining), both parties believe that to be successful one must be inventive and cooperative. One party seeks to achieve its interests by helping the other party realize its own interests. Creativity helps devise an agreement in which both parties will gain from the agreement rather than no agreement.[197] Following this method, both the buyer and seller seek gain by knowing and understanding the interest behind the positions taken by the other party. This knowledge leads to the identification of shared interests and concentration on finding ways to realize joint gains through bargaining.

Current policy permits the CO to reveal the other offeror's price, with the other offeror's permission. The CO also may now inform an offeror that its price is considered to be too high, or too low, and reveal the results of the government's analysis supporting that conclusion. In addition, the

CO also may reveal to all offerors the cost or price that the government's price analysis, market research, and other reviews have identified as being reasonable.

Figure 6-1, Negotiation Positions, illustrates the relationship between the buyer's and seller's negotiation objectives. It also portrays the buyer's and seller's BATNA. The seller's opening position is its offer that is on the table at the time discussions begin. During discussions the buyer moves from its minimum position toward its objective. At the same time the seller moves away from the proposal toward its objective. The entire shaded area between the buyer's and seller's objectives should be seen as the bargaining area. It represents possible agreements on issues that could not be improved on from the standpoint of either party without harming the other. It is within this area that negotiation skills and persuasion are used to change positions and to reach an ultimate agreement of stalemate. The closer both parties' initial objectives are to each other, the smoother the negotiations are expected to be. This is because both parties feel conformable in making concessions.

Bargaining with future relationships in mind: Negotiations between the parties do not end when the contract is signed. The "I win, you lose" attitude has the high probability of giving both parties a big headache during contract performance.[198] If the other side is crippled by the deal, it has nothing to lose by breaking the agreement. The Treaty of Versailles that ended World War I in

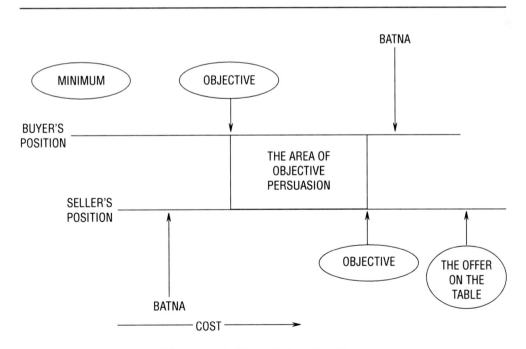

Figure 6-1 Negotiation Positions

1919 brought a win-lose deal dictated by the victorious allies that could not be carried out, and instead of creating peace, created further resentment by Germany. This resentment turned into a desire to seek revenge, leading to the rise of Adolph Hitler and World War II.[199] Therefore, the "last day of World War I was the first day of World War II"!

A survey of purchasing managers in the late 1990s concluded that they believed future negotiations will focus on win/win situations rather than heated debates. And, as competition to furnish the highest-quality product at the lowest price increases, the goal of industry will be to establish winning relationships that result in lower cost.[200] Acquisition doctrine is consistent with this trend, calling for participants in the process to work together as a team with a unity of purpose to achieve the acquisition goal.[201] This requires the parties follow a more cooperative course, in which both sides aim to achieve some of their goals, rather than a competitive approach in which one side wins while the other loses.

In *The Power of Nice*, Ronald M. Shapiro and Mark A. Jankowski state their belief that in reality there is no such thing as both parties getting all they want or winning equally. "One party is bound to get more than one less, *even if both sides are content with the outcome*." Both parties can be satisfied, but they cannot win to the same degree. Therefore, the stated objective should be win/win as opposed to win/lose, win/clobber, or win/ransack/pillage and obliterate. The way to accomplish this is "to get what you want by helping the other party get what they want." This is the best way to make an acceptable deal and achieve your most desirable goals by letting the other side achieve some of its goals. Both parties win, but you win bigger.[202]

CONTRACT AWARD

For negotiated contracts, award occurs when the CO provides the successful offeror either an executed contract document or a written notice of acceptance of an offer. Most government contracts are bilateral agreements. The contract is said to have been integrated when it is adopted as the full and final expression of their agreement.[203] Key to post-award contract interpretation is the determination by the courts and boards whether the contract document constitutes an integrated agreement. Contracts and solicitations generally considered integrated include a schedule; contract clauses; a list of documents, exhibits, and other attachments; and representations and instructions. This is important because the "rule (parole evidence) bars admission of evidence to contradict language in an integrated contract or to add language to a completely integrated contract."[204]

The contract document is also important because it: (1) represents the common language for the government/contractor acquisition team, (2) is written legal proof of the intent of the parties, and (3) authorizes the Comptroller to disburse funds because all obligations of the United States must be supported by documentary written evidence of a binding agreement. The only exceptions to this rule are contracts involving non-appropriated funds and the sale of government property.

If the award document includes information that is different than the latest signed proposal, as amended by the offeror's written correspondence, both the offeror and CO must sign the contract document signifying the award.[205] Note that the Rewrite of Part 15 permits the use of plain-paper formats in lieu of standard or optional forms. This was decided to conserve time if EDI is used. If plain paper is used, it must incorporate the agreement and award language of the OF Form 307.[206]

When an award is made for fewer than all the items that may be awarded and additional items are being withheld for subsequent award, options are a prime example. In this case, each notice shall state that the government may make subsequent awards of the additional items within the purposed acceptance period.[207]

The CO is responsible for determining when the contract requires Cost Accounting Standards (CAS) coverage. A CAS-covered contract is not to be awarded until the ACO has made a written determination that the contractor's disclosure statement is adequate, unless this provision is waived by the CO to protect the government's interest. The criteria for determining that a disclosure statement is adequate includes confirming that it is current, accurate, complete, and describes accurately the offeror's cost accounting practices. When this happens, the required disclosure statement will be required as soon as possible.[208]

Post-Award Debriefing

For the unsuccessful offeror, the post-award debriefing is the only means of determining if its proposal was fairly evaluated. The government's goals in providing a post-award debriefing are to gain the confidence of the unsuccessful offeror that its proposal was evaluated fairly, instill confidence in the acquisition process, and avoid a protest that could disrupt contract performance.[209] This latter goal overshadows the others because the SSA believes that the motive of the unsuccessful offeror is to obtain information that could be used in a protest. This apprehension sometimes influences the content of the debriefings through the fear of providing information that could be used to protest the award.

The Federal Acquisition Streamlining Act (FASA) establishes the offeror's right to a meaningful post-award briefing by mandating that when a contract is awarded by negotiation, an unsuccessful offeror may request a debriefing in writing. It further establishes a timeline for this to occur. Time is the critical factor when it comes to the unsuccessful offerors requesting and receiving a post-award debriefing (see Figure 6-2, Post-award Debriefing and Bid Protest Timeline). Failure to file within the time limit can re-

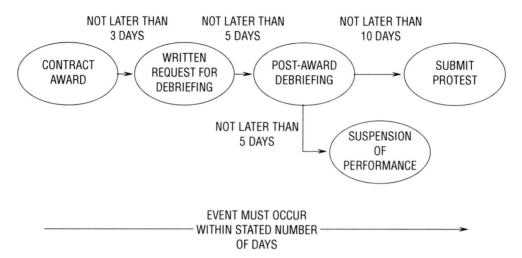

Figure 6-2 Post-award Debriefing and Bid Protest Timeline

---

sult in dismissal of the protest. FAR 15.506 establishes the following mandatory dates:

- Within three calendar days of receiving notification of contract award, the offeror must submit a written request for a post-award debriefing. This is critical because if an offeror fails to submit its written request within the three-calendar-day window, the buying agency is not obligated to provide the debriefing. An offeror that was notified it was excluded from the competitive range is entitled to one debriefing. Therefore, the offeror would only receive a post-award debriefing if it had previously requested the post-award debriefing in lieu of a pre-award debriefing within a time limit established in the FAR.
- The post-award debriefing should occur within five calendar days after receipt of the written request. The CO normally chairs the debriefing. The debriefing may be done orally, in writing, or by any other means acceptable to the CO, and it will be included in the contract file.[210]
- A bid protest is considered timely if it is filed within 10 calendar days of the required post-award debriefing by the CO. (Protests based on alleged improprieties in a solicitation shall be filed before bid opening or closing date for receipt of proposals.[211])
- Contract performance is to be suspended if the acquisition agency receives notice of the protest from the General Accounting Office (GAO) within five calendar days of the required debriefing. Suspension of contract performance is important to the protesting party. Without suspensions the contractor will begin to perform the contract, and government will likely obligate and expend funds. After the contract

has been awarded and contract performance has begun, to successfully suspend or terminate a contractor's effort, it must be shown that there was no rational basis for the award decision or that there is no overriding public interest precluding the issuance of an injection against continuing contractual performance.

Note that the time limit for filing a protest, within 10 calendar days of the post-award debriefing, is unrelated to the time limit to suspend contract performance, which is within five calendar days of the required debriefing. To meet the deadlines the unsuccessful offeror must file both its protest and request for a suspension within five days of the debriefing.

The debriefing is not intended to inform any offeror as to why the winning company was awarded the contract. At a minimum, the debriefing shall include:

- The government's evaluation of the significant weaknesses or deficiencies in the offeror's proposal, if applicable
- The overall evaluated cost or price (including unit prices) and technical rating, if applicable, of the successful offeror and the debriefed offeror, and past performance information on the debriefed offeror
- The overall ranking of all offerors, when any ranking was developed by the agency during the source selection
- A summary of the rationale for award
- For acquisition of commercial items, the make and model of the item to be delivered by the successful offeror
- Reasonable responses to relevant questions about whether source selection procedures contained in the solicitation, applicable regulations, and other applicable authorities were followed.[212]

The debriefing cannot be used to inform other offerors of source selection–sensitive information or proprietary information from the winning proposal. Therefore, some categories of data are not to be included in the debriefings:

- A point-by-point comparison of the debriefed offeror's proposal with those of other offerors
- Any information exempt from mandatory disclosure by FAR 24.202, e.g., classified information, trade secrets, confidential commercial and financial information, inter- and intra-agency memoranda, personnel and medical information, and names of individuals providing reference information about an offeror's past performance.

The debriefing should provide the unsuccessful offeror a perspective on its strengths and weaknesses as well as how it can improve its next competitive proposal. If errors are disclosed during these debriefings, the offeror should alert the buying agency to the need for corrective action to prevent an erroneous award.[213]

PROTESTS

Fairness to all offerors is the foundation of the entire acquisition system. Acquisition doctrine promotes full and open competition. One way to facilitate this objective is to enforce procurement laws and regulations. The CO's decisions to award contracts must be objective and justifiable on the basis of the solicitation. In addition, the process is based on the rule that all unsuccessful bidders must be offered a chance to protest decisions with which they do not agree.[214]

A protest is defined in the FAR as a written objection by an interested party to:

- A solicitation or other offers for a contract for procurement of property or services
- The cancellation of the solicitation or other request
- An award or proposed award of a contract
- Termination or cancellation of an award of the contract if it is based in whole or in part on improprieties concerning the award of the contract.[215]

Protests are administrative proceedings, not court suits. This is because the protester's objective is to obtain relief in the form of a judgment by the tribunal that the procuring activity committed an error and must correct the mistake.[216] The unsuccessful offeror may protest directly to the buying agency or to the GAO.[217] The record shows that at the GAO level, less than 15 percent of the protesters prevail.[218]

Although the unsuccessful offeror may have good reason to believe the government made a serious mistake during procurement, there is a potential downside that an unsuccessful offeror should consider prior to initiating a protest. The protest process can be expensive, and it inherently favors the government. In addition, if not handled carefully the protest can diminish the offeror's standing with the buying activity that may take years to erase.[219]

Protests to the Buying Agency[220]

On protests submitted directly to the buying agency, the CO is instructed to provide for inexpensive, informal, procedurally simple, and expeditious resolution of the matter. Other acceptable methods to resolve the protest are alternative dispute resolution techniques, as well as third party neutrals and other agency personnel. An independent review of the protest at a level above the CO, by a person not necessarily in the CO's supervisory chain, is also available to the interested party. Where practicable, the official selected to perform the independent review should not have had previous personal involvement in the procurement.

When a protest is received before contract award, the CO may not award the contract until the matter is resolved. However, a written determination can be made at a level above the CO that the award is in the best interest of the government. When the protest is received after contract award, the CO is instructed to suspend performance immediately pending resolution within the buying agency. Again, contract performance can continue for "urgent and compelling reasons" if it is judged to be in the best interests of the government by an official at a level above the CO.

Protest decisions are to be well reasoned and explain the agency position. The agency hearing the protest is to make its best efforts to resolve the protest within 35 days.

Protests to the GAO[221]

The unsuccessful offeror may file a protest with an organization outside the buying agency. The GAO, an arm of Congress, is formally recognized as that agency. The GAO began accepting protests from unsuccessful bidders in 1931. When the unsuccessful offeror files a written protest with the GAO, a copy of the complete protest is also required to be furnished to the official or location from the buying agency that was cited in the solicitation. This must be accomplished within one day of the original filing with the GAO. If the solicitation does not designate an official or location to send the protest, it should be furnished to the CO. If the contract has been awarded, it is the responsibility of the CO to notify the contractor of the protest. If no award has been made, the CO is to notify all parties that have a reasonable prospect of receiving the award if the protest is denied.

When no award has been made, the CO also is to furnish copies of the protest submission to these parties and instruct them to: (1) communicate directly with the GAO and (2) provide copies of their communications with the GAO to the CO. These parties can request access to the protest file, which is to be furnished within a reasonable time after submittal of the CO report to the GAO.

The CO is also responsible for compiling information of the acquisition and submitting a complete report to the GAO within 30 days of being notified by them of the protest. The GAO also can make a determination that this process needs to be expedited and can authorize the express option. In this case, the CO is to provide the information within 20 days. The CO also can apply for an extension to the submission date.

The GAO may issue protective orders, which can be used to safeguard the confidentiality of materials or information that may be disclosed as part of the discovery process. Information being protected is proprietary, business confidential, and procurement sensitive. Protective orders permit limited and controlled disclosure of this information. All personnel who receive this information are bound by the protective order not to disclose it to anyone not authorized to receive it, and they may not use the information for purposes other than prosecuting the protest.[222]

As in the case of a protest filed with the CO, contracts are not to be awarded if the protest is filed before award unless urgent and compelling circumstances that will significantly affect the interests of the United States will not permit waiting for the decision of the GAO. Contractor performance is also to be suspended if the protest is received after contact award. In this situation, urgent and compelling circumstances that significantly affect the interests of the United States unless the contractor's performance is permitted to continue can be cited to justify not suspending the contract effort.

Pre-award Protests

The objective of the unsuccessful offeror seeking a pre-award protest is seeking injunctive relief to block the award of the contract long enough to attain a judgment. This is because history has shown that judgments rendered after the contract has been awarded have been difficult to reverse.[223]

Protesting after Contract Award

When protesting a contract award, the objective of a majority of unsuccessful offerors is to obtain that contract by overturning the CO's award. Even if an order to terminate is issued, there is no certainty that the unsuccessful offeror will be awarded the contract. In some cases the only realistic remedy an unsuccessful offeror can aspire to gain is the cost of preparing and submitting its bid.[224]

There also have been examples of protests being filed with the objective of allowing the incumbent contractor to continue selling to the government. These "bad faith" protests easily crest ill will. A buying office can protect itself by overriding the suspension, and the protest could be dismissed summarily if it is without merit.

The Difficulty of Prevailing in a Protest

As noted earlier, unsuccessful offerors prevail less than 15 percent of the time when the protest is submitted to the GAO. There are two primary reasons for this: (1) the standard for review is based on the presumption that the CO acted properly, and (2) discovery is limited to documents in the possession of the agency. Consequently, the information needed to determine the probability of prevailing in a protest is not available unless the unsuccessful offeror files a protest.[225]

Questions that must be answered positively by the unsuccessful offeror to have any chance of prevailing in a bid protest are:

- Can the unsuccessful offeror demonstrate that there is no rational basis for the CO's decision eliminating them from the competitive range? Was any applicable regulation or statute violated? Had a government official exercised his or her discretion "in an abusive, unlawful, or irrational manner?"
- Is there any overriding public interest that would prevent any delay in making a contract award?
- Will the unsuccessful offeror suffer irreparable harm should the injunction not be issued? What is the probability the unsuccessful offeror will succeed in establishing that it has suffered irreparable harm?[226]

Protest Costs

To encourage legitimate protests, Congress has authorized successful protesters to recover the cost of protesting—including attorney fees and proposal preparation costs.[227] To recover these costs, the unsuccessful offeror must show that the government's conduct in considering its bid was arbitrary, capricious, or without a reasonable basis. The Court of Claims in Keco Industries, Inc. v. United States, 203 Ct. Cl.565,492 F 2d 1200 (1974) "marked out four subsidiary, but nevertheless general, criteria controlling all or some of these claims," i.e., claims of conduct that was arbitrary, capricious, or without a reasonable basis. The four criteria are:

1. Subjective bad faith on the part of the procuring officials, depriving a bidder of the fair and honest consideration of his proposal, normally warrants recovery of bid preparation costs.
2. Proof that there was "no reasonable basis" for the administrative decisions will also suffice, at least in many situations.
3. The degree of proof of error necessary for recovery is ordinarily related to the amount of discretion entrusted to the procurement officials by applicable statutes and regulations.
4. Proven violation of pertinent statutes or regulation can, but need not necessarily, be grounds for recovery.[228]

CONCLUSION

One of the most critical activities, which also has long-range implications, is the selection of the right source for supplies or services. The government's objective is to select a supplier that will provide the right quality of goods and services, at a reasonable price, and will furnish the level of responsiveness that will earn the satisfaction of the ultimate user.

As illustrated throughout this chapter, the idea of fairness underlies the entire source selection process. All potential suppliers, especially small and disadvantaged businesses, must not only be given the opportunity to compete for the contract, but the award decision must be made objectively. This is because the acquisition process is subject to public review, and it is easier to justify the award decision when it is based on criteria that are objective rather than subjective. The sealed bidding method of awarding contracts, which is characterized by formal advertising, public bid openings, and the contract being awarded to the low bidder, lends itself to meeting the tests of fairness. However, as the technical content and the uniqueness of some requirements increased, the government needed to consider factors other than price as a basis for making the contract award. In 1984 the Competition in Contracting Act recognized that negotiated procurements could be awarded competitively and that as long as they met the competitive criteria, they would be condoned by Congress.

Negotiated competitive procurement, with its best-value compendium, was included in a historic rewrite of FAR Part 15, Contracting by Negotiations, in 1997. In many places the Rewrite of FAR Part 15 is consistent with the goals of acquisition reform, i.e., to simplify the process and remove unnecessary regulatory constraints that impaired the ability of government personnel from being more innovative or from exercising business judgment. One place where this is particularly true is the establishment of the competitive range for a negotiated procurement. Here the CO has been given the ability to restrict the number of proposals admitted into the competitive range to enhance efficiency. The Rewrite also increases the scope of discussions, eliminates the use of mandatory forms to make the process "user friendly" in the information age, and streamlines the post-competitive range process. Just as significant is the emphasis placed on more open exchanges between the government and industry to improve the understanding of the requirements and foster teamwork that is so necessary in today's environment.

However, sellers have traditionally viewed the source selection process with skepticism that increases when FAR procedures permit the use of discretion or subjective judgment in the award of a government contract. The primary source of their apprehension is unclear. Is it because price has now been joined by additional evaluation factors and even subfactors, thus making it difficult for the seller to identify the buyer's criteria for selecting the source? Is it because the process does not include a clear-cut checklist that the SSA must check off while making the contract award decision? Or is it because the process for awarding a competitive negotiated contract makes it more difficult to determine if an unsuccessful offeror was treated fairly?

Industry feels that when it comes to discussions during the source selection process, the Rewrite of FAR Part 15 enormously expands the discretionary power of the CO.[229] It supports this contention with the following: (1) the "scope and extent of discussions (negotiations) are solely a matter of the CO's judgment,"[230] (2) an offeror can be eliminated from the competitive range "whether or not all material aspects of the proposal were afforded an opportunity to submit a proposal revision,"[231] and (3) the failure to require quantitative support of tradeoffs making the source selection decision.[232] At this point only time will tell if the COs will abuse this newfound authority or if they will fulfill their obligation to maintain the public trust in acquiring goods and services for the ultimate user.

Chapter 7 covers contractor performance after award. All the effort described so far has been directed toward delivering on a timely basis the best-value product or service to the customer while maintaining the public's trust and fulfilling public policy objectives.[233] As the old saying goes, "The proof of the pudding is in the eating."[234]

NOTES

[1]FAR 1.102.

[2]Witte, Robert D. 1989. Source Selection—A Treatise. Case Commentary. *Contract Management* (January): 38.

[3]Rider, Melissa D., Kenneth D. Brody, David B. Dempsey, and Bernard L. Weiss. 1997. *FAR Part 15 Rewrite*. Vienna, VA: National Contract Management Association, 18.

[4]Talbot, Terry R. 1997. Source Selection After Acquisition Reform: How Does It Stack Up Now? *Contract Management* (December): 45.

[5]Ibid.

[6]Talbot, 45.

[7]United States Code Service: 41 U.S.C.S. 405 note, Policy Regarding Consideration of Past Performance (1996); and Public law 103-355, Federal Acquisition Streamlining Act.

[8]Talbot, 44.

[9]Cibinic, Jr., John, and Ralph C. Nash, Jr. 1982. *Formation of Government Contracts*. Washington, D.C.: Government Contracts Program, George Washington University, 113.

[10]Cibinic, Jr., and Nash, Jr., *Formation of Government Contracts*, 113.

[11]Cibinic, Jr., and Nash, Jr., *Formation of Government Contracts*, 138.

[12]Cibinic, Jr., and Nash, Jr., *Formation of Government Contracts*, 139.

[13]Cibinic, Jr., and Nash, Jr., *Formation of Government Contracts*, 137.

[14]FAR 9.104-1.

[15]FAR 9.4.

[16]Cibinic, Jr., and Nash, Jr., *Formation of Government Contracts*, 151.

[17]Nash, Ralph C., Jr., Steven L. Schooner, and Karen R. O'Brien. 1998. *The Government Contracts Reference Book*, 2d ed. Washington D.C.: The George Washington University Law School, 158.

[18]Cibinic, Jr., and Nash, Jr., *Formation of Government Contracts*, 173.

[19]10 U.S.C. § 2305(c) and 41 U.S.C, 253(b).

[20]FAR 14.406-3.

[21]Nash, Jr., Schooner, and O'Brien, 203.

[22]Witte, Robert D. 1987. Mistakes in Bids—Legalism versus Business Judgment. *Contract Management* (April): 47.

[23]FAR 14.406.

[24]FAR 14.406-3(a).

[25]FAR 14.406-3(f).

[26]FAR 14.406-3(a).

[27]FAR 14.406-3(b).

[28]FAR 14.406-3(c).

[29]FAR 14.404-1(a)(1).

[30]FAR 14.404-1(a)(3).

[31]FAR 14.404-1(d).

[32]FAR 14.404-1(b).

[33]FAR 14.404.

[34]FAR 14.404-1(f).

[35]FAR 14.405.

[36]FAR 14.201-6(q).

[37]FAR 14.407-1.

[38]Cibinic, Jr., and Nash, Jr., *Formation of Government Contracts*, 500.

[39]FAR 14.408-4.

[40]FAR 14.201-8

[41]Gifis, Steven H. 1984. *Law Dictionary*. Woodbury, CT: Barrons Educational Series, Inc., 297.

[42]Nash, Jr., Schooner, and O'Brien, 357.

[43]Gifis, 298.

[44]Nash, Jr., Schooner, and O'Brien, 531.

[45]FAR 15.302.

[46]Rider, Brody, Dempsey, and Weiss, 18.

[47]Rider, Brody, Dempsey, and Weiss, 19.

[48]FAR 15.101-1.

[49]Rider, Brody, Dempsey, and Weiss, 20.

[50]Rider, 22.

[51]FAR 15.101-2.

[52]FAR 15.101-2(b).

[53]FAR 15.303(b).

[54]FAR 15.303(c).

[55]FAR 13.000.

[56]FAR 13.106-2.

[57]Shariati, Linda. 1999. Bid Protests Decisions Related to Commercial Items: Raising Unanswered Questions. *Contract Management* (June): 7.

[58]FAR 15.305(a).

[59]Talbot, 45.

[60] Burt and Pinkerson, 135.

[61]FAR 15.305(a)(1).

[62]FAR 15.405(a).

[63]FAR 15.404-1(2).

[64]Nash, Jr., Schooner, and O'Brien, 403.

[65]Nash, Jr., Schooner, and O'Brien, 139.

[66]FAR 15.404-1(c).

[67]FAR 15.401.

[68]Dempsey, 45.

[69]FAR 15.304.

[70]FAR 15.304.

[71]Arnavas, Donald P., and William J. Ruberry. 1994. *Government Contract Guide Book.* Washington, D.C.: Federal Publications Inc., 4–6.

[72]Rider, Brody, Dempsey, and Weiss, 56.

[73]FAR 15.304.

[74]FAR 15.305(a)(3).

[75]Bodenheimer, David Z. 1997. Past Performance: A Sequel. Topical Issues in Procurement Services. *Contract Management* (September): 2.

[76]United States Code Service: 41 U.S.C.S. 405 Policy Regarding Consideration of Past Performance (1996); and Public Law 103-355, The Federal Acquisition Streamlining Act.

[77]FAR 15.404(c)(2)(iii).

[78]Bodenheimer, 4.

[79]Bodenheimer, 5.

[80]FAR 15.305(a)(2).

[81]Rider, Brody, Dempsey, and Weiss, 62.

[82]FAR 15.306(a)(2).

[83]Bodenheimer, 6.

[84]Beausoleil, Joseph W. 2000. Past Performance is Not Working. *Contract Management* (July): 29.

[85]Bodenheimer, 5.

[86]FAR 15.306(b).

[87]FAR 15.306.

[88]Dempsey, 46.

[89]FAR 15.306(b).

[90]Dempsey, 46.

[91]Stanley N. Sherman. 1991. *Government Procurement Management*. Germantown, MD: Wordcrafters Publications, 264–268.

[92]FAR 52.215-1(f)(4).

[93]FAR 15.306(c)(1).

[94]Rider, Brody, Dempsey, and Weiss, 68.

[95]Dempsey, 46.

[96]Williamson, Edward L. 1999. The New Competitive Range Standard: Raising the Bar. *Contract Management*. (July): 9.

[97]Williamson, 11.

[98]FAR 15.306(b)(1).

[99]Williamson, Edward L. 1998. The New Debriefing Procedures: Where Time Is of the Essence. *Contract Management*. (May): 8.

[100]FAR 15.505.

[101]Williamson 1998, 9.

[102]FAR 15.505(a).

[103]Williamson 1998, 14.

[104]FAR 15.505.

[105]FAR 15.404-1.

[106]FAR 31.000.

[107]FAR 31.101/102.

[108]FAR 15.404-3(a).

[109]FAR 15.404-1.

[110]FAR 15.404-1(b).

[111]FAR 15.404-1(c).

[112]FAR 15.404-1(d).

[113]Carroll, Thomas D. 1994. Cost Realism. *Contract Management* (May): 22.

[114]FAR 15.404-1(e).

[115]FAR 15.404-1(f).

[116]FAR 15.404-1(g).

[117]Dobler, Donald W., and Davis N. Burt. 1996. *Purchasing and Supply Management*. 6th ed. New York: McGraw-Hill, 340.

[118]Burt and Pinkerson, xi.

[119]Burt and Pinkerson, 152.

[120]FAR 15.404-3(a).

[121]FAR 15.404-2.

[122]FAR 15.404-2(d).

[123]Nash, Jr., Schooner, and O'Brien, 483.

[124]Nash, Jr., Schooner, and O'Brien, 484.

[125]FAR 15.308.

[126]Ibid.

[127]Rider, Brody, Dempsey, and Weiss, 83.

[128]Cibinic, Jr., and Nash, Jr., *Formation of Government Contracts*, 424–426.

[129]Nash, Jr., Schooner, and O'Brien, 196.

[130]Nash, Jr., Schooner, and O'Brien, 363.

[131]Karrass, Chester L. 1993. *Give and Take, the Complete Guide to Negotiation Strategies and Tactics*. New York: Harper Collins, 4.

[132]Sherman, 268.

[133]Sherman, 269.

[134]Sherman, 269.

[135]FAR 15.306(d).

[136]FAR 52.215-1.

[137]Sherman, 267.

[138]Sherman, 267.

[139]Dobler and Burt, 315.

[140]Dobler and Burt, 370.

[141]Karrass, Chester L. 1976. *The Negotiating Game: How to Get What You Want*. New York: Thomas Y. Crowell, Publishers, 56–57.

[142]Dobler and Burt, 365.

[143]FAR 15.406-1.

[144]Dobler and Burt, 366.

[145]Shapiro, Ron M., and Mark A. Jankowski. *The Power of Nice: How to Negotiate So Everyone Wins—Especially You!* New York: John Wiley & Sons, Inc., 54.

[146]FAR 15.405(b).

[147]Fisher, Roger, and William Ury. 1983. *Getting to Yes: Negotiating Agreement Without Giving In*. New York: Penguin Books, 101.

[148]Fisher and Ury, 102.

[149]Fisher and Ury, 103.

[150]Nash, Jr., Schooner, and O'Brien, 196.

[151]FAR 15.306(d)(2).

[152]FAR 15.306(b).

[153]Kennedy, Gavin. 1994. *Field Guide to Negotiation: A Glossary of Essential Tools and Concepts for Today's Manager*. Boston, MA: Harvard Business School Press, 30.

[154]FAR 15.405(b).

[155]FAR 15.306(d).

[156]FAR 15.306(d)(2).

[157]FAR 15.306(e)(1).

[158]Rider, Brody, Dempsey, and Weiss, 72.

[159]FAR 15.306(d)(3).

[160]Witte, Robert D. 1989. Source Selection—A Treatise. Case Commentary. *Contract Management* (January): 39.

[161]FAR 15.306(d)(4).

[162]FAR 15.307.

[163]Ibid.

[164]Nash, Jr., Schooner, and O'Brien, 45.

[165]Rider, Brody, Dempsey, and Weiss, 75.

[166]Sherman, 257.

[167]Rider, Brody, Dempsey, and Weiss, 78.

[168]FAR 52.215-1(f)(4).

[169]Miller, Michael F. 2000. Negotiations: A Lost Art in an Era of Online Auctions? *Contract Management* (May): 11.

[170]Williamson, Edward L. 2000. The Right to Remain Silent. *Contract Management* (May): 19.

[171]Williamson 2000, 19.

[172]Miller, 10.

[173]Ibid.

[174]Nash, Jr., Schooner, and O'Brien, 414.

[175]Nash, Jr., Schooner, and O'Brien, 245.

[176]FAR 15.404-4.

[177]FAR 15.405(b).

[178]Sourwine, Darrell A. 1997. DOD Profit Policy: Resolving the Confusion. *Contract Management* (August): 12.

[179]FAR 15.404-4(d).

[180]In the early 1980s organizations outside the DoD, e.g., The Grace Commission, Defense Finance and Investment Review, and the General Accounting Office, reviewed defense acquisition processes. They concluded that DoD's profit policy was giving more weight to the contractor's effort, including G&A, than it did in capital assets. Consequently Congress, in the 1987 Appropriations Act, directed that negotiated contracts emphasize facilities capital and contractor risk and not include profit based on specific elements of cost, e.g., G&A. However, the FAR was not changed to exclude profit from being applied to G&A. This was accomplished by not including G&A on the DD Form 1547, which is used to calculate weighted guidelines. No other government agency precludes awarding profit on G&A. (Sourwine, 13).

[181]FAR 15.404-4(d).

[182]Dobler and Burt, 379.

[183]FAR 15.406-1.

[184]Rider, Brody, Dempsey, and Weiss, 117.

[185]FAR 15.406-2.

[186]FAR 15.406-3.

[187]Ibid.

[188]Miller, 10.

[189]FAR 1.102(a).

[190]Miller, 11.

[191]Drucker, Peter. 2000. *Wall Street Journal* January 1.

[192]FAR 37.602-3.

[193]Total Federal Snapshot Report, SF279. Actions Reported Individually on SF279, FY1999 Through Fourth Quarter.

[194]Berkowitz, Donna. 1997. Negotiating Strategies, Tips & Techniques for Commercial and Federal Contracts. *Contract Management* (June): 4.

[195]Lax, David A., and James K. Sebenius. 1986. *The Manager as Negotiator.* New York: The Free Press, 30–33.

[196]Fisher and Ury, 20.

[197]Lax and Sebenius, 30.

[198]Casey, J.R. 1997. Keys to Successful Negotiations: Observations from the Trenches. *Contract Management* (June): 14.

[199]Shapiro and Jankowski, 12.

[200]Duffy, Roberta. 1999. Where Are We Headed? *Global Purchasing and Supply Chain Management.* London: World Markets Research Center (October): 104.

[201]FAR 1.102-3.

[202]Shapiro and Jankowski, 49.

[203]Gifis, 239.

[204]Cibinic, Jr., John, and Ralph C. Nash, Jr. 1986. *Administration of Government Contracts,* 2d ed. Washington, D.C.: The George Washington University, 135.

[205]FAR 15.504.

[206]FAR 15.504(c).

[207]FAR 15.504(b).

[208]FAR 30.202-6.

[209]Williamson 1999, 9.

[210]FAR 15.506.

[211]FAR 33.103(e).

[212]FAR 15.506(d).

[213]Adelson, Dennis. 1996. The New Bid Protest Procedures: A Cautionary Note. *Contract Management* (June): 6.

[214]Wilson, James Q. 1989. *Bureaucracy: What Government Agencies Do and Why They Do It.* New York: Basic Books, 127.

[215]FAR 33.101.

[216]Adelson, 7.

[217]FAR 33.102.

[218]Rosen, William M. 1996. Considerations When Deciding Whether to Challenge Federal Procurements. *Contract Management* (June): 23.

[219]Rosen, 21.

[220]FAR 33.103.

[221]FAR 33.104.

[222]Adelson, 6.

[223]Cibinic, Jr., and Nash, Jr., *Formation of Government Contracts,* 646.

[224]Cibinic, Jr., and Nash, Jr., *Formation of Government Contracts,* 656.

[225]Rosen, 23.

[226]Cibinic, Jr., and Nash, Jr., *Formation of Government Contracts,* 649–652.

[227]Gabig, Jerome S., Jr. 1988. Speaking Out: Curbing "Bad Faith" Protests. *Contract Management.* (September): 22.

[228]Cibinic, Jr., and Nash, Jr., *Formation of Government Contracts,* 660.

[229]Rider, Brody, Dempsey, and Weiss, 73.

[230]FAR 15.306(d)(3).

[231]FAR 15.306(d)(4).

[232]FAR 15.308.

[233]FAR 1.102.

[234]deCervantes, Miguel, 1547–1616.

Contract Performance

Until now this book has concentrated on the pre-award activities rather than the numerous post-award actions required to fulfill the requirements of the contract. The contract performance phase begins with contract award. One need not be reminded that no work is to begin until the contract is awarded unless the contractor is willing to assume the total risk or the CO has authorized work in advance of contract award. (The latter is sometimes done to obtain material with long lead times.)

Successful contract completion is entirely dependent on an effective inter-organizational relationship between the government and the contractor during contract performance. A task force headed by the Office of Management and Budget issued a report in December 1992 criticizing the lack of agency management attention to contract administration. The report, titled *Summary of the SWAT Team on Civilian Agencies Contracting: Improving Contracting Practices and Management Controls on Cost-Type Federal Contracts*, identifies 10 major issues pertaining to contract administration. Although the agencies surveyed for the report did not include DoD, its conclusions were "reminiscent of the FY 1986 Department of Defense (DoD) Authorization Act in its criticism of the government's contracting practices and the proposed imposition of significant restrictions on contractors."[1] The SWAT Team's report first and foremost criticized the lack of management attention to contractor performance: "More than one agency reported because bureau management concentrates on the attainment of mission goals, the primary focus is on contract award and obligation of dollars in order to attain these goals. Monitoring contractor performance and cost is not emphasized."[2]

With the end of the Cold War came reductions in overall federal spending. There is increased competition for fewer dollars, especially in the area of defense. To be successful, firms in the government market will need to offer a quality product with a competitive cost of ownership. Maximum use of commercial items has become another key element of acquisition doctrine. Acquisition streamlining has also given members of the acquisition team an increased opportunity to be innovative and exercise good business judgment during the acquisition process. As noted earlier, if a policy or procedure is not specifically addressed in the FAR nor prohibited by law, Executive Order, or other regulations, the government member of the acquisition team should not assume that it is prohibited. Contemporary doctrine emphasizes the need to have a close working relationship and an attitude of mutual confidence and respect between government and contract members of the acquisition team. The objective is to create an environment that cultivates open communications and the elimination of duplicative, and sometimes unique, processes at the contractor's plant by adopting a single commercial-like process.[3]

During the performance phase, the role of the government representatives is to ensure that the contractor complies with the terms and conditions of the contract. In recent years this role has been evolving from managing items to managing suppliers. This is being done by eliminating government standards and replacing them with best commercial practices, such as ISO 9000, as well as opening the door to supplier alliances.[4] The net result has been the adoption of plant-wide processes rather than numerous process tailored to the individual contracts.

THE CONTRACT

When a contract is formed, there are underlying presumptions that accompany each contractual agreement. If any one of these presumptions proves to be false, it must be dealt with because it can jeopardize the outcome of the contractual effort. Actions by both parties during the performance phase are directed toward ensuring that the original intent of the parties is fulfilled. The six presumptions upon which a contract is founded are illustrated in Table 7-1, Presumptions Upon Which a Contract Is Founded. These are:

1. **Performance feasibility:** Although not specifically stated, there is a fundamental presumption that it is possible to perform the proposed work. If this is not the case, there is a risk that the procurement objectives will not be fulfilled and that a significant financial loss will occur if the situation is not recognized and corrected early in the performance phase.
2. **Competency:** Although the buyer has a duty to assess the seller's capabilities prior to contract award, the seller also has an obligation to perform the work satisfactorily after contract award.

Table 7-1. Presumptions Upon Which a Contract is Founded

- It is possible to perform the work
- Seller has capability and capacity to complete the work successfully
- Contract agreement is sound
- Parties will cooperate
- There are no material mistakes regarding objectives and nature of effort
- No unconscionable burden will be placed on either party

---

3. **Document soundness:** The contract is the *common language* between the buyer and seller. The contract document should be a complete and accurate expression of the original intent of both parties.
4. **Cooperation:** This presumption imposes the duty on both parties to cooperate. The contractor's obligation to cooperate is well understood. The government's duty to facilitate performance by providing the information and suitable government-furnished equipment (GFE) when they are needed to perform the work cannot be overemphasized.
5. **Absence of mistake:** Mistakes are endemic in human relationships and do not disappear when the parties enter into a written agreement. When contracts are formed, mistakes occur that are classified as mutual or unilateral. The burden resulting from a mistake can be substantial, and the parties must resolve the situation quickly by determining the cause and how the impact of the mistake will be handled.
6. **Conscionability:** Supervening events, misunderstandings, and optimistic analysis can create contract requirements that impose an obligation on the performing party to operate contrary to its best interests. The contractor usually bears most of an unreasonable burden, e.g., when the cost of performance is not in proportion to the benefits.[5]

Keeping in mind the risk associated with these presumptions, the acquisition team must develop its plan to administer the contract. The character and scope of contract administration activity varies from contract to contract. The depth of the government's participation in the contractor effort is also mixed. In some cases it can be characterized as complete involvement. In others it is almost complete disengagement. Factors that influence the government's involvement include the nature of the work, type of contract, and experience and attitudes of the personnel involved. An off-the-shelf item requires much less government involvement than does a firm-fixed-price contract for performance of unique services or complex equipment. The degree of government involvement in a cost reimbursement contract is much greater than in a firm-fixed-price contract.[6]

Acquisition doctrine has ushered in a change to the perspective of the government-contractor relationship. No longer should the government-contractor relationship be approached as being a command-and-control association. As David Lax and James Sebenius of the Harvard Negotiation Roundtable write, "With the rise of complexity and interdependence, with increasing professionalization, with heavier emphasis on the role of information, with new organizational forms, and with the continuing decline in the automatic acceptance of formal authority, indirect management skills promise to be ever more necessary."[7] Indirect management is the name given to the phenomenon of concentrated responsibility but shared authority.[8]

Acquisition doctrine calls for the creation of the acquisition team consisting of all participants in the process, including the customer as well as representatives from the technical, supply, and procurement communities and the contractors who provide the products and services.[9] The acquisition team fits the indirect management model.

To create the product or service required by the ultimate user, the acquisition team must harmonize interests among its members. This is because although accountability is established by the contractual relationship, control of the resources needed to accomplish the contractual effort are diffused among many stakeholders, e.g., Congress, superiors in the agencies, peers, parallel organizations, or subcontractors.

The success of the contract performance phase is measured by how the product performs in the hands of the user while meeting the cost objective as well as delivering the product on a timely basis. This calls for the team to exercise personal initiative and to be able to accommodate changes while at the same time maintaining the discipline imposed by the contract. The contractor is interested in the product's performance and follow-on business as well as profit. Realization of these objectives also requires discipline, on the part of both the buyer and seller, to maintain the productivity balance that is present at the time of contract award.

CONTRACT ADMINISTRATION SERVICES

The term *contract administration services* (CAS) refers to "steps taken by the government representatives responsible for ensuring government and contractor compliance with the terms and conditions of the contract."[10] It is not a one-way street. It is important to point out that the government representatives responsible for administering contracts are also charged to set up systems to mitigate the risk to both the government and the contractor when problems surface.[11] The scope of the contract administration task is not one-dimensional.

The procuring Contracting Officer (CO), who awarded the contract, has the authority to designate a contract administration office (CAO) responsible for the administration of the contract. A primary goal during the contract performance is to avoid any type of destructive breakdown in the working relationship of the acquisition team.[12]

The CO also can appoint an Administrative Contracting Officer (ACO) to engage in the day-to-day administrative tasks of the contract. Sometimes the CAO and the ACO are located with the prime contractor. Other times they are separated from the place of contract performance, and the delegated contract administration tasks are performed on an itinerant basis. The extent and scope of this delegation should be described in Part G of the applicable contract.

Some contracts have a contracting officer representative (COTR) whose job is to perform contract administration tasks as they pertain to technical matters. The COTR's role is to provide technical guidance to a contractor on issues that fall within the scope of the contract. Frequently the authority of the COTR is defined in a technical direction clause. Rarely is the COTR given authority to enter into contractual matters.[13]

Contractors with more than one operational location often have corporate-wide policies, procedures, and activities applying to all locations. This often affects the performance of the CAS duties of more than one ACO. Specifically, these include:

- Determining final indirect cost rates for cost-reimbursement contracts
- Establishing advanced agreements or recommendations on corporate/home office expenses
- Administering Cost Accounting Standards (CAS) applicable to corporate-level and corporate-directed accounting practices.[14]

If workload warrants, a Corporate Administrative Contracting Officer (CACO) may be assigned to deal with corporate management and perform selected CAS functions on a corporate-wide basis. Location of the CACO depends on the distribution of workload among the ACOs at the various contractor locations as well as the location of the corporate office, corporate records, the major corporate plants, the cognizant government auditor, and overall cost effectiveness.[15]

The source of the rules governing contract administration are the statutes, regulations, and precedents established by legal and board decisions. FAR 42.302(a) lists some 70 CAS functions that may apply to each contract. The CAO is automatically delegated the responsibility to perform all of these functions, to the extent they apply to the contract, unless authority to do so is specifically withheld by the CO. Table 7-2, General Contract Administration Functions, contains a list of many of these functions.

FAR 42.302(b) also identifies 11 other functions that are performed by the CO unless specifically delegated to the CAO. The extent of this delegation is at the discretion of the CO. The functions are:

- Negotiating or negotiating and executing supplemental agreements incorporating contractor's proposals resulting from change orders issued under the Changes clause. Before completing negotiations, changes to the delivery schedule must be coordinated with the CO.

Table 7-2. General Contract Administration Functions

- Review contractor's compensation structure
- Conduct post-award orientation
- Negotiate forward-pricing rate agreements
- Determine allowability of cost
- Establish final indirect cost rates
- Attempt to resolve issues
- Determine adequacy of disclosure statement
- Make payments when prescribed
- Timely notification of cost status
- Analyze quarterly limitation on payments
- Process and execute duty-free entries
- Issue work requests under M, R, & O contracts
- Negotiate and execute convenience terminations
- Process and execute navigation agreements
- Screen property for disposal
- Manage facilities contracts
- Assist COs in priority allocations
- Perform traffic management services
- Ensure compliance with quality requirements
- Perform engineering surveillance
- Report inadequacies in specifications
- Review engineering change proposals
- Monitor restrictive marking program
- Evaluate socioeconomic programs
- Perform supporting CAS
- Issue administrative changes
- Negotiate and execute supplemental agreements
- Accomplish administrative closeout
- Support program reviews
- Evaluate environmental specifications
- Review contractor insurance plans

- Evaluate contractor's proposals
- Negotiate advanced agreements on cost
- Issue intent to disallow costs
- Establish final indirect billing rates
- Cost accounting standards
- Approve/disapprove requests for payment
- Manage special bank accounts
- Monitor contractor financial condition
- Issue tax-exempt forms
- Administer industrial security program
- Negotiate and execute supplemental agreements
- Negotiate and execute cancellation charges
- Approve special test equipment requests
- Issue modification on excess GFP
- Perform pre-award surveys
- Monitor contractor industrial relations
- Evaluate packing and packaging processes
- Ensure safety requirements
- Evaluate adequacy of logistics and maintenance
- Perform engineering analysis of proposals
- Evaluate requests for waivers and deviations
- Consent to placement of subcontracts
- Maintain surveillance of flight operations
- Ensure submission reports
- Release shipments
- Cancel unilateral purchase orders
- Evaluate drug-free workplace program
- Evaluate environmental practices
- Deobligate excess funds after final closeout

- Negotiating prices and executing priced exhibits for unpriced orders issued by the CO under a basic ordering agreement (BOA).
- Negotiating or negotiating and executing supplemental agreements changing contract delivery schedules.
- Negotiating or negotiating and executing supplemental agreements providing for the de-obligation of unexpended dollar balances excess to contract requirements.
- Issuing amended shipping instructions and negotiating and executing supplemental agreements incorporating contractor proposals resulting from these agreements.
- Negotiating changes to interim billing prices.
- Negotiating and defining adjustments to contract prices resulting from exercise of economic price adjustment clauses.
- Issuing change orders and negotiating and executing resulting supplemental agreements under contracts for ship construction, conversion, and repair.
- Executing supplemental agreements on firm-fixed-price supply contracts to reduce required contract line item quantities and de-obligate excess funds when notified by the contractor if such actions are deemed to be in the best interests of the government.
- Executing supplemental agreements to permit a change in place of inspection at the origin specified in firm-fixed-price supply contracts awarded to nonmanufacturers to protect the government's interests.
- Preparing an evaluation of the contractor's performance.

Authority of Government Personnel

Contractors who deal with government personnel are affected by a legal rule, unique to government contracting, that the government is not bound by the unauthorized acts of its employees. Therefore, when dealing with a government employee it is important that a contractor understand the scope of that individual's authority. The apparent authority doctrine does not apply to a government contract.[16] Boards and courts have rejected the apparent authority rule, which is applicable to private agency law, by holding that actual authority is required to bind the government. In Federal Corp. Insurance Corp. v. Merrill, 332 U.S. 380 (1947), the court stated:

> Whatever the form in which the Government functions, anyone entering into an arrangement with the Government takes the risk of having accurately ascertained that he who purports to act for the Government stays within the bounds of his authority.[17]

As we have seen, numerous government personnel and organizations can be involved in administering a contract at various locations. Authority to commit on behalf of the government is limited and sometimes fragmented. This raises the question when dealing with the government of how the contractor determines the authority of the person it is dealing with. Boards and courts have frequently granted contractor relief on the basis of "implied authority." Authority to bind the government is generally implied when it is an integral part of the duties assigned to the employee, for example, a quality assurance inspector. Although under the implied authority doctrine the contractor is not obligated to appeal to the CO, it would be prudent to do so when there is a question.[18]

In addition, an unauthorized act may be ratified if the ratifying official, usually a CO, has actual or constructive knowledge of the unauthorized act and, expressed or implied, adopts the act. Ratification has the same effect as if the act were authorized originally. The ratifying official must have the power to perform or authorize the unauthorized act.[19]

To ensure that the CAO is aware of all contractual issues, the FAR specifies that the CO is to forward all correspondence relating to assigned contract administration functions through the cognizant CAO to the contractor. Or, if urgency requires sending correspondence directly to the contractor, a copy is to be sent directly to the CAO. In addition, when government personnel visit a contractor's facility in connection with a contract, they must notify the CAO organization in advance. Early communication permits making the necessary arrangements with the contractor so the purpose for the visit can be achieved. Another reason for this procedure is to eliminate duplicate reviews, investigations, and requests for audit.[20]

Protecting the Public Interest

Public interest, i.e., the interest of the United States, is the term frequently used when broad authority is granted to an officer of the government. For example, 10 U.S.C.§ 2304(c)(7) and 41 U.S.C.§ 253(c)(7) permit award of contract without full and open competition when the head of the agency determines that such actions would be in the public interest.[21] In addition to obtaining the needed goods or services, government officials also should beware of their obligation to protect the public interest. Not only is this interest concerned with the effective expenditure of public funds, but it also includes the maintenance of the integrity of the competitive system. In the latter case the CO should take no action after the contract is awarded that will give the contractor an advantage that would not have been given to the other competitors. To preserve the contract the COs should:

- "Require full performance to specifications (this is referred to as the strict compliance standard)

- Obtain appropriate price reductions (or other considerations) when less-than-full contract performance is acceptable to the government
- Hold contractors responsible for damages suffered by the government resulting from the contractor's failure to perform as agreed
- Make certain that the government does not fail to perform its obligations, thereby relieving the contractor of performance responsibilities
- Preclude the issuance of unnecessary or excessively priced change orders or contract amendments."[22]

CONTRACT AUDIT SERVICES

Contract auditors, although they are organized separately from procurement and contracting administration activities, are the principle advisors to the CO on financial matters. Normally the Defense Contract Audit Agency (DCAA) is the responsible government audit agency. However, there may be cases in which an agency other than DCAA desires cognizance of a particular contractor for audit purposes. When this happens, it is to be resolved by an agreement on the most efficient approach to meet contract audit requirements.[23]

An audit is defined as "the systematic examination of records and other documents and the securing of—confirmed by physical inspection or otherwise—for one or more of the following purposes: determining the propriety or legality of proposed or consummated transactions; ascertaining whether all transactions have been recorded and are reflected accurately in accounts; determining the existence of recorded assets and the inclusiveness of recorded liabilities; determining the accuracy of financial or statistical statements or reports and fairness of the facts they represent; determining the degree of compliance with established policies and procedures of financial transactions and business management; and appraising an accounting system and making recommendations concerning it."[24]

The auditor is responsible for:

- Submitting information and advice based on the auditor's financial and accounting records or other related data as to the acceptability of the contractor's incurred and estimated costs to the requesting activity
- Reviewing the financial and accounting aspects of the contractor's cost control systems
- Performing other analysis and reviews that require access to the contractor's financial and accounting records supporting proposed and incurred costs.[25]

DCAA also performs operations audits to confirm the allowability of costs claimed on cost-reimbursement contracts. Audits like this provide a basis for cost realism reviews. Here the auditor provides data on the contractors's estimating methods, forward pricing factors, reliability of prior cost estimates, and other areas specified by the CO.[26]

Although opinions have been expressed that audits represent an intrusion into management's prerogatives, the right to examine records is included in the FAR and is a fundamental condition of most government contracts. FAR clause 52.215-2, Audit Negotiations, which is incorporated by reference in Part I of cost-reimbursement, incentive, time-and-material, labor-hour, and price-redeterminable contracts, gives the government the right to examine and audit "books, records, documents, and other evidence and accounting procedures and practices, regardless of form or type, sufficient to reflect properly all costs claimed to have been incurred or anticipated to be incurred in performing the contract."[27]

POST-AWARD ORIENTATION (CONFERENCE)

One of the most important but difficult responsibilities for both parties after contract award is to maintain a harmonious working relationship during the performance phase. John Cibinic, Jr., and Ralph Nash, Jr., in *Administration of Government Contracts*, describe the situation accurately: "Cooperation between the parties is essential if the work is to be performed and yet the parties are, in a very real sense, adversaries. The government's right to insist on strict compliance with contract obligations does not relieve the government from its duty to cooperate with the contractor in the performance of work. While the government is not required to assume the contractor's obligations, in many cases the government's assistance and cooperation will be required."[28]

One of the first opportunities both parties have to get the performance phase off to a good start is by having a post-award orientation. It is an initial step in the management of risk. It is especially crucial when risks to the contractor or the government have not been adequately addressed in the contract. The orientation is not a substitute for a full understanding of the work requirements by both parties. The process is designed to help government, contractor, and subcontractor personnel gain a clear understanding of all contract requirements in a joint environment as well as identify and resolve potential problems before occurrence. The post-award orientation is not a way to alter the agreement.[29]

The orientation also provides the acquisition team an opportunity to define focal points for specific tasks, establish a communication protocol, and establish operating relationships among the functions that make up the team. This is very important because, as noted above, only a limited number of personnel can authorize a change to the contract. An important element of this communication protocol is the communication process and administrative structure to be followed for managing risks and opportunities.

The orientation should be held as soon as practical after the award of the contract. There are two forms of post-award orientation. The first is a conference, or video conference, with key government, contractor, and subcontractor personnel participating. The CO chairs the orientation conference. This forum is most appropriate if the CO believes the contractor does not have a complete understanding of the scope, technical requirements, or their obligations under the contract. It is also possible to provide the needed information via a letter advising the contractor of the government's principal concerns. This method is appropriate when the procurement is not complex. When the contractor has previous experience producing the items or performing the services, and it has previously worked on government contracts, a letter may be appropriate.

It is up to the CO to decide if a post-award orientation is needed and what form is most appropriate. When making this decision the FAR instructs the CO to consider at a minimum:

- The nature and extent of the pre-award survey and prior discussions with the contractor
- The type, value, and complexity of the contract
- The complexity and acquisition history of the product or service
- The requirements for spare parts and other equipment
- The urgency of the delivery schedule and relationship of the product or service to critical programs
- The length of the planned production schedule
- The extent of subcontracting
- The contractor's performance history and experience with the product or service
- The contractor's status, if any, as a small, small disadvantaged, or women-owned small business subcontracting programs
- Safety precautions required for hazardous materials or operations
- Complex financing arrangements, such as progress payments, advanced payments, or guaranteed loans.[30]

There is no standard format for the agenda for an orientation conference. Table 7-3, A Sample Post-award Conference Checklist, was adapted from Stanley Sherman's *Contract Management Post Award*.[31] The agenda must be tailored to the acquisition. Subjects covered most frequently are:

- Special contract clauses (including warranty provisions, if appropriate)
- Critical contractual events
- Key elements of the contractor's ISO 9000 process
- Special reporting requirements
- Billing and paying procedures

Table 7-3. Sample Post-award Orientation Checklist

Technical and quality issues
- Quality assurance/inspection system compliance
- Procedure for design-drawing approval
- Policy toward waivers and deviations
- Qualification and pre-production samples
- Value engineering incentives/program questions
- Inspection, testing, and acceptance
- Data requirements and manuals
- Adequate of facilities and availability
- Program-unique issues or concerns

Contract administration issues
- Personnel matters
  - Authority and responsibility of managers
  - Key personnel
- Overall management issues
  - Contract management plan
  - Contract management schedule
  - Communication protocol
  - Questions concerning terms and conditions

- Office space for government personnel
- Reports and intellectual property rights
- Classification and plant security requirements
- Priorities and allocations
- Modification of contracts

Production and progress management
- Technical direction authority
- Production surveillance procedure and work-in-progress reports

Finance, cost, and payment issues
- Financial reporting
- Funding schedule
- Invoicing, billing procedure, and payment information
- Change order accounting

Procurement and subcontracting matters
- Procurement system approval status
- Subcontract consent

Social-economic policy objectives

Property management matters

Transportation and shipping

- Roles of the government's acquisition team members
- Roles of the contractor's acquisition team members.

WHAT DOES THE CONTRACT SAY?

The written contract document is the primary evidence of the parties' agreement in virtually all cases involving government contract interpretation controversies.[32] The contract document should be thought of as the common language for the government/contractor acquisition team. The contract is the record of the parties' intention at the time the offer is accepted.

One thesis of this book is that the integrated contract has taken on even greater importance than before. This is because with the advent of the Internet and the capability to have a project/contractual home page, each member of the acquisition team can call up a current integrated contract at his or her work station. The contract is an encyclopedia of requirements and a reference point for all members of the acquisition team. Placement of this document on the project's home page means it must be clear and easily understood. Therefore, it is imperative that the document defines the requirements in generally prevailing terms, establishes the obligations of the parties, and describes how the risk is allocated. The importance of having a contract document that will stand up in a court of law is another reason it should be free from ambiguities.

The process of determining what the parties agreed to in the contract is referred to as *contract interpretation*. The contract interpretation process involves determining the meaning of words, supplying missing terms and filling gaps, resolving ambiguities, and sometimes ruling that the parties are bound to perform in a manner that appears to be contrary to the words in the contractual document.[33] The process begins with examining the language in the document as well as evidence outside the contract itself. This includes considering such facts or circumstances as requests for clarification of the solicitation, performance of the parties after award, and information presented at the pre-proposal conference. If a clear interpretation is found, the question is resolved. Ambiguity may remain when other factors are discovered that require further examination, or even litigation. As an alternative to litigation the parties can seek a solution through the alternative disputes resolution (ADR) process.

The cardinal rule of contract interpretation: The cardinal rule of contract interpretation is to carry out the original intent of the parties. This rule is founded in common law.[34] "Courts and boards interpret contract language in the way it would be interpreted by a reasonably intelligent person familiar with all the facts and circumstances surrounding contract formation. Under this approach parties are held to appropriate standards of knowledge and experience."[35]

Chapter 5 discusses the "duty to inquire rule," in which there is an obvious, or patent, ambiguity. This rule is designed to prevent post-award disputes by making it clear that offerors have a duty to seek clarification before bidding.[36] This obligation applies only to obvious errors, gross discrepancies, or inadvertent and glaring gaps. Unlike the other rules of contract interpretation, it does not focus on intent. When failing to inquire as to the meaning of an obvious ambiguous provision in the solicitation, the non-drafting party probably has assumed any risk associated with contract performance.

The rule regarding the duty to inquire represents a way to stop one party from taking advantage of conspicuous flaws in the drafting of the agreement. A criterion of the "duty to inquire rule" is whether either party, by failing to divulge mistakes, stands to profit from the failure.[37] To determine if a discrepancy is obvious, the offeror should look for these two indicators:

- The provision has a significant affect on price
- The provision significantly increases the amount of work.

Secondary rules of determining the original intent of the parties: It is important to point out that by following the "duty to inquire rule" before bidding, the contractor may prevent having to consider any of these secondary rules.

It should be understood that before being able to prevail in a dispute using these secondary rules of contract interpretation, the burden of proof is on the party to show that it actually relied on the protested interpretation. The secondary rules of contract interpretation are listed below:

- **The party must read the contract as a whole:** The contract rule is based on the precept that all parts of the contract have meaning and that no one part should be given more weight than any other. However, if a provision can be interpreted in two ways—one that is consistent with the other clauses in the contract and one that conflicts with the others—the consistent reading is preferred.[38]
- **Express language prevails:** The express language rule, as the description implies, states that when there is only one reasonable interpretation, that interpretation should prevail. This rule assumes that the professionals understand the language of their own specialties. The expressed language rule overcomes the parties' relevant behavior prior to any dispute arising. The rule also does not permit the government to avoid the consequences if the express language was "imprudent for the agency."[39] Often there are situations in which it is necessary to list items that are part of the contractor's effort or are to be furnished by the government. There are two rules that apply to the interpretation of these provisions:
  1. Where the contract contains a specific list of items without words of qualification, the contractor may reasonably assume that items not on the list are not included unless there are provisions to the contrary.
  2. When words of qualification that have doubtful meanings are used, the context of others words with which they are associated will determine their meanings.[40]
- **Conduct of the parties:** The conduct of the parties rule can apply if the expressed language of the contract does not resolve the disagreement. This has been referred to as the "action speaks louder than words" guideline because it demonstrates the parties' intent. "How the parties act under the arrangement, before the advent of controversy, is often more revealing than the language of the written agreement by itself."[41] Discussions after contract award but before the disagreement may be an indication of the reasonableness of one party's interpretation.[42] The courts generally give a great deal of weight to the pre-dispute actions of the parties as evidence of their intent.

The pre-bid or pre-proposal conference is an integral part of the solicitation process and therefore is a primary source of information as to whether the contractor did or did not seek clarification on an obvious ambiguity or term and conditions contained in the solicitation. The courts have held that statements by authorized government officials made at such conferences can be taken into account in ascertaining the parties' intentions and joint understanding of the contract requirements.[43] However, most often without a written modification to the contract, oral agreements by government representatives to amend the solicitation will not be recognized.[44]

- **Knowledge of the other party's interpretation:** Entering into a contract knowing the other party's interpretation was objectionable means the other party's interpretation is the one that is binding. This rule means that failure of one party to object is regarded as acquiescence to the interpretation expressed by the other party.
- **Prior course dealings:** The prior-course dealing rule focuses on the parties' actions on past similar contracts. The criterion is that there must be a series of similar contracts between the same party and the government to be considered precedent setting.[45] Both parties must have actual knowledge of the prior-course dealings and of their significance to the contract. The burden of proof is on the party seeking relief to establish the existence of prior-course dealings. "A prior-course dealing cannot be established based on similar contracts with another party."[46]
- **Custom in the trade:** Parties entering into a contract are presumed to be competent in the subject mater of their contract. Similar to the rule of prior-course dealing, there is an expectation that trade practices will be observed unless the parties specifically agree to do otherwise. The burden of proving that the practice is well established in the trade is on the party stating that the other party should have followed the method in question. If there is an obvious variance from normal trade practices in the solicitation, the duty to inquire rule also applies.[47]

Other rules that need to be applied to the interpretation of a contract are that: (1) a specifically drafted clause cannot contradict a general clause that is required by law or regulation having the force or effect of law; (2) handwritten or typed terms have precedence over printed terms because it is assumed they are tailored to the specific contract; and (3) words used in one sense are to be interpreted in the same sense throughout the entire contract unless there is a specific reason to do otherwise.[48]

- **Order of precedence:** If inconsistencies still exist after considering the above secondary rules, the FAR contains Order of Precedence clauses, FAR 52.214.29 (Sealed Bidding) and 52.215-33 (Negotiated Contracts), that establish a hierarchy for each of the schedules within the contract. When two or more provisions are in conflict, this is a mechanical means whereby a solicitation can be resolved. However, the use of this structured method does not guarantee that the original intent of the parties will be carried out.[49] Order of precedence provides a method for inconsistencies to be resolved by giving precedence in the following order:[50]

1. Schedule (Part I, Section A, Solicitation/Contract Form; Section B, Supplies or Services and Prices; C, Description/Specifications/Work Statements; D, Packaging and Marking; E, Inspection and Acceptance; F, Deliveries and Performance; G, Contract Administration Data; and H, Special Contract Requirements) excluding specifications
2. Representations and other instructions (Part IV, Section K, Representations, Certifications, and Other Statements of Offerors or Quoters; L, Instructions, Conditions, and Notices to offerors or Quoters; and M, Evaluation Factors for Award)
3. Contract clauses (Part II, Contract Clauses)
4. Other documents, exhibits, and attachments (Part III, List of Documents, Exhibits, and Other Attachments, consisting of Section J, List of Attachments)
5. The specifications.[51]

As a note of caution, the Order of Precedence Clauses cannot be used to circumvent the cardinal rule, the whole instrument rule, nor the duty to inquire in the event of an obvious ambiguity. Consequently, they are used infrequently to resolve disputed interpretations.[52]

- **Interpreted Against the Drafter:** A rule that comes into play after all others have been exhausted has been called the "rule of last resort." This rule places the responsibility for the lack of clarity on the party responsible for drafting the provision in dispute. Frequently referred to by its Latin name, *contra preferentem*, it is based on the premise that the least culpable party should be responsible for the dispute. In most instances it is invoked against the government, but there have been exceptions.[53] To apply the rule, the drafting party must be identified, and the non-drafting party must demonstrate that it relied on its interpretation during bid preparation or performance. *Contra preferendum* does not apply when the controversial provision was coauthored, nor does it apply to clauses that have their basis in either statutes or regulations that have the force and effect of law.

APPLICATION OF UNIFORM COMMERCIAL CODE

The Uniform Commercial Code (UCC) is the primary source of commercial contract law in the United States. It covers contracts for the sale of goods, commercial paper, bank deposits and collections, letters of credit, bulk transfers, warehouse receipts, bills of lading, investment securities, and secured transactions. The objective of the UCC is to simplify, clarify, and modernize the law governing commercial transactions by making it uniform throughout the various jurisdictions. The UCC has been adopted by 49 states and the District of Columbia, and a significant portion of the code is applicable in the state of Louisiana. Under the UCC buyers and sellers are left to develop their own terms and conditions. On the surface it seems as though applying the UCC to regulate the purchase of commercial goods and services for the federal government fits right in with the objectives of acquisition streamlining. There are two reasons, however, why this is not entirely so.

First, it must be pointed out that the UCC also does not apply to the sale of services or real estate transactions. Both comprise a significant segment of what the government purchases. In 1999 government contracts for services accounted for 41 percent of the total dollar value of government purchases.[54]

Second, the UCC is state law and is subject to the views and customs of each state's legislature. Contractual disputes involving the UCC are interpreted by state courts. Consequently, there are differences in the code from state to state. In short, the UCC is not uniform.[55] In a 1996 dispute involving a federal procurement, a court in Oregon ruled that Oregon's UCC was not applicable because "Federal common law, not state-adopted UCC, governs questions or the rights of the United States arising under nation-wide federal programs."[56]

Contract law is founded on the precedence established by existing law as well as legal concepts previously established by the courts. "The UCC is not directly applicable to government contracting, but it is used by analogy and for guidance when the terms of a contract or the regulations do not deal directly with the subject."[57] Where there is no precedence or guiding principle on an issue, the courts may refer to legal concepts from other jurisdictions to aid in formulating their legal opinions. The Court of Appeals for the Federal Council stated: "[t]o the extent existing federal law is not determinative on the issue and permits an area of choice between the merits of competing principles, the best modern decision and discussions, including the general principles of contract...law should be taken into account."[58] Therefore, UCC can be an area of choice for guidance in situations where federal law is not determinative on the issue. The GAO has ruled in certain cases that the government should follow the UCC "to maximum extent practicable in the interest of uniformity where not inconsistent with federal interests, law, or court decisions."[59] The courts have also supplied strong arguments for applying UCC principles to the interpretation of federal contracts. "Only when a particular issue has been directly addressed in the FAR does the UCC not apply."[60]

PERFORMANCE MEASUREMENT

With acquisition reform has come a renewal of the need for management to track actual achievement and compare it to the planned performance schedule. The objective is to be able to measure actual achievements continuously against a detailed performance plan, to be able to predict the final cost and schedule results for the project or operation, and to be able to implement timely actions that will ensure attainment of the acquisition objectives.

The method that has been designated by DoD as the management tool for the acquisition team is the Earned Value Management System (EVMS). EVMS is a combination of PERT (Program Evaluation Review Technique) and COST that evolved into Cost/Schedule Control Systems Criteria, or C/SCSC, in the early 1970s. C/SCSC was seen primarily as a financial reporting system and a method for the government to use in evaluating progress payments. Those who attempted to use the C/SCSC as a management tool to identify potential problems found the data were not available in sufficient time to initiate effective action.

The introduction of EVMS as the means of measuring performance is designed to address four problems. These are:

- The need to control work that, although authorized, had not been negotiated in terms of cost and schedule
- The need to provide the government with the ability to determine reasons for changes in cost and schedule through audit
- The need to eliminate the tendency of contractors to borrow budget value from downstream activities by applying it to current work
- The need to provide a method of identifying and reporting variances from the plans.[61]

EVMS is now seen as a business management tool that facilitates contract management by allowing the acquisition team to initiate corrective action at the earliest possible time.[62] It recognizes that cost data alone—or schedule data alone—can lead to distorted perceptions of performance. Earned value is the budgeted cost of work successfully performed by a contractor. This technique regularly compares budgeted cost of work performed with the actual cost of work performed. EVMS relates resource planning to schedules and technical performance requirements.

For illustrative purposes, the cost or price of every contract can be expressed by the following formula:

$$IB + MR = TC + E_{ann} + OR + UW$$

Where:
IB = sum of internal budgets allocated to managers
MR = management reserve held for contingencies
TC = contract target cost
E_{ann} = estimate of authorized but not negotiated work
OR = an addition to cost of performance, e.g., overrun
UW = work under dispute, e.g., unclassified work[63]

The left side is the sum of the internal planning budgets (values) allocated to the subordinate managers and an amount retained by management to resolve problems during contract performance. The right side of the equation represents the value of the planned contract effort plus authorized work yet to be negotiated, cost overruns, and unclassified work. The latter situation occurs when the contractor is performing work believed to be over and above contract requirements and the CO has taken the position that the work is already part of the negotiated agreement. Both authorized work yet to be negotiated (E_{ann}) and unclassified work (UW) occur when the contractor has submitted contract changes under the changes clause. The right side of the equation gives the acquisition team a current estimate of the cost of all work proceeding under the contract. Overrun (OR) and unclassified work (UW) do not represent additions to the contract cost, but they provide management an estimate of all the work. (For accounting purposes, their value is negative and therefore would not increase the contract cost.)

Key to having an effective EVMS is the quantification of the planned value $TC + E_{ann}$, which represents the contract baseline. To do this satisfactorily requires a record of the negotiated agreement that can be quantified. The contract baseline not only documents the boundaries for the scope of work, but it also places a monetary value on the technical requirements in the form of the cost for labor and material needed to perform the planned work. DoD refers to the quantification of the above equation as the Integrated Baseline Review (IBR). The IBR must be completed soon after contract award. Its objective is to "[en]sure that the contract performance measurement baselines captures the entire technical scope of work consistent with the schedule requirements and have adequate resources assigned."[64]

Under EVMS the value of internal planning budgets can be tracked to determine how the performance is conforming to the plan. To accomplish this, the contractor's management system must be able to compare the budgeted cost of work performed for a designated amount of work with the actual cost of work performed for a specific reporting period. The government does not specify any management system but looks to the contractor to have a system capable of meeting the following standards:

- **Organization:** The contractor must define the effort through the use of a work breakdown structure (WBS) of discrete work packages that can be expressed as a budget for the work to be performed. These must be tied to the contractor's management structure to establish responsibility for the performance of the work contained in the WBS.
- **Planning and budgeting:** This includes a description of the scope and schedule for each WBS. In addition, all indirect cost must be allocated to the budget in relation to time of performance. Being able to trace the budget to the WBS is vital.
- **Accounting:** The contractor's cost accounting process must be able to record direct cost in a manner consistent with the budget and WBS.

- **Analysis:** The contractor's system must be designed to permit a comparison of planned and actual costs at an appropriate level throughout the WBS. Variance analysis should be generated on a monthly basis.
- **Revisions of work plans:** The contractor must have the ability to revise work plans on a controlled basis without loss of historical records. It is especially important that the contractor have a method for estimating the effects of change orders and internal re-planning actions on the overall contract. The system must provide the capability to reconcile revised cost estimates with the original performance baseline.[65]

EVMS is a management system that uses quantitative indicators that are generated by the contractor's cost accounting system and a coordinated WBS that relates the products to be delivered to the work to be performed, providing the acquisition team a framework for managing risk and opportunities. Using as an example Figure 7-1, The Earned Value-Time-Cost Relationship, the acquisition team can proactively track the status of the contract effort, report the financial status, mitigate risk, or take advantage of opportunities as they present themselves.

During the contract performance phase, the acquisition team should continually address progress in two areas. The first has to do with the contract baseline and the resources, expectations, and risks associated with the work remaining to be performed on the contractual agreement. To illus-

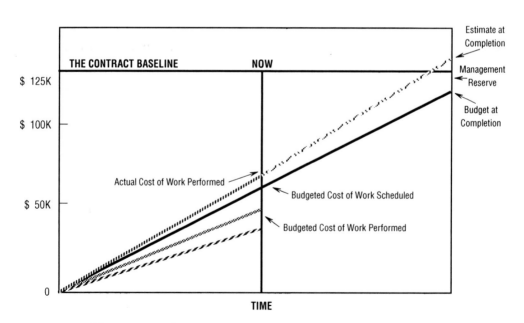

Figure 7-1 The Earned Value-Time-Cost Relationship

trate, in Figure 7-1 the value of the contract baseline is $125,000. The figure shows that the original budget at completion is approximately $120,000, leaving approximately $5,000 in management reserve. The second area of concern involves actual performance. Management should concentrate on tracking performance, identifying variances from contractual objectives, taking corrective actions, and managing changes to the contract. As Figure 7-2 shows, what is planned and what is actually performed are not consistent, and an out-of-balance condition exists.

In this example, on the cost side the Actual Cost of Work Performed (ACWP) exceeds the Budgeted Cost of Work Performed (BCWP) by approximately $18,000 (ACWP-BCWP). This equates a cost overrun of around $18,000 at the time of the report. As for the schedule, the figure shows that at this time approximately $58,000 of work was scheduled to be completed (Budgeted Cost of Work Scheduled, or BCWS). However, approximately $48,000 of scheduled work had been completed (Budgeted Cost of Work Performed, or BCWP). This means there is a variance of around $8,000 between work scheduled to be performed and what has ac-

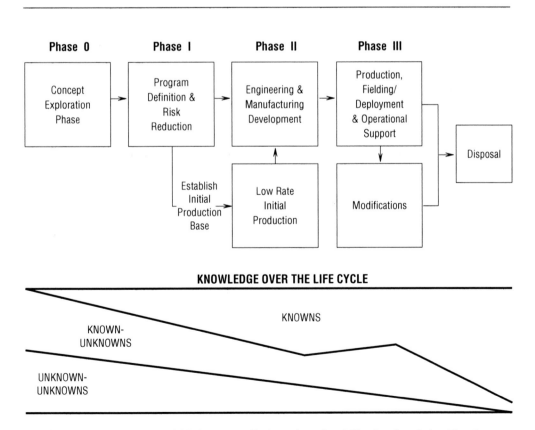

Figure 7-2 Technical Unknowns Related to the Life Cycle of the Product

tually been accomplished (BCWS-BCWP). Consequently, the contract not only is in a cost overrun, but it is also behind schedule. Armed with this information the acquisition team can identify likely causes and initiate corrective actions. Referring again to Figure 7-1, it appears the corrective action taken is expected to reduce the overrun significantly at contract completion.

MANAGING RISKS AND OPPORTUNITIES

Managing Risk—Acquisition doctrine calls for a shift in focus from risk avoidance to one of risk management because the cost to the taxpayer of attempting to eliminate risk (in an acquisition) is prohibitive.[66] In Chapter 2 we covered the management of risk. Risk is an assessment of the future. It is the probability of an undesirable significant event occurring that will have a negative impact on the goods or services being purchased. The contemporary goal of acquisition management is to mitigate risk through identifying and creating measures to reduce the probability of the feared event occurring. DoD Instruction 5000.2 defines risk management as "an organized method of identifying and measuring a risk and developing, selecting, and managing options for handling risk." As a system enters into system development and demonstration, the types of risk identified in DoDI 5000.2 include, but are not limited to, "schedule, cost, technical feasibility, threat, risk of technical obsolescence, security, software management, dependencies between a new program and other programs, and risk of creating a monopoly for future procurements."[67]

Managing risk begins with requirements determination and continues as a key management task during the entire acquisition process. It is a well-accepted fact that as knowledge increases over time, the level of risk declines as the operational concept transitions through its life cycle and becomes a mature product. Technical unknowns related to the life cycle of a product were reviewed in Chapter 4. For example, Figure 4-10, presented here as Figure 7-2, Technical Unknowns Related to the Life Cycle of the Product, contains a conceptual illustration of how knowledge evolves over the life cycle of a product. The diagram portrays the relationship between knowns, known/unknowns, and unknown/unknowns as the product matures. For example, during conceptual design the magnitude of the unknowns associated with the product performance is much greater than during full-scale production. Not only is the quantity of unknowns reduced during this period of time, but the development and testing programs also expose the unknown/unknowns. An effective risk management program, which includes proactive risk-handling techniques, contributes to this decline. As one would imagine, the risk management program for each acquisition is a function of where the product stands in its life cycle. Consequently, the risk management program must be tailored to the acquisition.

The proactive risk management process is a systematic management technique designed to identify and deal with potential problems that could have a negative impact on the acquisition. Plans to handle risk by implementing these techniques during the performance phase should be developed during post-award orientation. The purpose of this orientation is to minimize any risks associated with the contractual agreement that have been unresolved. This is a most appropriate time for communication with the key participants in the risk management process, as an understanding of the contractual allocation of risk is fresh in everyone's mind. The fact that there is a contract does not eliminate the business risk. The contract document can introduce new risks. Unresolved contractual issues should be integrated into the overall risk management process, along with risks associated with programmatic, technical, software, supportability, and cost risk.

Risk cannot be managed until it has been identified, analyzed, and characterized. The result of this risk analysis provides extremely valuable information that can be used in presentations to acquisition team and upper management. The following factors, which should be identified during risk analysis, are used to describe the characteristics of each risk:

- Description of the undesirable event
- Possible causes of the undesirable event
- Probability (cumulative) of occurrence of each cause
- Consequences of the undesirable event
- Time window during which action must be taken to deal with the risk
- Risk aversion strategy, along with milestones and responsibility.

Identification of this information on an item of risk is a product of analysis and interviews with the various stakeholders in the acquisition process. Stakeholders include the ultimate user, PM, CO, prime contractor, subcontractors, design engineers, systems engineers, production personnel, test engineers, quality assurance personnel, software engineers, configuration management personnel, and logistics (supportability) personnel.

The amount of exposure to risk can be determined by determining the probability of occurrence and multiplying it by the severity of the consequences if the event occurred.

Risk Exposure = PO · SC

Where:
PO = Probability of Occurrence
SC = Severity of Consequences

The Defense Management College published *Risk Management Concepts and Guidance*, in which it is recommended that a risk management rating system should probably be very simple, with ratings such as high, medium, and low. A conceptual diagram for a risk rating mechanism is illustrated in Figure 7-3 as example of a Risk Rating Mechanism.

The handling of risk represents a critical task during the performance stage. At this time the stakeholders (acquisition team) can use the above risk-ranking mechanism or similar rating methodology to rank individual risk to prioritize their actions as well as track and record actions taken.

Managing Opportunities—Contemporary procurement members of the acquisition team are now being called on to act as business advisors and to develop long-term business strategies to acquire the best overall solutions and to develop future partnerships with proven suppliers. This requires them to track cost and schedule during contract performance and closeout as never before envisioned. There may be opportunities to exceed the project's expectations, which could result in a compensatory change to the contract. In these situations cost-benefit tradeoffs need to be made to determine if the added performance is worth the additional cost. This analysis should be completed and a change to the contract approved before any action is initiated.

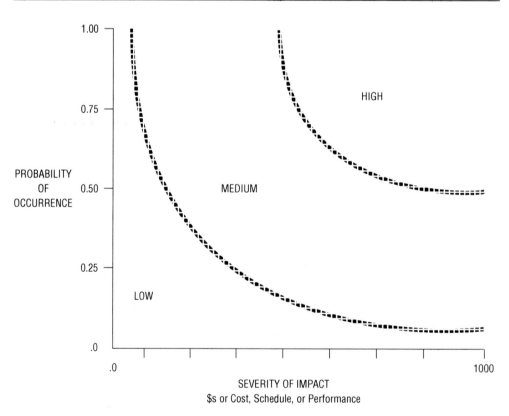

Figure 7-3 An Example of a Risk Rating Mechanism

On the contractor's side, the primary objective of a business is to maximize the wealth of the shareholders (owners). The contractor's performance represents a continuous balancing act of cost vs. total sales, overhead vs. profit, accounts receivable and inventories vs. current and fixed liabilities. Internally, it is the return on assets (ROA) and return on investment (ROI) that are measures of a business organization's profitability, i.e., the effectiveness with which capital is being utilized. Delivery schedules, payment frequency, financing provisions, and other provisions of a contract can significantly affect a contractor's cash flow and ROA.

An overall excellent performance by the contractor provides an opportunity for follow-on business. The contractor is motivated to long-term profits by producing quality products that will result in follow-on business. The best way to attain this goal is to meet performance, schedule, and cost goals.

The FAR also includes a procedure, i.e., the Value Engineering clause, whereby the contractor can gain a share of any cost reduction it initiates. The contractor must initiate a Value Engineering Change Proposal (VECP) proposing a reduction to the contract price without impairing the functions or characteristics of the product. In theory the VECP is intended to provide the contractor an incentive to develop ways to be more efficient by including a contract provision on how the amount of cost reduction will be shared. Use of the VECP clause eliminates any question of defective pricing if the contractor changes the method of performance after its disclosure during negotiations and the certifying cost or pricing data.

The Handling of Risk and Opportunities process (see Figure 7-4) begins with expectations (objectives) of the procurement as they are defined at the beginning of the acquisition process. It is a method whereby the risk and opportunities are continuously assessed during all phases of the acquisition. The process not only implements the risk management philosophy defined in acquisition doctrine, but it also provides a method whereby benefits can also be realized by taking advantage of potential opportunities. It is not a plan that is developed and then placed on the shelf. This technique includes identifying, analyzing, and developing handling plans beginning in the requirements determination process and proactively monitoring each risk or opportunity continuously throughout the acquisition process. Under the risk management philosophy the acquisition team identifies what could go wrong and create a future problem, as well as the probability of occurrence and the potential impact. However, it does not end there. This information then becomes the foundation of an action plan, which is continuously tracked and adjusted as conditions warrant during the life cycle of the acquisition. The objective is to provide a structured management technique whereby risk and potential opportunities are analyzed and handled proactively. A tool that lends itself to this concept is the earned value management approach, discussed earlier.

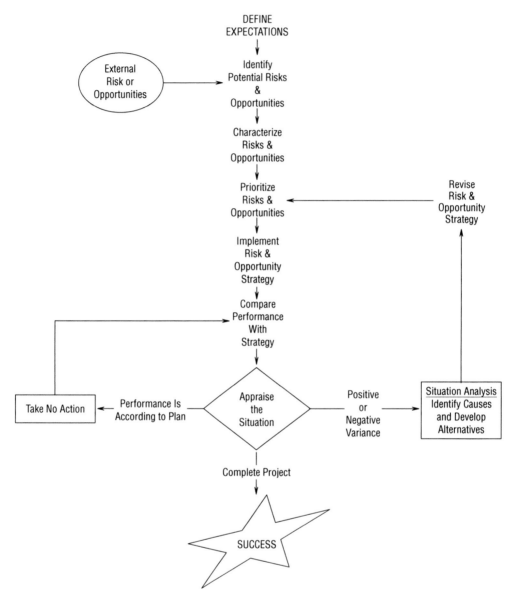

Figure 7-4 Handling Risk and Opportunities

The amount of time the integrated acquisition team spends on this process depends on the complexity of the procurement. For highly technical and complex projects/programs, a formal risk and opportunity program is appropriate.

The Handling of Risk and Opportunity plan consists of two parts. The first includes actions that can be taken to reduce risks that are likely to become problems. The second addresses potential opportunities that may surface during the acquisition process. Each part should: (1) describe the likely cause, (2) state the probability of occurrence, (3) explain the probable impact if the risk becomes a problem or the opportunity presents itself, (4) describe a plan to reduce or enhance the likely effects, and (5) define a method of tracking each risk or opportunity that can be used by the acquisition team to trigger timely action.

CONTRACT CHANGES

It is unrealistic to assume that the original contractual agreement will not be modified or adjusted during its lifespan. Change is driven by advancements in technology as well as shifting priorities, funding constraints, and economic issues. In the private sector changes to contractual agreements are usually made bilaterally. "If one party acts to change the relationship without concurrence of the other party, a breach of the contract occurs, thereby permitting sanctions to be imposed by the injured party through legal action."[68] Under the UCC, "agreements to modify a contract need no consideration to be binding."[69] The change must meet the test of good faith, i.e., the observance of reasonable commercial standards of fair dealing in the trade, a total absence of any intention to seek an unfair advantage to defraud another party; and honesty in fact and in the conduct or transaction concerned.[70]

In the public sector the rules pertaining to changing or modifying contracts differ significantly. The unilateral right of the CO to modify a government contract is founded on the sovereign powers of the government and the need to act in the public interest. This right provides the government the ability to adjust unilaterally to the shifts in the user's needs, to accommodate improvements in technology, to correct errors or omissions, and to order additional work. The only constraint is that the changed work must be within the "general scope" of the original contract.

In exchange for the power of unilateral modification, the contractor is promised an "equitable adjustment" if it causes an increase in the cost or time of performance.[71] The right to submit an equitable adjustment proposal is done in exchange for the contractor including contingency costs in the initial contract.[72] Consequently, the submission of a request for equitable adjustment by the contractor should be viewed as a normal part of the contracting process as opposed to an undesirable event. When the CO unilaterally directs the contractor to perform in a manner that differs from the contract without first negotiating any cost or schedule impact, the government is in fact assuming the risk of a potential price increase. This means the government assumes the added cost risk of such events as design changes, delays caused by conditions outside the control of the contractor, changes in inspection methods, defective or late government-furnished property, stop work orders, and differing site conditions, as well as actions or omissions by the government that add work.

Therefore, most government contracts contain a changes clause that gives the government the right to order changes to contract work during the performance phase. This can be a unilateral act by the CO to change or modify the contract document. The FAR contains five changes clauses. The first is for fixed-price contracts (FAR 52.243-1). The second is for cost-reimbursement contracts (FAR 52.234-2). The third pertains to time-and-material or labor-hour contracts. The fourth is applicable to construction as well as dismantling and demolition or removal of improvements (FAR 52.243-4). The fifth, FAR 52.243-5, pertains to small purchases and is limited to ordering changes to drawings and specifications.

Only COs, acting within the scope of their authority, are empowered to execute a contract modification on behalf of the government. One of the basis tenets of contracting is the right of all contractors not to do work that is not required by the contract. The FAR encourages the pricing of contract modifications before their execution if doing so does not adversely affect the interest of the public.[73] This includes modifications that could have been issued unilaterally. Therefore, the authority of the CO to order a change to the contract is contingent on the CO having a certificate of fund availability. Alternatively, the modification is contingent on the availability of funds, and the change contains a limitation of funds clause. This certificate should be based on a negotiated price unless the modification is executed prior to a negotiated price agreement. When this occurs the certificate or limitation of funds clause should be based on the best available cost estimate.[74]

All changes clauses limit the use of changes to those that are: (1) "within the general scope of the contract" and (2) "within the descriptive words" contained in the changes clause itself. Boards and courts have ruled that "within the general scope of the contract" means the change must be consistent with the original intent of the parties. The function of the work must be generally the same as was called for in the original bargain. The type of changes that can be made to the contract work is governed by the descriptive words contained in the applicable clause. For example:

1. The clauses allow changes to technical details of the end product or service. This is usually accomplished through changes to the drawings and specifications. This has been broadly construed to include the written description of work to be done. In fact, a board of contract appeals held that the government could change specific conditions under the changes clause because such provisions are listed as part of the specifications.[75]
2. Increases or deletions of major portions of the items to be furnished are not generally authorized because doing so is thought to alter the entire agreement.

3. Changes to the time of performance have traditionally been judged to be outside the clause. However, this view was altered for construction contracts because the contract schedule was part of the specifications. Construction contracts now include acceleration as a type of change that is permitted.
4. Changes to the method and manner of contract performance have generally been permissible under the changes clause. The government has been judged to be entitled to deductive changes when the same individual has performed two functions.
5. A few cases have held that defective government-furnished property (GFP) is covered under the changes clause because it is equivalent to a defective specification.
6. Changes in the place of delivery are also permitted under the clause.[76]

One of the key provisions of the changes clause is that the contractor has a contractual duty, in the public interest, to proceed with the contract as it has been changed, even though the contractor may not agree with the direction given by the CO. However, the clause gives the contractor the right to an equitable adjustment within 30 days from the receipt of a written change order. Failure to agree to any adjustment to the contract shall be a dispute under the Disputes clause in the contract.[77]

There are two types of contract modifications (changes):

- Bilateral modifications (supplementary agreement) are signed both by the CO and the contractor before the initiation of any work. They are used to: (1) make negotiated equitable adjustments resulting from the issuance of a change order, (2) define letter contracts, and (3) reflect other agreements of the parties modifying the terms of the contract.
- Unilateral contract modifications are signed only by the CO. They are used to: (1) make administrative changes; (2) issue change orders; (3) make changes authorized by the property clause, option clause, and suspension of work clause; and (4) issue termination notices.[78]

FAR 43.102(a) states that other government personnel shall not: (1) execute contract modifications, (2) act in a manner that would lead the contractor to believe they had the authority to bind the government, and (3) direct or encourage the contractor to perform work that should be the subject of a contract modification.[79]

Contractors also can benefit from the changes clause because it provides them with the means to: (1) submit engineering change proposals (ECPs) that will modify the product or service; (2) propose changes to the contract to implement a more effective method of performance, as in the example of a value engineering change proposal (VECP); and (3) provide an administrative process whereby the contractor may submit requests to be compensated for extra work resulting from action or inaction by the government under the doctrine of "constructive changes."

The Doctrine of Constructive Change

The doctrine of "constructive change" was established in case law and is unique to government contracts. When a contractor performs extra work beyond what is required by the contract without a formal change order from the CO, or when the government causes added work, the contractor can obtain relief by following the administrative procedures contained in the changes clause. This administrative process is in contrast to common law, where situations like the ones described above would likely be considered a breach of contract or implied contract.[80] It must be emphasized that the burden of proof is on the contractor to show that action or inaction by the government directly caused the situation requiring compensation.

There are four categories of constructive changes (see Table 7-4, Categories of Constructive Changes):

1. **Disagreement over the contract requirements:** Examples include extra work "within the general scope of the contract" that clearly could have been ordered by issuing a change order; government directly ordering the contractor to perform the work in a specific manner while stating that the order shall not be considered as a change order; government interpretation of specifications; rejection by the government of a method permitted by the contract; and an order by a government inspector without formal CO authority, resulting in extra work. There are also cases in which appeal boards have applied the rules of constructive change to work outside the changes clause. Other examples include improper exercise of an option after it has expired, improper withholding of progress payments, government action forcing the contractor to pay higher wages, and government-ordered changes in the accounting system. Appeal boards and the courts also have ruled that suggestions by government personnel that the contractor should perform work in such manner are not constructive changes. The doctrine of constructive change is not a "one-way street"

Table 7-4. Categories of Constructive Changes

- Disagreement over the contract requirements
- Defective specification and government nondisclosure of information
- Acceleration
- Failure of the government to cooperate during performance

because the government can use it to obtain an equitable adjustment for cost saved through actions of its officers and employees.[81]

2. **Defective specification and government nondisclosure of information:** The doctrine of constructive change has been applied when the government was at fault and breached its implied duties to disclose information or implied warranty of specifications, impracticability, misrepresentation, and nondisclosure. Examples include a contractor who was able to include cost incurred from the inception of the contract in the cost of a contract change issued by the government to overcome defective specifications; non-disclosure of incorrect information that resulted in extra work on the part of the contractor; and when the government enforces the specifications in a way that was not foreseen by the contractor at the time of bidding.[82]

3. **Acceleration:** Speeding up performance in an attempt to deliver the product earlier than anticipated can be compensated for when the government orders such an effort. This includes situations in which the government requires the contractor to meet the contract delivery schedule in spite of excusable delays that would entitle the contractor to a schedule extension. An essential element of constructive acceleration is an act or communication that can reasonably be construed to be an order to accelerate. Acceleration costs are recoverable against the government if they are incurred in mitigation of the effects of a government-caused delay. Boards have also ruled that a threat to terminate the contract for default constitutes an acceleration order.[83]

4. **Failure of the government to cooperate during performance:** The government has an obligation to cooperate with the contractor and not to hinder, interfere with, or delay contractor performance of work. The most common cause of the breach of this duty is to require performance of work beyond that called for by the contract. Examples include the government insisting that the contractor perform in a more expensive manner, overzealous inspection interfering with the contractor's performance, and inaction by a CO to correct a delay of another contractor that affects work. In addition, the rules of constructive change have been applied when the government has been unreasonable in exercising its discretion. An example is when the government forces the contractor to perform work in a certain sequence by using its right to approve progress schedules.[84]

The Configuration Management Process: Key to Contract Change Control

Configuration management is defined as a procedure for applying technician and administrative direction and surveillance to identify and document the functional and physical characteristics of an item or system, control any changes to these characteristics, and record and report the change process and implementation status. The goal of configuration management is to ensure that continuous changes to a product do not result in unacceptable growth.[85] It is based on the concept of using an orderly, well-documented part from a program's first baseline through the last.[86] This process interfaces with specification tree, contract work breakdown structure (WBS), software, firmware, engineering management, and the contract change processes.

The four principal elements of configuration management are:

1. Approval or disapproval of engineering change proposals: This decision is vital to change control because all contractual changes should follow the steps of the configuration management system.
2. Identification and documentation of the configuration of the item or system: Some level of configuration control should be applied to all programs. Larger and more complex programs require a much greater degree of control than simpler systems.
3. Reduce support requirements, cost of ownership, for the end product.
4. Prevent slippage in an approved production program.[87]

Delays

Every contract is based on a presumption that nothing will interfere with the delivery of goods or services according to the delivery schedule. Nevertheless, interruptions in performance can and do occur. The contractor is responsible for meeting the delivery schedule outlined in the contract and bears the risk of both time and cost for delays caused by the contractor. Key to managing the risk of delays is a knowledge and identification of potential problems. "A contractor is expected to know or have reason to know of those facts that are within the scope of its business operations pertaining to or possibly affecting its conduct. Boards and courts have consistently ruled that existing causes of delay are considered to be within the scope of the contractor's implied knowledge and are not unforeseeable."[88]

In their text *Administration of Government Contracts*, authors John Cibinic, Jr., and Ralph Nash, Jr., state that the contractor is generally entitled to a time extension if there is an excusable delay and to additional compensation if there is a compensable delay.[89]

The primary function of the excusable delays provision is to protect the contractor from sanctions for late performance. If the delay is caused by factors outside the contractor's control and is not foreseeable, it is usually judged to be excusable. To the extent the delay is excusable, the contractor is protected from default termination, liquidated damages, actual damages, or excess costs of re-procurement or completion.[90] Occurrences that are considered to be "beyond the control" and therefore excusable are acts of

God, strikes, fires, floods, and market conditions, unless the circumstances surrounding the incident made it foreseeable. Examples of events that have been judged to be beyond the control of the contractor are the oil embargo of 1973, a strike that prevented the contractor from obtaining steel bar joists from its supplier when the cost from other suppliers was excessive, when the CO failed to act promptly on the contractor's request for a time extension, and when the operation of the government priority system diverted needed components to a higher-priority program. Events that were judged to be within the control of the contractor included delivery delays by a subcontractor when supplies were available elsewhere and the shortage of skilled specialists that existed at the time of the agreement.[91]

A compensable delay is one that requires the government to compensate the contractor. There are two standard FAR clauses that provide compensation. They are the Suspension of Work clause, FAR 52.242-14, and the Government Delay of Work clause, 52.242-17. The former must be used in all fixed-price construction and architect-engineering contracts. The latter must be used in all fixed-price supply contracts, except those for commercial or modified commercial items. These clauses reimburse the contractor a price adjustment, excluding profit, when an unreasonable delay is caused by an act or failure to act on the part of the CO in the administration of the contract. When there is an unreasonable delay and a clause covering compensable delays is not in the contract, the contractor may be compensated if the delay was caused by the government under the breach of contract theory.[92]

In determining the consequences of delays, guidance can be found in the general principles of risk allocation, e.g., the time and cost effect of delays are dealt with separately and are allocated to the party that caused the delay. When contracting with the federal government, standard contract clauses deal with the effect the delay had on delivery schedule separately from any added cost attributed to the delay. The Suspension of Work, Government Delay of Work, and Stop Work Order clauses define circumstances that permit the contractor to be compensated for delays or prohibit the contractor from recovering any increased cost associated with delays.[93]

The Suspension of Work clause was first used by the Corps of Engineers during World War II. It gives the CO the right to order the suspension of all or part of the work on construction or architect-engineering contracts. This procedure in turn led to the Board of Appeal establishing a precedent by granting price adjustments. This has also been applied to contracts for supplies and services. Under the Suspension of Work clause, the contractor may submit a request for an equitable adjustment if the CO fails to act within a reasonable time for any increase in the cost of performance of this contract (excluding profit) necessarily caused by the unreasonable suspension, delay, or interruption.[94]

The CO may use the stop work order if the situation warrants any negotiated fixed-price or cost-reimbursement supply, research and development, or service contract. In this circumstance the contractor must stop work on all or any part of the work for a period of 90 days. After that period, unless the two parties have agreed to extend the stop work order, the CO must order the effort to proceed or to be terminated for default or convenience. The contractor is also able to initiate a request for equitable adjustment if the government's actions cause an increase in the time required for the performance of any part of the contract.[95]

Stanley Sherman enumerates six reasons that could lead to a delay in delivering the needed goods and services under the terms of the contract. All can create extra effort to overcome the impact on the contractor's delivery obligations. The six categories are:

1. Technical or management failure
2. Failure of subcontractors to meet the requirements of their contract
3. Supervening events, such as strikes or fires
4. Defects in the requirements or specifications
5. Changes in the specified requirements
6. Interference by the purchaser or other contractors performing in the same area.[96]

At face value, the contractor bears the risk associated with the first two and thereby bears the responsibility for the consequences. The third cause is usually outside the control of the contractor. Here the contractor can gain schedule relief if the incident can be shown to be unforeseeable. However, the contractor is not granted any reimbursement for any additional incurred cost unless the government insists that the original schedule be met. The last three causes imply that risk of occurrence is the responsibility of the government. Consequently, the government can be responsible for both time and added cost resulting from delays it causes. All six potential problems must be considered in assessing candidates for the risk management program.

Negotiating Changes to Government Contracts

Being able to adjust the contract price as work proceeds is unique to government contracts. The prerequisite is that the increase or decrease must have been caused by an event covered in a standard contract clause that provides for "equitable adjustments." This includes events such as contract changes, differing site conditions, defective or late government-furnished property, and the issuance of a stop work order. Requests for "equitable adjustments" cover claims that would be classified as damages for breach of contract in the private sector. Therefore, breach of contract claims or other types of price adjustments are relatively rare when contracting with the government.[97]

When negotiating the equitable adjustment request, the overriding rule is to return the parties to the same relative positions they held prior to the event that caused the need for a price adjustment in the first place.[98] The equitable adjustment method attempts to limit the effect of re-pricing on the effect of the change and not alter the basic profit or loss position of the contractor before the change occurred. Therefore, the basic pricing formula for pricing adjustments includes determining the reasonable cost of: (1) work added, (2) work deleted, and (3) actions that substitute one item of work for another item of work. This method has been described by boards of contract appeals as "the difference between the reasonable cost of performing without the change or deletion and the reasonable cost of performing with the change or deletion."[99] The test of cost allowability, allocability, and reasonableness are also applied when determining the value of these changes.

For purposes of determining if cost or pricing data are required, the total price is determined by including the cost of the added effort and the cost of the effort deleted. Pricing added work is fairly straightforward, except when the contractor has proceeded with the new effort pending the receipt and negotiation of the equitable adjustment. Here the question is if the cost incurred by the contractor for the added work is reasonable. Attempts to judge the cost of the adjustment by what would have been incurred by other contractors generally have been rejected by the boards and courts. They have ruled that because the purpose of the equitable adjustment process itself is to safeguard the contractor against increased cost, any determination of the cost incurred requires one to recognize the situation the contractor found itself in at the time the cost was incurred.[100]

The party claiming the adjustment must submit sufficient data to convince the other party the cost is reasonable and the adjustment warranted. To be in a position to do this, the contractor's accounting system must be able to segregate and record the direct cost of the change. Categories of direct cost to be segregated under the change order accounting clause are:

- Nonrecurring cost, e.g., engineering costs and cost of obsolete or pre-performance work
- Cost of added distinct work caused by the change order, e.g., new subcontract work, new prototypes, or new retrofit or back-fit kits
- Cost of recurring work, e.g., labor and material costs.[101]

In all situations in which the contractor requests an equitable adjustment, the contractor must be able to identify the cause, to show the effects of the event on the cost of performance, and to prove that it was caused by government. Wherever used in government contracts, the term "equitable adjustment" has become a term of art, and it is given the same interpretations.[102]

Pricing Deleted Work

The basic rule for deleted work is that it should be priced at the amount it would have cost the contractor had it not been deleted. (The amount cited in the proposal is not considered.) This is referred to as the "would have cost" because the government is entitled to a price reduction based on the amount the contractor would have spent to perform the deleted work.[103]

Boards and courts always prefer actual costs when evaluating the value of deleted work that has been completed. However, estimates must always be used to establish the cost of deleted work not yet performed. These are particularly vulnerable when not supported by statistical techniques such as learning curves, expert testimony, industry statistics, and historic cost. Estimates supported by "similar to" data are often used.

Pricing Added Work

The fundamental goal in pricing added work is to establish that the cost estimate, or cost incurred, is reasonable. If the costs have not yet been incurred, then the two parties rely on negotiations to establish their reasonableness.[104] Incurred costs are measured by the net cost increase to the contractor.

Unabsorbed overhead can represent a significantly large expense that can be affected by changes in the work content of a contract. Contractors have been permitted to recover additional overhead for the effect of delays and disruptions because additional overhead costs are incurred when the period of performance is extended and the contract has not absorbed its share of the overhead. Unabsorbed overhead has been allowed to compensate the contractor for idle facilities, inability to use manpower, plant maintenance, or cost of opening the facility, but there is less in the direct cost base over which to allocate overhead.[105]

CONTRACTOR SURVEILLANCE

Although the contractor is responsible for timely performance to protect its interests, the government maintains close surveillance over the contractor's performance. A key contract administration task is surveillance of the contractor's performance. The goal is to ensure that supplies and services being purchased conform to quality, quantity, and other requirements specified in the contract. It is deemed in the public interest because late deliveries or other kinds of unsatisfactory performance may cause costly program delays.

Contract administration personnel play a large role in the management of risk and opportunities; therefore, they need to be proactive in working with the contractor in the identifying and mitigating risk. Because of their location, the CAOs are readily able to:

- Obtain data on contractor performance to identify potential delinquencies
- Perform inspection and acceptance tasks as defined in the contract
- Isolate specific performance and other risks that could cause problems
- Support contractor requests for information, assistance, or approval
- Point out the need for government assistance, approvals, and contract changes
- Attend periodic meetings of the acquisition team to obtain as well as provide pertinent information on contract status
- Identify and report government-caused delays
- Report actual or anticipated default.

Onsite performance monitoring of government contracts dates back to the early days of the republic when Captain John Barry, the "Father of the American Navy," was given the duty of overseeing the construction of the U.S.S. United States in the early 1790s. (There is a statue of Captain Berry outside Independence Hall in Philadelphia. It will be left up to the readers to draw their own conclusions as to what episode in the Captain's illustrative service to the nation is being commemorated.) In World War I government inspectors were assigned to aircraft contractor plants to improve the quality of aircraft being built and delivered to the American forces in France. During World War II government inspectors were routinely assigned to major defense plants to inspect supplies and equipment being produced.

After World War II the role of government personnel at contractor's facilities was mainly devoted to physical inspection and acceptance of goods and services. With the realization that you cannot "inspect quality into the product," this philosophy evolved to where the government representative's responsibilities centered on verifying that the contractor had an adequate inspection or quality assurance system for the product being purchased.[106] In the 1970s the contract administrators working for the Air Force went further when they introduced "a structured approach which emphasizes a systematic appraisal of contractor management systems ... as a review mechanism to perform its contract administration services responsibilities." The thought behind this approach, which was titled the Contractor Management System Evaluation Program (CMSEP), was to encourage contractors to develop and maintain effective management systems, thereby increasing the probability that the product would also be satisfactory. Contractor management systems that were subject to surveillance were industrial management, manufacturing operations, quality assurance, safety, subcontract management, contract administration, engineering and integrated logistics support, and flight operations.[107] Government onsite personnel's role was to evaluate these systems continuously to determine if they were documented, adequate, and were being complied with.

The early 1980s witnessed an escalation of the adversarial relationship between industry and government. In 1988 the DoD introduced a program called CRAG (Contractor Risk Assessment), which signaled a shift in oversight philosophy. CRAG was designed to reduce oversight and audits where the contractor had demonstrated to the DoD's satisfaction that its internal control systems adequately protected the government's interests. Unfortunately, contractors had mixed reviews as to the results when it came to reducing overlapping audits, reviews, and inspections by DCAA, CO, IG, GAO, ACO, and various functions within DCAS.[108]

As noted earlier, in the mid-1990s acquisition reform called for increased cooperation between the two parties. The contractor has been given a greater status as a member of the acquisition team, with the implied responsibility to "tell it like it is." It remains to be seen if the call of closer working relationships will lead to an increase in mutual trust that will result in a reduction in the number of government personnel devoting their time to surveillance.

Today the CO, in conjunction with other members of the acquisition team, should determine the scope of the government's onsite surveillance over the contractor's in-plant performance. Factors that should be considered when establishing surveillance requirements include:

- Priority designator assigned to the contract
- Contract requirements for reporting production progress
- The contract performance schedule
- The contractor's production plan
- The contractor's history of contract performance
- The contractor's experience with supplies or services on contract
- The contractor's financial capability
- Supplementary written instructions from the contracting office.[109]

Production Progress Reporting

Production progress reporting is usually required to be submitted by the contractor to the government. If the contractor delays in submitting this report, the CO may withhold up to $10,000, or 5 percent of the amount of the contract.[110] It is the job of the CAO to verify the accuracy of these reports and advise the CO if any action is necessary. If there is a potential or actual delay, the applicable CO or inventory manager (if one has been designated) should be informed in sufficient time to take necessary action.

If appropriate, the CAO also should provide a definite recommendation as to the required corrective action.

Quality Assurance

The contractor is responsible for establishing, documenting, and maintaining the processes necessary to ensure that a conforming product is delivered to the user. Key to an effective contractor quality program is realization by management that delivery of a quality product is the end result of high standards and processes that are working in harmony. Product quality is ensured only when tasks are done consistently and processes are under control. The foundation of a continuous improvement program is having measurable standards in place, collection and recording of performance, and corrective actions that address the source of the variance. Table 7-5, Philosophy of a Quality Assurance System, summarizes the Total Quality Management philosophy that guides the government quality assurance policy. The scope of a contractor's quality assurance program encompasses subcontractors as well.

Table 7-5. Philosophy of a Quality Assurance System

- Quality of product is result of total contractor's processes
- Product inspection alone cannot verify quality of complex products
- Product quality is ensured only when process is under control
- Control of process occurs only when verifiable standards:
  - –Are applied
  - –Are recorded
  - –Corrective action is initiated
- Verifiable measurement standards are:
  - –Consistent in-process inspections
  - –Consistent in-process testing
  - –Statistical estimates
- Control of process depends on measuring and verifying:
  - –Incoming and in-process material
  - –Equipment calibration
  - –Cleanliness
  - –Technical data
  - –Records system
  - –Capabilities and presence of personnel
- Consistence performance is achievable by producer alone
- State of processes can be verified through:
  - –Random reviews and testing
  - –Review of contractor quality records
- Least costly is system that delivers 100 percent conforming quality

Chapter 4 pointed out that as the DoD increases its reliance on an integration of the civil-military industrial base, commercial quality standards like ISO 9000 will have a significant influence on the quality of goods and services delivered to the government contractor. ISO 9000 was developed by the International Organization for Standardization, which is based in Switzerland. This is an organization with a global perspective and a membership of over 100 countries, whose quality management guidelines were created through international consensus. ISO 9000 represents a set of requirements describing what standards for products, processes, and information technology must be accomplished. The "how" is left up to the individual organization. These guidelines are also generic and can be applied to many types of businesses, e.g., manufacturing, software, and services. Benefits from an ISO 9000 Quality Management System cited by ISO include:

- Access to global markets
- Ability to sell to customers who require ISO 9000 from their suppliers
- Reduction or elimination of scrap and rework
- Reduction of warranty and customer support costs
- Reduction of management time spent on "putting out fires"
- Improvement of productivity by "doing it right the first time."[111]

Managing Subcontracts

This book has highlighted the increasing amount of purchasing materials and services that are being purchased from subcontractors. A fact of contemporary contracting is that performance of the supplier not only can affect the prime contractor's bottom line; subcontractor performance can also mean the difference between a successful and unsuccessful program. "The development and maintenance of collaborative relations with key suppliers is a necessary and indispensable element required to reduce development cycle time and production time significantly.[112] Contemporary contractor surveillance evaluates prime contractors on their ability to involve the major subcontractors in the acquisition as members of their integrated acquisition team.

Each subcontractor's role in an acquisition is defined by the current phase of the product's life cycle. The purchasing of material begins with its design and continues through product support. This includes three integrated stages: product design, purchasing, and post-award management. The prime contractor's actions during these stages should be tailored to the events that occur during these stages.

A critical step in the design process is determining what to purchase initially. Product design is the only point in the life cycle of the product when the often conflicting objectives of the ultimate user and the engineering, manufacturing, purchasing, and financial elements of the product cost can be addressed. It is becoming more and more common in the commercial sector for prime subcontractors to participate in product development, beginning with the statement of needs. Early in the life cycle of the product the prime contractor's purchasing department, by working closely with the design engineers, can foster earlier supplier involvement and closer participation in product design. This action also sets the stage for supplier participation in manufacturing and product support later in the cycle.

The contractor's purchasing policy and planning system must ensure that the prime contractor complies with applicable government regulations governing maximum use of commercial products and gives a large number of firms an opportunity to compete for the subcontract. Are the types of contracts selected justified on the basis of technical or other risk assessment? Were pre-award surveys used to determine vendor capabilities? Are satisfactory flowdowns of prime contract terms and conditions, including data requirements, incorporated into subcontracts? Does the prime contractor have a vendor rating system? Is a form of cost or price analysis performed on purchases as the situation warrants?

After the award the surveillance role turns to the prime contractor's method of validating subcontract status, data, and reports. What visibility does the prime have over the subcontractor's cost, schedule, and performance? Does the subcontract procurement manager have an effective interface with technical personnel and current data regarding the product performance? Is the standard for progress payments to subcontractors the same as those applicable to the prime contractor? Does the prime contractor have a procedure to notify the acquisition team, on a timely basis, of potential as well as actual problems?

The criteria for determining the extent of contract quality requirements, including contractor inspection and testing requirements, are usually based on the classification of the supplies or services. The three determining factors are its technical description, its complexity, and the criticality of its application.[113] Chapter 4 described the extent of contract quality assurance needed by the government. The government quality assurance specialists, in coordination with other members of the acquisition team, should develop a quality assurance surveillance plan tailored to the source and characteristics of the product and the type of contract. The criteria of an effective contractor's quality system include the following attributes (see Table 7-6, Attributes of an Effective Contractor's Quality System):

- A comprehensive contract review to identify inspection and test requirements that lead to the development of inspection and test plans for hardware, software, and services at the earliest practical phase of contract performance
- Clear written procedures and work instructions for all work to be performed by contractor quality personnel that are compatible with manufacturing and software development processes

Table 7-6. Attributes of An Effective Contractor's Quality System

Initial comprehensive contract review
Clear, written procedures and work instructions for manufacturing and software
Current, accurate, and complete record of performance of contractor's system
Effective measurement of completed item's overall quality
Timely and effective corrective action to eliminate root causes of poor quality
Ensure that written procedures and drawings are available at place of inspection
Maintain effective metrology and calibration system standards
Control and monitor status of calibration on production tooling
Identify, segregate, control, and dispose of nonconforming material
Provide for effective use of sampling plans
Provide for adequate control over quality of purchased material
Ensure that inspection and test operations are performed under controlled conditions

---

- A provision for recording current, complete, and accurate records on the performance of the contractor's quality systems
- A provision for an effective measurement of the completed item's overall quality
- An assurance that timely and positive corrective action is taken to eliminate the root causes of nonconforming products or that the contractor's processes are unsatisfactory
- An assurance that written procedures and work instructions are consistent with drawings, specifications, and inspection records and are available at the time and place of inspection and the control of the software library
- An effective metrology and calibration system standards for measuring and test equipment
- A means of controlling and monitoring status calibration/certification of production tooling
- A provision for the identification, segregation, control, and disposition of nonconforming supplies
- A provision for effective use of sampling plans
- A provision for adequate control over the quality of purchased materials
- Assurance that an inspection and test operation are established and performed under controlled conditions and completed satisfactorily in proper sequence at the prescribed time.

INSPECTION AND ACCEPTANCE

All FAR inspection clauses give the government the right to inspect the contractor's work at any place and time, providing that doing so does not unduly delay contractor performance. These broad and comprehensive rights have been upheld by courts and boards to be in the public interest. These government inspection rights do not create a duty to inspect, nor do they relieve the contractor from its obligations to inspect goods and services before tendering them or before they are accepted.[114] For government contracts, inspection means examining and testing supplies or services, including appropriate raw materials, components, and intermediate assemblies to determine whether the supplies or services conform to contract requirements.[115]

Government Quality Policy: The acquisition team is to ensure that:

- Inspection and other quality assurance methods are performed, including warranty clauses, when appropriate, that are determined necessary to protect the government interest
- Supplies and services tendered by contractors meet quality requirements
- Government quality assurance is conducted before acceptance or is undertaken by government personnel
- No contract precludes the government from performing inspection
- Nonconforming supplies or services are rejected, or, if it is judged by the CO to be in the best interest of the government, nonconforming supplies or services may be corrected or replaced, at no additional cost to the government, by the contractor when it can be done within the required delivery schedule.[116]

Government Inspection Rights: A fundamental rule of government contracting is that the government has the right to enforce strict compliance with the terms and conditions of the contract. One of the reasons for this is because the government has limited rights to require that the contractor correct non-conforming products after they have been accepted.[117] Other reasons behind this strict compliance policy are to: (1) ensure that the product will satisfy the user's requirements, (2) ensure that public funds will not be spent improperly, and (3) protect the integrity of the competitive system by requiring the contractor to deliver the product at the same standard agreed to at the time of contract award. The government is entitled to force this strict compliance standard by:

- Rejecting the work
- Requiring the contractor to repair or replace non-conforming work
- Receiving a reduction in price as consideration for non-conforming work.

Acceptance in government contracting is defined as an act by an authorized representative of the government assuming ownership of existing supplies tendered or approving specific services rendered as partial or complete performance.[118] This rule is significantly different from the rights of the buyers after acceptance in the private sector. Under the UCC there is an implied warranty that the product will be of a quality generally acceptable for that line and is fit for its ordinary purpose. There also can be an implied warranty that the product is fit for a particular purpose when the seller has knowledge of that purpose.[119] Under the UCC acceptance of goods with patent defects precludes the buyer from subsequent rejection, but it does not preclude the recovery of damages.[120]

Unlike the commercial contracts, with their all-encompassing warranties for "merchantability" and "fit[ness] for a particular purpose," the rights of the government buyer are not legally extended after acceptance unless the item is being procured under a cost-reimbursement contract for supplies, a fixed-price services contract, a time-and-material contract, or a construction contract. Acceptance of goods under a fixed-priced contract represents an acknowledgment that the supplies or services delivered and accepted conform to the quality and quantity requirements defined in the contract. In fixed-priced contracts acceptance is conclusive, except for latent defects, fraud, gross mistakes amounting to fraud, or as otherwise provided in the contract.[121] The latter exception applies to contracts containing a warranty clause.

The government enjoys the broad latitude to choose where inspections will be conducted, the time they will be conducted, and the number of inspections that will be conducted. One recurring issue on this subject involves the government's liability for delays and added cost resulting from actions of its inspectors. Government inspectors have the duty to interpret contract specifications and make evaluations as to whether or not the contractor complied with the contract. Inspectors do not have the authority to order changes to the contract, waive contract requirements, or cause the contractor to perform to a standard that is higher than established by the contract. If an inspector exceeds his or her authority, a constructive change can result.[122]

The government does not have to specify the tests to be performed in the contract, and it can impose unspecified tests. When an unspecified test imposes a stricter standard of performance, the contractor may be able to recover the cost caused by the unspecified test. In addition, a test that does not reasonably measure contract compliance is considered an erroneous test and should not cause rejection of the product. The government also has the right to inspect items or services it had inspected previously. When the re-inspection is inconsistent with prior inspections, it is considered improper. Also inappropriate is re-inspection for acceptance at destination when supplies had been accepted previously at another location. In each of these examples, the burden of proof is on the contractor to show that government action caused any delay and increase in cost.

The First Article Inspection Clause: For new products, the government often inspects pre-production samples to confirm the quality characteristics of the product as well as prove that it is workable. Responsibility for conducting a first article testing can rest with the contractor or with the government. The CO is required to provide written acceptance of the first article rest results.[123] The Armed Services Board of Contract Appeals (ASBCA) has stated, "the primary purpose for requiring a first article submission is to prove the capability of the contractor to produce end products that will meet requirements .... Deficiencies in a first article that are correctable in production are not a valid basis for an outright disapproval of a first article. The first article approval clause also expressly provides for conditional approval. The contract (clause) does not expose the contractor to the risk of a default termination without any opportunity to correct defects or when defects in the first article are of such a nature as they can be corrected during production."[124]

Under the first article inspection procedure, the strict compliance standard does not apply. Government inspection rights are generally limited. However, in some situations the first article approval clause permits immediate termination for default if the contractor either fails to deliver any first article on time or delivers an unacceptable first article.[125] Tests used during first article testing become established as the appropriate method of conducting performance tests.

Government Quality Assurance: As noted earlier, the trend in government contracts is to place the responsibility on the contractor to conduct inspections and testing before tendering the product for acceptance to ensure the supplies are in conformance with contract requirements. Nevertheless, the government often retains the right to approve or witness contractor-conducted tests. The contractor is required to retain records of inspections and tests available for government review during contract performance. The role of the government's representative is to ensure that the contractor has an adequate inspection system in place and that it is being complied with. This places increased importance on defining the extent of the contractor's inspection obligations in the contract and during post-award orientation.

The quality assurance plan, developed by the acquisition team in conjunction with the statement of work, should be used by the contract administration activity to determine the work requiring surveillance as well as the method of surveillance. Government inspection is to be performed by or under the direct supervision of government personnel and is to be documented on the inspection of the receiving report or commercial bill of lading/packing list. Locations where the government reserves the right to perform quality assurance inspections are designated in the contract. These locations may not be changed without CO authorization.[126]

The government is to perform quality assurance inspections at the source when: (1) performance at any other place would be uneconomical; (2) there would be a considerable loss from the manufacturer and shipment of unacceptable supplies; (3) special test equipment, gages, or facilities are available only at the source; (4) inspection at any other place would destroy or require the replacement of costly special packaging material; (5) government during contract performance is essential; and (6) it is determined to be in the best interest of the government.[127]

Government quality assurance inspections can be performed at the destination when: (1) supplies are purchased off the shelf and no technical inspection is required, (2) necessary test equipment is located only at the destination, (3) subsistence supplies are purchased within the United States (supplies destined for overseas will be inspected at the port of embarkation), (4) brand-name products are authorized for resale, (5) products are purchased under direct control of the National Institutes of Health or the Food and Drug Administration, (6) services are performed at the destination, (7) it is determined to be in the best interest of the government.[128]

For acquisitions at or below the simplified acquisition threshold, the government normally relies on inspection by contractor. Government inspection at the destination is limited to type and kind, quality, damage, operability, and preservation. The scope of detailed government inspection may be reduced to periodic checks when the contractor has a history of defect-free work. However, if the application of the product is critical or its characteristics are special or likely to cause harm to personnel or property, inspection may be at the source. Other situations when it might be advantageous for the CO to designate the source as the location of government inspection are the criticality of the supplies or services, the amount of possible loss, and the likelihood of uncontested replacement of defective work.[129]

Government quality assurance inspections on subcontracted supplies or services shall be performed only when required in the government's interests. Examples of situations when this is appropriate include: (1) when the item is to be shipped from the subcontractor's plant directly to the user and inspection at the source is required, (2) when conditions of quality assurance at source are applicable, (3) when the contract specifies that certain quality assurance functions are to be performed only at the subcontractor's plant, or (4) when it is determined to be in the best interests of the government. It is appropriate to point out that the government does not enjoy any privity of contract. Therefore, all oral or written work statements or terms and conditions need to be worded so as not to affect the contractual relationships between the prime contract and the subcontractor, the prime contractor and the government, or to establish a contractual relationship between the government and the subcontractor. It is also important that it does not constitute a waiver of the government's right to accept or reject the supplies or services.[130]

Acceptance: This not only constitutes acknowledgment that the supplies or services conform to the quality and quantity provisions of the contract, but it also affects the rights of the government to correct deficiencies after acceptance. Acceptance is the responsibility of the CO unless it has been delegated to the CAS office or some other agency. The contract is to designate a point of acceptance. Acceptance based on a certificate of conformance may also be used instead of source inspection when: (1) it is in the best interest of the government; (2) the loss would be small in the event of a defect; or (3) the supplier's past performance has shown it is likely the supplies or services will be replaced, corrected, or repaid.[131]

Title to supplies also passes to the government on formal acceptance regardless of where the government takes physical possession. However, unless the contract states otherwise, the risk of loss or damage to supplies remains with the contractor until the supplies are delivered to a carrier when transportation is f.o.b. origin. This does not apply if the supplies tendered are non-conforming. In this case, the risk of loss or damage remains with the contractor. The contractor is not liable for loss or damage to supplies if it was caused by the negligence of the government acting within the scope of its authority.[132]

POST-ACCEPTANCE RIGHTS

In the private sector acceptance of goods with patent defects prevents the buyer from later rejecting the goods, but it does not bar recovery of damages.[133] This is because formal acceptance of goods and services tendered to the government imposes major limitations of the government's rights to retract acceptance later. The inspection clause for supplies acquired under a fixed-price contract states: "Acceptance shall be conclusive except for latent defects, fraud, gross mistakes amounting to fraud, or as otherwise provided in the contract."[134]

Latent Defects: A latent defect is a defect in the contract work that is not readily discoverable by observation with the use of reasonable inspection methods.[135] A latent defect overcomes the finality of acceptance in the Inspection of Supplies—Fixed-Price clause.

Key to determining whether a defect can or cannot be reasonably discoverable is first to establish what type of inspection or test would have discovered the defect. Next, one must determine if it would have been reasonable for the government to have used that inspection or test procedure under the circumstances of the acquisition and product being procured. If a defect could have been discovered by an inspection or test specified in the contract, it is not latent.[136] Another determining factor is what inspection and test procedures are used in the industry for similar products. If an inspection procedure that is a normal practice in the industry could have discovered the defect, then the defect is not latent. If an inspection or testing method that would have discovered the defect was not in the contract or is not a normal method used in the industry, then the defect probably would be judged to be latent. In this case the government's act of acceptance could also be retracted.

Other essential elements that must be confirmed to determine if a defect is latent include:

- The defect must have existed at the time of acceptance
- The defect must have been hidden from sight or unknown
- The defect could not have been discovered through the exercise of reasonable care
- The defect cannot be discovered readily by ordinary examination or test.[137]

Fraud: Fraud involves an intentional act of deception of the government by the contractor. To revoke acceptance and charge the contractor with fraud, the burden of proof is on the government to show that it suffered an injury because its acceptance was induced by its reliance on a misrepresentation of fact, actual or implied, or the concealment of a material fact. The government also must prove that the contractor had knowledge of its falsity, reckless or wanton disregard of facts, and the intent to mislead the government. If the government cannot prove that the contractor knew of the error or that it relied on the misrepresentation, then the government's claim will probably be denied.[138]

The False Claims Act also covers fraud. Therefore, it might be advantageous for the government to seek relief under the False Claims Act.

Gross Mistakes Amounting to Fraud: There two differences between fraud and gross mistakes amounting to fraud. The first is that there is no requirement to prove intent to mislead in establishing gross mistake amounting to fraud. Second, the level of the mistake must be so major that the error cannot be reasonably expected or justified by a responsible contractor. As in the case of fraud, the government must also demonstrate that: (1) acceptance of defective items was caused by the gross mistake amounting to fraud and, (2) it was harmed by the mistake.[139]

Effect of Contractor Certificate of Conformance: Situations in which the government permits the use of a certificate of conformance executed by the contractor in lieu of government inspection raise the question of how its use affects the rights of the parties. Boards have ruled that when the government relies on the certificate of conformance, it enjoys a greater degree of protection because the certificate survives acceptance. This ruling is based on the logic that it is reasonable for the government to conduct a more limited inspection by relying on the certificate of conformance. Cases cited in Cibinic, Jr., and Nash, Jr., were dealt with as though they were "latent defects."[140]

Warranty: A warranty represents "a promise or affirmation given by the contractor regarding the nature, usefulness, or condition of supplies or performance of services furnished under the contract."[141] The use of warranty clauses in government contracts is optional, and no longer do defense contracts require warranties when acquiring weapon systems under a production contract. In Chapter 4 we covered the factors a CO must consider when determining if warranty was appropriate for the supplies or services being acquired and the terms and conditions that should be included in the solicitation when the government decides a warranty is in its best interest.

The implied warranty of merchantability in UCC 2-314 and fitness for particular purpose in UCC 2-315 may be applicable to describe the quality requirements in government contracts in appropriate circumstances.[142] When the inspection and acceptance clause does not contain the language that makes acceptance final and conclusive, the UCC implied warranty can be applicable. However, when FAR clauses 52.246-17(4) (Warranty of Supplies of a Noncomplex Nature); 52.246-18(6) (Warranty of Supplies of a Complex Nature); and 52.246-19(10) (Warranty of Systems and Equipment Under Performance Specification or Design Criteria) are used, the implied warranties of merchantability and "fitness for a particular use" are not applicable because both are specifically excluded in each of the clauses.[143]

The scope of the warranty clause is entirely dependent on the language in the clause. Quite often it is limited to a guarantee that the work is free from "defects in material and workmanship and conforms to the requirements of the contract." Care must be exercised when dealing with all warranty clauses because slight changes in the language can change the contractor's obligation significantly.[144]

Normally, the warranty clause also limits the period of time the government must give the contractor notice of the defect. For example, "the Contractor warrants that for [CO shall state specific period of time after delivery...] all supplies furnished under this contract will be free from defects in material or workmanship and will conform with all requirements of this contract...." The warranty usually begins with delivery and acceptance. The end of the warranty period can be stated in calendar time, operating hours, miles, etc. It is key that the period of warranty have a definable beginning and end. Usually this clock begins to run at delivery and acceptance. However, if the time specified in the clause requires the government to provide notification within a certain period of time after discovery, the warranty becomes an open-ended obligation that could extend indefinitely.[145]

If the contract contains a warranty clause, it must be covered as part of post-award orientation. At a minimum, the parties need to know: (1) the extent of the contractor's warranty, (2) the contractor's obligation to the government in the event of a breach of warranty, and (3) the government's administration and enforcement of procedures.

CONTRACTOR ACCOUNTING SYSTEMS AND INTERNAL COST CONTROLS

The government has a great deal of interest in the adequacy of the contractor's accounting records, methods, and internal controls because when price competition is not adequate, cost analysis is used to establish the basis for negotiation or contract prices. Therefore, the adequacy of the contractor's cost accounting and controls is an important consideration when cost reimbursement contracts are being used. With proper accounting systems and internal controls, the government has some assurance as to the accuracy and integrity of the information present. Before awarding a cost-reimbursement contract to a contractor without a history of federal government contract, the government should conduct a survey to determine the adequacy of the contractor's accounting system. The accounting system must provide: (1) proper segregation of cost that is applicable to the proposed contract, (2) data required for contract re-pricing and negotiations, (3) a method to exclude unallowable cost, and (4) segregation of pre-production and production costs.

Cost accounting standards are a series of accounting standards issued by the Cost Accounting Standards Board under Public Law No. 91-379, 50 U.S.C. APP §2168 that are intended to achieve uniformity and consistency in measuring, assigning, and allocating cost to contracts with the federal government. Nineteen cost accounting standards (CAS) have been issued by a CAS Board (see Table 7-7, Cost Accounting Standards). Each standard consists of six parts: purpose, fundamental requirement, technique for application, illustration, interpretation, and exemption.[146]

Table 7-7. Cost Accounting Standards

CAS 401—Consistency in Estimating and Accumulating and Reporting Costs
CAS 402—Consistency in Allocating Costs Incurred for the Same Purpose
CAS 403—Allocation of Home Office Expense
CAS 404—Capitalization of Tangible Assets
CAS 405—Accounting for Unallowable Costs
CAS 406—Selection of Cost Accounting Periods
CAS 407—Use of Standard Costs for Direct Material and Direct Labor
CAS 408—Accounting for Costs of Compensated Personnel Absence
CAS 409—Depreciation of Tangible Capital Assets
CAS 410—Allocation of Business Unit G & A Expense to Final Cost Objective
CAS 411—Accounting for Acquisition Cost of Material
CAS 412—Composition and Management of Pension Cost
CAS 413—Adjustment and Allocation of Pension Cost
CAS 414—Cost of Money as an Element of Cost of Facilities
CAS 415—Accounting for Cost of Deferred Compensation
CAS 416—Accounting for Insurance Cost
CAS 417—Cost of Money as Element of Cost of Capital Assets under Construction
CAS 418—Allocation of Direct and Indirect Costs
CAS 420—Accounting for IR&D and Proposal Cost

Public Law 100-679 (41 U.S.C. 422) requires designated contractors and subcontractors to comply with CAS and to disclose in writing their cost accounting practices. They must also consistently comply with their disclosure statement. The CAS has had a considerable impact on accounting systems of government contractors. Contractors must comply with CAS when: (1) the total value of all government contracts awarded to the contractor exceeds $50 million or (2) the value of a negotiated contract exceeds $500,000, unless otherwise exempt.[147] CAS does not apply to sealed bid contracts or contracts with small business concerns.

During contract performance the CAO and cognizant auditors ensure that the contractor's estimating system and methods of accounting for incurred cost are consistent and meet the intent of the CAS standards, if they are applicable. If CAS applies, it is the duty of the CAO to determine the effectiveness of the contractor's program to ensure compliance with all of the CAS standards and FAR provisions on the administration of CAS.

Disclosure of Accounting Practices: Contractors whose cost accounting systems must meet the standards established by the CAS Board are also required to provide the government with a written description of its accounting practices and procedures. This statement is to be certified and submitted to the cognizant contract auditor. After its submission, the disclosure statement is reviewed for adequacy by the cognizant auditor and ACO. After it has been determined to be adequate, the contractor then must follow the disclosed accounting practices, or a change to the disclosure statement must be requested.[148]

A separate disclosure statement must be submitted for each profit center, division, or organizational unit. As a condition of filing, the disclosure statement is not made available to the public because of the proprietary nature of the data it contains. However, it is recommended that contractors designate portions of the statement they wish to be kept confidential to ensure that information is not released under the Freedom of Information Act (FOIA).

Contract Cost Principles and Procedures: Cost principles and procedures are the rules developed over the years by the government to define which costs are allowable in the negotiation and administration of government contracts. The FAR recognizes that cost and procedures have different characteristics depending on the type of organization that is involved. Therefore, FAR Part 31, Contract Cost Principles and Procedures, groups the principles by organizational type, i.e., commercial concerns, educational institutions, construction, architect-engineering, facility contracts, and contracts with state and local governments.[149]

Determining if an Incurred Cost Is Allocable and Allowable: For the government to permit the contractor to recover cost incurred during the performance of a contract, the cost must be allocable as well as allowable to the contract.

An allocable cost is one that is assigned to one or more cost objectives in accordance with the relative benefits received or other equitable relationships defined or agreed upon by the contracting parties. A cost is allocable to a government contract if it:

- Was incurred specifically for the contract
- Benefits both the contract and other work and can be distributed in reasonable proportion to the benefits received
- Is necessary to the overall operation of the business, although a direct relationship to any particular cost objective cannot be shown.[150]

The following factors are considered when determining if a cost is allowable. To be allowable the cost must be:

- Reasonable, i.e., ordinary and necessary for the conduct of business or performance of the contract; generally accepted sound business practices; and consistent with the contractor's responsibilities to the government, other customers, the owners of the business, employees, and to the public at large
- Allocable (reference previous paragraph)
- Consistent with the standards promulgated by the Cost Accounting Standards Board
- Consistent with Generally Accepted Accounting Principles and practices appropriate to the particular circumstances
- Consistent with the terms and conditions of the contract
- Consistent with the cost principles contained in FAR sub part 31.2.[151]

Disallowance of Cost: The government has the right to refuse to recognize a cost as being allowable.[152] The notice of intent to disallow costs clause is required to be included in solicitations and subsequent cost reimbursement contracts, fixed-price incentive contracts, or contracts providing for price re-determination.[153] A notice of intent to disallow cost usually is the result of an audit or a program to monitor contractor costs. The clause gives the government the right during the course of performance to issue notices of the intent to disallow costs, including costs that have already been incurred. The goal of the notice is to inform the contractor as early as possible that an incurred cost or planned incurred cost is not allowable. This should then lead to a satisfactory settlement of the issue through discussions with the contractor. If the contractor disagrees with the post-incurring disallowance, it may file a claim under the disputes clause.

Approval or Disapproval of Payments to the Contractor: It is the responsibility of the cognizant CO, which is often delegated to the ACO, to approve or disapprove vouchers received from the contractor. Contracts that provide for the disallowance of cost during the course of performance and after the cost has been incurred include cost-reimbursement contracts, cost-reimbursement portions of fixed-price contracts, letter contracts that provide for reimbursement of costs, and time-and-material and labor-hour contracts. The approval or disapproval can be done with or without assistance from the auditor. However, contract auditors may be authorized to: (1) receive disbursement vouchers direct from the contractor, (2) approve payment of acceptable vouchers, and (3) suspend payment of questionable vouchers.

When the examination reveals a question regarding the allowability of cost under terms of the contract, informal discussions are held with the contractor; if the issue is not resolved, a notice of contract cost suspension or disapproval is issued to the contractor, disbursing officer, and the CO. When the contractor disagrees with the deduction it may:

- Submit a written request to the cognizant CO to consider if the unreimbursed cost should be paid and to discuss the finding of the auditor
- File a claim under the disputes clause that the cognizant CO will process in accordance with agency procedures
- Both of the above.[154]

After review, approved vouchers are forwarded directly to the cognizant contracting finance office for payment.[155]

PRICING RATE AGREEMENTS

Rate agreements are written, interim pricing agreements between the government and the contractor to make certain that rates, e.g., labor and indirect and material usage, are available for use during a specified period of time in pricing contracts or contract modifications. These administrative agreements cover forward pricing factors and overhead and affect all government contracts being performed by a specific contractor. They are developed to expedite pricing of proposals, negotiations, and billings.

Forward Pricing Rate Agreement: When a contractor has a significant volume of government contracts, it is the role of the ACO to make a determination if the government would benefit from having forward pricing rate agreements (FPRA) negotiated and in place. Chapter 5 emphasized the importance of having FPRAs when evaluating and negotiating contractor proposals. The purpose of an FPRA is to ensure that rates are developed for such indirect costs as labor hours, material and labor variances, material handling rates, and efficiency factors, while making allowances for obsolescence. Headquarters of large contractors are required to account for home office expense in one pool and allocate them to divisions to the maximum extent possible.[156]

When an FPRA or forward pricing rate recommendation (FPRR) is not in place, the ACO is responsible, in conjunction with the cognizant auditor, to evaluate the validity of the rates used in contractor proposals.

The ACO is responsible for determining if the benefits to be derived from having an FPRA are commensurate with the amount of effort needed to develop the rates and negotiate the agreement. When making this decision the ACO must consider: (1) the volume of future pricing actions, (2) the reliability of the contractor's cost accounting data and cost estimating practices, (3) if the period of time the rates will be in effect justifies the administrative effort needed to monitor the rates, (4) if the period of time the rates will be in effect represents an unacceptable risk, and (5) the effect the characteristics of the contractor's operations and product mix will have on the agreement. This information can then be used to gain agreement from all government agencies doing business with the applicable contractor as to the conditions under which the FPRA will be used.[157]

The process for developing these rates is for the contractor to submit to the ACO a proposal, along with appropriate cost of pricing data current at the date of submission. The ACO, the cognizant contract auditor, and applicable COs jointly participate in developing a government objective for rate negotiations. The corporate FPRA, which is negotiated by the cognizant CACO, is also incorporated into the subordinate corporation's rate. At the conclusion of negotiations, the price negotiation memorandum is prepared by the ACO and forwarded along with the FPRA to the cognizant auditor and all COs affected by the agreement.[158]

It is the responsibility of the ACO to monitor the agreement and to determine if the conditions upon which it was founded are the same or have changed. The FPRA contains specific terms and conditions covering expiration, application, and data requirements for systematic monitoring to ensure the validity of the rates. When the government conducts an overhead monitoring program, it includes tracking actual costs and comparing them to the budgets on which the rates were founded. Changes in business volume, changes in market conditions regarding material and labor, savings resulting from initiatives to reduce cost, and changes in the treatment of direct and indirect costs can all alter the agreement.

Continuous monitoring allows the rates and factors to be modified when they are no longer applicable. The standard FPRA contains a provision permitting either party to cancel the agreement as well as a requirement that the contractor will notify the cognizant auditor if there are any significant changes to cost or pricing data. When an FPRA is invalid the contractor should submit a new proposal that reflects the changed conditions. Until a revised FPRA is negotiated, the ACO issues an FPRR to the buying activities.

Final Overhead Rates: Final overhead rates are necessary to determine the cost incurred under cost-reimbursement contracts, incentive contracts, and fixed-price re-determinable contracts, as well as other contracts that require settlement of indirect costs before establishing the final contract price. Determining the final overhead rate begins within 90 days of the expiration of its fiscal year. At that time the contractor is required to submit to the ACO a final overhead rate proposal for the period based on actual cost. A final overhead rate is generally computed as a percentage or dollar factor that expresses the ratios of indirect expenses incurred in a period to direct labor, total cost input, or some other appropriate base of the same period.[159]

Failure by the parties to agree on a final annual indirect cost rate shall be a dispute within the meaning of the disputes clause.

Billing Rates: Until final annual indirect cost rates are established for any period, the government reimburses the contractor at billing rates that have been established by the CO or by the cognizant auditor, when authorized. These rates are temporary overhead rates and are used for interim reimbursement purposes. They are subject to adjustment when the final rates are established.[160]

It is also the responsibility of the cognizant ACO to monitor payments to make certain they are close to actual expenditures. When they are over or under by a significant amount, the rates need to be adjusted.

TERMINATIONS

The federal government has the right to terminate a contract, in whole or in part, if the CO determines it is in the best interest of the government to do so. The CO is instructed to terminate contracts only when it is in the interest of the government to do so.

There are three methods by which a government contract can be terminated. These are termination for default, termination for convenience, and a no-cost cancellation. A no-cost settlement is used instead of issuing a termination when: (1) it is known the contractor will accept one, (2) government property was not furnished, and (3) there are no outstanding payments.[161]

Default Termination: Private contracts have three circumstances that can result in a breach of contract. These are:

- Failure to deliver on time
- Failure to demonstrate an inability to perform either managerial or technical functions, which cannot be caused by an impossibility or impracticability to perform
- Declared unwillingness to perform amounting to a repudiation of the agreement.[162]

The federal government has the right to terminate a contract completely or partially because of the contractor's actual or anticipated failure to perform its contractual obligations. This right is included in all government contracts.[163] Under the standard termination for default, certain clauses give the government the right to declare the contract terminated for default if the contractor fails "to make progress so as to endanger performance of this contract."[164] This represents a declaration of a breach of contract prior to the event occurring. Therefore, courts and boards place the burden of proof on the government to prove that timely performance is impossible.

A default termination is the government's ultimate method of dealing with a contractor's unexcused present or prospective failure to perform in accordance with the contract specifications and schedule.[165] With a default termination the government is effectively saying to the contractor that its failure to perform releases the government from its obligations under the contract while exposing the contractor to potential liability because of its failure. Under default termination procedures for a fixed-priced contract for supplies, the government is not liable for the contractor's cost on undelivered work and is also entitled to the repayment of advance and progress payments applicable to undelivered work. The contractor may be liable for re-procurement costs. The CO may also elect to have the contractor transfer title and deliver to the government completed supplies and manufacturing materials. The CO must also protect the government from overpayment that might result from failure to provide for any potential liability to labor and material suppliers for outstanding lien rights against the completed supplies and materials after the government has paid for them.[166]

Under a cost-reimbursement contract the contractor's potential liability is not as substantial as it is under fixed-price contracts. For a cost-reimbursement contract, the contractor is reimbursed for all allowable costs whether or not the government accepts the work. In addition, the contractor will also receive a portion of the negotiated fee based on a percentage of work accepted.[167]

The decision to terminate a contract should be taken only after full consultation with the government members of the acquisition team. Before making a decision to go forward with the administrative actions required when considering default termination, the team needs to assure itself that satisfactory work cannot be completed and delivered on time. Sources of data to prove performance is endangered are scheduled project milestones, on-site inspections of the contractor's work, and the contractor's monthly progress reports. When the reason for possible termination is a contractor's alleged "failure to comply with other provisions of the contract," boards and courts have held that the provision must represent a "material requirement" of the contract. Examples of failures to perform other material provisions include: failure to provide a performance bond required by the contract, failure to provide a reproduction sample, failure to perform duties under the warranty clause, tender of nonconforming material, failure to provide the required insurance certificates, the contractor's lack of properly licensed drivers, and milk that fails to meet sanitary standards.[168]

It is important to understand that the government has the right to terminate. The decision to terminate is left up to the discretion of the CO. The

CO's decision must be fully justified and in no way be arbitrary or capricious.[169]

The FAR includes alternative courses of action that the CO may take in lieu of terminating for default when it is in the government's best interests. These include negotiating a schedule extension, permitting the contractor the surety to continue performing under a revised schedule, permitting continued performance by means of a subcontractor or other business arrangements, and termination for convenience of the government.[170] When a default termination is contemplated prior to proceeding, the CO must render a judgment based on the business considerations listed below:

- Terms of the contract as well as applicable laws and regulations
- The specific failure of the contractor and excuses for failure
- The availability of supplies or services from other sources
- The urgency of need for the supplies or services and the period of time required to obtain them from other sources, as compared to the time delivery could be obtained from the delinquent contractor
- The degree of essentiality of the contractor in the government acquisition program and the effect termination for default will have on its capability as a supplier under other contracts
- The effect the termination will have on the ability of the contractor to liquidate guaranteed loans, progress payments, or advance payments
- Any other pertinent facts and circumstances.[171]

The CO has a reasonable amount of time to investigate the facts surrounding the contractor's performance and to determine what course of action is in the best interest of the government. A postponement of the decision to terminate the contract for default is known as *forbearance*.[172] The facts and circumstance of the case determine the length of time that is considered reasonable to delay a decision to terminate. Once the forbearance period has expired and no action has been taken, the government is said to have waived its right to terminate for default, and it must then reestablish a delivery schedule through a bilateral agreement if it wishes to pursue termination for default further.

Boards and courts have not been hesitant to hold terminations improper when the government has failed to observe the termination procedures that were established to protect the contractor's rights. Both default clauses FAR 52.249-8, Fixed-price Contracts for Supplies and Materials, and FAR 52.249-6, Cost-Reimbursement Contracts, require a notice of delinquency, i.e., "cure notice," be sent to the contractor prior to termination.

When the delivery date has not expired for a fixed-price contract, a written 10-day cure notice is to be sent to the contractor notifying it of the delinquency. If the time remaining does not permit the 10-day cure notice, it should not be issued. Failure to issue a cure notice when it is required will result in an invalid termination for default. In this case the termination for default will be terminated for convenience. Termination prior to the expiration of the 10-day period is also improper.

If the contractor fails to respond to the cure notice or to give the government adequate assurances, the CO is justified in terminating the contract for default. Examples of adequate assurances include hiring additional employees and performing additional work.[173]

A "show cause notice" may be given to the contractor by the CO when a default termination is possible. The notice informs the contractor of its deficiencies and warns of possible termination for default. A key provision of this notice is the request that the contractor "show cause why the contract should not be terminated for default." This notice may also state that failure by the contractor to provide an explanation may be taken to mean that no valid explanation exists. The notice may also invite the contractor to meet with the ACO to discuss the matter.[174] Unlike the "cure notice," the use of a "show cause notice" is not mandatory, nor does it grant the contractor an automatic extension in the period of performance.[175]

The FAR also includes information the CO should provide the contractor if it is determined that a default termination is proper. In addition to identifying the contract, the CO's notice must:

- Identify the acts or omissions that constituted the default in a statement that the contractor's authorization to proceed further under the contract, or specified portion of the contract, is terminated
- State the supplies or services terminated and that the contractor maybe held liable for any excess re-procurement
- State that the contractor has the right to appeal the CO's determination that the contractor's failure to perform was not excusable under the disputes clause
- State that the government reserves all rights and remedies provided for under the law, in addition to charging excess re-procurement cost
- State that the termination notice constitutes a decision that the contractor is in default and the contractor has the right to appeal under the disputes clause.[176]

The case law shows that the strict compliance standard that applies to the issuance and content for the "cure notice" does not apply to the formalities outlined above in issuing a default termination.[177]

The default clause for fixed-price supply, services, and construction contracts gives the government the unique right to assess the contractor's excess costs as well as the right to collect actual damages if they can be proved. Although the assessment of excess cost permits the contractor to contest the propriety of the default termination itself, the CO often uses it to ensure government reimbursement for any excess costs incurred for similar supplies or services acquired under a re-procurement contract.[178] To obtain excess cost of re-procurement, the burden of proof is on the government to show that the re-procurement contract did not increase the costs assessed.[179]

Settlement of a cost-reimbursement contract terminated for default follows many of the rules that apply when a contract has been terminated for the convenience of the government. The contractor is reimbursed allowable cost incurred, and there is an appropriate reduction to the total fee. Some differences are that the terminated contractor does not get reimbursed for the cost of preparing the termination proposal and that the terminated contract does not contain any provisions for recovery by the government of excess repurchase cost after termination.[180]

Termination for Convenience of the Government: Termination of contracts has been used extensively as a means to end massive procurement efforts accompanying wars, dating back to the Civil War. In 1876 the Supreme Court ruled that the government had the right to terminate a contract unilaterally, even though there was not a provision in the contract permitting it to do so. In the landmark case *United States v Corliss Steam-Engine Company*, the Navy directed the contractor to discontinue work on a contract for engines and boilers. Although the contractor and the contracting officer had reached an agreement on a settlement, the comptroller of the treasury refused to approve the certification for congressional appropriation of funds. The Court of Claims ruled in favor of the contractor receiving a financial settlement. It also supported the Supreme Court decision that confirmed the necessity for the government to have the power to terminate a contract in the public interest. The Supreme Court decision stated in part: "the contracting officer, when representing the public's interest, must have the right to suspend or terminate otherwise contractually agreed to work ... with the improvements constantly made ... some parts originally contracted have to be abandoned; and other parts substituted, and it would be of serious detriment to the public if the head of the Navy Department did not extend to providing for all such possible contingencies by modification or suspension of the contract and settlement with the contractor...."[181]

The termination for convenience of the government clause is required to be in every government contract. In ruling on *G.L. Christian & Associates v. United States*, the court stated that if a clause is required to be included in a contract, it will be read to include it even though it is not physically incorporated in the document. There is converse ruling. The Armed Services Board of Contract Appeals ruled in a case involving Charles Beseler Co. that if a certain clause is prohibited, it will be read out of the contract even though it is physically present.[182]

The government uses the termination for convenience of the government clause to terminate a contract, in whole or in part, when: (1) completion of the contract is not practical or economical, (2) the contract was erroneously terminated for default, or (3) there was an improper award.

When the same item is under contract with both large and small business concerns and it is a necessary part of the unit, preference is to be given to continuing the performance of the small business concern.[183]

In no other area of contract law has one party been given such complete authority to escape its contractual obligations.[184] This unilateral power of the government to terminate a contract without cause and to limit the contractor's recovery to cost incurred, profit on work completed, and the cost of preparing the termination settlement proposal is unique to government contracts. The major impact of the termination for convenience procedure is to relieve the government from the contingent liability of paying anticipated profits for unperformed work if it terminates the work.

It should also be pointed out that a termination for convenience in effect converts a fixed-price contract to a cost-reimbursement contract for the work performed up to the termination. In addition, under the termination for convenience of the government clause, a terminated contractor cannot recover consequential damages, e.g., cost of bankruptcy, loss of existing business, loss of future contracts, or damage to the company's reputation.[185] In addition, contractors are exposed to a financial loss if the most profitable portion of the effort is terminated.

The possibility of termination for convenience is often cited as a factor inhibiting commercial firms from doing business with the government because it denies the contractor the ability to predict with certainty the length of production runs.

There are also limits on the government's right to terminate. For example, termination for convenience is not permitted if it demonstrates bad faith. However, the burden of proof is on the contractor to show that the government has exercised bad faith. The courts have ruled that the government should not use the clause to avoid anticipated profits unless there has been a change in circumstances. The courts also have ruled against termination for convenience when it is used to violate or avoid other government policies, e.g., the government's failure to file an environmental policy or to correct an arbitrary and capricious action that occurred during the source selection process.[186]

Upon receipt of the notice that the contract is being terminated for convenience of the government, the contractor is instructed to stop work immediately on the terminated work and to continue working on any work not terminated. The contractor is also instructed to stop placing subcontracts, terminate all subcontracts on the terminated work, and to preserve and protect government property in possession of the contractor.[187] The contractor is also told to minimize the impact on personnel if the termination will result in a significant reduction of its work force.[188]

After issuing the notice of termination, the terminating contracting officer (TCO) is responsible for negotiating any settlement with the contractor, including a no-cost settlement, if appropriate. It is the responsibility of the TCO and auditors to complete audit reviews promptly.[189] The TCO's responsibilities also include directing the actions required by the CO; examining proposals of prime and subcontractors; and promptly negotiating a settlement agreement.

A subcontractor has no contractual rights against the government when the prime contract has been terminated. The contractor's contract with the prime contractor may include rights against the prime contractor in the event of a termination. However, the termination clause permits the settlement proposal to include the cost of settling and paying termination costs to subcontracts.[190] Interpretation of the termination clauses has been that the prime contractor must have paid the subcontractor's claim or have reached a binding agreement with the subcontractor before the prime contractor can recover the amount of the subcontractor's claim.[191]

MANAGEMENT OF DISPUTES

A dispute is defined as a disagreement between the contractor and the CO regarding the rights of the parties under the contract. A dispute is different from a protest because it occurs during or after the performance of a contract. As we have seen in earlier chapters, a protest occurs prior to contract award and involves a prospective contractor who is protesting the conduct of the solicitation process or the award of a contract.[192]

This is another example of how government contracts differ from private contracts. When agreement cannot be reached on a commercial contract, the contractor can stop work and seek a remedy in the state courts. A federal contractor has a legal duty to proceed "diligently" and comply with the direction of the CO, even if in the opinion of the contractor that direction represents a material breach of the contract.[193] The logic of having the contractor proceed pending resolution of the dispute is "rooted in the concept of public interest, which do[es] not permit interfering with the government operation that may involve the public welfare or the government's political position in its worldwide commitments and responsibilities."[194]

Historically, it has not been easy for a government contractor to seek or obtain equitable relief for material breach of contract by the government as a contractor performing work in the private sector. However, for many years contractors in the public sector could obtain legal or equitable relief only when Congress waived the government's right to sovereign immunity or to apply to Congress for a private bill. As the requirement to obtain goods and services from the commercial sector increased, government contracts began to include provisions for handling disputes. In 1887 Congress passed the Tucker Act, waiving sovereign immunity for "any claim founded upon either the Constitution, or any Act of Congress, or any regulation of an executive department, or upon any express or implied contract with the United States...."[195]

Finally, the Contract Disputes Act of 1978 establishes a disputes process that is applicable to all government agencies and defines the types of claims subject to the Act. All contracts for goods and services entered into after March 8, 1979, fall under the provisions of the Act. It is appropriate to note that the government may also make claims against contractor under the Act.[196]

The types of claims covered under the Act include:

- Disputes "concerning a question of fact arising under the contract."[197] This has been interpreted by the courts to cover only situations where the contracts provided for the remedy requested by the contractor. Standard clauses in most contracts include a changes clause that covers extra work ordered by the government; a suspension of work clause covering government delays of the contractor; and a differing site conditions clause, which is included in construction contracts when a contractor encounters unforeseen physical conditions.[198]
- Breach of contract claims in which the contractor alleges that the government failed to perform an expressed or implied duty for which no relief is available under the terms of the contract[199]
- Mistake claims after award in which the contractor is seeking contract rescission or reformation[200]
- Tort claims in which action by the government failed to carry out a contractual duty.[201]

Excluded from coverage under the Act are claims involving fraud, statutory penalties, or forfeitures under specific jurisdiction of another federal agency.[202] In addition, subcontractors do not have the right to file a direct appeal with the government unless they are in "privity of contract with the government." Privity of contract is the legal relationship between the government and the prime contractor. The prime contractor has privity of contract with the first-tier subcontractors. But there is generally no privity of contract between the government and subcontractors. Claims of contractors against the government must be asserted by the prime contractor or in the name of the prime contractor.[203]

A claim by the contractor triggers an obligation on the part of the CO to make a timely decision. A 1995 ruling established that there was no requirement that there be a dispute prior to filing of a claim unless the issue involves nonpayment of vouchers, invoices, or routine requests for payment. Previously, there had to be a dispute followed by a claim.[204]

The Act specifies that a claim "shall be in writing and submitted to the CO for a decision."[205] The submission of the claim also starts the period of interest. The claim must be a "demand or assertion" by one party or the other.[206] The format for submitting a claim is included in FAR 52.233-1, Disputes. The CO is advised to follow closely the instructions included in the FAR so as not to be charged with failure of due process in not providing sufficient notice to the contractor, which means "not a final decision," and the contractor wins the appeal.[207]

It is the stated objective of the government to resolve all claims at the working level through a negotiated agreement between the CO and the contractor. At this level the parties are in the best position to know and understand the facts involved with the dispute. In addition, it requires less time, is less disruptive, and is less expensive. A final decision under the disputes clause has always been regarded as a last resort.

The CO has the authority to reach a binding mutual agreement with the contractor. The final decision of the CO can be either to accept or challenge the decision by appealing it to a board of contract appeals or to the U.S. Claims Court. The CO's final decision is considered the first step in the formal litigation process.[208]

Alternative Dispute Resolution: With the passage of the Administration Disputes Resolution Act (ADRA), Congress provided a way to test arbitration and mediation in government contract disputes. The legislation is contrary to the long-standing doctrine that the government cannot submit to binding arbitration, which had its roots in English common law.[209] It represents another major evolution in government contracting.

An alternative dispute resolution (ADR) offers a means of streamlining, reducing cost, and lessening the business disruption that comes with litigation. ADR is any procedure or combination of procedures voluntarily used, in lieu of litigation, to resolve issues in controversy. These alternative procedures include settlement negotiations, conciliation, facilitation, mediation, fact-finding, mini-trials, and arbitration. ADR is used when the CO and a contractor cannot resolve an issue through normal contracting procedures. It is intended to resolve issues faster than the traditional litigation process, which brings into play courts or an agency board of contract appeals. It also has the advantage of being less costly than the formal litigation process. The essential elements of ADR include:

- Existence of an issue or controversy
- A voluntary election by both parties to participate in the ADR process
- An agreement on alternative procedures and terms to be used in lieu of formal litigation
- Participation in the process by officials of both parties who have the authority to resolve the issue in controversy.[210]

ADR procedures may be used any time the CO has the authority to resolve the issue in controversy. A written agreement to use ADR will specify the maximum award that may be issued by the arbitrator as well as any other conditions limiting the range of possible outcomes. A neutral party may be used to facilitate resolution of the issue using the procedures chosen by the parties. If either the CO or contractor rejects a request by the other party to follow ADR procedures to resolve the controversy, they are required to inform the other party of the reason for rejection.[211]

In addition to being less costly and less time consuming, the benefits of ADR include: (1) less disruption caused by the requirement to use technical experts during litigation, (2) the fact that the manager has greater control over the decision process than does the traditional litigation process, and (3) reduced potential for long-term damage to the buyer/seller relationship.[212]

CONCLUSION

Writing in *Contract Management*, John Nichols observes:

> Most lawyers experienced in contract litigation will trace the root cause of most disputes to failure of interpersonal relationships. As is often the case with shattered marriages, effective communication has broken down. No doubt stress and the competing goals play a large part in this. Since people in this failed relationship are having difficulty communicating with each other effectively, they begin to get suspicious of each other and grow increasingly unaffordable because they realize they have lost control over the situation. Mistrust then leads to animosity and people begin playing hardball.[213]

Nichols goes on to say that mistrust can begin during negotiations and recur later during contract administration. His advice is that the acquisition team should never lose sight of its common goal. Business issues must be confronted and worked to resolution so they do not interfere with the common goal. This is best accomplished when all parties have a level of mutual trust that facilitates communication.[214]

Chapter 8 will cover contract closeout.

NOTES

[1]Knight, Steven D. 1993. New Initiatives In Contract Administration: The SWAT Team Report Repeats History. *Contract Management* (February): 16.

[2]Knight, 18.

[3]FAR 1.102.

[4]Gansler, J.S. 2000. The Road Ahead. Under Secretary of Defense, Acquisition and Technology. Washington, D.C.: (June 2), 3.

[5]Sherman, Stanley N. 1986. *Contract Management Post Award*. Gaithersburg, MD: Wordcrafters Publications, 111.

[6]Cibinic, Jr., John, and Ralph C. Nash, Jr. 1986. *Administration of Government Contracts*. 2d ed. Washington, D.C.: The George Washington University, 2.

[7]Lax, David A., and James K. Sebenius. 1986. *The Manager as Negotiator: Bargaining for Cooperation and Competitive Gain.* New York: The Free Press, 314.

[8]Lax and Sebenius, 12.

[9]FAR 1.102.

[10]Nash, Jr., Ralph C., Steven L. Schooner, and Karen R. O'Brien. 1998. *The Government Contracts Reference Book: A Comprehensive Guide to the Language of Procurement.* Washington, D.C.: The George Washington University, 121.

[11]*Basic Contract Administration.* Federal Acquisition Institute, Office of Acquisition Policy, General Services Administration. Vienna, VA: National Contract Management Association, 1–3.

[12]Cibinic, Jr., and Nash, Jr., 5.

[13]Nash, Jr., Schooner, and O'Brien, 509.

[14]FAR 42.603.

[15]FAR 42.602.

[16]Witte, Robert D. 1998. Authority of Government Officials. *Contract Management* (May): 40.

[17]Cibinic, Jr., and Nash, Jr., 22–23.

[18]Cibinic, Jr., and Nash, Jr., 31–33.

[19]Cibinic, Jr., and Nash, Jr., 35.

[20]FAR 42.401.

[21]Nash, Jr., Schooner, and O'Brien, 424.

[22]Cibinic, Jr., and Nash, Jr., 7.

[23]FAR 42.101(b).

[24]Nash, Jr., Schooner, and O'Brien, 45.

[25]FAR 42.101(a).

[26]Kruse, Peggy.1998. DCAA Adapting to Customer' Changing Needs. *Contract Management* (April): 10.

[27]FAR 52.215-2.

[28]Cibinic, Jr., and Nash, Jr., 3.

[29]FAR 42.501.

[30]FAR 42.502.

[31]Sherman, 95.

[32]Cibinic, Jr., and Nash, Jr., 109.

[33]Cibinic, Jr., and Nash, Jr., 102.

[34]Cibinic, Jr., and Nash, Jr., 103.

[35]Cibinic, Jr., and Nash, Jr., 104.

[36]Cibinic, Jr., and Nash, Jr., 170.

[37]Gabig, Jerome S. 1989. A Guide to Interpreting Contracts. *NCMA Journal* (Summer): 60.

[38]Gabig, 56.

[39]Gabig, 56.

[40]Cibinic, Jr., and Nash, Jr., 119–120.

[41]Gabig, 57.

[42]Cibinic, Jr., and Nash, Jr., 122.

[43]Cibinic, Jr., and Nash, Jr., 126.

[44]Cibinic, Jr., and Nash, Jr., 123.

[45]Gabig, 58.

[46]Ibid.

[47]Gabig, 59.

[48]Ibid.

[49]Cibinic, Jr., and Nash, Jr., 116.

[50]Nash, Jr., Schooner, and O'Brien, 377.

[51]Nash, Jr., Schooner, and O'Brien, 529.

[52]Gabig, 60.

[53]Ibid.

[54]Total Federal Snapshot Report, SF279. Actions Reported Individually on SF279, FY 1999 Through Fourth Quarter.

[55]Rindner, Corey. 1998. Can Government Really Contract Commercially? *Contract Management* (November): 6.

[56]Petersen, Daniel R. 1998. Government Procurement & the UCC: How the Code Affects Federal Contracting. *Contract Management*. [November]: 9.

[57]Nash, Jr., Schooner, and O'Brien, 529.

[58]*Prudential Ins. Co. v. United States,* 801 F.2d 1295,1298 (Fed. Cir. 1986).

[59]Petersen, 9.

[60]Summerill, Joseph, and Todd Bailey. 1998. The Use of UCC-Implied Warranties in Public Contracts. *Contract Management* (November): 13.

[61]Sherman, 235.

[62]"Don't Just Survive, Thrive." 2000. *The Contract Professional as a Business Manager.* Vienna, VA: National Contract Management Association, 6-1.

[63]Sherman, 237–238.

[64]Abba, Wayne F. 1997. Earned Value Management—Reconciling Government and Commercial Practices. *Program Manager.* (January-February): 62.

[65]Sherman, 242–244.

[66]FAR 1/102-2(c)(2).

[67]DoD Instruction 5000.2, Operation of the Defense Acquisition System. Paragraph 4.7.3.2.3.4.1, January 4, 2001.

[68]Sherman, 308.

[69]UCC § 2-209.

[70]UCC § 2-103(1).

[71]Cibinic, Jr., and Nash, Jr., 280.

[72]Alston, Frank M. et al. 1984. *Contracting with the Federal Government.* New York: John Wiley & Sons, 359.

[73]FAR 43.102(b).

[74]FAR 43.105.

[75]Cibinic, Jr., and Nash, Jr., 290.

[76]Cibinic, Jr., and Nash, Jr., 290–296.

[77]FAR 52.243-1, FAR 52.243-2, and FAR 52.243-3.

[78]FAR 43.103.

[79]FAR 43.102(a)

[80]Cibinic, Jr., and Nash, Jr., 320.

[81]Cibinic, Jr., and Nash, Jr., 324–335.

[82]Cibinic, Jr., and Nash, Jr., 324–339.

[83]Cibinic, Jr., and Nash, Jr., 339–352.

[84]Cibinic, Jr., and Nash, Jr., 352–357.

[85]Nash, Jr., Schooner, and O'Brien, 114.

[86]Gregory, Linda J. 1995. The Role of Configuration Management in the Acquisition Process. *National Contract Management Journal* 26(I): 23.

[87]Sherman, 310–313.

[88]Cibinic, Jr., and Nash, Jr., 412.

[89]Nash, Jr., Schooner, and O'Brien, 104 and 173. There are two standard clauses for which the government is required to give compensation. These are FAR Clauses 52.242-14, Suspension of Work, and 520242-17, Government Delay of Work.

[90]Cibinic, Jr., and Nash, Jr., 410.

[91]Cibinic, Jr., and Nash, Jr., 412–425.

[92]Nash, Jr., Schooner, and O'Brien, 104.

[93]Cibinic, Jr., and Nash, Jr., 409.

[94]Cibinic, Jr., and Nash, Jr., 450–451.

[95]FAR 52-212-12.

[96]Sherman, 337.

[97]Cibinic, Jr., and Nash, Jr., 479.

[98]Sherman, 369.

[99]Cibinic, Jr., and Nash, Jr., 482.

[100]Cibinic, Jr., and Nash, Jr., 491.

[101]FAR 43.203.

[102]Cibinic, Jr., and Nash, Jr., 481.

[103]Cibinic, Jr., and Nash, Jr., 484.

[104]Cibinic, Jr., and Nash, Jr., 491-492.

[105]Cibinic, Jr., and Nash, Jr., 530–531.

[106]Sherman, 247.

[107]AFCMD Regulation 178-1, 7 June 1983, Department of the Air Force, Headquarters Air Force Contract Management Division (AFSC), Kirkland AFB, New Mexico, 1–5.

[108]Menestrina, Robert W. 1989. CRAG: Just Another Four-Letter Word? *Contract Management* (April): 9.

[109]FAR 42.1104, Production Surveillance and Reporting.

[110]FAR 52.242-2.

[111]2000. Executive Overview. ISO 900 Quality Management System, Sept. 10.

[112]Burt, Davis N., and Richard L. Pinkerton. 1996. *A Purchasing Manager's Guide to Strategic Procurement*. New York: American Management Association, 221.

[113]FAR 46.203.

[114]Cibinic, Jr., and Nash, Jr., 569.

[115]FAR 46.101.

[116]FAR 46.102.

[117]Cibinic, Jr., and Nash, Jr., 568.

[118]FAR 46.101.

[119]UCC §2-316 (3).

[120]UCC § 2-607.

[121]FAR 52.246-2 (k).

[122]Cibinic, Jr., and Nash, Jr., 570.

[123]FAR 9.3, First Article Testing and Approval.

[124]Cibinic, Jr., and Nash, Jr., 603.

[125]Cibinic, Jr., and Nash, Jr., 604.

[126]FAR 46-401.

[127]FAR 46.402.

[128]FAR 46.403.

[129]FAR 46.404.

[130]FAR 46.405.

[131]FAR 46.504.

[132]FAR 52.246-16.

[133]Cibinic, Jr., and Nash, Jr., 631.

[134]FAR 52.246-2.

[135]Nash, Jr., Schooner, and O'Brien, 322.

[136]Cibinic, Jr., and Nash, Jr., 633.

[137]Cibinic, Jr., and Nash, Jr., 632.

[138]Cibinic, Jr., and Nash, Jr., 637.

[139]Cibinic, Jr., and Nash, Jr., 640–641.

[140]Cibinic, Jr., and Nash, Jr., 641–648.

[141]FAR 46.701.

[142]Cibinic, Jr., and Nash, Jr., 655.

[143]Cibinic, Jr., and Nash, Jr., 656.

[144]Cibinic, Jr., and Nash, Jr., 649.

[145]Cibinic, Jr., and Nash, Jr., 653.

[146]Nash, Jr., Schooner, and O'Brien, 137.

[147]Peckenpaugh, Jason. 2001. Contractors to Benefit from Relaxed Purchasing Rules. *Government Executive*, January 12.

[148]Nash, Jr., Schooner, and O'Brien, 194.

[149]FAR Part 31.

[150]FAR 31.201-4.

[151]FAR 31.201-2.

[152]Nash, Jr., Schooner, and O'Brien, 193.

[153]FAR 42.802.

[154]FAR 42.803(2).

[155]FAR 42.803.

[156]FAR 30.403-20.

[157]FAR 42.1701.

[158]FAR 42.1701.

[159]FAR 52.216-7(d).

[160]FAR 52.216-7(e).

[161]FAR 49.101.

[162]Sherman, 389.

[163]Nash, Jr., Schooner, and O'Brien, 513.

[164]FAR 52.249-8 through 52.249-10.

[165]Cibinic, Jr., and Nash, Jr., 667.

[166]FAR 49.402-2.

[167]Cibinic, Jr., and Nash, Jr., 673.

[168]Cibinic, Jr., and Nash, Jr., 696–703.

[169]Cibinic, Jr., and Nash, Jr., 742–749.

[170]FAR 49.402-4.

[171]FAR 49.402-3(f).

[172]Nash, Jr., Schooner, and O'Brien, 257.

[173]Cibinic, Jr., and Nash, Jr., 750–755.

[174]FAR 49.402-2(e).

[175]Cibinic, Jr., and Nash, Jr., 757.

[176]FAR 49.402-3(g).

[177]Cibinic, Jr., and Nash, Jr., 758–759.

[178]Cibinic, Jr., and Nash, Jr., 760.

[179]Cibinic, Jr., and Nash, Jr., 788.

[180]FAR 49.403.

[181]Alston, et al., 381.

[182]Cibinic, Jr., and Nash, Jr., 18.

[183]FAR 49.101(e).

[184]Cibinic, Jr., and Nash, Jr., 817.

[185]Cibinic, Jr., and Nash, Jr., 841.

[186]Cibinic, Jr., and Nash, Jr., 821–825.

[187]FAR 49.104.

[188]FAR 49.102.

[189]FAR 49.101(d).

[190]FAR 52.249-2 (b)(5), 52.249-3(b)(5), and 52-249-4(b)(5).

[191]Cibinic, Jr., and Nash, Jr., 855.

[192]Nash, Jr., Schooner, and O'Brien, 197.

[193]FAR 52.233-1(h).

[194]Sherman, 393.

[195]Cibinic, Jr., and Nash, Jr., 944.

[196]Cibinic, Jr., and Nash, Jr., 944–950.

[197]Cibinic, Jr., and Nash, Jr., 948.

[198]Cibinic, Jr., and Nash, Jr., 948.

[199]Cibinic, Jr., and Nash, Jr., 952.

[200]Cibinic, Jr., and Nash, Jr., 953.

[201]Cibinic, Jr., and Nash, Jr., 955.

[202]Cibinic, Jr., and Nash, Jr., 956.

[203]Cibinic, Jr., and Nash, Jr., 963-965.

[204]Nash, Jr., Schooner, and O'Brien, 197.

[205]Cibinic, Jr., and Nash, Jr., 967.

[206]Cibinic, Jr., and Nash, Jr., 970.

[207]Ewart, Loel A. 1988. The Disputes Process: Are Final Decisions? *Contract Management* (April): 16.

[208]Cibinic, Jr., and Nash, Jr., 986.

[209]Babbin, Jed L., and Garylee Cox. 1992. Saving Time and Money—Arbitration and Mediation of Government Disputes under the ADRA. *Contract Management* (January): 20—22.

[210]FAR 33.214.

[211]FAR 33.214.

[212]Babbin and Cox, 23.

[213]Nichols, John. 1994. Trust, Teamwork, and Effective Communication—An Alternative to the Disputes Process. *Contract Management*. (May): 53.

[214]Nichols, 54.

Contract Closeout

Contract closeout is defined as "the process of settling all outstanding contractual issues to ensure that each party has met all of its obligations and documenting the contract file accordingly."[1] The primary objectives of contract closeout include the:

- Identification and resolution of uncompleted obligations or pending liabilities on the part of either party. This includes the final audit and the negotiation of the final overhead rates and the price (for fixed-price contracts) or cost and fee (for cost-type contracts). For the government this action will probably result in the recouping of unobligated funds remaining on the contract and applying the unspent balances to other approved programs. The contractor also benefits because it not only receives final payment but is also reimbursed the 15 percent fee retained by the government to liquidate progress payments or other any form of contract financing.
- Disposal of government-furnished property (GFP), special tooling, residual inventory, scrap, and classified documents that were required in the performance of the contract.
- Review and disposal of the contract files: FAR 4.805 defines the policy for storage, handling, and disposing of the contract file. It includes information on retention of the various document files after contract closeout.

A contract is physically complete when: (1) all required work has been delivered or performed, inspected, and accepted, and all options have been exercised or have expired; or (2) a contract termination notice has been delivered to the contractor. When the contract effort has been completed, the government and the contractor must initiate joint action to close out the contract.[2]

The administrative contracting officer (ACO) is the individual usually responsible for performing contract closeout. Other government officials who are key to the successful closeout of a contract include the auditors, property administrators, payment officers, and the legal council.[3]

On the contractor's side a contract manager (CM) is usually the focal point for all closeout actions. Also involved is the project or program manager, accounting, security, functional managers, and subcontract manager/administrators. Principal actions that are required to be performed by the contractor as part of closeout include:

- Ensuring that all remaining deliverable products and services will be completed within the time period specified in the contract. This includes a notice of physical completion that is performed by the contractor and confirmed by the ACO.
- Developing plans to close out contract labor charges. This includes a schedule for final close out of contract work authorizations for members of the prime contractor acquisition team.
- Closing out all subcontracts and inter-divisional work authorizations. Resolving any claims or terminations related to purchase orders; coordinating the disposition of GFP or government-owned inventory as part of property clearance or plant clearance procedures.
- Disposing of GFP, classified documentation, special tooling, residual government-owned inventory, and scrap as instructed by the government's CO; completing the property clearance report; receiving confirmation that assigned GFP has been disposed of by the government property administrator; verifying that the contractor's property records reflect the revised balances.
- Managing the plant clearance and performing the plant clearance report. The plant clearance period begins on the effective date of contract completion or termination and ends 90 days after the CO receives an acceptable inventory schedule for each class of property.[4] The plant clearance period can be extended if the CO agrees. Actions to be accomplished during this period include transferring any excess contractor material inventory so it can be used on other contracts and selling excess for scrap if it cannot be returned to the supplier for credit. Any excess inventory belongs to the contractor if it is a fixed-price contract. If it is a cost-reimbursement contract, the contractor can purchase excess property at fair market value. It may also be transferred to follow-on contracts with the contract being closed out given credit for the amount transferred. The government also may order the contractor to sell any excess inventory, with the contract being credited for amount sold plus expenses incurred to advertise and manage the sale.

- Advising the appropriate government office of all patents, inventions, or innovations. Complete required patent applications. Verifying all patent and royalty obligations.
- Completing final reconciliation. This includes settling all interim or disallowed costs and prior-year indirect cost rates.
- Submiting the final invoice.

The following standards for closing out the contract files have been established:

- Files for contracts using simplified acquisition procedures are to be considered closed when the CO receives evidence of physical delivery of the property and final payment.
- Fixed-price contract files should be closed within six months after the CO receives evidence of the physical completion.
- If the contract requires audit, negotiation, and settlement of indirect cost rates, as is the case in a cost-reimbursement contract, the contract files are to be closed within 36 months of the CO receiving evidence of physical completion.
- Files for the remaining contracts are to be closed within 20 months of delivery of physical completion.[5]

A survey by the Defense Contract Management Command (DCMC) identified the five biggest problems that prevented timely closure of contracts as awaiting final overhead rates (26 percent); awaiting final invoice (25 percent); awaiting final payment for reasons of posting errors, not enough of the correct fiscal year funds (15 percent); awaiting final results (7 percent); and awaiting reconciliation (6 percent).[6]

The contract closeout process is time consuming because the need to review and audit the contract documents and complete the plant clearance process is labor intensive. The resources needed to accomplish these tasks are often reassigned to other acquisitions before completing the tasks required to complete closeout. To establish an appropriate priority, the benefits the government gains from the release of de-obligated funds need to be quantified. The contractor must also realize that it will benefit from the release of the 15 percent withheld by the government to liquidate progress payments.

When the amount of unsettled indirect costs are not significant, "quick closeout" procedures can be used. This procedure permits the CO to negotiate the settlement of indirect costs for a specific physically complete contract in advance of the determination of final indirect cost rates. Indirect costs are considered insignificant when the total allocated to any one contract is less than $1,000,000, unless the cumulative unsettled indirect cost to be allocated to one or more contracts in a single fiscal year does not exceed 15 percent of the estimated, total unsettled indirect cost allocable to cost-type contracts for that fiscal year. Even then, the 15 percent restriction may be waived when, after assessing the characteristics of the contractor's accounting, estimating, purchasing systems, and any concerns of the cognizant contract auditors, the CO concludes that risk is acceptable. The CO also must determine that a reasonable agreement can be reached on an estimate of allocable dollars. The FAR policy does caution against applying any over- or under-recoveries of costs allocated or allocable to the contract covered by the agreement and is a binding precedent when establishing the final indirect cost rates for other contracts.[7]

CONCLUSION

There are benefits to be gained when a contract has been closed out. The government benefits from the recouping of funds that have been de-obligated because they can be applied to other requirements. The 15-percent fee retention that may still remain on the contract is a financial benefit to the contractor. Prompt initiation of action to closeout of the contract is important because personnel are available who understand the terms of the contract and recall events that occurred during performance. To recreate a contract history years after the contract has been completed consumes time and money.

NOTES

[1]Nash, Jr., Ralph C., Steven L. Schooner, and Karen R. O'Brien. 1998. *The Government Contracts Reference Book: A Comprehensive Guide to the Language of Procurement.* 2d ed. Washington, D.C.: The George Washington University, 97.

[2]FAR 4.804-4.

[3]FAR 4.804-5.

[4]Nash, Jr., Schooner, and O'Brien, 397.

[5]FAR 4.804-1(a).

[6]Thibodeaux, Lynett M. 1996. Contract Closeout—An Introduction. *Contract Management* (August): 25.

[7]FAR 42.708.

Index

Determination of Eligibility, Small
Business Administration, 96
DFARS. *See* Department of Defense,
FAR Supplement
DFAS. *See* Defense Finance and
Accounting Service
direct charges, 115
direct labor pricing data, 258
disadvantaged groups, program that
favor, 26
disagreements over contract
requirements, 356–357
discrepancies, addressing, 225–226
disputes, 387–390
Distributive Electronic Order
Processing System, 205
DO-rated orders, 129
Doctrine of Constructive Change,
356–357
document imaging, 27
document soundness, contract
presumption, 329
DoD. *See* Department of Defense
DoDISS. *See* Department of Defense,
Index of Specifications and
Standards
downsizing, government, 22
Doyle, Michael, 30
DPAS. *See* Defense Priorities and
Allocations Systems
draft contractual documents, 225
Drake, Daniel, 120
Drucker, Peter, 28–29, 39, 231
Drug-Free Workplace Act, 271
dual-sourcing, 4
Dun and Bradstreet reports, 98, 268
DX-rated orders, 129

E

e-cats. *See* electronic catalogs
e-commerce, 146
Earned Value Management System
(EVMS), 344–345
earned value systems, 19
ECP. *See* Engineering Change Proposal
EDI. *See* electronic data interchange

efficiency ratios, 230
EFT. *See* electronic funds transfer
Eisenhower, President Dwight, 98
electronic catalogs (e-cats), 77
electronic commerce, 23
electronic communications, 23
electronic data interchange (EDI)
government dependence upon, 3
importance of, 27–28
integrated acquisition team, 43
paperless procurement environment,
146
electronic data transfer, 3
electronic funds transfer (EFT), 27–28
electronic mail (e-mail), 27
Electronic Signatures Act of 2000, 28,
145
embezzlement, 271
employees, empowering, 21
encrypted signatures, 146
engineering, 53
Engineering Change Proposal (ECP),
85, 355
ENIAC, 27
environment, programs that protect,
26
equal opportunity, 27
Equipment Under a Lease or Purchase
Arrangement (FAR Part 7.4), 108
European Recovery Program, 6
evaluation process
cost or price evaluation, 280–282
importance of, 279–280
even playing field, maintaining, 10
EVMS. *See* Earned Value Management
System
evolutionary acquisition, 208
executive branch, 7
expert estimates, 255
extrapolation, costs, 255

F

F-22 Engineering and Manufacturing
Development Program, 56
F-22 System Program Office (SPO), 60
facilities capital cost of money, 258